Case Files of the
East Area Rapist /
Golden State Killer

KAT WINTERS

with
KEITH KOMOS

CCW Books

http://www.coldcasewriter.com

Copyright © 2017 Kat Winters, Keith Komos

ISBN: 0999458108

ISBN13: 978-0999458105

Cover design by Kat Winters

For more information:

Web: https://www.coldcase-earons.com

E-mail: coldcase.earons@gmail.com

Twitter: https://www.twitter.com/coldcasewriter

DEDICATION

It's the nature of the beast that far too much time is spent talking about the criminal and not enough time is spent talking about the victims. This book is dedicated to the people whose lives were changed forever or even taken away because of these crimes. Thinking about the lost years of love, joy, promise, and potential brings an overwhelming sense of loss and sadness to anyone, but it also becomes the fire that fuels the quest for justice. Hopefully this book can contribute to that in some way. This case is eminently solvable, and we join with those who dream of that day.

Table of Contents

Supplemental Material

Introduction

The East Area Rapist / Golden State Killer case is one of the most terrifying and complex cold cases in American history. For over forty years, this baffling case has remained unsolved.

He was the ultimate villain. Always one step ahead. He couldn't be tracked, he couldn't be spotted, and he couldn't be identified. Police couldn't catch him, and he flew under the radar so well that neighbors often shrugged him off. He was careful, so careful that in all the years that he offended, police weren't sure if they even had his fingerprint. He was prolific, attacking in over a dozen communities over a five-hundred mile range and over a ten-year period.

This methodical and deadly rapist-turned-killer was on the loose in California. Deadly—but one knew *how* deadly. There were too many pieces of the puzzle, and the pieces were spread too far apart. None of them seemed to fit. Time and time again, the offender would emerge from the night, terrorize or kill, then vanish like a ghost.

But there was nothing supernatural about this offender. He was careful, methodical, and *lucky*, but he was a man, and he has a name— a name other than the one the FBI has given him. Until we learn what that name is, we call him the "East Area Rapist," the "Golden State Killer," or sometimes the "Original Night Stalker."

With over one hundred burglaries, fifty rapes, and possibly a dozen murders, the "EAR" / "GSK" was truly one of history's most vile and heinous criminals. He seemed to appear out of nowhere in the mid-1970s near Sacramento, California, where he began a series of rapes that left police baffled and communities on-edge. As time wore on, he began moving away from the Sacramento area and he began targeting surrounding communities like Modesto, Davis, Concord, San Ramon, San Jose, Danville, Fremont, and Walnut Creek. In the latter half of 1979, he appeared in Southern California and began murdering couples and single women in Goleta, Ventura, Dana Point, and Irvine. He vanished for five years, then returned for one more murder in 1986.

It's a complex case, and naturally, there's a great amount of confusion about even the basic facts. When I first became aware of this case, the learning-curve was steep and it was quite a challenge to make sense of the information that was in the public space (which over time, had become quite dizzying and convoluted). To smooth out the process, I gathered a team to create a website for the general public (located at https://www.coldcase-earons.com), and while we were fairly successful in our efforts, it was clear that much more could be done. Other projects were started, the website gained more traction, I assumed a moderator position at the main discussion forum dedicated to the case, and several victims, survivors, and even past/present Law Enforcement officers generously spent their time assisting me with my work and research. As all of these things started to come together, not only had we simplified the presentation and information about the East Area Rapist / Golden State Killer, but I suddenly found my finger on the pulse of this case in a very unique way. Through the people who e-mailed my site every day, the forum members I assisted, the discussions I led, and the contacts I made, I found myself at the nexus of a diverse and comprehensive set of vantage points related to the public's informational needs regarding the "EAR/GSK" case. These perspectives allowed me to get a real sense where the knowledge gaps were, how the interplay and dynamics among the different parts of the cold-case ecosystem worked, and a sense of the evidence and materials people were looking for when they started to learn about the case.

What's more, I could clearly see that my goal of streamlining the information of this case for everyone had not yet been met, and that there was an entire segment of the population that needed an off-web presentation. From that frame of reference and the ones described above, I set about the task of compiling the narrative and facts of the case into an even more comprehensive and accessible medium. This book is the result of those efforts.

The "EAR/GSK," by any measure, is one of the most prolific, enigmatic, and dangerous criminals to ever haunt the night—and he remains unidentified and unpunished to this day. Despite the fact that he's still at large, the public knows almost nothing about this offender. That needs to change. While it's true that many years have passed, this case has not yet fallen into the abyss of history. Actuarial tables estimate that the killer is still alive, and in the interest of justice, everything possible must be done to capture and convict this violent offender. The statute of limitations will never expire for his homicides, and the statute of limitations for the pain and loss he's caused thousands of people will never run out, either. "Justice delayed" is not ideal, but "justice denied" is unthinkable.

Every move the assailant made, every word he spoke, every wardrobe choice he made, and every sighting of a suspicious person or vehicle in the vicinity of the crimes has the potential to blow the case wide open. As the years have worn on, more and more jurisdictions have come forward with unique clues and findings that weren't shared at the time of the actual crimes. More is known about the assailant now than ever before.

This book contains an exhaustive rundown of all of the information available on this criminal, with plenty of new facts never released before and additional analysis to help provide context. Each and every attack is covered, with information culled from every source possible—including information taken from conversations with victims and survivors who have never spoken to authors or the media about the case before. Going over the complex details of this case with such granularity is a worthwhile exercise. This case is solvable. The clues to his identity are in here.

Because as they say, *the Devil is in the details*.

The East Area Rapist

The killer got his start as a home-intrusion burglar/rapist, operating prolifically in a group of neighborhoods east of Sacramento in the mid-1970s. His proclivity for attacking in that general location earned him the nickname "East Area Rapist," a monicker that residents of California got very tired of seeing in the paper as the months and years started to wear on.

The rapist struck a particularly fearful chord in the communities he operated in because of the apparent randomness of the crimes and the fact that he was targeting middle and upper-middle class people in their own homes in the middle of the night. There was a pervasive feeling among regular, everyday people that any one of them could be "next" and be subjected to the brutality of the masked rapist.

The typical East Area Rapist (or "EAR") attack involved the victim(s) being awakened from a sound sleep in the middle of the night by a flashlight beaming into their eyes. They'd barely catch a fleeting glimpse of a masked intruder (one who wore a different mask to every single crime) before their hands were bound tightly (so tightly that circulation was restricted to the point that the hands would turn purple). The man, speaking through a harsh whisper and clenched teeth, would often claim that he was just looking for "food and money" and he'd begin ransacking the residence. If a couple rather than a lone woman was being attacked, the woman was led out of the room and dishes from the kitchen were stacked on the man's back so that the assailant would hear him if he tried to escape.

The assailant would sexually assault the woman, usually multiple times, amidst a barrage of constant threats with a gun or a sharp weapon. After lording over the house for up to three or more hours, the offender would silently make his escape, taking with him a few personal items belonging to his victims and most of whatever cash was lying around.

The silence of his departure and the difficulty that victims had in breaking free from their restraints often meant that the police weren't summoned for several minutes or more after he left. As a result, responding officers couldn't locate him, tracking dogs could only lead down a trail that ended abruptly, and not a single blatant clue to his identity could be found. Time and time again, month after month and year after year, the East Area Rapist eluded police.

As he moved into Southern California in 1979, it seemed he was no longer satisfied with simply raping his victims and he began killing. First with a gun, then with bludgeoning. This phase of the crime spree earned him the name "Golden State Killer" decades later. Even with the increased manpower given to the homicide investigations, nothing substantial related to the killer's identity could be uncovered. Because the killer kept moving around, the crimes weren't immediately tied together.

But many years later, we have the luxury of hindsight and history. The thousands of clues left behind do begin to add up, even though they couldn't be aggregated at the time. Patterns begin to emerge from the noise, and modern communication and technology is tightening the circle around the offender.

In order to present this case properly, we must start at the very beginning and go step by step, examining the clues along the way until we reach the end. Somewhere throughout the journey, something might come together for someone, or an unknown witness might recognize that one elusive clue that could open up an exciting lead. Someone out there has the key that could finally solve this case once and for all.

1973 Burglary

Date: March 7th, 1973
Victim: 16-year-old girl
Location: Dawes Street, Rancho Cordova

The confirmed attacks of the East Area Rapist began in an area east of downtown Sacramento called Rancho Cordova. At the start crime spree, the neighborhood had been around for about twenty years. Most people in the community had come to live there for one of two reasons: they were military, or they worked for Aerojet.

In 1970, the population of Rancho Cordova was 30,451. In 1980, it had grown 41% to 42,881. Over one thousand of the households were closely associated with the local military installation, Mather Air Force Base, and military culture widely influenced the tone of the area.

Aerojet was the predominant economic force in Rancho Cordova for many years, employing nearly 21,000 people in 1963. By 1974, a slowdown in the space race and other hits to the industry had brought that number down below 2,000—a very steep drop in economic terms. Many of the families who were displaced financially by this downturn remained in the area and built a comfortable life for themselves in other professions. Many of them moved away, and the volatile nature of the job market in the early 1970s and the transient nature of the nearby military personnel certainly put areas of this quiet town in flux from time to time.

It was in this environment that the confirmed attacks by the East Area Rapist began.

While the first canonical attack wasn't until the summer of 1976, there were indicators as early as 1973 that a unique brand of offender was cutting his teeth in the area. The most suspicious burglaries, in hindsight, occurred on and around a particular intersection—Dawes Street and Dolecetto Drive.

As one of the main intersections in Rancho Cordova, the nexus of Dawes and Dolecetto was positioned in the middle of a residential area. The most distinctive feature of this intersection was (and still is) the cement-lined canal that ran through it, almost like a backbone to the neighborhood. Even to this day, the canal winds through most of the city, running along countless residential backyards and past schools and green spaces. The significance of these types of canals, to be discussed later, wouldn't become evident until the rapist had committed nearly half a dozen attacks.

A burglary that seemed quite negligible at the time occurred on March 7th, 1973, very close to this intersection. A house was broken into, but the only damage inside was a bit of rummaging. Nothing of value was taken, save for a wine bottle full of coins and a single earring (from a pair) belonging to the teenager who lived there. Possible significance to this event would only be applied three and a half years later, when this teenage girl, even after having moved to a different house in Rancho Cordova, became the sixth victim of the East Area Rapist. By the time she was assaulted, it was clear that one of the unique elements of the East Area Rapist's modus operandi was to break in, rummage through a potential victim's personal things, and steal small and personal items of little value.

Some of his favorite things to steal? Coins. And he often stole a single earring from a pair.

Due to the nature of the crime, the location, and the teenager's status as a future victim of the East Area Rapist, some feel that this was the community's first small taste of the carnage to come.

Spring 1974: The Dog

Date: Spring 1974
Victim: Family dog
Location: Dolecetto Drive, Rancho Cordova

The first victim of the killer might not have been a human—it might've actually been a dog.

In the Spring of 1974, a future detective on the EAR case (Richard Shelby) responded to a house on the corner of the aforementioned intersection, Dawes Street and Dolecetto Drive. The cops had been called because a prowler was in the backyard of a residence situated near the intersection. The owners of the house were out of town, so it was the next-door neighbors who had made the call.

Three officers examined the perimeter of the property, but no intruder could be found. They left, but were barely down the street when the call came in once more from the same neighbors. Officer Shelby returned, and as he pulled up to the curb, he noticed that the garage door to the residence was open. When he had left the scene just moments before, it had been closed.

The neighbors met him outside and explained that the prowler had reappeared just as the cops had left. In fact, they'd peered out their window to find a young man literally jump off of their roof. He'd landed upright on both feet, run to the back fence, and leapt over it easily to make his escape. Shelby immediately went to the fence and peered over it, but of course, the subject was gone. All he could see from that vantage point was thick foliage, the dry pavement of the cement-lined ditch that wound throughout the shadows of the neighborhood, and a sliver of nearby Cordova High.

The garage was searched, and a log measuring about a foot and a half was found. It was drenched in blood.

The officer entered the house, apprehensive of what he might find. Room after room seemed pristine and unspoiled, with no signs of rummaging. It wasn't until he reached the master bedroom that something out of the ordinary was found. Lying near the bed was the family dog. It had been bludgeoned to death while trying to crawl under the bed to hide from the intruder.

Like the burglary in March of 1973, this event would not seem significant until years later. You'll find out why as we make our way through the crimes: the bludgeoning, harm to a family dog, location, and physical description of the assailant warrants its inclusion here as a possibly-related crime.

The culprit was reported to be a white male, late teens, 5'9", with blonde hair. He was dressed in military fatigues. This matches the general description of the East Area Rapist.

October 21st, 1975

Date: October 21st, 1975 4:00 AM to 6:30 AM
Victims: Mother (36), 18-year-old daughter, 7-year-old daughter
Location: Dawes Street, Rancho Cordova

Over a year later, a significant crime (in terms of its possible relation to this series) would again be committed near the intersection of Dawes and Dolecetto.

In the early hours of October 21st, 1975, a man entered the unlocked garage door of a home on Dawes Street. He silently made his way through the door that led from the garage to the kitchen, and he crept through the house until he located the room of an eighteen-year-old girl. She suddenly found herself being threatened with a knife, then promptly tied up with strips of torn towel and cord. The intruder then quickly made his way into the bedroom where her mother was sleeping, corralled her into the room with the teenager, and bound her in a similar fashion. Feeling confident that they couldn't move or escape, he wandered through the rest of the house, located a seven-year-old, tied her up, and left her in her room.

He returned to the room where the older women were tied. They begged for him to leave them alone, but their pleas were answered continually with "shut up" whispered harshly. The intruder purposely didn't move his mouth when he spoke, and every word he said was through clenched teeth (perhaps in an effort to disguise his voice). He called them "ladies" over and over again.

He raped the mother and daughter. At one point he began

ransacking and rummaging through the house, and he moved the seven-year-old girl into the room with the two women and committed what was termed as "sex perversions" on the young girl. He raped the two women "repeatedly."

He finally left the house at 6:30 AM, stealing a ring and some coins on his way out.

The victims didn't get a very good look at the assailant due to the trauma of the situation and the fact that the room was dark. They initially felt that he was a black male in his early twenties and 5'6" or 5'7". He appeared to wear a homemade mask, military-style camouflage clothing, and he wielded a large buck knife. At a follow-up interview with police, the victims revealed that it was too dark to determine the race of the assailant, and that he could've been white.

Once the rest of the East Area Rapist crimes got going, the police revisited this attack and felt that it was the EAR. For over a year, as far as police documentation and the media were concerned, this was the first canonical EAR assault. As the crime spree wore on, the details of the case were revisited, and due to the unresolved question about the race of the offender and a few variations from what became the established modus operandi of the East Area Rapist, this attack was dropped off of the official list. It's currently only listed as a "possible" attack, when it's even listed at all.

The biggest departure from what his M.O. eventually became was the act of "sex perversions" on the young girl. This type of behavior didn't occur in any of the other attacks, at least not on a girl so young. An argument can be made that in the first EAR Stockton attack, a child may have had a near-miss. The East Area Rapist *did* assault a twelve-year-old and a thirteen-year-old, along with numerous other girls in their teens. If this attack *was* him, perhaps he was "experimenting" with a broader range of perversions before figuring out his attack style and narrowing down the activities he "liked" and "didn't like" to engage in.

Either way, there's plenty here to suggest a possible connection. I encourage you to revisit this attack after you've explored the rest of the book and make up your own mind.

Attack #1

Date: June 18th, 1976 4:00 AM to 4:20 AM
Victim: 23-year-old woman
Location: Paseo Drive, Rancho Cordova

Pre-Attack Events

May 1976
Starting in May, the victim (a twenty-three-year-old woman living with her father) started to get the eerie feeling that she was being watched. An older, dark-green, medium-sized American car appeared to haunt her as she went about her daily life on Paseo Drive, a street located about half a mile to the southwest of the Dawes and Dolecetto intersection in Rancho Cordova. The car, whose driver would turn his face completely away from her (preventing her from even getting a glimpse of his profile) when she looked at him, finally stopped appearing in early June.

Mid-May 1976
The woman's father left town for the East Coast on a planned six-week trip.

Late May 1976
A neighbor near the intersection of Malaga Way and Paseo Drive began hearing someone climbing his fence late at night on a regular basis. The activity occurred for many weeks, both before the attack and for quite awhile afterward.

Early June 1976

Starting sometime in the two weeks before the attack (and coinciding with the disappearance of the apparent stalker in the car), the victim began receiving hang-up phone calls. There were only two of them, but they were still fresh in her memory at the time of the attack because they struck her as very odd. She'd answer the phone, and there'd be nothing but silence on the other end and the caller wouldn't hang up.

The Attack

The victim went to bed at a normal time, tired from working and uncomfortable from dealing with menstrual cramps. She slept soundly, so soundly that sometime after 3:00 AM, she didn't hear the neighbor's dog barking. She didn't hear the commotion in her backyard as a man tried to cut her telephone wire, or the sound of him chipping away at her doorjamb and freeing her deadbolt. It was the sound of someone tapping on the frame of her bedroom door that finally jarred her from sleep.

Her bedroom light was flipped on. Squinting in the brightness, she saw a masked man. He had no pants on and his penis was erect. Instinctively, she drew the covers over her head. At once he was on top of her, ripping them off and digging a knife into her temple.

Snarling hoarsely through clenched teeth, he issued a warning: "If you make one move or sound, I'll stick this knife in you." He'd already, in fact, dug it in so deeply that he'd inflicted a wound, one which was rapidly soaking part of her pillow with blood.

Then, he announced the reason for his intrusion.

"I want to fuck you."

He stood beside her now, flashing his knife and tersely ordering her to remove her nightgown. As she did, he wandered through the room with an air of apparent anxiousness until finally stopping in front of her.

"Take it out," he commanded, referring to her tampon. She

removed it and let it fall to the floor.

"Roll over," he snarled. She did. He pulled her arms behind her back and tied her hands very tightly with ligatures he'd brought with him (some kind of rope or twine). Again he was moving about the room, rummaging and collecting items that he could use to reinforce her bindings. He supplemented the ligatures on her wrists with a cloth belt from her closet.

Again he ordered her to roll over, and then he raped her. During the sexual assault, he touched her breasts only briefly. When he pulled out, he wiped his penis with the bed sheet and tossed the bedding onto the floor. She couldn't tell if he'd climaxed or not, but would find out much later from a crime lab report that he had.

When the horrendous assault was over, he asked her if there was money in the house. She began to answer, but he interrupted her, ordering her through clenched teeth to "shut up."

Again he wandered the bedroom, collecting more items to tie her up with. He bound her ankles together with the cord from her hairdryer, and reinforced it with a bra that he found in the room. He also picked up her slip and wrapped it around her head to gag her.

With his victim even more secure, he began moving through the bedroom once more, rummaging and ransacking as he went. He returned to her side, held the knife close, and warned her that if she made any movements he'd kill her.

Then he was gone... but just from the room, not from the house. She heard him tearing the residence apart, pulling at drawers loudly, and opening and closing a paper bag as he wandered through the rooms.

At one point she heard whispered voices, as if two people were talking. A louder whisper said "I told you to shut up!" The whispering continued as drawers and cabinets were opened and shut in various rooms. Despite the apparent conversation, the victim felt that the assailant was by himself, and that all of the whispered voices belonged to one person.

After a few moments, there was silence. No more paper bags opening, no more drawers being slammed, and no more hushed conversation.

Fearing that he could return at any moment, she began twisting and pulling at her bindings. Her legs broke free, and she moved stealthily through the house, praying that the assailant was indeed gone. The backdoor was open. She tried to close it with her feet, but the deadbolt was engaged and it wouldn't shut.

Her hands still bound, she knocked the phone receiver off the wall and tried to dial it. She couldn't manage. She attempted the same with the phone in her father's room, and fortunately was able to dial the operator and summon the police.

Immediate Aftermath

Law Enforcement arrived to find the victim lying on her father's bed, covering her nakedness as best she could. A quick search of the residence confirmed that the assailant had indeed left. They cut her bindings, which freed her cold, numb hands. The rapist had bound her so tightly that they had turned black from the restricted circulation. A cursory medical examination was performed, and a deep scratch on her temple was noted (which she had actually been unaware of), as well as a scratch on the right side of her chest.

The interior of house was in disarray from the assailant's frenetic rummaging. Drawers were open and their contents were strewn about the floor. There were two pieces of rope or twine found, and it was determined that the assailant had brought them with him to the attack. The police took the bed sheets as evidence, and in the bathroom, they found two towels balled up along with a bottle of Johnson's Baby Oil (which had probably been used by the assailant to lubricate himself before waking the victim). Those items were also taken for analysis.

As the officers made their way outside, they noticed that the doorjamb of the back door had been chipped down with a knife. The victim's purse was found on the patio and its contents had been dumped onto the lawn. The plastic birdbath had been repositioned to be on top of a block of wood directly under the telephone wire. Closer inspection revealed cutting marks on the wire—but only the outer lining of the wire had been cut, leaving the main wire intact and the phone operational. It appeared that the birdbath had cracked under the assailant's weight, which had probably caused him to abandon his attempt to sever the phone line.

Ten dollars were stolen from the scene, some silver dollars were taken, and some packs of Winston cigarettes were missing as well.

Suspect Description

The attacker was described as a white male, early twenties, 5'9", 160 lbs. He was broad-shouldered, with a fairly muscular build. His legs were muscular with dark hair, and his arms had a lot of dark hair as well. He was described as "not well-endowed."

He wore a dirty white or gray tight-fitting mask made of a coarse-knitted material, which was constructed with a seam down the middle. It had eye holes, but no holes for the nose or mouth.

His clothing consisted of a dark navy blue or black t-shirt with short sleeves and a pocket on the left breast. He wasn't wearing any pants. His gloves were a coarse material similar to the mask, with elastic bands near the wrist (similar to garden gloves). He wore tennis shoes.

His knife was three or four inches long with a tapered end, and it may have been a pocket knife. He held it in his left hand, and wielded it in a way which may have indicated that he was left-handed.

The assailant whispered hoarsely through clenched teeth. His jaw didn't seem to move when he talked.

Post-Attack Events

Two weeks after the attack

Over a period of two weeks, the victim reported five or six more hang-up phone calls. This is interesting to note because as the East Area Rapist attack series wore on, it became clear that almost all of the hang-up calls to victims and neighbors occurred *before* the attack—almost never afterward.

March 26th, 1977

Nearly a year after the attack, while the East Area Rapist's crime was in full-swing, the towels and bed sheets from this case were removed from the evidence locker and sent to the crime lab. The goal was to examine the semen to determine the blood type of the attacker.

May 2nd, 1977

The results from the analysis were completed, and it was learned that the rapist was a "non-secretor." This is a medical situation where a person's blood type cannot be determined from a semen sample. It's a trait shared by about a fifth of the population.

January 2nd, 1978

A year and a half after her attack, the victim received several strange phone calls. One of them, where the caller repeatedly threatened to kill her and called her a "bitch," was recorded. The victim identified the voice of the caller as the man who had attacked her. A full transcript of this call, and several others, is printed later in the book.

Context and Analysis

A common axiom exists among criminologists–look at a serial offender's first attacks, and you can find clues to his or her origins. The proximity of the events described thus far in the book, while they may or may not be related, are important to look at as a group, especially since they all occurred just over a thousand feet from the Dawes and Dolecetto intersection that we've been discussing. Often a serial offender, due to inexperience, will make most of his or her mistakes early on in the series. Rancho Cordova may or may not be ground zero for this criminal, but there are certainly important clues to be gleaned from studying it.

The "fence hopper" noted in the Pre-Attack Events section is almost certainly the attacker, which would indicate a period of traversing the area well in advance of the attack. If the East Area Rapist arrived at this location by car, it seems he didn't park terribly close by if he had to use backyards to get around. The predominant theory is that he used the nearby canals and railroad tracks to traverse Rancho Cordova, and then went through backyards until he arrived at this victim's house.

The attempt to cut the outside line is a fairly unique feature of this particular attack when taking into account the rest of case. EAR frequently severed the lines in attacks, but from here on out he'd pretty much do it exclusively from inside the residence. Is this attempt at breaking the line from the yard, then not attempting again, an example of a new offender learning as he went? An alternate theory that's been put forth is that he wasn't trying to cut the line at all, but he was actually tapping into it and listening to the victim's phone calls. It didn't seem that the birdbath was designed to have someone stand on it though, so even if that's true, he couldn't have listened for long.

The victim's menstruation didn't deter the assailant. His seeming familiarity with the tampon and that part of a female's life has led some current investigators to believe that this offender started out on the older side of the age range, possibly mid-twenties rather than late teens.

You've probably noticed that we avoid trying to guess at or describe the emotions/thoughts that run through the victim's head during these events, and that we shy away from coloring or characterizing the perpetrator's actions unless it's relevant or unless it's something very obvious to the victim. Presenting these cases in such a "dry" and objective format is important to us—we feel that the reader can best be served by the facts of the case rather than a sensational retelling of events. The circumstances as they play out are tense and dramatic enough on their own. This isn't done as an effort to minimize the trauma and fear that the victims felt... far from it. This victim, and all subsequent victims, were uniform in their description of the utter fear and terror that they felt, as well as the firm belief that the assailant would've killed them at any moment and not thought twice about it. The distress and panic that washed over the victims at every turn is something that we don't have the words to describe. It's a given, and one of the primary purposes of this book is to someday dampen that fear by in some small way helping to put a name and a face to this man.

While this first attack occurred in Rancho Cordova and the third attack would occur only a few houses away, one of the main components of the EAR/GSK crime spree is that he would move around geographically and rarely commit an attack in the same area back-to-back. That's an important point to remember for any researchers trying to find early events that may or may not be related to the offender. Even though we've only discussed Rancho Cordova up to this point, finding an EAR-style burglary or assault in another part of the city or even another part of California does not automatically disqualify the event as being a part of the EAR/GSK series.

1976 Garage Beating

Date: July 16th, 1976 4:45 AM
Victim: Man (early 60s)
Location: Carmichael

Directly to the north of the area we've discussed so far is Carmichael, a community in East Sacramento separated from Rancho Cordova by the American River. In the early 1970s, a population of 37,000 resided in the eleven square miles and two zip codes that made up Carmichael, and at any given time, one could find dozens of joggers and bikers enjoying the ten miles of paths that made up a prominent area on Carmichael's southern edge called the American River Bike Trails. Fair Oaks Boulevard, a street paralleling the American River, was a major thoroughfare, and Rio Americano High School was the main school in the area.

Unfortunately, this quiet, serene location would be the East Area Rapist's next target. Before we look at the first attack in Carmichael though, it's worth looking at an event that happened the day before it (and in the same small area).

On July 16th, 1976, at 4:45 AM, a man leaving his house by way of the garage surprised an intruder in the act of rummaging through the man's tool box and cabinets. A confrontation ensued and the intruder responded violently, beating the homeowner with a club. The man made attempts to get away from the attacker, but he was unable to disengage from the onslaught. After suffering multiple savage blows, he was able to finally pull away and take cover under his car. The intruder by this time had unsheathed a revolver, and the man, stuck in a vulnerable position under the vehicle, awaited the inevitable gunshot.

It never came—the intruder ran off into the early morning and disappeared. The man made his way out from under the car, evaluated his wounds, and realized that they were quite severe. He had to be taken to the emergency room for treatment.

The police interviewed him, and the part of the description that stood out to investigators later on in the crime spree was the description of the club that the attacker was wielding. It was vintage military training club, short, with a white pad on the end. A club similar to this one would be used in Attack #3, an August attack in Rancho Cordova. Later, it was found that a club of this type had been stolen in one of the last known crimes of another California criminal named the "Visalia Ransacker." It was the first of many tenuous connections between these two offenders, who some think might even be the same person. We'll explore that later.

It wasn't until the East Area Rapist crimes were in full swing when it was determined that the event could've been more than a simple prowling—ties to the EAR became apparent. In addition to the club, the timing, and the geographic similarities, a young woman who fit the basic victim profile of the rapist had been living at the house until only a short time before the incident. It was theorized that she could've been a target.

Luckily, the man who was attacked in this case ended up making a full recovery from his wounds, and the young woman never became an EAR victim.

Attack #2

Date: July 17th, 1976 2:00 AM to 4:40 AM
Victims: 15-year-old girl. Her 16-year-old sister was bound
by the attacker but not raped.
Location: Marlborough Way, Carmichael

The Attack

On this mid-July weekend at a residence on Marlborough Way, two teenage sisters were enjoying the novelty of having the house to themselves while their parents were away on a four-day hiking trip with their church. Because they were by themselves, the girls made sure that all of the doors and windows were locked before they turned in for the night. It was about 10:30 PM when they went to bed.

A few hours later, the older sister was awakened by someone sitting on her back. She felt a knife against her neck and heard a hoarse whisper telling her that if she made a sound, she'd be stabbed and killed. The assailant reached over and yanked the phone out of the wall, then tied her up.

She caught several glimpses of her intruder as he threatened her again and again. He told her that he was going to "steal some stuff and be gone in half an hour."

The intruder woke the younger sister, who was fifteen, in the same manner (he sat on top of her and clamped his gloved hand over her mouth). She tried to scream.

"Shut up," he snarled though clenched teeth. "I have a knife and if you don't shut up I can kill you. If you make a move, I'm going to stab this right through your neck."

The girl rolled off the bed and took a swing at him, but her aim was off and she only hit his thigh. Realizing that she hadn't done much damage, she escaped into the hallway. "Goddamn it, what's this queer doing in here?" she shouted. She began yelling for her sister.

The intruder caught up with her and hit her on the back of the head three or four times. She fell to the floor and continued calling her sister's name. He hit her twice more and ordered her to "shut up," then informed her that the sister was already tied up.

The girl pretended to be unconscious, which angered the assailant. "Get your hands behind your back," he hissed, grabbing her arms and tying her hands tightly with string. He leaned in and whispered into her ear. "You do everything I want and I'll fill my bag and leave."

He put a sock in her mouth to gag her and tied a belt around her head to keep it in. He tied her feet and then grabbed her by the waist and began dragging her to the bedroom. He swung her up onto the bed and positioned her onto her stomach.

"If you move or make the bed twinge, I'll kill you."

He left the room. Both sisters could hear drawers opening and closing loudly throughout the house. He came back to check on the younger sister a few times, and on one trip, he tied a strip of towel around her eyes to blindfold her.

Several minutes later, he returned once again to the younger sister and flipped on the light. What he did next would become one of the strongest M.O. links in the entire rape series.

Still on her stomach, the victim felt his weight on the bed and she felt him looming over her. Her hands, still tied very tightly behind her, were starting to go numb. She could feel him draw closer, and then she felt his wet, lubricated, erect penis in her bound hands. "Play with it," he ordered. "Play with it."

She couldn't move her hands due to the restraints. He rocked back and forth. The victim could smell baby lotion.

He got close to her face and whispered loudly into her ear. "Have you ever fucked before?"

She shook her head.

Her feet were untied, and then she was forced onto her back. He raped her for a minute or two, lifting her t-shirt up and fondling her breasts very quickly while he did. Then he stood up and retied her feet.

"Where's the money?" he asked. She nodded toward the dresser, where she kept sixty dollars. She heard him moving things around. He opened drawers, pulled them out of the dresser, dumped them out, and then discarded the drawers onto the floor.

She had a picture of her and her boyfriend from the junior prom on the dresser. The photo was labeled as such on the back.

"When I saw you at the junior prom, I knew I had to fuck you," he said. She felt that he was lying (having read the back of the photo) and she didn't believe that she had ever met him.

He left the room and made his way to the older sister's room, where he threatened again to kill her with a knife.

Then he returned to the younger sister's room. He straddled the victim from the other side (with his head facing her feet). He put his penis in her hands and again ordered her to "play with it." "I'm in love with it," he said. "I'm in love with your fucking body."

Leaving her on her stomach, he got up, untied her feet, and raped her for a second time. After a few minutes he got up and walked around the room, then returned to her and raped her once more. He left the room. She heard him rummaging through the house for several minutes. He returned to her and raped her a final time. After this assault, he took some of the sheets and wiped between her legs.

"Where's the doctor's drugs?" he asked. "I looked in the refrigerator and they're not there."

The girl didn't know, so she shook her head.

The assailant seemed very angry at her answer. He breathed heavily through his mouth a few times, something she'd noticed he had done a few times earlier in the attack when he'd gotten angry. Then he left the room.

A moment later, the house was silent. Both girls waited and listened, and they heard a car engine start up and leave. The vehicle sounded like a standard four cylinder car.

Immediate Aftermath

The younger sister waited about thirty minutes before moving, just to be sure that the attacker was gone. After a safe amount of time had elapsed, she struggled with her bindings. She was unable to get free, but her blindfold came off, so she hopped over to her sister's room. The older sister had just freed herself, so she got scissors and cut the bindings off her younger sister's hands. They ran to their parents' room and called the operator for help.

Law Enforcement transported the victims to Sacramento Medical Center, and their parents arrived from out of town shortly afterward. The sisters were treated and then interviewed by Law Enforcement. Interviewers confirmed that only the younger sister had been sexually assaulted, but both of them had been hit and injured by the assailant.

The police processed the crime scene. They determined that the intruder had entered the residence by prying open the rear sliding glass door. Scuff marks on the fence indicated that he'd probably come and gone by way of backyards rather than the street. Footprints were found outside the older sister's window but not the younger sister's.

Four equal lengths of string were located in the house—they were the ligatures the rapist had used to tie the hands and feet of the girls. He had brought them with him to the scene.

Two empty beer cans were found in the kitchen, but the girls hadn't smelled alcohol on the assailant.

Suspect Description

The victims described their attacker as a white male, just under twenty years old, 5'10" to 6' tall, with a muscular frame.

He was wearing a light-brown mask with just eye holes, a print t-shirt, and blue corduroy pants. His shoes were waffle stompers (hiking shoes). Neither girl remembered him wearing gloves, but no fingerprints were found, so he probably was.

The younger sister clearly remembered him wearing a multi-colored stocking cap, but the other one did not.

Context and Analysis

The East Area Rapist's first victim was twenty-three years old, but here we already have him attacking a young teen. Sadly, many young girls would be assaulted before the crime spree ended.

The discrepancy in the description with the stocking cap was eventually resolved. The older sister was the first one to see him, and she'd gotten a good look at him. He definitely didn't have a multicolored stocking cap on his head at that point. But when the *younger* sister first encountered him, the assailant *was* wearing a multicolored stocking cap. What had happened was that after the rapist had tied up the older sister, he'd rummaged through her closet and removed a ski cap and some mittens. He'd put the ski cap on his head and left the mittens in a dresser drawer. Later on in the attack, he deposited the ski cap in that same dresser drawer. Since the wearing of the stocking cap didn't appear to have any practical use, this has been considered an example of perhaps the attacker "goofing off," and is sometimes pointed to when folks are trying to figure out his age or maturity level. Perhaps there was a practical purpose though... maybe he used the stocking cap to hide the shape of his head, hide some hair, hide a hole in his mask, or he might've even intended to use it as a blindfold for one of the girls.

It's difficult to tell how much planning went into this attack. Did he know that the girls would be alone? If so, how? How much planning would a novice offender have to do in order to mount an assault on a house with two individuals in it? Is it a sign that the offender had been committing these types of crimes already? It's interesting to note that the house was laid out in such a way that once inside, he had to pass the younger sister's room in order to get to the older sister's room. He'd obviously had a plan of some sort to secure the older sister first. Whether he came up with it on the spur of the moment, or whether he'd stalked the girls for a couple days while their parents were out of town, there's no way of knowing.

Investigators who interviewed the girls were intrigued by the assailant's use of the word "twinge" in the attack. They were also unclear as to how he knew that there was a doctor in the household, although they decided that the doctor's bag in the master bedroom might've given it away, or perhaps some mail or envelopes on a desk or counter. Asking for refrigerated drugs was an interesting aspect of the case as well, because only certain types of drugs require refrigeration.

The two beer cans found in the kitchen, without the girls smelling alcohol on the assailant's breath, would become a common theme at these attacks. The attacker's use of baby lotion to lubricate his penis and the fact that he didn't put his full weight on the girl that he raped would become common themes in future attacks as well.

At this point, Law Enforcement did not know that a serial offender was on the loose. The first attack in Rancho Cordova had been attributed to possibly a "local teen." This particular rape was considered very odd in the early days because it was unknown how the East Area Rapist selected these victims. Even today, investigators can't be sure. Perhaps it was through prowling neighborhoods after dark, something that was most likely becoming routine for him. One of the best guesses put forth was that perhaps he had initially seen the younger sister on the American River Bike Trails, a place that she visited several times every week. Perhaps it was at one of the girls' many school functions. Several options were thoroughly explored, including inquires to anyone who knew that the girls would be alone for those nights and anyone who had done construction work on their house. Nothing concrete was ever developed.

Attack #3

Date: August 29th, 1976 3:20 AM
Victims: Failed attack. Mother (41) and her two
daughters (12 and 15) were in the house. The mother
was beaten badly.
Location: Malaga Way, Rancho Cordova

Six weeks after the attack in Carmichael, the East Area Rapist resurfaced in Rancho Cordova. For this attack, he targeted a street called Malaga Way. Even though the house he attacked was on a different street from Attack #1, they practically shared a backyard. This makes for yet another incident in the very small geographical area near the intersection of Dawes and Dolecetto.

Pre-Attack Events

August 28th, 1976 10:00 PM
A neighbor near the intersection of Malaga Way and Paseo Drive (the same neighbor mentioned in the chapter about Attack #1) was still hearing noises at his fence. It had been going on since before Attack #1. After months of this, he'd even had to replace fence boards a few times. The fact that the activity had been noticed didn't deter the prowler, and the new fence boards were frequently broken. The neighbor's side gate had been left open quite a few times during the night as well, and the homeowner responded by nailing his gate shut (investigators would later learn that open side gates were one of the hallmarks of a visit by the East Area Rapist). This neighbor had never

reported any of this on his own, but when officers were canvassing the neighborhood for clues after Attack #1, he'd told them about some of the strange activity. Unfortunately, even the nailed gate wasn't a deterrent. On the night of August 28th, at 10:00 PM, the homeowner again heard the tell-tale sound of someone scaling his fence.

The Attack

Thirty minutes after the neighbor had heard the prowler at his fence, a man living in a house virtually next door to the victim from Attack #1 *and* virtually next door to the house where the fence-jumping was occurring had just left his family for the night. He was working his new shift at SMUD, Sacramento's utility company. This was only his second night working the night shift. His wife and two young daughters (twelve years old and fifteen years old) were to be home alone until morning.

The youngest daughter slept with her window open. At around 3:20 AM, the sound of the wind chimes on her curtain rod woke her up. Turning to look, she saw the dark silhouette of a masked man at her window and a gloved hand prying at the window screen. Realizing that he'd been spotted, the man stared at her for a moment, then sunk into the darkness and disappeared.

Frightened, the girl ran to her mother's room and shook her awake. Upon hearing the girl's story, the mother jumped up with a start and ran to look out the window. She didn't see anything, but she caught a faint whiff of a sweet-smelling aftershave that she didn't recognize. She was now on high alert and ran to wake up the older daughter. The teenager seemed unfazed by the story. She recommended that they call the police, turned over, and went back to sleep.

The mother considered calling the Sheriff, but she wanted to check the backyard again to see if the man was gone. As she and her younger daughter walked into the girl's bedroom, they saw that he'd returned to the window. Seeing the mother, the masked man turned and ran toward the back fence. The mother grabbed her daughter and

29

went quickly to the kitchen. She grabbed the phone and crouched down on the floor to dial the operator for assistance. Before the number could even be dialed, they heard a crash from the younger girl's room and the tell-tale sound of the wind chimes hitting the floor. Looking up, they saw the masked man running into the kitchen. He was armed with a gun in his left hand, a club in his right hand, and he wasn't wearing pants or underwear.

"Freeze or I'll kill you," he hissed at them. "Hang up the phone! Now!"

She hung up the phone.

"Who else is in the house?"

"Only my sister," the daughter replied.

The intruder approached them. As he did, the woman's maternal instinct kicked in.

She jumped up, grabbed at the man's gun, and pushed it away from her child. Fortunately, she found her adversary to be fairly weak, and she quickly began overpowering him. As she wrestled the gun away, he started pummeling her with the club in his free hand. She tried to dodge his blows, but the hits kept coming. She could hear her daughter screaming in the background. He knocked her back, then hit her over the head with the barrel of the gun. The woman crumpled to the kitchen floor.

"Don't worry," the man whispered at her, "all I want is your money. You won't be hurt if you cooperate."

He pulled her up and led her and the daughter to the couch. He began tying their hands behind their backs. The woman caught her second wind and began to resist again. "You need to accept God!" she cried as she struggled with the assailant.

The mother was able to overpower him and push him away, after which she began running for the front door with her daughter in tow. The club reappeared, hitting her over and over again, but she was able to open the door and usher her daughter out. She fought off the assailant one last time, then stumbled outside. They ran for their lives toward a neighbor's house, screaming as they went. The neighbor's door opened and they quickly sought refuge inside.

The commotion was enough to wake up the older daughter, who wisely made her escape through her bedroom window. She jumped the fence and, seeing her mother and sister disappear into the neighbor's house, followed the same route.

Immediate Aftermath

Several neighbors heard the victims screaming, but despite the street being well-lit, most of them didn't see the assailant.

The neighbor across the street got a pretty good view of the action, however. Alerted by the screams, she looked out her window and saw four people running from the house. One of them was a masked man with "white shorts" on. She watched as he ran across the street directly into her yard and then hid in the bushes. He waited there, watching the three girls go into the house. Then he simply stood up and started walking away. The neighbor turned her back for a moment and when she looked at the street again, he was gone. She later said that he didn't seem to be in a hurry at all—that he'd simply started walking off. She described him as walking upright, with a military bearing or the bearing of a police officer. She was quite surprised when she found out he was actually nude, not wearing "white shorts."

Upon arrival at the neighbor's house, the mother fell unconscious. They placed a towel around her head, and her injuries were so severe that she bled through it.

The police received the call at 3:28 AM, which was roughly five minutes after the women had arrived at the neighbors. Responding officers were only two blocks away, but by the time the call came through and they arrived, the assailant had been gone for several minutes.

They went to examine the scene. The front door was still open, and they noticed that it had blood on it. As they entered the house, they noticed blood on the floor and walls as well. A shattered picture frame was on the floor. In the kitchen they found more blood, and they noted that the phone cord had been ripped from the wall. There was a black shoelace on the arm of a chair near the couch where the intruder had intended to tie up his victims, and a black shoelace was located on the floor nearby. There was an off-white towel in the living room, and a two-inch by twelve-inch piece of torn towel on a couch cushion. Neither the towels nor the shoelaces belonged to the family.

The officers examined the backyard. Under the window leading to the youngest daughter's bedroom, officers found that the intruder had relocated a small wooden patio chair to give himself something to stand on. The screen had been removed from the sliding glass window and the curtain rod had indeed crashed down on one side. The mother told the officers that she thought the assailant might've had his pants on when he was in the backyard, so they searched it expecting to find his pants, but they were unsuccessful.

The mother was taken in an ambulance to Kaiser Hospital. Fortunately, the bleeding had stopped on its own, but her injuries were severe enough to need medical attention and stitches.

Suspect Description

The combined description of the assailant was that of a white male, between eighteen and twenty years old, though maybe as old as twenty-five. He was 5'9" or 5'10", slim, about 165 lbs, and was lacking upper-body strength. His legs were thin, tanned, and appeared to be muscular. They didn't have any noticeable hair. His pubic hairs were dark. He didn't have an erection when he confronted them and his penis seemed fairly small. The younger sister felt that he might have been blonde because of his complexion, and she noticed that the skin tone on his butt was much lighter than his legs.

The mask he wore was hood-like, not knit but maybe nylon, though not like a nylon stocking. It was tight-fitting, with a slit for the eyes and no holes for the mouth or nose. He had on a light brown t-shirt that went to his hips and black leather gloves. He had on ankle-high dark-brown shoes—possibly boots—with laces. His belt was shiny, three or four inches wide, and brown. The mother compared it to "lineman's belt" (something that someone working for the utility company might wear). The noted similarity to a lineman's belt and the usage of that term might've been influenced by the victim's familiarity with SMUD, the local utility company for which the victim's husband worked.

The attacker had held a gun in his left hand and a club in his right. The gun was very small—possibly a two-inch revolver. Its description made it sound similar to an off-duty police officer's weapon. The club that the assailant wielded was about a foot long, made of wood, was either light brown or yellowish, and possibly had some leather on it. It wasn't a modern design; it was perhaps surplus military in style or vintage police-issue. When striking the victim, the assailant at one point moved the club to his left hand and seemed to prefer hitting with his left.

The assailant's voice was described as being "controlled," and he spoke through clenched teeth. It was described as a forced whisper, like he was trying to make his voice sound deeper than it really was— at least, initially. After he physically fought with the mother, his voice became much higher and it seemed to be shaky. The assailant never used any obscenities—a rarity in an East Area Rapist attack.

Post-Attack Event

August 31st, 1976 3:30 AM
A couple days after the failed attack on Malaga Way, the neighbor who had observed the assailant hide in her bushes suffered a break-in at her home. Thankfully, the intruder didn't confront her, and nothing was stolen from the residence. The time of night was almost exactly the same time that the house across the street had been invaded just two days before.

Context and Analysis
Thankfully, after already inflicting so much damage and pain to East Sacramento, the rapist was foiled. The contusions on the mother's head (two on the back and one on her forehead) required thirty-two stitches. She had bruising on her arms, shoulders, face, and sternum. These were battle scars to wear proudly—this brave and selfless

woman had certainly spared her family from many horrors.

The EAR/GSK case is one with thousands of tiny details, but so many of them come from eyewitness reports, which are inherently difficult to work with. Only a small percentage of the details can be regarded as hard facts. Geography is one of those things that can be categorized as unquestionably factual. Investigators can deal with timing and geographical information unencumbered by forty years of lost reports, conflicting statements, myth, and hearsay. Attack #3 is one of the most important pins on the map because of the very close proximity to Attack #1, and we can explore what that might tell us about the offender's early activities and situation.

Does this proximity to Attack #1, in addition to the assailant seemingly traveling on foot both nights and arriving with no pants on for both attacks, point to an offender who lived nearby? That's the $50,000 question (or whatever the reward money is at the time you're reading this). Could he still have driven a car or traveled on a bike to the scene? Malaga Way wasn't as built up back then as it is today, and there was a place to hide a vehicle or bicycle at the end of the street. And consider this: someone driving a car with no pants looks exactly the same as someone driving *with* pants. Someone biking with no pants does tend to stand out, though.

It's unfortunate that Law Enforcement (and the neighbor with the fence activity) didn't have enough context to understand that a serial rapist was using the backyards as an expressway. And the brazenness of the criminal to see fence boards replaced and a gate nailed shut but still continue to travel the same path without wondering if he'd be discovered says a lot about the perp—either his recon ability or his foolhardiness, at least. Perhaps both.

The use of a club here, in conjunction with the garage attack in Carmichael, is definitely interesting, and it's something that helps tie some of these initial attacks together. The military or police overtones to the offender in this attack are also notable... we have a club that's similar to an old police-issue weapon, a revolver with similarities to an off-duty weapon, and the assailant that seemed to an eyewitness (and the mother as well) to be someone who might have been a policeman or in the military because of his posture and bearing.

Then we have the odd situation of the offender wearing something like a lineman's belt to attack the family of a utility employee. The East Area Rapist / Golden State Killer is not thought of as one who made poetic statements, so it could be an odd coincidence, or the victim could just be using terms that she's familiar with to describe an item that was actually something else. It could've been military in origin, or something else entirely.

The police departments serving the Sacramento area were not winning awards for interdepartmental communication at this time in history, and almost nothing was computerized because of the time period, so the possibility that a serial offender was at work was not yet on the radar. Despite the attack being thwarted, it was certainly brought it into the fold rather quickly once it it became obvious that East Sacramento was being terrorized by a serial rapist due to its proximity to Attack #1. But those dots had not yet been connected at the time of the attack.

In addition to the continued fence hopping, an example of the offender's nerve and tenacity is that he continued his attack even though he'd been spotted twice by the occupants of the house. That's a unique boldness. The calmness with which he walked away after the failed assault is also interesting, especially considering that the police were only two blocks from the scene (though he probably didn't know that). It seems trickier somehow to make daring escapes without pants on, so one would've expected him to move a little faster. The seemingly casual nature of his escape could say a lot about where home base was, or perhaps it's a peek into his unique brand of psychopathy or the overconfidence of a fledgling offender.

How had this family come to be on his radar? Had he seen them while jumping fences to get to or from (or near) Attack #1 on Paseo Drive? How familiar was he with them before he attacked? He had asked them who else was in the house, but did he already know? Was this a sign that he didn't know, and that the attack was more spontaneous? This was only the husband's second night working the nightshift. The fence noise had come thirty minutes before the husband left, so had the assailant watched the husband leave for work? The family only owned one car, so anyone familiar with the street and going by the front of the house would've known that he wasn't there. Was the rapist indeed familiar enough with the household to know that they only had one car? The foliage at this residence, especially in the front, was quite thick. Was this part of the reason that the offender chose this location? Since the husband had only been working that shift for a very short time, there couldn't have been *too* much planning put into this attack. Perhaps that's why it failed?

Also: who was the intended victim? Law Enforcement at the time assumed it was the teenager, especially since she had a lot of physical similarities to the rape victim in Attack #2. But it was the twelve year-old's room that was entered. Did the rapist plan on tying up the younger sister, and then plan on going off to assault the older sister like he had done in the previous attack (but with the ages reversed)? How did he plan on controlling the mother? Or was he hoping that he could be quiet enough to where she wouldn't awaken? Was he being reckless by escalating so quickly, first trying to control one victim, then two, and now three? Was he overconfident in his abilities?

There are certain echoes of the October 21st, 1975 attack in this one. Perhaps the plan was to tie up the daughters one by one, then the mother, then bring some of them into the same room with each other before assaulting them.

Thankfully, this attack was thwarted, so, short of the EAR/GSK being apprehended and confessing, we'll never know the answers to some of these questions.

Attack #4

Date: September 4th, 1976 11:00 PM to 2:00 AM
Victim: 29-year-old woman
Location: Crestview Drive, Carmichael

Attack #2 had occurred in mid-July and Attack #3 had occurred in late August, but all was not quiet on the EAR front during those intervening weeks. All throughout August, there were prowling incidents on a street called Crestview Drive, a location in Carmichael positioned a full six miles north to the scene of Attack #2, the other Carmichael assault. Despite the distance between them, the locations of Attack #2 and Attack #4 were almost directly connected by Carmichael's main thoroughfare, a street called Fair Oaks Blvd (and later down the road, Manzanita Avenue).

Pre-Attack Events

Mid-August 1976
Two doors down from where the attack would happen, a neighbor spotted a prowler in his backyard. The prowler appeared to be in his late teens.

Late August 1976
Within a day or two of Attack #3, another house on Crestview Drive was forcibly entered. Strangely, nothing was taken.

The Attack

On the evening of September 4th, 1976, a twenty-nine-year-old divorced mother of two decided to stop by her parents' house to do laundry (her own washing machine was broken and her parents were out of town). She arrived at 6:00 PM, and because of the early hour and the mild weather, she left the garage door open.

By 11:00 PM she'd finished, and she had just put her laundry into the trunk of her car when she felt a hand on her shoulder. She was forcibly spun around and just barely caught a glimpse of a masked man before a fist slammed into her face. Her nose was broken and she briefly lost consciousness as she fell to the ground. Blood from her face soaked into the driveway. The next thing she remembered was seeing a small knife and hearing threats.

"Don't look at me. If you look at me I'll slit your throat."

He pulled her to her feet and began to push and drag her to the side of the house. "All I want is money to get to Bakersfield.," he told her. He also told her that he wanted her car, and repeated his threat that if she looked at him, he'd "slit her throat."

He tied her hands tightly behind her with white shoelaces and then pushed her into the house. "Is anyone expected home soon?" he asked as he dragged the woman from room to room.

The assailant checked every area of the house and then took her to a bedroom. He forced her onto the bed, positioned her on her stomach, tied her feet together, and then gagged and blindfolded her. He left her there and began wandering through the house by himself. He rummaging through closets and drawers and spent time in the kitchen, where she thought she heard him eating. Eating in victims' homes would become another East Area Rapist / Golden State Killer hallmark.

Every few minutes he returned to check on her, threatening to kill her if she moved or made a sound.

At one point, she heard him down the hall, talking in a very low voice. It sounded like he was talking on the telephone, but the victim couldn't be sure.

He checked on her again, only this time she didn't hear him leave the room. She heard a sound which she later realized was the assailant applying lotion to himself, and then she felt his weight on the bed. He straddled her, and then she felt his penis in her bound hands.

"Do it right or I'll kill you," he said, moving back and forth. He cut her clothing off with a knife, held the knife against her throat, and threatened to kill her yet again. He turned her over, then told her that she had a "nice body" and asked her if anyone else had ever told her so. He orally copulated her and raped her.

During the assault, he bragged that when he was "in the army," he had made love to "all the girls" and had never met one that "didn't like it."

Throughout the nearly three hours that he was in the house with her, he raped her twice, sodomized her, forced her to masturbate him, and ejaculated onto her leg. He climaxed into her mouth twice and forced her to swallow it and repeated his comment about her "nice body." All the while, she was dizzy from the pain of her broken noise, her face was stained with blood from the injury, and her hands were numb and turning black from the ligatures.

When he was through torturing her, he dragged her outside and tied her to a patio post, then stole her car to make his getaway.

Immediate Aftermath
The police were called, and the victim's sister arrived to assist her. She was taken to Kaiser Hospital.

Responding officers took inventory of the scene. All of the lights in the house were off except for one, and the air conditioner had been unplugged. There were two empty Coors beer cans in the kitchen, and the assailant had propped the back door open with a chair.

September 5th, 1976 7:00 AM
Her stolen car was found abandoned on Oakgreen Circle, a street located a little over a quarter mile away from the scene.

Suspect Description

The victim described her attacker as a white male, 5'8" or 5'9", with a slender build. She didn't see any of his hair, but his pubic hair was dark and he had a lot of lighter hair on his legs.

The mask appeared to be homemade—a gray flannel hood with holes for the eyes and mouth. He had on a dark green t-shirt, black imitation leather gloves, and a black belt.

He spoke by whispering through clenched teeth.

Context and Analysis

This attack is significant to the series for a number of reasons. While Attack #3 might have given indication that the rapist was stalking a small area or street in advance of his assaults, the events on Crestview Drive helped confirm that several days or perhaps several weeks of reconnaissance was being performed before some of the attacks. What's interesting is that the prowling on Crestview Drive took place a week before the attack on Malaga Way, which indicated that multiple areas were being cased at the same time.

Geographically, this was the furthest that the assailant had struck from the initial epicenter area of Dawes Street and Dolecetto Drive. The other Carmichael attack, Attack #2 on Marlborough Way, was closer to bike trails and the main school. A school and a park bordered the east side of this attack (Thomas Kelly Elementary and Del Campo Park).

It's long been theorized that this was a crime of opportunity, because the assailant couldn't have known that the woman would be at that house doing laundry. Also, he asked her if anyone was expected home. It's possible that he didn't know if she was telling the truth or not, which is why the back door was propped open with a chair, allowing him a quick means of escape.

This attack is also notable for its brutality. As the series wore on, it would become apparent that an attack committed after a failure would almost always be more sadistic. Perhaps the failure of Attack #3 was responsible for the violence shown, and also the reduced time between attacks (Attack #3 was only a week before this one). Either there was a certain anger at the failure, or perhaps whatever frustration or compulsion that drove this offender to commit these crimes had not been released in Attack #3 and had pent up to a boiling point. Regardless of whether being rerouted in Attack #3 had anything to do with this, once these crimes were connected, it became clear that the offender was escalating.

Attack #5

Date: October 5th, 1976 6:45 AM to 8:20 AM
Victim: Mother (29). Her 3-year-old son was also in the house.
Location: Woodpark Way, Citrus Heights

Crestview Drive in Carmichael had suffered several prowling incidents and break-ins throughout the month of August, leading up to Attack #4. In September, a similar cloud of odd activity settled over a small area in Citrus Heights, another community in East Sacramento. While there was evidence of simultaneous stalking in #3 and #4, the stalking here seemed to begin around the time that the stalking for the area of Attack #4 was completed, with very little overlap.

Pre-Attack Events

Late August and Early September 1976
This is the approximate time period that prowlers, burglaries, and hang-up phone calls began in the area of Woodpark Way.

September 4th, 1976
This is the approximate date that the victim started receiving hang-up phone calls. After the victim would answer the phone, the person on the other end would sit in silence for a few moments and then hang up. These types of phone calls were being received by several neighbors. They continued up until the week of the attack.

September 21st, 1976

A burglary occurred at the victim's home. The first indication that someone had been in the home was the presence of some cheap jewelry that didn't belong to the victim. Upon investigating the perimeter of their house and the possible entry points, she and her husband noticed pry marks on their son's bedroom window. They took inventory of their own jewelry and discovered that a bracelet and some inexpensive earrings were missing from a jewelry box in the bedroom. The expensive items were left untouched.

Responding officers determined that the son's bedroom window had indeed been the entry point, and they noticed that a nearby flowerbed had been trampled. The bedroom window faced the backyard, which backed up to a giant field. In the middle of the field, a sock belonging to the victim's husband was found.

The jewelry that had been left in the house was examined, and as it turned out, it belonged to a neighbor several houses away. Apparently they too had been burglarized. In fact, there were burglary incidents happening all up and down Woodpark Way. Junk jewelry belonging to one house was being left in another, and all the while, hang-up phone calls were continuing to happen in the neighborhood.

October 1st or 2nd, 1976 6:15 AM

This is the approximate date that a woman living on a nearby street (the southeast corner of Shadow Brook Way) saw a strange man standing in her driveway next to her car. When the man discovered that he'd been spotted, he stood and stared at her for over a full minute, then calmly walked across the street, got into a dark green car (possibly a Chevy Vega), and drove away. She described him as a white male in his thirties, 5'10", 170 lbs, with thick dark hair. The stranger's car was parked exactly where the bloodhounds would later lose the East Area Rapist's scent after the attack.

October 2nd, 1976

This is the approximate date that the victim had a strange encounter with an unknown male at the club on Travis Air Force Base. The victim had arrived to meet friends, and she decided to go to the bathroom before joining them. As she entered a dark hallway, a man approached her from the shadows. She immediately felt anxious and didn't turn to look at him. "Excuse me," he said, "I haven't seen you here before. Do you mind if I ask your name?" Something about his voice scared her. Still without looking at him, she told him she was with friends, and that her husband was a captain. "Sorry, I didn't mean anything," he replied, and then he turned and entered the men's bathroom. She caught a only a glimpse of him as he disappeared. He was described as short, with a thin build, wearing a white t-shirt and camouflage pants. He spoke without moving his mouth.

October 4th, 1976

The victim was at home with her young son, and her husband was at work. The phone rang, and she was greeted with silence on the other end, just as she had been for several weeks. By now she was fed up with the silent, hang-up phone calls, and she began shouting at the person on the other end. "Who is this? Stop calling like this. The police know about it and they know who you are."

"I'm going to kill your husband," the voice on the other end whispered.

She hung up, tried to reach her husband by phone but wasn't able to, so she called the police. There wasn't much the police could do. They initially felt that it was a prank and tried to reassure her.

The Attack

The victim's husband woke up at 5:00 AM. Her son climbed into bed with the her at 6:30 AM, and a few minutes later, her husband left for work.

About ten minutes later, the woman heard two clicks, like a light being flipped on and off quickly, and then she heard footsteps running down the hallway. A masked figure suddenly appeared at her bedroom door. She screamed and pulled her son close while the man approached. He held a knife above his head as he walked.

"Shut up. All I want is your money. I won't hurt you. Shut up and stay there. Cooperate and you won't get hurt. I have a knife." Now standing beside the bed, he held the knife against her body.

"Please don't hurt us. I'll tell you where my money is, just please take it and leave us," the victim said.

He poked her with the knife several times and put it to her neck. He told her that if she didn't do what he wanted, he would kill her and her son. He ordered her to roll onto her stomach. She complied. Unable to see him now, she heard him tearing cloth.

Using shoelaces he'd brought with him, he pulled her hands behind her back and tied them. He blindfolded and gagged her with the towels he had torn into strips, pulled the sheets away from her feet, and tied her ankles together.

"Take my money and go. Please go," she said over and over as she was bound.

"Shut up or I'll use this knife. I swear I'll use this knife." With his victim tied securely, his threats became angrier. "All I want is money," he hissed repeatedly.

He was now tying her son's hands and feet. He lifted the boy off the bed and placed him onto the floor. With both residents secured, the intruder began rummaging through the house. He went through every drawer and inspected every closet, returning to check on the victim every few minutes. Occasionally while checking on her, he'd slide the blade of his knife along her body. Other times he would quietly stand beside her. There were times when she didn't know if he was standing near her or not, so she'd try to ask a question through her gag. If he was there, he'd tell her to "shut up" and again threaten to stab her.

During one of his ransacking spells, she heard him moving a chair to the front door.

He returned to the bedroom and told her that he'd found money and that he was going to leave soon. She heard him tearing cloth again near the bed and then heard a different sound, one that she would soon realize was the sound of lotion.

He leaned over her, and she felt his weight on the bed. He put his penis into her bound hands and told her to "play with it." She tried to tell him that her hands were tied too tightly, and he promptly told her to "shut up." She tried once more to protest, and he replied with "Shut up and do what I say or I'll use this knife." She noticed that his penis felt very small. It was lubricated with lotion.

He untied her feet and raped her. "Do it like you do with the captain," he told her. "You looked good at the Officer's Club." He also told her that he had seen her at a "dance with the captain" at the McClellan Air Force Base Officer's Club. He remarked that she had a "beautiful, big pussy," and asked her if his dick was "like the captain's." She could tell that he was becoming aroused by saying these things, both before and after the actual rape, and later learned that he had climaxed.

When he pulled out, he put his penis into her hands again and once more told her to "play with it."

After the assault, he told her that he was "going into the kitchen to prepare something to eat," and that if he heard any movement in the room, he'd come back and kill her. She heard him in the kitchen with a frying pan.

Next she heard him at the back sliding door. Even though she was fairly certain that he was gone, to be safe, she waited over thirty minutes before removing her gag and blindfold. Her three-year-old son was beside her, tied up with towels, and she wondered if he had witnessed what had happened. She told him to stay put, and she was able to make her way to the back sliding door, which the assailant had closed when he'd left. She worked it open, despite her hands and feet being tied, and hopped around the side of the house to the gate. She was able to get the attention of neighborhood children, and they went for help.

Immediate Aftermath

The police got the call around 8:30 AM. When they arrived, they brought a bloodhound with them to track the assailant. The dog was turned loose in the backyard, and he picked up the scent immediately. He went in a winding path all across the backyard and stopped under the son's window—the same one that had been used by the burglar several weeks prior. He then went in a straight shot from the window to the rear fence. They put the dog over the fence, and the scent was followed across an overgrown field, past a house trailer that was located on the west side of the field, through some trees that were being bulldozed, and then onto Shadow Brook Way, a street on the west side of the field that had some newer homes. There were only two houses that bordered the field on Shadow Brook Way, and the dog stopped at an oil spot on the street at the curb across from them. Investigators at the scene determined that the assailant had probably parked a car there.

It was the spot where the woman had seen the strange man just a few days prior, and the same car that he'd been driving was actually seen again on the morning of the attack. This time it was described as a dark-colored car, possibly a 1952 Chevy Coupe. It was seen parked at that spot a little before 7:00 AM. Another neighbor left for work sometime after 8:00 AM and neither he nor his wife saw a car parked there at that time.

The victim was taken to Sacramento Medical Center for an examination. Her hands had turned black from the tightness of the ligatures, and there were deep indentations on her wrists. She had a minor wound on her left shoulder.

The assailant had entered the house through the same bedroom window that had been used in the burglary, and he'd left through the back patio door. Two black shoelaces that had been tied together were used to bind the victim, and white shoelaces were also found in the house. The assailant had brought them with him. Two hairs were found on the laces. He had used towels belonging to the victim. Fingerprints were found at the scene, but they did not come from the assailant. He stole $160 during the attack.

Suspect Description

The attacker seemed to be a white male in his thirties, 5'9" or 5'10", and medium weight.

He wore a ski mask that was either khaki or a grayish green. It had eye holes but no nose or mouth holes. He also wore a jacket.

Based on the pattern of a wound on the victim's shoulder, police were able to determine that the knife used in this assault had a serrated edge.

His voice was described as a quiet whisper, probably through clenched teeth. Not as hoarse as in the other attacks. He'd used the phrase "shut up" several times, even when he'd asked the victim a question and she'd tried to answer it.

Post-Attack Event

Mid-February 1977

The victim in this case had a possible sighting of her attacker over four months after her assault. She spotted a man walking in the neighborhood heading toward Greenback Lane. He seemed very suspicious and he reminded her in some way of her attacker. She drove by him twice to get a better look. After getting a look at different angles, she was even more convinced that it might be him. She called the police, but by the time they arrived, the suspicious man was gone.

Context and Analysis

The most striking thing about this attack in relation to the others is the time of day. It occurred during the early daylight hours, a factor that tremendously increased the risk of the assailant being seen. But since the victim lived with her husband, and her husband was home at night, the rapist probably determined that if he wanted to target this particular victim, then the early daylight hours were his only option. He was clearly lurking nearby, waiting for the husband to leave. Does this indicate a familiarity with their schedule?

We've talked about victim selection a bit already, and we'll take a break in the next chapter and talk about it at length. When it comes to selection and stalking, this one stands out quite a bit because of that strange incident a few days before the attack that might actually have been the EAR making contact with his victim in-person. That would be an extreme rarity in the EAR/GSK case as far as we know. In addition to that, at the time of the attack, the victim truly did feel that her attacker knew her from the club at Travis or McClellan. Again, if any of these in-person contacts were actually EAR, this was an extremely rare occurrence. If true, would that be an added thrill for the assailant? Was it an early part of his M.O. that he decided to drop because it was too risky? Was there something so "special" about this victim that it warranted the added risk? Did the attacker need to "justify" his assaults somehow, and her rejection of him in the hallway served as a sort of twisted reason to attack?

To recap quickly, the very first EAR attack seemed well-planned and contained many elements that would continue throughout the series. Attacks #2 and #3 seem to be more of a mystery as far as stalking and victim selection, and #4 seemed spontaneous, despite the extensive stalking that had gone on in the neighborhood prior to the assault. This attack is the first one that contained a fairly complete example of what would be known as the EAR/GSK's stalking M.O.: hang-up phone calls, break-ins, prowling, parking across fields, stealing insignificant items, etc. We can't be sure, but because of the timing and large area hit by burglaries and phone calls, it does seem that the neighborhood was selected and targeted before the EAR zeroed in on the victim, although it does seem he zeroed in on her fairly quickly. So that brings up an interesting question—did he come to know her at Travis or McClellan like he said, or did he come by her while prowling this street? The fact that other neighbors were getting phone calls and prowlers before she was indicates the latter, which would mean that the attacker was lying about knowing her from the base, probably in an effort to throw off investigators. The dropping of "red herrings" like this to mislead the police would seemingly become a common theme with this well-organized offender, though it can't be proven that all or most of what he said during attacks was a lie. Perhaps his victim selection method here was a little of both: maybe he came across her while prowling the street, and then stalked her at the Officer's Club at Travis or McClellan? A scenario like that would require him to be military (either a solider or employed as a steward or janitor or something) or family of military—a lead that's been explored for decades.

Geographically, it seemed that the field was a main draw to the area for him (very easy to walk along fences and peek into backyards), but it's worth noting that there was a cement-lined ditch to the north of the attack area as well that could've appealed to him.

The M.O. used during the attack might seem a little formulaic to you by now. One of the big differences between the very first attack and some of the subsequent ones though is the act of the assailant forcing his victim to masturbate him with their bound hands. Another difference, a bit more subtle, is that in the first attack, the rapist rummaged through the house after the sexual assault. The last few completed attacks have shown though that he now preferred to start rummaging before *and* after the sexual assault. He also began staying longer in the houses, perhaps a sign that his confidence was growing.

The responding deputy felt that the sock left in the field at the pre-attack burglary was probably used as a glove by the assailant. That would mean that until he found the sock in the house, he'd potentially have left fingerprints all over the place, or at least on the window that he pried. Nothing viable was found, however.

During the attack, he moved a chair to the front door, most likely so that anyone entering the front door would make a loud noise and alert him. Also, the "game" of moving jewelry from one house to another makes no sense to an outside observer, yet it occurred here and it would occur a few more times in the crime spree.

This was the first time that we can be fairly positive that the EAR's car was seen. What's interesting is that it's description matches up fairly well with the car that Victim #1 thought was stalking her, and it roughly matches the noise that the victims in Attack #2 had heard. A lot of suspicious vehicles would be associated with the offender as time wore on, but at this point, we've only got one basic description.

And if that was truly the EAR's vehicle, then the sighting of the man on Shadow Brook Way could've been the first clear sighting of the EAR. What's interesting is that it varies in fairly significant ways from the countless sightings that would follow, but this sighting is incredibly hard to discount. The man sighted was described as heavier, in his thirties, and with thick, dark hair. In the coming years, the description would typically be that of a younger, trimmer man with light brown or blonde collar-length hair.

Thankfully, the victim's young son was not traumatized by this incident. He didn't at all comprehend what was happening and actually thought that the assailant was a doctor who was applying bandages. After having not discussed the attack at all while the young man grew up, his mother finally asked him if he had witnessed the sexual assault. She learned that the rapist had moved her son to another room before the rape, and then moved him back when it was over.

This victim, a truly incredible woman, has come forward and participated in a lot of advocacy work for this case. She's a gifted speaker, and in addition to all of the work she's done on the road and on television, she's written a compelling book about her life and her experiences related to this attack. The book is titled "Frozen in Fear" by Jane Carson-Sandler. It's a fantastic read, and I highly recommend it.

Occupational Ties

While there were some strong geographical links early on, as the number of attacks began to mount it became more difficult for investigators to wrap their heads around the possible methods that the offender was using to select victims. The perimeter of the attacks expanded and the demographics of the victims became more diverse, so a strong thread of commonality simply didn't seem to exist.

Forty years later, we have many more data points than the original investigators did, and still, the exact methods can't be cracked. It's worth discussing which angles seem to come up the most, and you can look for some of these connections and form some of your own ideas as you work through the rest of the attacks.

The first five assaults provide an example of almost every major theme that exists throughout the rest of the entire crime series, or at least every theme that exists in a statistically significant way. Some of these might be coincidences, or they might be proof that the offender used far more than geography to find his prey. Something about some of the victims' occupation(s) or activities could have possibly led them into his crosshairs.

Victim #1: Insurance Rater for Pacific Bell Telephone
This victim worked for the phone company, and throughout the crime spree there are little hints here and there that the offender might've had some kind of ties to utilities or some kind of association with phones. The most notable oddities regarding potential phone manipulation occur with Attack #23, the first Stockton attack. The

insurance industry, another facet of her job, doesn't come up very much until the murder series in Southern California. It's interesting that the first victim and some of the final victims share this tie.

The victim's father was retired from the Air Force, and he had spent several years stationed at Mather Air Force Base (which was fairly close to many of the attacks). The victim herself had been to the hospital associated with that base when her mother was ill and died. As you'll soon notice, military and medical connections abound in the EAR/GSK cases.

Victim #2: Father was a Cardiologist

Out of all of the potential connections among victims, the connections to the medical industry are the strongest. Strong medical ties occur in over fifty percent of the attacks. There are several doctors, nurses, pharmacy clerks, medical students, folks who had just undergone major procedures, and the like. The vast amount of locations that the assailant operated in makes the offender's connection to any one particular hospital or medical field less likely, but this connection remains notable, even if we don't know exactly what it means.

Victim #3: Utility Company

We've discussed phones briefly, but other utilities come up in this case a few times as well, particularly the water departments. Not only were two victims directly related to the water company targeted, but there were a couple attacks were a suspicious vehicle was spotted in areas that were only accessible to employees of the water company. The stalking opportunities afforded by a job with a utility would seem to fit what is known about the offender.

Victim #4: Education and Government

This victim worked downtown for the California Department of Community Colleges, and her ex-husband worked at Sierra College in the Social Sciences Department. Additionally, a neighbor that was seemingly burglarized by the EAR/GSK worked near the Capitol

Mall in downtown Sacramento (at the California State Motor Pool). These types of links to government and education (particularly in downtown Sacramento) come up quite a bit.

Victim #5: Registered Nurse in the Air Force Reserves

This victim worked as a flight nurse at Travis Air Force Base with the Sixty-Fifth Aeromedical Evacuation Squadron. She spent most of her time at work caring for the wounded soldiers returning from Vietnam. Her husband was a captain in the regular Air Force and worked at McClellan. With this victim, we have both the military *and* the medical connection. Additionally, this victim was attending California State University in Sacramento, which provides a tie to the educational field as well. The military connection, which is very strong in Sacramento, begins to dissipate once the offender begins attacking elsewhere, suggesting the possibility that perhaps the military angle *was* chance, and that the amount of military installations in the East Sacramento area could've been responsible for this trend.

A great many of the other victims had similar occupational profiles. There's no one single thread connecting them, but there are quite a few similarities. Forty years of research and questions have yet to smoke out the exact selection methods used by the EAR/GSK, but as we work through the attacks, no doubt these elements will jump out at you again and again—far more than mere chance should account for.

Attack #6

Date: October 9th, 1976 4:30 AM to 5:30 AM
Victim: 19 year-old woman
Location: El Segundo Drive, Rancho Cordova

The assailant seemed to be comfortable hitting new neighborhoods, but he had no problem returning to ones he'd already been to. Attack #6 occurred fairly close to Attacks #1 and #3, on a fairly short street called El Segundo which ran parallel to Paseo Drive (where the first attack occurred), and ran right into Malaga Way (where the third attack occurred). Five-hundred feet to the northeast we find the infamous Dawes and Dolecetto intersection.

Pre-Attack Events

March 7th, 1973
This burglary, covered at the beginning of the book, occurred while the victim was living with her family on Dawes Street. The house was broken into, but the only damage inside was a bit of rummaging. Nothing of value was taken, save for a single earring from a pair belonging to the victim and a wine bottle full of coins.

October 4th, 1976
This is the approximate date that a neighbor on the southern part of El Segundo spotted a prowler in her backyard.

<u>October 9th, 1976 3:30 AM</u>
An hour before the attack began, a neighbor's dog began to bark.

The Attack
The victim, home alone for the weekend, went to sleep around midnight. Sometime around 4:30 AM, she heard someone whispering her name. She started to stir and as she did, a gloved hand clamped over her mouth. She felt something sharp jab into the top of her shoulder near her neck.

"Don't scream or I'll kill you," an voice hissed at her. She was forcefully turned over onto her stomach and her arms were pulled back. "Shut up or I'll kill you," the intruder said. He tied her wrists tightly with shoelaces, wrapped some cloth around her eyes for a blindfold, and shoved cloth into her mouth to gag her. He tied a piece of towel around her head to hold it in place.

He demanded money, telling her that he needed a "fix." "Better have money," he warned her. He threatened to kill her if she screamed, and then he stood next to her. His breathing came in short, rapid breaths.

"Get up," he hissed. She felt him pull her up, grab her arm, and begin leading her blindly down the hallway. He told her to duck down, and he wove her left and right as they moved forward. Occasionally she felt something like rope scrape against her bare back.

He pushed her onto the patio outside and told her to lie down on a rug. He whispered loudly into her ear, telling her that he'd been "dreaming about" her and that he had "always wanted to fuck" her, and then he bound her feet together. She heard him leave and go back into the house, and then she heard him come back. He began walking around in the backyard.

After a few moments, he went back into the house and came out again. He asked her for money once more, and repeated that he "needed a fix." "Better have money," he warned again. Then he went back into the house.

When he returned, he stood next to her very closely. She could still hear him breathing in those short, rapid breaths. Then, there was a new sound. He was masturbating.

He bent down and she felt something very sharp against her skin. "You better let me do this," he hissed at her. He turned her over onto her stomach and straddled her, then put his penis in her bound hands and moved back and forth a few times. He turned her over once more, unbound her feet, put her legs up in the air, and rested them on his shoulders. Then he entered her for a short time. He climaxed inside.

He went into the house for a little while, came back out, and raped her again. Then he put his penis into her hands again and moved back and forth, telling her once more to "play with it." He entered her for a third time, and climaxed inside of her again.

He got up, and she heard him move to the other side of the yard. She could hear him putting something into a paper bag. She couldn't be sure, but it sounded like he might've entered the house and carried out additional paper bags, as well.

The assailant bound her feet and pulled the rug (with her on top of it) up to a post on the patio and tied her to it. He took the rings off of her fingers and told her that he was leaving. He warned her that if she screamed, he'd be able to hear her because he "lived just down the street" and he'd come back and kill her.

She didn't hear him open the gate, but she figured he must've left after the threats.

Immediate Aftermath

She waited until she was sure that he was gone, and then tried to struggle free. She was able to get her gag and her blindfold removed, and eventually she worked her way free from the post. Her hands, bound behind her very tightly, wouldn't shake free. She hopped into the house to use the phone to call for help, but the lines on both phones had been cut. She gave up and decided to wait for someone to discover her. A friend arrived about two hours later.

After she was rescued, they went directly to the friend's house so that the victim could shower. The police were called while the victim cleaned up. The call came in to the dispatcher around 9:00 AM.

The police arrived and processed the scene. They were able to determine that the method of entry was the window to the dining room. The screen had been removed, and it was found nearby leaning against a bush. There was a candy dish on the ground (the intruder had reached in and removed it prior to entering). The sliding door at the back patio was still open, as was the side gate. The patio still had the rug next to it, as well as the rope tied to the post and a knotted strip of towel. More torn strips of towel were found on the victim's bed, along with some white shoelaces. The victim's bedroom had been ransacked and the drawers had been emptied onto the floor. The kitchen had also been ransacked extensively.

The most interesting thing that they had found, by far, was the unique "cat's cradle alarm system" that the assailant had rigged up in the house. Before waking the victim, the attacker had taken clothesline from the victim's backyard and stretched it tightly throughout the house. The clothesline had been woven intricately from doorknob to doorknob, possibly to keep the doors shut or to slow down anyone who entered the house during the attack. The rope started at the master bedroom door, then stretched over to the brother's bedroom door (where it was tied to the doorknob). Then it went to the victim's bedroom door and to the kitchen, then stretched to the bathroom in the hall where it was secured to the bathroom faucets. The way it was woven indicated that he knew which bedroom belonged to the victim. Despite the intricate alarm system that appeared designed to secure the attack area, the rapist still took her outside.

In addition to the rings he stole from her fingers, the assailant had also stolen three single earrings from the scene, an unsettling echo of the March 7th, 1973 burglary.

The victim, accompanied by her friend, was taken to Sacramento Medical Center.

Suspect Description

The young woman never got a good look at her assailant. She felt that he was probably white, maybe about twenty-five years old. He was wearing a ski mask. She got a good look at his legs below the knees, and described black, square-toed, patent-leather shoes.

His voice sounded like an adult's, and he spoke in an angry, forced whisper.

The Suspect

Thousands of viable suspects have been looked at and dismissed in the EAR/GSK case over the years, and it doesn't do a lot of good to discuss a suspect that's been cleared. However, a unique "person-of-interest" was developed from this particular attack, and he intersects with the case in enough ways to where it's impossible to discuss Attack #6 without mentioning him. Plus, readers that are already familiar with this case might not be aware that this suspect was cleared, or of the unorthodox way in which he was checked off the list, so it's worth discussing.

While officers were processing the scene, a young man showed up at the door. He seemed keenly interested in the scene, and he explained that from his house, he could see clearly into the victim's bedroom window (even though she had attempted to obscure it with a hanging plant). He claimed he didn't know that the attack had occurred, and seemed very interested in knowing if the victim was okay. He also explained that his house had been burglarized, and presented a deputy with a small bag of cheap jewelry, mostly rings. He said that he had found it in his mother's room. His parents were out of town and he didn't think it was theirs.

Police took an interest in him because he was the right age and the right size, and he had told them that he knew that the victim was alone for the weekend. They investigated him a little further and learned that he'd moved back in with his parents sometime in April 1976, a few months before Attack #1. He had been driving a green Chevy Vega, which was a vehicle tied to Attack #5.

As promising as he was, the suspect was eliminated a couple of weeks later. In the early morning hours of October 18th, right after Attack #7 occurred, the police retrieved this suspect. They brought him to the tracking dog used in Attack #7 while the dog still had the scent of the East Area Rapist. The dog sniffed him and didn't react, confirming that he was innocent. Just to make sure, Law Enforcement continued to watch the suspect. He was confirmed to be in his house when a later attack occurred.

Context and Analysis

Again the Dawes and Dolecetto area comes into focus due to the location of this attack and the odd burglary that the victim had suffered more than three years before the assault. The events near the intersection that we've discussed so far help to form an interesting "ring" around a group of addresses that has been the focus of investigation for decades. Unfortunately, this hot zone has yet to deliver us the elusive East Area Rapist.

This was still early in the crime spree, so not as much is known about aspects of the attack that would later become familiar to investigators as EAR trademarks, such as whether the victim had hang-up phone calls or if there were houses for sale in the area (a trend that developed later). A year after this assault occurred, and when more of these EAR calling cards were known about, the victim was interviewed again and she didn't recall any unusual phone calls from the time period or anything particularly strange. During the investigation, it was discovered that there was a man painting addresses on the curb prior to the attack, but no other utility workers or odd men were described. The victim told police that she never locked her bedroom window, so it's likely that nothing *too* frightening could've been happening in her world at the time of the attack.

The use of rope throughout the house here is spectacularly interesting, and it's really the only known time in the entire Golden State Killer canon of attacks that such a thing was done so elaborately. I see it as a precursor to the "dishes trick," a much simpler technique he would employ later where he would stack a cup and saucer on a doorknob or person, which would then crash down and alert him to any movement in the house. The added benefit of the rope trick over the dishes seems to be that it could keep doors shut and allow him more time to escape, but it must've been too unwieldy to weave at the scene (or not as useful as it appears to be) or it surely would've been employed more. It was possibly abandoned because it not only limited his victim's mobility throughout the house, but it limited the offender's mobility as well. As it stands, this is just one more odd thing that the EAR did only once at a scene. For an offender who seemed to stick rigidly to an attack pattern and even a "script," he was not averse to what seemed to be experimentation at his attacks. Or, perhaps this and the removal of the victim to the patio was a rudimentary effort to keep his attacks from being connected. If so, it failed. Detectives had by now figured out that they were dealing with a serial rapist.

One final thought about the rope—did EAR not know that the victim was home alone for the weekend? He tied down the master bedroom and the brother's room so that it would be difficult for them to open from the inside, so... did he think someone could be in there? It's also interesting that he set all of this up before he woke her, which was probably when he cut the phone cords, as well. For a perpetrator who seemed to thoroughly stalk his victims and know their comings and goings, did he really not know who was in the house? What does this say about victim selection, or preparation? Footprint evidence showed that he had looked into her bedroom window, where she routinely slept nude, so was voyeurism a part of this? Was he just prowling Rancho Cordova that night, looking into windows, and found someone he wanted to strike? Did he have a group of houses or potential victims that he routinely checked on, and that night he'd decided that he wanted to attack someone and she just happened to be vulnerable? If so, would that mean that he's not connected to the 1973 burglary? Or had he been keeping tabs on her all this time, waiting for the perfect time to strike?

There's a connection to Mather Air Force Base here as well. For a couple of years before the attack, the victim had been going to dances at Denker Hall, a venue located on the base. In order to attend those dances, she'd been providing her name and address, which could potentially allow someone from the base to track her down.

This victim had a brother who lived in the house, which was rare, statistically, for households that the East Area Rapist struck.

The assailant using her name to wake her is notable. Was he trying to make her think that he knew her, therefore giving us another example of a red herring being dropped by the assailant? Was he doing it to instill more terror? He could've known her name since 1973, or he could've possibly come across it by rummaging through her purse before waking her up. With this offender, you never know.

Attack #7

Date: October 18th, 1976 2:30 AM to 5:15 AM
Victim: A young mother. Her son (10 years old) and
daughter (4 years old) were also in the house. The
son was bound by the rapist.
Location: Kipling Drive, Carmichael

Have you noticed it yet? So far, every Rancho Cordova attack has been followed by an attack in Carmichael, and with Attack #7, the trend continues. In this attack, the home of ayoung family was invaded while the father was out of town. A few notable things happened in this attack, including evidence that this family was potentially an "alternate" victim, a moment where the attacker appeared to be knocked "off-script," and a phone call purportedly from the assailant nearly fifteen years later.

Pre-Attack Events

October 17th, 1976 9:00 AM
The area near this attack was built up quite a bit in the decades that followed the incident, but at the time of the attack, the victim's house was situated in front of a large, vacant field. It was in this field that a neighbor saw car headlights five hours before the attack.

October 18th, 1976 12:15 AM

A neighbor living nearby heard his side gate open. He looked outside and saw that whomever had just used his gate had left it open, but he found nothing else amiss so he went back to bed.

The Attack

A young boy on Kipling Drive heard his dog barking at 2:30 AM. He got up to let him out into the backyard. When he opened the sliding glass door and turned on the porch light, it illuminated a masked man standing in their yard. The dog shot out the door and bounded after the figure, while the boy scrambled to shut and lock it down. The man, pursued by the small dog, ran to the fence and climbed it quickly. He sat there, perched on top of it, watching the dog yap at him from below.

Determining that neither the dog nor the boy were a threat, the masked man lowered himself back down into the yard. The dog made a lot of noise but didn't attack him. The man walked nonchalantly past the family pet and toward the open kitchen window. The boy watched him approach for a moment and then ran in terror to his mother's room. As he did, he heard a noise in the kitchen indicating that the man was making his way into the house.

The boy woke his mother up and tried his best to explain the situation, but his panic made it hard to get the words out. The mother told him that he'd had a bad dream, and she began dialing the operator as a precaution. It rang sixteen times. She heard a thump in the kitchen, as if someone had jumped from a ledge and landed on the kitchen floor. She had just begun dialing a friend's number when she heard a flurry of footsteps in the hall. The door to her bedroom burst open, and a masked intruder stood in the doorway with no pants or underwear on.

"Sssshhhut up!" he hissed as he moved toward them. He pressed a short, thick knife against her throat. "Do exactly as I tell you or I'll kill you. I'll butcher you all to pieces. Don't scream. Do as you're told or both you and your son will die. Who else is in the house?"

The dog was still making noise, and it seemed to concern the assailant. "I'm going to kill you if you don't get him," he hissed. "Shut him up!" The woman was forced to move the dog to another room.

"Who else is in the house?" the assailant repeated. The woman told him that her young daughter was in the house as well, and she begged him not to hurt her. He quickly stepped out to close the door to the daughter's room.

"My husband is out of town," the woman said, hoping that by offering information, the intruder would calm down and curb his violent demeanor. He responded by going over to the telephone and roughly yanking the cord out of the wall. Without looking back at her, he left the room, and then came back with a towel in his hand. Using his teeth, knife, and hands, he ripped the towel into thin strips. His movements appeared to be laced with rage.

He grabbed her arms and angrily pulled the woman to her feet. He spun her around, pinned her arms behind her, and, using cords that he had cut from their blinds, tied her hands together. He then tied her son to the headboard and forcefully tied his feet together, causing a deep cut to the boy's foot in the process.

"If you move, I will kill you," the man threatened. The boy told his mother that he was afraid of dying. The intruder threw a blanket over the boy's head.

"Don't move," he told the mother, and then he began to speak in a stuttering whisper. "If you do, it will take s-s-seconds off his life. If you do what I s-s-say, you won't get hurt. I'll be gone in a little while. If you don't do as I s-s-say, I'll k-k-k-kill you all."

He took her by the arm and started pushing her toward the family room. He ordered her to sit on the couch.

"Where's your money?"

"There's some in an envelope in my purse. It's for the Heart Association. That's all I have."

He knelt down in front of her. Using strips of towel, he tied her ankles together. He left the room, and she heard him rummaging through drawers and ransacking cupboards. Then he was back.

He leaned close to her face. "You're beautiful," he whispered.

"Please don't hurt me.," she pleaded. "I'm pregnant."

He blindfolded her with a strip of towel, and then a sweet smelling cloth was forced into her mouth. Another strip of towel was tightened around her head, anchoring the cloth to her mouth.

He lifted her to a standing position, then led her back to the bedroom and pushed her onto the bed next to her son. The assailant began rummaging through the drawers in the dresser. When he was done, he pulled her off of the bed and again led her back to the family room. Instead of the couch, he ordered her onto the floor. Due to her hands being tied and her eyes being blindfolded, she stumbled a bit while trying to lower herself. He pushed her backwards roughly. She hit the ground, rolled onto her side , then then fell onto her back.

He unbuttoned her shirt slowly, then lifted her waist off the floor and removed her underwear. "You have a beautiful body," he whispered. "Do you lay out in the sun?"

She shook her head. She felt his mouth on her, going over it and moving progressively lower. She could tell that he was no longer wearing a mask, and as his hands violated her body, she could tell that he had removed his gloves as well.

He forced her knees apart and his unmasked face moved between her legs. He orally copulated her briefly, then pulled away and tied her ankles together.

He disappeared into the kitchen, where she heard him moving things around. Then he was back at her side, and he placed the knife against her cheek.

"You lied," he hissed. "You said there was no more money. I'm going to k-k-k-kill you for lying. There was m-m-more m-m-money in the desk."

She couldn't answer because of the gag, so she shook her head— she'd had no idea that there was money in the desk.

The knife left her face, and then he began to run it in a pattern across her body. He traced a vertical line down her torso, across her stomach, down each side of her hips, and then back up her body, shoulder to shoulder. Then he guided it up to her neck, and then back and forth across her throat.

"If you don't do as I say, I'll kill you and the kids," he told her. Then he rolled her onto her stomach, and she felt his lubricated penis in her hands.

"Play with it," he whispered. He untied her gag as he moved back and forth in her hands. The cloth was removed from her mouth.

"If you scream or do anything, I'll kill you. You better not fight me."

He grabbed her hand and started pulling on her rings. Her fingers were swollen from the tight ligatures and the rings wouldn't come off. The victim could feel him getting very angry as he violently pulled at her hand. "I'll cut your fuckin' fingers off," he hissed.

She begged him to get some soap, but he didn't understand. She tried to explain several times that soap would help the rings slide off of her fingers. He went to the sink for some soap and rubbed some on her hands, but the swelling was such that the rings still wouldn't come off. Still grabbing at the rings, he decided to cut her ligatures off to allow circulation to return.

"Take the rings off or I'll kill you," he said. She struggled, and was eventually able to remove them. He retied her hands.

"Your body is beautiful," he whispered. He lifted her to a sitting position. She felt another piece of towel being tied around her eyes and then a hood of some kind being slipped over her head.

"Suck on it," he ordered. She felt the hood being raised and then felt his penis against her mouth. He moved back and forth against her face for a moment, then pulled away. He rolled her onto her side. Again his penis entered her mouth, and at the same time, she felt the knife against her back. He took it out of her mouth, moved down, and penetrated her.

The victim's terror grew, and she tried to think of a way to get out of the situation.

"You're such a good lover," she said, hoping that her lie would get him to stop. It did. He pulled away from her.

"No one ever said that before. Most people just laugh at me."

"Do you like to be complimented?" she asked.

"Yes. People make fun of me, especially since something happened to my face." Then he paused for a brief moment. "I need to know what time it is. Where's your clock?"

"In the kitchen."

He went to the kitchen and began opening and closing the refrigerator and drawers. She heard him eating.

Then the house was silent. She wondered if the ruse had worked.

Unfortunately, it hadn't. He returned and was on her again, this time attempting to sodomize her.

"Oh, God, you're hurting me!" she cried as his penis pushed hard against her rectum. He moved her to the couch, placed her head on the seat, put her knees against the front of the couch for a better angle, then tried to sodomize her again. This time he was successful. She cried out.

After the horrific event was over, he tied her leg to the coffee table, and she heard him walk away.

"You better not move or I'll kill your mother," she heard him say from down the hall.

He walked back to the family room and stood there in silence for several moments.

"When will your husband be home?" he asked. "You better tell me the same as your son or I'll kill you all. Don't lie to me."

"He won't be home until Friday," she replied.

Again he was on her, sodomizing her. He was only in her briefly, and then he pulled out. He walked away, but soon came back. The hood was still affixed to her, and he lifted it a bit and put his penis in her mouth again. He then positioned her on her back, unmasked himself, and put his face between her legs. Then he raped her once more.

The barrage of assaults was too much to take, and she was being driven to hysterics. Her body began shaking and convulsing.

"I'm cold," she stammered. Moments later, she felt a blanket being thrown on top her her. He sat her up, pulled the hood up again and once more put his penis into her mouth. Still shaking, she fell onto her back. He hovered over her, then raped her yet again. She blacked out for a moment.

When she next became aware, the house was silent. She heard the engine of a large American car start up. It seemed to be coming from the large open field behind her house.

He was gone.

Immediate Aftermath

A neighbor also heard the car engine. It started up shortly after 5:00 AM, warmed up for a few minutes, and then drove off.

The police brought a bloodhound to the scene. The dog determined that the assailant's route had started from the middle of the open field located to the east of the victim's residence. This corresponded with the direction of the car engine that the neighbor and victim had heard. There were large tire tracks in the mud, but the dirt was too wet to make proper castings and identification of the tires couldn't be made. There was a small section of tracks that passed over a gutter, which gave them a small sample to analyze. From this, they were at least able to determine that the car was large and probably American-made.

From where the assailant had parked in the field, the dogs determined that he'd traveled on foot for about a hundred yards in a straight line to the fence of the victim's next-door neighbor, then over the fence, then straight to a window of the neighbor's house. He had then circled the perimeter of that house and made his way through the side gate to one of the neighbor's cars parked in front. He'd circled the car, then he'd gone straight to the victim's backyard, up to the kitchen window, and then the patio door.

It was this bloodhound who ended up clearing that promising suspect from Attack #6. Police retrieved the young man, and the bloodhound had no reaction to him at all.

There were two empty beer cans found at the scene that didn't belong to the victim or her family. The assailant stole several rings, including her wedding rings.

Several fingerprints were found, and one of the fingerprints lifted from the scene remains unidentified even to this day. It was found on a closet door on the west side of the southern-most hallway in the house. The victim was able to verify that there were times in the attack that the assailant did not have gloves on, so it was (and still is) a promising piece of evidence.

In addition to the trauma of the attack, the victim had minor abrasions on her ankles and knees, as did her son. They were treated at the hospital.

Suspect Description

The suspect was described as short, no more than 5'7". He had dark eyes and heavy dark hair on his arms and legs.

He had on a black mask, a dark blue t-shirt, and black tennis shoes. He wasn't wearing any pants or underwear, but when the young boy initially saw him in the yard, the assailant might have been wearing white underpants. The boy didn't know if the assailant had gloves on when he was in the backyard, but he did have gloves on for most of the assault inside the house. The gloves were dark, maybe white and black.

He had a small penis, which the victim especially noticed when she was ordered to "play with it."

He spoke in a whisper through clenched teeth, and sometimes stuttered.

His weapon was a three or four inch knife, possibly a pocket knife, and very sharp. It was originally described as maybe an ice pick.

The young boy thought he saw what might've been a tattoo on the assailant's right leg, but he wasn't sure. He also noticed that the assailant had a distinctive gait—he walked a little slouched or slightly bowlegged.

Post-Attack Event

October 23rd, 1976

The victim was cleaning her house a few days after the attack and came across a spoon underneath the couch where she had been assaulted. It didn't belong to the house. Other than being bent almost halfway over, there were no scratches or marks on the spoon. She turned it over to the police, who spent months trying to trace the its origin. They came away empty-handed—it was too common of an item.

Sometime between 1990 and 1992

The victim received a phone call, and she recognized the voice on the other end as the voice of the rapist. The caller whispered harshly into the phone, saying "You know who this is" or "Do you know who this is?" The victim was on the line with him for about a minute. There was the sound of children crying and maybe a woman in the background, which could've potentially come from a television or some other source. At an interview with police, the victim positively identified the caller as the man who had attacked her in 1976. The family had moved to a few different cities and states over the years, but their phone numbers were usually listed in the places they moved to.

Context and Analysis

Now that more geographic data points were available and the previous attacks were gathered under the umbrella of a serial offender, it appeared to investigators that the East Area Rapist had made the American River area his hunting grounds. Attacks were happening on both sides of it, and as discussed in the intro, even alternating back and forth.

The victims' residence was a one-story home situated in a part of town that was a bit more affluent than some of the other attacks up to this point. It was in the process of being sold, and a TRW Real Estate Company sign was still in the front yard. They were planning a move to Danville, a move that was completed about a month later. Interestingly, Danville was the site of a few EAR assaults two years later. In this attack, the EAR seemed to have come from a greenbelt paralleling the river. The large, open area behind the victims' residence is now dense with houses, but back then it was expansive and bare. On the night of the attack, it was muddy from the previous day's rain shower.

Thanks to the bloodhound, a strong case can be made for this attack being an example of the EAR "settling" for an alternate victim. The rage and brutality inflicted on the woman he attacked could possibly have been from the frustration of finding his primary victim unexpectedly out for the night. The woman living at the house next door (the place the bloodhound indicated that the EAR visited first) fit the victim profile of the East Area Rapist. The husband was an eye doctor for the Air Force (there's that medical and military connection again), and he'd studied at UC Davis, a place that would be connected to the EAR later on. His wife was close to thirty at the time of the attack. It turned out that the couple was almost always home at the time of night that the EAR visited, but they'd had an unplanned change of routine and were out of town.

On the night of the attack, neighborhood dogs were making a lot of noise, and several neighbors even heard the victim scream. A few of them looked outside, didn't see anything, and shrugged it off. It's a almost criminal that the police weren't called, but neighbors minding their own business (to the detriment of the victims) is a common theme in this case.

The vehicle associated with this attack was larger than a Chevy Vega (which was the car associated with Attack #5 and possibly Attack #1). This is the first probable instance of the EAR having access to more than one vehicle, and also notable is the fact that this was the first time that the assailant had worn tennis shoes to a scene.

This is also the first clear example of the offender having a stutter. A stutter comes up a few times over the years, with varying opinions on its authenticity. Several victims felt that it was a genuine stutter that broke through when his anger, nervousness, or fear got to be too much. In some of the attacks, he would stutter on only one letter (like the letter "L") but in others, like this one, he seemed to be an equal-opportunity stutterer, getting stuck on the letters "S," "M," and "K." Related to this discussion is the way that the assailant spoke at every assault—a "controlled whisper" through "clenched teeth," "barely moving his mouth." While it's almost assuredly a forced way of speaking in order to sound more menacing and to disguise his voice, it's been theorized that this was possibly a manner of speaking that could've helped control a stutter.

The bent spoon was an interesting find. There are a few examples of the East Area Rapist / Golden State Killer leaving some oddities under couches, and even more examples of him leaving behind items at one scene that he had taken from other scenes. This spoon could be an example of both. The presence of the beer cans, too, is odd, because the assailant didn't seem to have a bag with him, and he wasn't wearing pants.

Here the assailant was described as having dark eyes, heavy hair, and possibly a tattoo on his right leg. These descriptors don't come up very often, especially the tattoo, but it *is* interesting to chart the change in victims' descriptions of his body hair, especially on his legs.

This was the last time the assailant would enter a house without pants on, after having decided to appear fully-clothed for the previous few attacks. The reason he did it initially was probably because it was part of his "fantasy," but perhaps there was a practicality to it (an effort to not leave any evidence behind). The reason he stopped doing it was probably related to control. If he entered a residence with no pants on and claimed that he only wanted food and money (which was a claim he started making in almost every attack), his victims wouldn't be likely to believe him and might offer resistance. Also, it's risky to vault fences with male anatomy at stake if the offender had to get away from a scene quickly.

The supposition that the rapist showed "compassion" to the victim (purportedly because she'd complimented him earlier) by clothing her with a blanket after she complained of being cold has become a popular myth in this case, but now that the whole story has been told about the scope of violence before and after the blanket was callously tossed on her, I'm hoping that the myth can die.

There was certainly no compassion shown to the victim when she revealed that she was pregnant, either. He could've seriously injured her. Neither pregnancy nor menstruation seemed to deter the offender.

The intricate pattern that he traced over his victim's body is notable. He'd done something somewhat similar in Attack #5 but not nearly as ornate, and he would go on to do something similar in Attack #13. Detective Richard Shelby, who worked on the EAR case at the time, noted that the pattern that the EAR had traced was very similar to the "Y" incision used in autopsies. Does it show a fascination with cutting open a woman's body? Does her pregnancy have anything to do with it what he did? Is it possible that even at this early stage in his crime spree, the fledgling Golden State Killer was already associating sex and death? Or did he simply get a thrill from running his knife along the bodies of his victims to instill terror?

He really, really wanted her rings. Instead of giving up when they wouldn't come loose, he actually went a pretty risky route by allowing the victim to be unbound so that he could take her rings with him. He'd removed rings in Attack #6, and he would remove several more before the crime spree would be done. The lengths that he went to make sure that he had this woman's rings goes to show how important it was that he take those types of items with him. It seemed essential that he take personal jewelry or a personal item from the victim.

For readers new to this case, the phone call in the early 1990s might merely be an interesting footnote right now, but as you learn more about the criminal, you'll learn that this phone call could be monumentally important. The last known Golden State Killer activity was in May of 1986, and from there he seemingly stopped offending and, for all we know, he stopped existing. This phone call, if the victim is indeed correct about it being the assailant, is proof that he at least survived until the early 1990s. A similar call was made in 2001. That's very important.

Finally, the victim's tactic of paying him a compliment in order to ward him off was smart thinking under the circumstances, though unfortunately, it didn't do much. And going back to the phone call, it's even been speculated that her compliment of him is what caused him to think of her fifteen years later and reach out by phone. Regardless, his response at the attack is interesting. In Attack #4 he'd boasted about how "all of the women enjoy making love" to him, and here, he claimed that they "laugh" at him. Of course we don't know if either of these statements are remotely true. His comment about something happening to his face shouldn't be taken too seriously. It's possible that his response here was genuine, but taken in context of the brutality he was inflicting, telling a little lie or two wouldn't be something he'd be morally opposed to. Since with every attack that he was committing he was leaving witnesses who could potentially identify him, fibbing about his appearance was probably something that made sense for him to do.

Attack #8

Date: October 18, 1976, 11:00 PM to 11:35 PM
Victim: 19-year-old woman
Location: Los Palos Drive, Rancho Cordova

We've just discussed the EAR bouncing between Carmichael and Rancho Cordova, so since the previous attack was in Carmichael, I doubt it comes as any surprise that this attack was in Rancho Cordova. What *might* come as a surprise is that this attack occurred less than twenty-four hours after Attack #7. At the risk of sounding like a broken record, this attack is located very near the intersection of Dawes and Dolecetto... only a few houses away from the 1974 dog-beating incident, actually.

The Attack
The victim, returning home from work, pulled into her driveway around 11:00 PM. She opened her car door and turned back for a moment to check on her dog in the backseat, and suddenly she felt someone outside the car grabbing her head and tearing her from the seat. She fought, trying desperately to break free from the gloved hands, and injured her elbow in the process. The assailant pulled out a knife and held it to her throat so closely that he cut her.

"Stop fighting," he hissed. "I only want your car. I won't hurt you. Don't move or I'll kill you." She obeyed and went limp.

"Get out," he ordered. She obeyed. Her father and brother would be home in about thirty minutes, and she thought about what might happen if she didn't' survive until then.

The masked man closed the car door and led her to the side of her house and then into the backyard. They stopped close to the fence at a spot where it was the darkest.

"Turn around," he ordered. He put her on the ground, then pulled her hands behind her. She begged him to leave her alone, but her pleas were answered with "Shut up." He tied her wrists very tightly with her own clothesline.

She struggled a bit as she was bound. "Don't look at me," he ordered. She continued to struggle, and he told her that if she didn't stop struggling that he'd "cut her up."

"Do you have any money? All I want is money and your car keys. I'm not going to hurt you."

"I've only got a dollar. It's in my wallet," she replied.

"Shut up," he said. He held the knife against her chest, then turned and rummaged through her purse. He threw it down, then turned and grabbed her arm roughly. She was led back to the driveway and reunited with her car. She begged him to leave her dog alone.

"Shut up," he told her. "I'm not going to hurt your dog."

He moved her across the lawn, past the house next door, and toward the corner of the block. She tripped, but he held her up. They went through an open side gate and into someone else's backyard. She noticed that the house was dark and appeared to be empty.

"Sit down," he ordered. He grabbed her shirt and pushed her down, but his grip on her shirt kept her from falling all the way. Nearby were three strips of towel neatly arranged on the ground. He set his knife on the ground, tied her ankles with a piece of white cord, and used one of the towel strips to blindfold her. He gagged her with another strip of towel while she moved her head in protest.

"Shut up," he hissed, needling the knife into her ribs. He forced her onto her side and straddled her. The final strip of towel was wrapped around her head to hold her gag in place.

He stood up and loomed over her silently for a moment. Then he jangled her keys over her.

"I'm going to leave for five minutes. If you move, I'll slit your throat and cut your guts out. If you move, blam, blam, blam."

She didn't hear him leave, but a short time later she heard her car start. It backed up and disappeared down the street.

She freed herself quickly (apparently she'd been tied much more loosely than the other victims) and summoned help.

Hours later, the police found her vehicle parked on El Segundo (yes the same street as Attack #6), a little ways south of where this victim was attacked and very close to Attacks #1, #3, and #6. The keys were gone and the dog was locked in the trunk, scared but unharmed.

Suspect Description

The assailant was 6' tall and about 170 lbs.

His mask seemed to be a almost like a man's sock, grayish brown and made of wool, with two holes cut out for the eyes. He had on a heavy gray jacket with buttons. His gloves were a brown wool, and he wore brown desert boots.

He spoke only in a whisper through clenched teeth.

Post-Attack Events

December 1977

Over a year after the attack, this victim received a threatening phone call from a voice that sounded just like her assailant. The phone call took place during a time period where the offender seemed to be making a lot of phone calls and sending communications. A couple months after the call, the police brought her in to listen to a tape made of the EAR in January 1978, and she confirmed that the voice matched the call that she had received, but she wasn't sure if it was the man who had attacked her in 1976.

Context and Analysis

EAR sure was in a hurry to strike again, with this one following so closely on the heels of Attack #7. Does this give any clue as to his work pattern, sleep pattern, mindset, or day-to-day life? Was he on some kind of time crunch, with maybe a wife or parents gone for the weekend? Did he have to leave town and go back to school, or did he have a big job coming up that would take him out of the area? As brutal and elaborate an attack as he committed with Victim #7, it's just surprising that he still felt the need to attack again so soon.

EAR threatened her with a "blam, blam, blam," but despite the threat, the victim felt that he didn't have a gun. She did, however, feel that he would've killed her in an instant if he'd felt inclined to or if she hadn't cooperated.

It's very fortunate that this victim wasn't sexually assaulted, but for a criminal who so far had always raped his victims once he had them bound and helpless, it's curious that she wasn't. Was he familiar with her schedule, aware that she had family arriving home shortly? If so, why give himself such a tight window in the first place? Was he overconfident in his ability to move things along quickly? And why risk going back to her house to take the car if he knew that the men of the house would be home so soon? He didn't ask who else was home, or who else lived with her or when they would be home, so it's possible that he *did* know. He'd been asking those questions at other scenes. If that's the case, it's no coincidence that he abandoned the attack at the time that her family members normally returned home. Another reason that he might not have attacked her sexually is that he might've been physically spent after all of the torture and abuse that he'd inflicted on Victim #7. The fact that he would even try again so soon might point to an inexperienced offender who didn't know his own limits.

To expand on some of those ideas, there's still a lot of talk about how spontaneous this attack seemed, and debate about whether this was a crime of opportunity or not. There are certainly a lot of parallels to Attack #4, and both theories could be argued, but I definitely lean toward this victim being a target and this not being a spontaneous attack. She was normally only home alone from 11:00 PM to 11:30 PM, and the EAR struck at 11:00 PM and left promptly at 11:30 PM without sexually assaulting her—either a lucky coincidence or he knew her schedule. The pieces of towel seemed to be laid out in preparation in a nearby yard, so it seems EAR was intending to attack *someone*. The owners of the backyard where the towels were laid out were an elderly couple, so they probably weren't intended as victims. Another reason that this was possibly not a spontaneous attack was the fact that he called her on the phone more than a year later. None of these by themselves prove anything, especially the phone call since it's possible Victim #7 wasn't an intentional target either and she received a phone call much later, but taken together they tip me toward this victim being his priority target.

Another interesting element is that the driveway where she was attacked was well-lit by a nearby street light, which added risk for the assailant. Attacking in the driveway is a strong parallel to Attack #4, and also like in Attack #4, EAR decided to take the victim's car for a joyride. Those are interesting similarities. What was the purpose of borrowing the car in either attack? And one has to honestly wonder if he kept his mask on while he drove. That might've attracted a fair amount of attention, even at that time of night. He didn't drive very far in Attack #4 and he *really* didn't go very far in this attack. How much of a hurry he was in to get away from the crime scene, and was that was a factor? Did he put the dog in the trunk before or after he drove away? If there was no practical reason for borrowing the car (getting to his bike, house, or own vehicle more quickly), then there must be a psychological reason. Inflicting more terror (the victim thought her car was stolen), violating the victim further, "becoming part of" the victim... could any of those be the reason? Simply a juvenile thrill?

Not to spend too much time on the car, but I mentioned earlier that geography can offer us some of the most reliable clues in this case, so there could be a clue here in regards to where he parked the car. The place he parked it was in the direction of and just a couple hundred feet away from the first and third attacks. As mentioned earlier, it was also the same street as (and naturally, very close to) Attack #6. Again, he could've been parking near his residence or parking near his own transportation, or he could've parked the car and then disappeared somewhere on foot. Perhaps this was a favorite area for entering the cement-lined canals that he most likely used to navigate the neighborhoods. As far as that goes though, if he was looking to get back to the canals, it would've been much easier to enter them on foot from the crime scene, because they pass right by Victim #8's house (and in fact, are almost certainly the way he *arrived* at the crime scene due to their proximity). It's possible that he was doing it to evade tracking dogs, which had been used on his crimes a couple of times already, though he probably didn't have any way of knowing that since he had apparently driven to and from both of those attacks. If he *was* concerned about tracking dogs, then in my opinion it points to an offender who lived close by and had to obfuscate his trail by using a car, or else the dogs would've led right to his doorstep.

As with the others, it wasn't clear how the victim might've been selected. She worked as a receptionist at the Sacramento Army Depot, which provides us with a quasi-military connection.

Attack #9

Date: November 10th, 1976 7:00 PM
Victim: 16-year-old girl
Location: Greenleaf Drive, Citrus Heights

EAR's first October in the limelight had given police plenty of angles to work on, with three different attacks in a short period of time. After this, he returned to offending once per month again for a little while like he'd been doing during the summer. But busy Octobers were a trend that generally continued throughout the rape series.

In this attack, it's clear that the EAR had started to gain a comfort level with his widened attack circle. He reached Citrus Heights again, hitting a home just three or so blocks away from Attack #5.

This particular attack is interesting because, like Attacks #4, #6, and #8, it again featured the outdoors, and like Attack #8, the EAR chose to not sexually assault the victim. There was perhaps a curious case of mistaken identity involved, and the EAR took his victim far enough from her home to possibly warrant an abduction charge.

The Attack
The victim's brother was in the hospital. The parents went to visit him at 7:00 PM, leaving their sixteen-year-old daughter home alone. A quiet evening of watching television was interrupted by a loud "bang" somewhere in the house. Seconds later, a masked man rushed into the room. The victim screamed and her dog barked furiously.

The intruder closed the space between them and held a knife to her throat. "Shut up or I'll kill you," he told her. He kicked the barking dog and threatened to "stab it" if she couldn't "shut it up."

"All I want is your money," he said. His face was so close to hers that she could hear him breathing. His breath was foul. A terrible odor seemed to emanate from his body.

He ordered her off of the couch and used black shoelaces to tie her hands very tightly behind her back. Once she was secured, he led her into the backyard and sat her down on the concrete. As she sat there, she noticed more black shoelaces hanging from the handle bars of her bike. He used them to bind her ankles. A fear that he would kill her kept her from screaming for help.

"Don't move or you'll be dead and I'll be gone in the night," he said. He went back into the house and spent a few minutes inside. He came out to check on her occasionally, but kept going back in. The victim later found out that he was turning off the television, turning on the heater and lights, and trying to make the scene look as if the girl had left for the evening. On one of his final trips outside, he replaced the window screen that had been removed when he had initially entered the residence. With the living room window screen on and the rest of the house put back together, he had eliminated any sign that he had been there.

"Where's your money?" he asked. She told him that she didn't have any. He asked if her parents had any, and she said that they'd taken it with them.

"Damn, no money. Ah, man, no money," he said. He made one more trip into the house and then came back out, locking the door behind him.

"Do you like to fuck?" he asked her. She didn't reply. He asked more questions, sexual in nature. She shut her eyes. After he was done with the questions, the victim's ankles were freed and she was pulled to her feet. He began pushing her, and then they were on the move. He took her over a low fence and into the neighbor's backyard, and they headed toward the canal that ran behind her street.

He led her down the shallow canal. The victim was barefoot and walked in an inch of water, and the assailant walked next to her on the dry slope. Dogs barked as they passed by—the only witnesses to the terror unfolding. She petitioned him to let her go, but her pleas were answered with a gruff "Shut up."

"If you don't shut up you'll be silent forever and I'll be gone in the dark," he told her.

After walking for a few minutes, they approached a large weeping willow tree.

"Sit down." He retied her ankles, then walked a short distance away, then returned and untied her ankles. A moment passed, and again he tied her ankles and walked away. When he returned, he flashed his knife, then orbited behind her, untied her feet, and once again retied them. He reappeared in front of her and used something to blindfold her. It slipped a little bit on her left eye, and she watched silently as her kidnapper paced back and forth several times. He stopped, bent over, and pulled at his sock. She observed as much as she could and memorized details.

He moved in and started cutting at her jeans with his knife. As her legs became bare, she began to squirm. He put his hands on her thighs until she stopped moving.

One leg came free, but he was having trouble with the other one. "This isn't working right," he said. He kept cutting away, and was eventually able to get her jeans and underwear cut all the way off.

With the victim now nude from the waist down, he leaned in close, again allowing the victim to smell the bouquet of awful stenches that emanated from his pores.

"I know you from somewhere, don't I?" he hissed.

"No," she replied.

"Do you go to American River College?"

"No."

The assailant held his knife against her neck with his left hand. She told him that she went to San Juan High School.

"You're lying," he said. "What's your name?"

She made up a name, and he didn't respond. He stood silently for a moment, and then started pacing back and forth.

"I have to wait for my parents to leave so I can go home," he muttered. "I'm going to take off in my car."

He turned back to address her. "Within the next twenty minutes, make one move and you'll be silent forever and I'll be off in the dark."

A moment later, the darkness swallowed him and the victim was alone.

She worked free from her blindfold and her ankles came loose almost immediately, but she was unable to make any progress on the tight bindings around her wrists. She waited close to an hour before moving again, afraid that the assailant would suddenly reappear. After she felt safe enough, she made her way toward her house. As she emerged from the ditch, she spotted her neighbor across the street and ran to him. The neighbor cut her free and phoned her parents, who had arrived home at 8:30 PM but had thought that their daughter was out on a date.

Suspect Description

White male, very light complexion, between eighteen and twenty-three years old, 5'10", 165 lbs. He had dark eyes, brown hair, and brown leg hair.

He wore a leather hood, which extended past his face and into his shirt. It had small slits for his eyes and his mouth. He wore a heavy coat, which may have been a military fatigue jacket. Under his coat he wore a gray sweater with front pockets. The sweater was zipped up. His pants were military fatigues. His gloves were tan and made of a soft leather, and his shoes were black and square-toed.

He initially had a knife, and a knife he used later in the attack might've been stolen from the victim's kitchen. When he threatened her, his knife appeared to be a six-inch serrated paring knife, and a knife exactly like that was missing from the house. He also had a flashlight, which the victim got a good look at. It was very small, so small that it disappeared completely into the assailant's hand. The beam was bright and about six inches in diameter.

He might have been right-handed. He cut her ties with his right hand, but he held the knife in his left hand at other times.

Context and Analysis

For the second time in a row, the East Area Rapist did not sexually assault his victim. Unlike most of the other "failures," where something outside of his control prevented him from completing his attack, in this case and in the previous one he seemingly called off the attack on his own. In the last attack, it could be argued that perhaps he knew that the girl's family would be looking for her, but in this case he staged the house in such a way that it completely fooled the parents—they had no idea that their daughter was in trouble and he had plenty of time to do what he wanted to, and he seemed to know it. He had his victim in a vulnerable position in a semi-private location, so why didn't he attack her? Tying and retying her, pacing back and forth, getting frustrated that he couldn't get her jeans cut off easily, and then the odd exchange about whether he "knew her" and the question of which school she went to made it seem like the offender was nervous or anxious. Additionally, the victim was menstruating, and her personal feeling was that her period was a big factor in preventing the assault. Of course, we know that it hadn't deterred the assailant in the past, but maybe it did this time. As far as tying her and retying her several times, some people feel that the rapist received sexual gratification from binding his victims. If true, that would be a decent explanation, but in this case it seems like nerves or a case of him planning as far as the abduction, but not knowing what to do once he had done it.

Perhaps the offender was already getting "bored" with his attacks, or maybe it was "routine" now. Maybe the compulsion that drove him to do it was overpowering the sexual component of the crimes. It's also possible that the whole "outdoors" thing just wasn't working for him and he didn't feel safe enough to carry out the attacks.

The act of the EAR leading his victim away from her house to a pre-appointed spot was very reminiscent of Attack #8, though this scene wasn't prepared as meticulously as the previous attack. He did prepare the patio, with the shoelaces hanging on the bike, so clearly he had a plan in mind.

There was physical evidence found by the willow tree that implied that the EAR was familiar with the area: there was a vacant lot nearby, on the north side of the ditch, and there was a well-worn foot trail in that area that contained his shoe prints. The foot trail was near Woodhills Way, a street west of Dewey Drive, near where he had taken her. The EAR had probably traveled that way to and/or from the area. In the canal itself, shoe prints pointing west were found, but none going east, leading investigators to believe that the EAR escaped from the willow tree back toward Woodhills Way. These shoe prints didn't match other crime scenes in style but they were roughly the same size. None of the victim's footprints were found, which confirmed the victim's statement that she had walked in the water while the assailant had walked next to her.

"I'll be off in the dark. I'll be gone in the dark. You'll be silent forever." These overdramatic phrases are not only a little haunting, but they give a little insight into the mindset of the assailant and the character or role he might've been trying to play. The phrases actually make him sound like a two-bit comic book character or villain from old Western movies. One of the most perplexing phrases in the EAR canon, "Give me a good drop," which we'll encounter much later, could probably be classified under this umbrella of phrases as well. There are many things that point to the offender being a little older than we usually peg him as, but these phrases sound juvenile to me.

One of the mysteries of this attack is the knife. There was a six-inch serrated paring knife missing from the kitchen. However, the EAR had flashed a knife when he had first encountered the victim, seemingly before he had spent any time in the house. Perhaps he used a different knife at the beginning of the attack, but liked the one that he found in the house and switched to that instead? Or perhaps he used the knife he brought with him for the duration of the attack, but took that one to use later or as a souvenir? Or maybe he moved the knife to somewhere else in the house (like with the bent spoon from Attack #7), or took it to leave somewhere else, like the jewelry in Attack #5?

"I have to wait for my parents to leave so I can go home," he muttered. "I'm going to take off in my car." He spoke so quietly and differently that the victim assumed he was talking to himself and not to her, but regardless, she didn't believe him and thought he was making up those statements for her benefit. The exchange about knowing her from American River College was equally suspicious. It seemed that the assailant was dropping in little tidbits to throw investigators off of his trail, which if true, would mean that the EAR did not go to American River College, did not live with his parents, and did not drive to the scene. It's very likely that he *did* walk to the scene, at least part of the way, given the footprints. But like everything EAR said during these attacks, there's this nagging feeling that part of what he was saying could be true. It's impossible to know. It's very likely that he mixed in a bunch of truth and plausible lies in order to keep detectives confused.

During their investigation, Law Enforcement officials explored the possibility that EAR had accidentally attacked the wrong victim. There was a lot of information indicating that the neighbor was the true target. She *did* go to American River College, and she and her boyfriend had run into a strange character resembling other witness sightings of the EAR several months before the attack. That neighbor, the one who might've been the intended target, had moved away from the neighborhood shortly before this attack occurred.

I previously mentioned the Visalia Ransacker, an offender who some think might be an early version of this offender. The Visalia Ransacker attempted to kidnap a teenage girl from her home on the night of September 11th, 1975, and it's thought that his intention was possibly to simply lead her off a little ways away and sexually assault her, which would be a bit of a parallel to this case.

I didn't post this in the main description because I couldn't corroborate it, but apparently some neighbors saw a suspicious male near the victim's house a couple nights after the attack. A case of mistaken identity, or an incredibly brazen criminal returning to the scene of the crime? Throughout the rest of this book, there'll be several examples of both.

Attack #10

Date: December 18th, 1976, 7:20 PM to 9:00 PM
Victim: 15-year-old girl
Location: Ladera Way, Carmichael

Pre-Attack Events

Late November 1976
Starting three weeks before the attack, the victim's family and the family of the girl next door started receiving hang-up phone calls. There were typically three or four calls every night.

Early December 1976
About a week before the attack, there was an incident on Galewood Way where an intruder forced his way into a house while the female resident was at home. She was on the phone when the intruder entered the house, and he left without interacting with her. This event took place about half a mile to the south of this attack.

The Attack
The victim was staying home alone while her parents went to a Christmas party. She was ill with a cold, so she planned on a relaxing evening to herself. After her parents left at 6:15 PM, she put a pizza in the oven and began playing the piano.

A loud cracking sound coming from outside startled her. She stopped playing for a few moments, but didn't hear anything else, so she resumed.

After a few minutes, she heard another sound—this one much closer. Suddenly she felt a knife at her throat.

"Make a move and I'll kill you," the man with the knife hissed. "Do you have any money in the house? You better not lie to me."

"No," she replied.

"When are your parents coming back? You better tell me so I'll know how much time I have."

"I don't know."

"Get up," he ordered. "Get moving. If you say anything or flinch, I'll push this knife all the way in and I will be gone in the dark of the night."

He began pushing her toward the utility room, and then to the door leading to the garage. They stopped, and he removed white shoelaces from his pocket and tied her hands behind her back. Then he began pushing her again. They went through the garage and into the backyard.

"You'll be okay. I won't hurt you. I'm going to tie you to a post. If you try and look at me I'll kill you."

He indeed tied her to a post, then he pushed her onto a picnic table and tied her ankles together. He removed cloth from his pocket, and the victim struggled against him as he forced it into her mouth.

"If you flinch or move, I'll kill you." She stopped resisting, and a second piece of cloth was tied around her head as a blindfold.

"I'll be watching you every ten seconds from the window," he said. She heard him enter the house through the back door (the one leading to the family room, not the door they had come out of), and she heard him opening and closing drawers and cupboards. It sounded like he was putting things into paper bags. "Oh, damn," she heard him mutter several times. Then he returned to her side.

"Have you ever fucked a guy?"

"No," she replied.

"You better not be lying to me or I'll kill you. Have you ever felt a guy's dick? I want you to play with mine."

He placed his penis into her bound hands and then he moved it back and forth. After he had done that a few times, she felt what she later learned was possibly an ejaculation.

He pulled her to her feet, unzipped her pants, and pulled them down to her ankles. He put his hand under her shirt, cut her bra in half, and then tore her shirt off.

The offender then untied her from the post and took her back into the house. He led her from room to room, and settled on the master bedroom, where he placed her on her parents' bed and raped her.

After that, he took her to the family room, forced her onto the floor, and raped her again. He turned on the gas fireplace and moved through the house a bit. He returned, put a knife to her throat, and ordered her to tell him that she "liked" what he was doing to her. She was raped a third time.

As he was getting ready to leave, he took her back outside tied her to the picnic table.

Immediate Aftermath

Once she was sure that he was gone, the victim was able to free herself from the picnic table and make her way back into the house. She used the phone to call the next-door neighbors for help. They came over, cut her free, and dialed the police.

Her parents arrived after the police did and sat with her while she gave a statement. The victim was then taken to Sacramento Medical Center. Once she was examined, it was found that despite being raped three times, the victim's hymen was still intact, which provided physical evidence that the assailant's penis was either on the smaller side or it wasn't fully erect during penetration.

During the interview with the victim, officers became interested in the loud crash that she had heard before the attack. It didn't take them long to figure out what had caused it. While examining the perimeter of the house, they found that the assailant had kicked the fence down. Why he did that, rather than jump over it as he had done in the past, was a mystery. Footprints found in the area and on the fence indicated that the assailant wore tennis shoes with a zig-zag pattern on the sole.

Because of the delay between the victim hearing the crash and encountering the assailant, officers at the scene wondered how long the intruder had been in the house before accosting the victim. They learned that the shoelaces used to bind the victim probably came from her older sister's tennis shoes, which meant that he was in the house for at least a few minutes before attacking her. In addition to those shoelaces, there were also some brown shoelaces, black shoelaces, and strips of town towel in the bathroom and on the family room floor.

A white shoelace was found hanging from a tree in the neighbor's yard. The victims clothes were also hanging in the neighbor's backyard, but they had not merely been tossed there. They were arranged there deliberately and specifically, for some unknown reason or purpose.

The house had been ransacked. According to the parents, a picture of the victim from the hallway had been moved. Furniture had been rearranged in the living room.

One of the most important pieces of evidence found in the entire case was a bloodied band-aid discovered near the picnic table in the backyard. Since the victim had not been wearing a band-aid, it was thought to be the assailant's. There was blood on it and an unidentified white or clear substance. The blood was analyzed and found to be type A+. Since the assailant's blood type could not be determined through seminal fluid, this was a significant breakthrough. Evidence found in later attacks would seemingly confirm that the assailant's blood type was indeed A+.

Suspect Description

The assailant was described as 6' tall with a regular build.

He wore a dark red ski mask and a dark nylon, ski-type jacket. It had a zipper in the front. He wore tennis shoes with a zig-zag pattern on the sole.

The victim felt that he had used lotion on his penis because she could smell it on her hands.

The assailant had a knife.

He spoke through clenched teeth, whispering loudly, and in the victim's opinion, he used a forced voice in order to sound tough or threatening. She felt that his natural voice was probably higher-pitched.

Context and Analysis

This attack has several things in common with Attack #9, and in some ways it feels like a repeat performance. Again he blitzes a victim and takes her outside. He must've somehow determined that it was safe for him to remain in the house, or perhaps he wasn't able to "perform" outside, so he took the victim back in. Unlike Attack #9, this victim was raped.

He didn't cut the phone line. Did he feel like he had control of this victim? Did he know the parents' schedule? Did he want to know if they were calling her? Or did he just forget to do it?

One of the parallels to Attack #9 is that the neighbor who cut her free had a daughter the same age as the victim. They had received hang-up phone calls as well, which might indicate that she too been on the rapist's radar as a potential victim.

In the early days, the assailant did more damage to fences than he did in the later attacks, but rarely did he flat out kick one down. That, plus the presence of a band-aid, could indicate that the assailant was injured in some way and not *able* to hop the fence. He wore tennis shoes in this attack, and the shoes he wore in the previous attack were square-toed shoes. Who knows, maybe extensive prowling had given him blisters or something.

This victim was a little different, physically, from other victims in the series. This was the first victim with her hair cut above her shoulders. Interestingly though, pictures of the victim hanging throughout the house all showed her with long hair. The victim had gotten her hair cut two weeks before the attack, which was after the hang-up phone calls had started. Had the attacker not physically seen her since then?

It's hard to tell if the timing of this attack is significant. Christmas was a week away. The victim was going to leave in three days for Bible camp, which would last two weeks. The attack occurred at a very "dark" time of year as far as daylight goes, which helped provide cover. All of this could've factored into the planning of the attack, if the offender was aware of all of this data.

The "I will be gone in the dark of the night" phrase was used again, which is yet another parallel to Attack #9.

The police took stock of the area and tried to determine how the assailant had arrived at the scene. They noted that if he traveled through backyards, there was only one possible route he could've taken because of the high percentage of mean dogs kept in the backyards of that particular area.

One of the strangest parts of this attack was the almost ritualistic way that the victim's clothes had been arranged in the tree. Any theories I might have on why this was done in this particular way is just pure speculation. It reminds me a little bit of the ritualistic way he would sometimes lay out strips of towel in preparation for a victim's arrival or transport. It's impossible to know why he did it, but it was intentional and it means *something*.

The geography of the case reveals a few of the usual clues, but nothing that sets off a lightbulb for me. There's a large ditch and a school nearby. The victim's family was interviewed a couple of times in an effort to help them recall anything strange that might've happened leading up to the attack, but they couldn't think of anything extraordinary except for the hang-up phone calls.

1976 Bicycle Incident

December 20th, 1976 2:00 AM or 2:30 AM

A strange and terrifying event, which may or may not have been EAR-related, took place just two days after Attack #10.

A woman was stopped at a stop sign at Oakcrest Avenue and Dewey Drive, an intersection in Carmichael. When she looked to her left to scan for traffic, she saw a person wearing dark clothing and a ski mask crawling on his hands and knees toward the front door of a residence. She quickly looked to the right to check for traffic, and when she turned back, the man was standing next to her driver's side door. They stared at each other for a moment, and then he knocked on her window. She floored it and shot through the intersection, leaving the masked man behind. Or so she thought.

She slowed down, stopped, and checked her rearview mirror. She could see the man turn, reach into some bushes, and pull a bicycle out from them. He got on it and began riding toward her. She stepped on the gas again. The last she saw of the man, he was still on his bicycle attempting to chase her. She lost him somewhere nearby.

Quite shaken by the incident, she told her boyfriend about it that night. He prodded her to report it, and she called the police about a week later.

Regardless of whether this event was related to the East Area Rapist or not, usually people crawling through neighborhoods in ski masks at two in the morning are up to no good. It happened just a little bit north of Attack #10, which makes it fairly suspicious to an EAR researcher. The incident took place just a little bit north of Del

Campo High School and northeast of American River College. Attack #4 happened just a little bit to the west (close to where Attack #13 happened, which we'll get to soon). Later on, the area was hit with Attack #17 and some odd break-ins during the summer of 1977. Attacks #5 and #9 happened north, off of Dewey Drive. So in other words, there was plenty of East Area Rapist activity in this small area.

If it *was* the East Area Rapist, I'm not sure what he hoped to gain by accosting a motorist. Was it an attempted car-jacking? Was he just trying to scare her? Did she witness something, and he wanted to eliminate her? Why pursue a vehicle if you're on a bike, when she can outdistance you with the simple press of her foot? Sometimes it's argued that some of his odd behavior can be explained by occasional drug use, and if anyone's looking for examples, this one might fit the bill. Perhaps he was angry at being spotted while prowling or while preparing for an attack, and he was simply lashing out? The bicycle stashed nearby makes me think that the man had planned on being in that area for a little while.

At this point in our narrative, bicycles haven't yet been associated with EAR, but they will be later. Another indicator that this incident might've been related.

Attack #11

Date: January 18th, 1977 11:30 PM to 3:30 AM
Victim: 25-year-old woman
Location: Glenville Circle, Sacramento

Pre-Attack Events

Late 1976
A neighbor living near the victim was burglarized.

Mid-December 1976
An unknown man unexpectedly walked out of a neighbor's backyard and startled him. The neighbor asked the man what he was doing, and the man replied that he was "taking a shortcut." Then he walked off. The man was described as a white male in his early twenties, 5'8" to 5'10", 165 lbs, with a muscular build and a dark complexion. He had a blue tattoo on his upper right arm.

January 11th, 1977 or so, 7:00 PM
A neighbor spotted a suspicious man peeking into the window of another house. To alert the prowler to the fact that he'd been spotted, the neighbor coughed loudly. The prowler turned and stared intently at the neighbor, then turned and started walking north on Glenville Circle. The neighbor who spotted the prowler was the same one that had recently been burglarized, so the police were called. They didn't show up. The prowler was described as a white male, late twenties, 6' to 6'1", medium build, with dark hair. He was wearing dark clothing.

January 12th, 1977 10:35 PM

A neighbor stepped outside onto her front walkway (which was well-lit by a porch light) and immediately spotted a man walking across her front yard. When the man saw her, he immediately took off running. She didn't get a good look at him, but she was able to describe him as being in his early twenties, 5'7" or 5'8", thin build, with a beige sweater and tennis shoes that had some sort of design on them.

January 13th, 1977

The same neighbor who had seen the prowler in her front yard found that her front porch light had been removed. That same light had been on the previous night and had allowed her to see the suspicious man.

January 17th, 1977

A blue sedan with one occupant was seen on Glenville Circle. No one in the neighborhood recognized the car.

January 18th, 1977 8:30 PM

One of the most detailed sightings occurred on the night of the attack, only a few hours before the EAR entered the house on Glenville Circle. In this instance, a dog in a house facing Glenville Circle began barking. The female who lived there looked out the front window and saw a man walk in from the street, through her side gate, and into her backyard. She went into her garage to make sure that her doors were locked, and when she came back, she looked out a different window and found herself staring face-to-face with the man outside. He immediately ran off and jumped the back fence. She called the police, but they told her they weren't interested since the prowler had left.

She described the man as a white male, thirty-five years old (based on his facial features, which looked older), 5'11", 175 lbs, and medium build with a small waist and broad shoulders. His hairstyle was a type worn in the 1950s, cut above the ears and combed up in front. His haircut seemed polished, as if he had just left the salon. The color was either grayish or blonde. No facial hair was seen. The woman thought he looked very athletic, and he was clearly very agile. He was wearing a dark blue, light-weight windbreaker and dark pants. She felt he was under-dressed for the cold weather. His appearance struck her as if he belonged in the neighborhood.

A few days after the attack took place, she was taken to the police station to view a high-tech photo system. She picked out seven or eight photos that matched the prowler, and these served as leads for the detectives.

The Attack
The victim was home alone. Her husband was out of town on business.

She awoke from a deep sleep to see a bright light shining in her face. "Who's there?" she asked.

An intruder approached her and held a knife to her throat. "Be quiet. I won't hurt you. All I want is your money. Just your money, and I'll be gone."

He tied her hands behind her back with electrical cord that he had cut up, and he blindfolded her with a bandana. Her panties were placed over her head to further restrict her vision.

She told him that she was five months pregnant, but it didn't seem to faze him.

He verbally threatened her multiple times, frequently telling her that he'd slash her or cut her up. He cut all of the phone lines in the house.

He stood near the victim, and she heard a popping noise. He asked her what she thought it sounded like. She guessed that he was shaking a can of spray paint. He was angry with her reply, and urged her to "keep guessing." She offered a few more ideas, and the assailant began to get furious. She eventually realized he was masturbating himself with lubricant.

He put his penis into her hands and told her to "massage it." Then he rolled the victim onto her back, put his penis in her face, and forced her to orally copulate him. He warned her that he'd kill her if she bit him.

He got on top of her and told her to put her legs up around his back like she does "with her husband." Then he raped her.

After it was over, he got up and ransacked the house. He ate in the kitchen.

For four hours he reigned terror over the house. He raped her again and ransacked almost every square inch of the residence. He took knives into the living room and began breaking the blades off of them. He took a photo of the victim and her husband, cut her out of it, and took the cutout.

She knew that he was finally gone when she heard her garage door open, then her car starting up and driving away.

Immediate Aftermath

After the assailant left, the victim was able to get her feet untied. She ran to her neighbor's house and they called the police. She was taken to Kaiser for treatment.

The assailant's method of entry had been a window in the backyard. He'd broken a small hole in it and removed a wooden dowel meant to keep the window from opening, and then was able to slide the window open easily.

In addition to the cutout from the photo, the criminal had taken some money, jewelry, and a digital clock.

January 19th, 1977 5:00 PM

The victim's vehicle was recovered later that day. It had been parked at an apartment complex on Great Falls Way, close to a mile and a half away from the attack. The keys were missing and the vehicle was locked. A tennis shoe impression, most likely belonging to the assailant, was located nearby.

Suspect Description

White male, 5'11", 180 lbs.

He had a ski mask on, pulled down to his neck. The victim

couldn't tell if it had holes for the eyes and mouth or if it was an open style. He had on a light jacket, leather gloves, and polyester pants. It was dark and she didn't get a good enough look at him to determine the color of his clothing.

Interestingly, she described the flashlight exactly the same way as Victim #9 did—very short, with a bright beam.

She noted that his penis was large compared to her husband's—about five inches but possibly as large as six inches.

He spoke through clenched teeth.

Context and Analysis

We've turned a corner here. After a series of experiments, blitz attacks, showing up with no pants, and hit-or-miss situations, the East Area Rapist had started to settle into a sickening and terrifying routine that he'd more or less retain for the rest of his known criminal career.

The victim was Asian, and this was the first time that the EAR had attacked an Asian woman. He seemed to be expanding his victim pool at this point—the previous victim was a deviation because of her hairstyle and this one because of her ethnicity. Many commonalities still existed however, such as her job—she worked in downtown Sacramento as a secretary at the State Capital building.

His victim selection pool wasn't the only thing that was widening—his geography was, too. This was the furthest south and furthest west that the EAR had struck up to this point. This victim's house was located very close to Watt Avenue, one of the main streets in East Sacramento. There was a large park on both sides Highway 50 to the west. La Riviera was a major street situated nearby to the north, and on that street just a few blocks west was where Attacks #18 and #27 happened later in the year.

Just like how Attacks #9 and #10 were closely tied together, this one can be tied to a few of them as well. It had the description of the flashlight in common with #9, and the strange vehicle theft in common with Attacks #4 and #8. This time, the stolen vehicle was located almost a mile and a half away. The quickest route between the victim's home and the apartment complex where the vehicle was found was to take La Riviera heading west, and then south on Occidental Drive. Who knows what route he actually took, though.

Like Victim #7, this woman was pregnant, and that information didn't do anything to stop the assailant.

"When he was standing in the bedroom near the victim, she heard a popping noise. He asked her what she thought it sounded like. She guessed that he was shaking a can of spray paint. He was angry with her reply, and urged her to keep guessing. She offered a few more ideas, and the assailant began to get furious." This sort of guessing game starts to become routine for a little while (with only minor variations, but the answer is always the same—he's masturbating), and it's one of the assailant's verbal idiosyncrasies that I use when trying to determine if an unconnected EAR-style attack was actually committed by him or not. Another one is telling the victims that he only wants "food and money," a phrase that will be appearing in the attacks on a regular basis very shortly.

Speaking of money, the assailant took her cash. A persistent myth surrounding the EAR is that he didn't steal a lot of money. As I've been diving back into each and every one of these cases, I'm finding that the myth just isn't true. There were a small handful of times where he didn't steal all of the spendable cash available at a victim's house, but those were few and far between, and these instances were noted by investigators simply because it *was* odd and out of the ordinary for him to leave money on the table. For the most part, the EAR stole whatever money was available.

It's worth noting that the weight estimate and penis size estimate from this victim was in the upper range for what was usually described by witnesses.

One of the hallmarks of EAR attacks was the length of time that he would stay in a victim's home. This one was in the upper range of that as well, with EAR staying in her house for *four hours.*

I'm sure you noticed at the beginning of this chapter that there were a whole lot of prowler sightings in the area. One of the descriptions that caught my eye was the one where the woman noted that the prowler looked like he "belonged in the neighborhood." There were other prowlers in the general area that I don't have enough details on to write about, so these sightings weren't included in the book at all (like a man who was seen in the bushes of a yard on Waterglen Circle. He was described as a white male in his early twenties, but that's all I have). There were many other strange happenings without any concrete details or dates assigned to them that I don't have corroboration on, and thus, they've been left out.

Previous EAR attacks had been in the outskirts of the city (Rancho Cordova, Carmichael, Citrus Heights), but this one was considered to actually be in Sacramento-proper. Media pressure had begun to mount on Law Enforcement, so between that and the offender attacking in the Sheriff's own backyard so to speak, a dedicated East Area Rapist Task Force of detectives and other personnel was formed in response to the growing threat.

Attack #12

Date: January 24th, 1977, 1:00 AM to 3:00 AM
Victim: 25-year-old woman
Location: Primrose Drive, Citrus Heights

Pre-Attack Events

A few days before January 24th, 1977
Over a three or four day period, two boys walking to Kingswood Elementary passed a dark-colored American-made car parked on Primrose Drive. Each time they passed it, the driver looked down and to his right as if looking at something on his seat. He looked away so completely that they never even caught a glimpse of his profile. The man's car was always parked at the same location about a block and a half away from the victim's home.

January 22nd, 1977 12:30 AM
A neighbor on Farmgate Way saw a man walking very quickly and quietly across the front yards of her neighbors' houses. He seemed to be intentionally traveling in a stealthy manner, staying close to the bushes and the shadows. As soon as the neighbor saw him, she employed some stealth maneuvers of her own and stepped back behind some bushes to observe him in secret. Apparently she wasn't as stealthy as she thought she was because the man, who by now was only twenty feet away, stopped mid-stride and turned to stare straight at her. A floodlight was shining on his face and she could see him very clearly. He showed no emotion or reaction of any kind. She

was frightened at this point, and stepped back to her door, turned, and called for her son to come outside. When she turned back around, the man had vanished. She scanned the area for him, and saw a man standing in front of a house at the corner of Primrose and Farmgate, but she wasn't sure if it was the same man or not. Police were keenly interested in this sighting, and she was able to provide a vivid description. A composite was made. Her description was of a white male, thirties, 6', 175 lbs, with a square face and dark curly hair. He wore a brown hip-length jacket and dark pants.

January 24th, 1977 12:30 AM

The same woman from the January 22nd sighting heard her dogs, which she kept in the backyard, barking fiercely. This was very close to the time that the EAR was most likely near the victim's home, ready to invade.

The Attack

A party at the victim's home had ended, and she'd just said goodbye to her final guest. She was in bed by midnight.

An hour later, she was awakened by someone grabbing her shoulders. She screamed and struggled against him. The intruder told her that if she screamed again he'd "kill her," and he held something sharp against her neck.

He forced her to lie on her stomach, and then he pulled at her hands and tied her wrists tightly with rope. He blindfolded her, gagged her, and bound her feet together. As he was doing this, she noticed that the intruder had an unimaginably bad body odor.

He threatened her again with the sharp object, which she realized was an ice pick. He placed it on her neck again and again, each time with renewed threats.

She was relieved when he disappeared for a moment, but he was back all too soon. She heard a popping sound, and deduced that the man was lubricating his penis and masturbating. He made her guess what he was doing, just like in the previous attack.

He forced his penis into her bound hands and urged her to "play with it." He then turned her over, removed his gloves, and raped her. She felt his bare hands on her body, and as he attacked her, he called her by her name several times. He spoke more in this attack than in most of the others, speaking to her in a vulgar way while he raped her and ordering her to repeat vulgar phrases. When she started to comply and repeat them, he ordered her to "shut up." He lifted her nightgown only briefly to expose her torso but he didn't touch her breasts. When he pulled out, she felt that he had not climaxed.

He rummaged through her house, stopping in the kitchen to eat. He returned after quite awhile and then raped her again. Again, he used her name and used vulgar phrases.

After over an hour and a half in the house, he untied the victim, then retied her with different ligatures. He took the original bindings with him when he left.

Immediate Aftermath

After she was sure that he was gone, the victim tried to free herself. She was bound and helpless, unable to even remove her blindfold, but she was eventually able to make her way off the bed and over to the telephone.

The police arrived, secured the scene, and called in a bloodhound. It was the same one that had been used in Attack #7. The dog followed the scent out the back door, around the corner, down the street, and around another corner, for a total of two blocks. The trail ended at a curb on Guinevere Way. Because of the way that the trail ended, the assailant had either driven away or had been picked up at that location.

As in other attacks, numerous tennis shoe impressions were located in neighbors' yards, and the victim's side gate was left open. Waffle-stomper-type shoe prints were found in a neighbor's backyard very close by on Farmgate Way, but not in the victim's yard.

Deputies found some partially-eaten cheese in the house. There were tooth marks on it, as if the assailant had taken a big bite out of the whole block. They also found two empty cans of beer.

It was determined that entry was made either through the sliding glass door or the door leading from the garage into the house. Both of them had been pried.

Suspect Description

The victim described her assailant as a white male in his thirties. His penis was "skinny" and measured about four or five inches.

He wore gloves throughout most of the attack, except during the first rape. He spoke in a low-sounding or hushed voice, and he smelled very badly of body odor.

Post-Attack Events

January 27th, 1977

The woman from the January 22nd, 1977 sighting (where the composite was made) found cigarette butts deposited below her living room window. The butt was a filter type with two thin stripes, which were determined to be Marlboro cigarettes.

January 28th, 1977 4:30 PM

The same woman was talking to the paper boy and as she did, she spotted a jogger. The paper boy saw him too, and they both commented that the man didn't appear to actually be a jogger, and his presence in the neighborhood was a little odd. She felt that he looked similar to the man she had seen on January 22nd, 1977. She got into her car and followed him, but unfortunately she lost him near the Birdcage apartments. As she was turning to leave, she saw him walking out of one of the apartments and she watched him get into a vehicle. She noted the license plate. Police investigated, and the registration of the vehicle came back to an Asian man who lived nearby, at Farmgate Way. The location he lived at was near the attack site.

January 28th, 1977 7:00 PM

On Juarez Way, a location not very near the crime scene, a woman spotted a prowler at a house under construction (and also for sale). The man saw her, and he took off running when she reached for the telephone. The description she gave was that of a white male, about 5'8".

Context and Analysis

This was one of the first times that someone had probably gotten a really good look at a prowler, but was it the EAR or was it an unrelated man who lived near the victims? Unfortunately, there wasn't anything terribly distinctive about the suspicious man that she saw. In many of the possible EAR sightings, the subject simply stops and stares at the witness once he's noticed. Other times the subject runs away quickly. Very rarely do any of the sightings involve a subject who speaks, but it does happen. This sighting was par for the course, whomever he was.

I think back to a psychological profile of the EAR/GSK that was released at some point, where it's stated that if he's encountered before an attack, the offender would probably be very calm and affable, but if encountered after an attack he would be skittish, violent, and shoot to kill. I wonder if his reactions to people who spotted him varied depending on whether he was just out doing reconnaissance (reacting calmly... after all he's not committing a crime, so why run?) or if he was out to do burglaries or attack (run for your life and shoot when necessary). Two very different mindsets to explain the two very different reactions that would sometimes occur.

Just like in the previous attack, he lubricated himself and asked the victim to guess what he was doing. It seems he'd begun talking nastier to some of his victims. By the time he moved out of Sacramento and down to Contra Costa County, he'd even begun speaking in a vulgar way on some of his hang-up phone calls from time to time, too.

One thing that I don't mention as often as I should is how tightly the EAR would bind his victims. This victim's hands were bound so sadistically that it took hours for feeling to return to them after the attack. And speaking of the bindings, this is an odd attack in the sense that he took the original bindings away with him. He did this frequently during the murder series but it was a rare occurrence during the rape series. Perhaps he hadn't found any suitable "souvenirs" in the house and decided that the ligatures used in the attack would be his mementos. Maybe he cut himself and bled on them, or they had become frayed during the attack and he wanted to make sure that the victim was secure before he left? Maybe they could've somehow been traced to him?

This is the second time that bad body odor was reported on the assailant. If there's a correlation between time of day, day of the week, time of year, or any other variable and his smell, I haven't found it yet.

Researching and diving into the details of this attack gave me the impression that the assailant was a little angrier than usual. He was in the house for a good four hours in Attack #11 so that was quite an involved attack as well. There were several times in this attack where the assailant would ask her to repeat a vulgar phrase, and as soon as she started to, he'd tell her to "shut up." Telling the victim to "shut up" while answering one of his questions or saying something that he had told her to say is a common feature of the East Area Rapist attacks, and it was on full display with this victim.

The victim had the impression that her assailant wasn't interested in the sexual component of the attack, and that he seemed to be more interested in the vulgarity of his speech and in his anger. Despite raping her twice, she felt that he had not climaxed at all during the attack. He rarely showed an interest in a victim's breasts, and for the amount of time that he usually spent in a victim's home, a relatively small percentage of it was spent actually engaging in lewd acts and more was spent rummaging and threatening.

He wielded an ice pick in this attack. At this point, the assailant was relying heavily on sharp weapons and didn't seem to be bringing a gun with him very often (he definitely had one in Attack #3, and in some of the other incidents that may or may not be connected). This is an important point when looking to tie him in with other offenders. When he began attacking couples, guns became his primary control weapon.

Folks didn't get to see EAR's mouth very often though, so the bite marks on the cheese were a rare clue. I've never heard of any castings being taken of this and I don't know if any photographs exist, so we may have lost our chance at any information we might have gleaned from his dental history up to that point.

This victim had many things in common with other victims, but unfortunately, none of it has led anywhere. The victim worked as an accountant in the Capitol Mall Blvd area in downtown Sacramento. Many EAR victims had an employment profile very similar to this. She was separated from her husband at the time of the attack, like many other victims. A real estate angle, which was becoming more and more apparent, exists here as well: her home was for sale at the time by JB&H Reality.

There were nine total detectives assigned to work the case full-time at this point. One of the activities they did immediately after this attack was to get in touch with nearly two dozen pawn shops in the area in an effort to locate items that the EAR had stolen. Unfortunately, they didn't come up with anything.

Attack #13

Date: February 7th, 1977 6:50 AM to 8:00 AM
Victim: 30-year-old woman. Her 7-year-old
daughter was in the house as well.
Location: Heathcliff Drive, Carmichael

Pre-Attack Events

Early January 1977
The victim's house was burglarized.

Mid-January 1977
One of the most bizarre sightings in the annals of East Area Rapist
history went down like this: a husband and wife who lived nearby
were finishing a walk around the neighborhood. A light show of blue
and red suddenly bathed the street, and they spun around to see three
squad cars turning from Heathcliff onto Crestview, heading north
and passing them as they went. Just seconds after the three squad cars
had passed, they saw a man in a dark ski mask and black clothes step
out from behind a bush. The man ignored the couple, walked out into
plain view, and stood in the middle of the sidewalk. He put his hands
on his hips and remained there, watching the squad cars fade into the
distance. The couple kept walking, and the masked man didn't bother
them or pay any attention to them. The only description that they
could give aside from his clothing was his approximate height: 5'9".

Late January 1977 through early February 1977

Hang-up phone calls began at the victim's house. They continued up until the attack.

February 6th, 1977

A husband and wife living nearby noticed a man in the park acting strangely. As they went about their business doing yard work, the wife noticed that every time she looked up, the man was staring at her. The husband didn't notice him staring, but saw the man looking up at the sky a lot. The man stood there for quite some time, and then walked away in an "awkward manner." The couple described him as a white male, thin build, with short blonde or brown hair. He was dressed in a blue leisure suit.

February 7th, 1977 6:15 AM or so

A neighbor living on nearby Moraga Way heard her dog growling in the backyard. She stood on the table to get a better view of what the dog might be upset about, and when she did, she saw two white males in their twenties positioned about two hundred yards away. When they saw that she had spotted them, they took off running. One of them turned and ran back, then ducked down behind a pile of asphalt. She didn't get a very good look at them, but she could describe one of them as wearing a knit cap, a dark blue pullover sweater, and dark pants.

February 7th, 1977 6:45 AM

Another neighbor (who lived three or four doors down from the victim) was looking out her window on the morning of the assault. She spotted a man who seemed very out of place in the neighborhood walking in the direction of the victim's house. As it turned out, this was only minutes before the EAR would begin his assault. She described him as a white male, early twenties, 5'11", with a thin build. His complexion was light, he had neatly-trimmed collar-length hair, and he had a full mustache.

The Attack

The victim's husband left for work around 6:00 AM. Their seven-year-old daughter was still asleep in her room. As the husband walked to his car, he told his wife that there was a suspicious white van parked in the school parking lot near their house that didn't belong to the neighborhood, and he suggested that she check all of the locks.

She went around the house, making sure that all of the doors were locked and that all of the deadbolts were secured, and assumed that the sliding door at the back of the house was locked. It wasn't.

She went back to the kitchen and stood at the sink. A moment later there was another presence in the room, and she thought that her husband had returned home or that her daughter had woken up. She turned around and came face-to-face with an armed intruder.

"Don't scream or I'll shoot you. I just want your money, I don't want to hurt you." He had on a ski mask and wielded a gun and a knife. He pointed the gun at her stomach.

"I'm going to tie you up. Do what I say or I'll kill you. Sit down in the chair."

She sat in the chair. He removed shoelaces from his jacket pocket, then pulled her arms back and tied her wrists tightly. She started to cry, and he immediately held a knife to her throat and told her "Shut up or I'll kill you."

"Get up," he ordered.

"No," she replied.

"I've got a gun. I just want to tie you to your bed."

He led her down the hall. They passed her daughter's bedroom door and she saw that the assailant had closed it before he'd accosted her in the kitchen. She was worried that he had harmed her.

They arrived at the bedroom, and he held the knife to her throat again. "On the bed," he ordered.

He positioned her on the bed and tied her ankles. She heard the sound of cloth being torn.

"I'm going to cover your face."

"No!" she cried, panicked about what could happen or might've already happened to her child. "Get the fuck out of here!"

As the woman became agitated, her dog took notice. "Get the man!" she ordered the dog. The dog did nothing but look confused.

She rolled onto her back and tried to leap off of the bed.

"Shut up!" the intruder hissed. He sat on top of her and placed his gloved hand over her mouth.

She continued to struggle. As she did, she felt the gun in his right jacket pocket. Despite the ligatures holding her hands together tightly, she started to grab for it. She managed to get it out of his pocket and she even grabbed ahold of it. Her fingers, numb from the tightness of the ligatures, found the trigger. She was about to pull it but she hesitated, fearing that a stray bullet might end up in her daughter's bedroom.

Seeing that he had lost control of his firearm, the assailant became extremely agitated and began punching her in the head. He hit her three times, very hard. She started to lose consciousness.

"Shut up or I'll kill your daughter! I'll cut off her ear and bring it to you!" The struggle seemed to agitate him greatly, and he began furiously stabbing the bed near the victim's head.

He tied a strip of towel around her eyes and stuffed a strip of towel into her mouth. She was still woozy from the beating she'd received.

"If you move, I'll kill you." He ran the knife down her cheek. "I'll cut up your face."

She heard him leave the room, and she quickly regained her wits when she realized that her daughter could be in danger. She began kicking her feet until the bindings fell off of them. She tried to swing off of the bed, but before she could, he was back.

He pushed her down and held her there. "If you move I'll cut off your toes. One for each time you move."

He pulled her jeans off and lifted her shirt. She tried to talk through the gag—she wanted to tell him that she'd just had an abortion and that he could seriously injure her.

"Shut up," he hissed, pressing the knife against her naked stomach.

He stood beside her, and she could hear him applying lotion on himself and masturbating. He pressed his mouth on her vagina, and his tongue went inside her. After only a moment, he pulled away. He ran the knife up and down her legs and then laid it on her stomach. Then he raped her, moving back and forth only a few times before groaning and then getting up.

The room became very quiet. She wondered where he had gone to and what he was doing. And then she heard a sound that terrified her. It was her daughter's voice.

"Be quiet or I'll cut you up," he told the little girl, who had accidentally encountered him while he was in the bathroom. "Go into the bathroom. I'm going to tie you up."

"No-no-no! You're going to kill us!" the little girl screamed. Her mother tried to order the assailant to leave her daughter alone, but the gag muffled her shouting.

The attacker tied the little girl up with cords cut from something in the house, then picked the daughter up and threw her onto the bed next to her mother.

At this point, the daughter had started screaming "NOOOO!" and crying. The mother started to make as much noise as possible, and the daughter began shouting "He's going to kill us! He's going to kill us!" The assailant went to both of the telephones in the house and ripped the cords out from the walls.

He tied the mother's ankles again, this time as tightly as her wrists. Then he left the room.

They continued shouting for a few minutes. Then the daughter asked her mother if the man was gone. There was no noise in the house, and the victim decided that he probably was.

Immediate Aftermath

They both began to hop and drag their way to the back door to yell for help, which caught the attention of a neighbor (incidentally, the same neighbor who had seen the strange man in the park the day before). The police were called.

When they arrived, the white van that the victim's husband had noticed was still in the school's parking lot. Police made contact immediately. Inside was a white male in his mid-twenties. He was interviewed by officers no less than three times, and each time he claimed that he was just there to "look at the stars." Looking at stars at 8:30 AM? Despite his suspicious excuse, it didn't seem that he was involved in the attack.

The assailant's point of entry was the rear sliding door, which had been left unlocked. Police found the regular things at the scene, but one thing in particular stood out: there were several cigarette butts in an ashtray in the victim's kitchen, and they were all the same brand except one. The family smoked Marlboros, but one of the cigarette butts was a Vantage. The victims didn't smoke that brand, and neither did any of their friends (note: one source puts the mysterious cigarette butt as being found during the pre-attack burglary, not in the aftermath of the actual attack).

The victim received medical attention. She'd been cut on her head during the struggle for the gun. The paramedic noticed that there was another spot of blood that didn't seem to be from the cut, and a sample of it was processed by the crime lab. The blood turned out to be type A+, and the victim's blood was type B. It had most likely come from the rapist.

Suspect Description

White male, early twenties, 5'11", 185 lbs. His eyes were hazel. His legs were hairy and very white.

He wore a dull, dark green, tight-fitting ski mask with a slit for the eyes. He had a dark blue waist-length nylon jacket, black pants, and white jockey shorts on underneath them. His gloves were a cheap black leather and he wore red, white, and blue tennis shoes.

His gun was described as "thin," with a long barrel and dark wooden grips. The knife was dull and about four or five inches long.

He whispered at her through clenched teeth, and his lips barely moved.

His penis was described as "extremely small." He was wearing a sweet-smelling aftershave lotion.

Sightings Immediately After the Attack

The neighbor who had come to the victim's aid after she'd cried for help actually sighted a strange man, probably the assailant, right after the attack. The neighbor spotted the man climbing a fence sometime close to 8:00 AM. The man seemed to disappear into a large cement drainage ditch near the park. He looked to be about twenty years old with short, light-brown hair. He was dressed in a blue jacket and pants, something that looked like maybe a blue leisure suit. Right after spotting this man, the neighbor heard the victim crying out that she'd been raped.

A neighbor living diagonally across the street from the victim saw a white male, early twenties, 5'9", slender build, with blonde hair coming from beside the victim's house. He was walking quickly and went toward a small grouping of trees next to the Kelley Grammar School (a school located near the victim's house).

Two young ladies who attended Del Campo High School were walking to school when they saw a white male running from near the victim's house. They watched as he disappeared into the park at the end of Heathcliff. They described him as a white male, early twenties, 5'8" to 5'10", "medium build but not skinny." He had short, light hair. He wore a blue, medium-weight jacket and dark pants which were possibly jeans.

Someone near Kelly Grammar School saw a man dressed in blue running across the park toward the Del Campo High School parking lot.

A teacher who worked for Kelly Grammar School saw a man running in the park area sometime that morning. He looked like he was in his mid-twenties, 5'8" to 5'10", medium build, and he was wearing a blue jacket.

The police investigated an area of trees near the Kelly Grammar School where one of the witnesses had seen the strange man, and they found a small trail there. On the trail were herringbone-style tennis shoe prints, Marlboro filter-tip cigarette butts, and empty beer cans.

Post-Attack Events

February 7th, 1977

Strangely, the man who delivered milk to the next victim (Attack #14), lived very close to *this* victim. The day of Attack #13, he found a screen removed from a rear window of his own home.

Approximately February 10th, 1977

Neighbors near the attack site began noticing a strange man in the neighborhood who regularly started parking his red and black sports car near the area where the man in blue had been seen on morning of the attack. For several days in a row after the attack had happened, this man would park his car there at about 10:00 PM and then would disappear on foot to the woods. He'd return at 6:00 AM and then drive off. After more than a week of this, a neighbor confronted the man as he returned to his car. He told the driver not to return, and if he did, then his car description and license number would be given to the police. The man snarled something about it "not being okay to park on the street anymore" and then left. He wasn't seen again. The vehicle description and license number was still given to the police, but records about what was done with the information have been lost.

Context and Analysis

A lot can be learned about the possible prowling and casing activities of the East Area Rapist by analyzing this attack. He brazenly times this attack to put his departure in the daylight hours, just like in Attack #5, but this time he's not nearly as lucky when it comes to stealth and evasive maneuvers. The suspicious man seen by so many people is almost certainly the assailant, given the timing. There was no composite made that I'm aware of, which could be because it doesn't seem like any of these people got a very close look at him.

There's some overlap here when it comes to stalking activities for Victim #12 and Victim #13 (and perhaps #13 and #14, judging by the milkman's experience). As the offender became more prolific and the attacks came in faster and faster, there's more and more overlap. It's very interesting how the East Area Rapist was able to keep his intel on different neighborhoods straight in his head. If an arrest had been made at the time, no doubt there were would be plenty of notes, maps, call logs, and various other forms of records found in his possession about these different attack areas.

Geographically, this incident was very close to Attack #4. This one was a corner house. A high, but not an overwhelming percentage of attacks committed by EAR/GSK were on houses that were directly on the corner, or just one house away from the corner.

Additionally, there was a park behind this victim's house, and then a parking lot, and then the Del Campo High School. These are also common features of attacks. I suppose they offered several tactical advantages, including the ability to hide during off hours and watch a residence from a distance, somewhere quiet to park at nights, and as far as a park goes, somewhere to blend in while you stalk. Another advantage of the schools is that if you cross one on foot, you can get out of the area faster than if you were crossing crowded blocks by vehicle. A lot of the streets on opposite sides of schools don't directly connect, so someone chasing you would have to make a few turns to catch up.

One of the important parts of this attack is the pre-attack burglary that took place about a month before the assault. Not only was this an EAR hallmark of sorts, but if this burglary was EAR, this shows an overlap with Victims #11 and #12. Was he truly stalking three or more locations at once? The offender appeared to be a smoker, or at least he wanted people to think that he was a smoker. The cigarette butts that were found in hiding/reconnaissance areas around the time of these attacks were just as interesting as any found at the scene itself.

I'm sure it took an incredible amount of courage for this woman to fight back so ferociously. Her struggle is one of the more nerve-wracking moments in the case. I completely understand why she hesitated when it came time to pull the trigger on him, but there's a "what if" game that you can play when you think about what could've happened if she'd somehow been able to lodge a bullet into his chest. The rapist didn't bring a gun to his next two attacks—maybe the memory of getting bested by a bound woman was still fresh in his mind.

The blood evidence is exciting. This attack, along with Attack #10, gives us a good indication that the East Area Rapist was blood type A+. Blood would be found at the next attack, but the analysis results have been lost so it's these two attacks, plus a metal spoon that'll turn up in a bit, that we rely on for blood type.

Running the knife up and down the stomach of the victim was very reminiscent of Attack #7. I can't tell here if he's doing it to strike terror into the victim or if he derives some kind of satisfaction or sexual pleasure from it.

There were so many post-attack sightings in this case... I can't get over how incredibly risky this one was for him, especially with school starting up around the time that he left. If the sightings were truly him, he was going past areas that were a whole lot more populated than the areas in Attack #5. Even in Attack #5, one of the two houses he seemed to park near noticed his vehicle. Folks like to talk about how "lucky" the assailant was and that might be true, but his luck, if anything, had to do with the time of day that he usually attacked. As the series progressed, he seemed to mostly restrict himself to very early morning hours before the sun came up, and I'm sure some of that is because of this attack right here. I wonder if he *knew* how many people actually saw him that morning (still assuming that the suspicious man in blue was him, of course). Whoever he was, he was running like the Law was after him.

The man in the white van raised a lot of eyebrows. The fact that he was still there after the police arrived makes me think that he was most likely ignorant of what was going on somewhere behind him, but still, having a man like that hanging around a school before it starts is unsettling whether he had something to do with EAR or not.

And that wasn't even the *strangest* sighting that this attack produced. One of my favorites is the the man in the dark ski mask and black clothing who stepped out onto the sidewalk to watch the police cruisers fade out. It's quite bizarre and brazen, and somewhat reminiscent of the man chasing the woman in the car while on his bike. A little more detail about the yard he emerged from: He came out from behind a bush in the middle of the lawn. It was the only spot available for cover in the whole yard, and it was located about halfway between the sidewalk and the house. The house he was hiding by was a corner house, the one on the northeast corner of Heathcliff and Crestview. Very close to the attack site so it's possibly related. But if it was EAR, what was he doing fully dressed in his "attack clothes," and who called the police on him and why?

EAR did not always completely avoid an area even right after he attacked it, or at least that's how it seems. In Attack #9 he was most likely spotted again a couple days later, and there's unconfirmed and uncorroborated EAR activity after a few of the other crimes we've discussed. Now we have this strange man parking his vehicle in the area for some days after this attack. I have a hard time believing that this is EAR, simply because he was seen so many times on the morning of the attack (potentially) and it would be incredibly risky to show his face again in the area and risk having someone recognize him, but I can't read the offender's mind and tell you what he would or wouldn't do. We know that he was obviously at least *somewhat* risk-averse, however, or else he would've been caught by now.

And there's still one more strange sighting to discuss. The idea of the offender having an accomplice, partner, or even mentor for some of these crimes might sound a little absurd given the homogenous footprint findings and the nature of the crimes, but we've got this sighting of the two men in their twenties being seen thirty minutes before the attack (and the way they reacted when they were spotted). Not much more to say about that, other than it's a head-scratcher. As the crime spree wears on there are a few more similar incidents.

Law Enforcement did their best to find connections between this victim and other victims, or to find some kind of way that this victim could've ended up on EAR's radar, but nothing solid ever materialized. She was going to school at Sacramento State College, and her studies were in the Social Sciences (actually focused on

Criminal Justice). She was doing internships at child care centers (two different ones, one of which was in North Sacramento). Her husband worked for the Cobbledick-Kibbe Glass Company, and he had been in the military and had served in Vietnam.

Even at this point, with thirteen confirmed attacks, nothing concrete or actionable could be found as far as patterns or intersections in the day-to-day lives of the victims. It seems likely that the offender changed up his victim selection methods from time to time, or that he used several different ones. If that's the case, it's amazing that at least *one* of his victim selection methods hasn't been fully discovered and somehow generated a lead to his identity. Using one semi-foolproof way of finding victims is understandable, but possibly being able to use several, and have none of them be discovered for decades, is beyond frustrating.

Ripon Court Shooting

Date: February 16th, 1977 10:30 PM
Victim: Teenage boy
Location: Ripon Court, Sacramento

Ripon Court, a street near Sacramento State College (which came up in Attack #13), had always been a quiet street, tucked snugly away near the Lincoln Highway. But the night of February 16th, 1977, things changed, and an incident that may or may have been related to the East Area Rapist tainted the street with violence.

A woman heard a noise in her backyard—it sounded like someone had bumped into something on the patio. She and her husband turned on the back porch light, but nothing out of the ordinary was seen. The woman was convinced that she'd heard something, so her husband and their teenage son took a flashlight outside to investigate. There was nothing in the backyard, so they walked around the house and into the street.

The older man swept his flashlight across the neighbors' yards, and as he did, he saw movement out of the corner of his eye. He trained the flashlight on the suspicious area just in time to see a prowler jumping over a fence. Both father and son began shouting at the prowler, and the son took off in the prowler's direction.

He reached the fence quickly, scrambled up, and just as he was about to swing himself over to the other side, he heard the sound of a gun cocking. He tried to halt his momentum, but it was too late. The last thing he remembered seeing was a man crouched beneath him, holding a gun in his left hand.

The sound of a gunshot shattered the stillness of the night. The bullet tore through the boy's abdomen, and he toppled backward.

His father reached the fence and threw himself on top of his son just as another shot rang out. He covered the young man completely, waiting for more, but none came. The father then pulled his son to safety and waited for an ambulance. About this time, a witness a couple blocks away spotted three men running from the area.

The boy was taken to Stutter Memorial Hospital and was rushed into surgery. He underwent an extensive operation that sought to put his intestines, bladder, and colon back together. The operation was mostly successful and the boy survived, though he still struggles with medical issues related to this encounter.

A spent casing and a live 9mm round were found at the scene. Officers couldn't determine where the second shot had landed.

The suspect was described as a white male, twenty years old, 5'10", 170 lbs. He had long, straight blond hair.

He was wearing a blue watch cap, blue sweatshirt, dark pants, and white tennis shoes. Three composite sketches were made of the shooter.

While it's not confirmed that this was an East Area Rapist incident, most investigators are convinced that it was.

An interesting geographical note about this event, before we move on: this incident occurred less than five hundred feet away from where the EAR had left Victim #11's stolen car.

Attack #14

Date: March 8th, 1977 4:00 AM to 6:00 AM
Victim: 37-year-old woman
Location: Thornwood Drive, Sacramento

Pre-Attack Events

February 7th, 1977
As mentioned in the section about Attack #13, the man who delivered milk to this location lived very close to the previous victim. The day of that assault, he found a screen removed from a rear window of his own home.

February 1977
The victim received multiple phone calls where the caller didn't speak, but didn't hang up, either. These lasted throughout the month and stopped a week or so before the attack.

February 1977
A neighbor and her two daughters received the same type of phone calls throughout the month. The caller didn't speak at all until the very last call, which was received by one of the daughters. The caller was a woman asking for the girl's mother. By the time the mother got to the phone, the caller had hung up.

Early/Mid-February 1977

A family living a few houses away from the victim found a cloth bag hidden away in their hedges. Inside the bag was a ski mask, a pair of gloves, and a flashlight. Thinking that this was a pretty strange thing to find in their yard, the family called the police, who instructed them to simply throw it away. They threw everything away but the flashlight.

Late February and Early March 1977

A fifteen-year-old girl spotted an old yellow pickup a few times over a period of three weeks. The truck parked near the house on Woodcrest Drive located directly behind the victim's house. The vehicle seemed to usually arrive around 7:00 PM. It looked like an old-style truck with a rounded roof, no rear bumper, and chains with rubber tubing on them attached to the the tailgate. There was a small dent next to the right headlight. It had a California license plate with the letter "J," followed by either a "1" or "L." The DMV provided Law Enforcement with the registration information for every yellow pickup of that era, but despite a lot of legwork being done, nothing ever came of this lead. The last time the teen saw the truck was during the week of February 28th. The people who lived at the house where the truck had been parking had noticed the truck too, and had seen it several nights in a row. They also saw the driver. He was a white male, probably in his twenties, about 5'9". He'd park the truck on the curb between their house and the neighbor's house, and then they'd see him walk toward the back of their neighbor's yard. Because of the rounded design of the hood, fenders, and cab, they thought it was probably a vintage truck from the 1940s or 1950s.

February 28th, 1977

A thirty-two-year-old woman spotted a man with a nylon stocking over his head looking into her living room window. Her husband turned on the porch light and went outside to investigate. The bushes were moving as if someone had just left, but a prowler couldn't be found.

Early March 1977

The neighborhood dogs barked frequently throughout the week leading up to the attack.

The Attack

The attack began with the assailant noisily entering the victim's bedroom while she was sleeping.

"Do you feel this butcher knife?" he asked her. "If you scream or anything, I'll kill you. All I want is your money. I won't hurt you if you don't scream."

He tied her very, very tightly, blindfolded her, and then gagged her.

He rummaged and ransacked through the house. When he sexually assaulted her, he used a lot of vulgar language, which seemed to arouse him.

He removed his gloves during the rape. This time he actually fondled her breasts, but only for a brief moment.

He did something strange and slightly sadistic in this attack—he took the victim's hand and squeezed her thumb very hard with his fingers until the pain was almost unbearable.

He haunted her halls for two hours and fled before sunrise.

Immediate Aftermath

At 6:30 AM on the morning of the assault, a neighbor saw a man standing on a porch looking into someone's window. The house he was peeping into was at the corner of Thornwood and Montclair. The man was described as 5'8" to 5'9", with a medium build. He wore a gray sweatshirt and looked like a jogger.

Meanwhile, the victim was struggling with her bindings. She wasn't able to contact the police right away, and by the time she did, it was already after 7:00 AM. The police arrived a few minutes later.

On the outside of the house, officers immediately discovered the point of entry. A small crack had been made in the corner of a window, and the window pane had been bent back to allow the assailant to reach in and open the lock. Impressions from tennis shoes (wavy with a zig-zag pattern) were found below the bathroom window. The bathroom curtain on the inside of the house didn't cover the window completely, and police discovered that someone standing where the shoe prints were found would be able to see the woman taking a bath and also see all the way into the bedroom. There were several shoe prints in the backyard, and they matched the ones under the window. Salem cigarette butts were found in the yard.

Matching shoe prints were found a few doors west of the victim's house (at the house where the cloth bag had been found in the hedges). There was a large tree in front of this house, and under the tree the police found a large concentration of the shoe prints. Cigarette butts were also found, ones with striped, light-colored filter tips.

Inside the victim's home, responding officers found the black and brown shoelaces that had been used to tie up the victim. When the victim received medical attention, some blood was found on her thumbnail where the rapist had squeezed her. The blood sample was taken to the crime lab, but the results of the analysis have been lost to time. A tracking dog was used by police at this scene, and the results of that, too, have been lost.

Suspect Description
Unfortunately, the victim didn't get a good look at her attacker. She felt that he was a white male, and he wore a shiny jacket and gloves that felt like rubber. He spoke in a clear and angry whisper, and had no accent or anything identifiable about his speech pattern.

Post-Attack Event

April 6th, 2001
This victim received a phone call from a man who whispered "Remember when we played?" She positively identified the man as the voice of her attacker. This phone call came just two days after the breaking news that the East Area Rapist crimes had been tied by DNA to the murders in Southern California.

Context and Analysis

One of the first questions I always have about neighbors who get multiple phone calls before the attack: is this person an alternate victim or is he trying to figure out their schedule so that he can time his attack better? Or does the other household getting the hang-up calls look like they were actually the primary target? Were a lot of the hang-up phone calls made for the purpose of finding out who lived at a residence? When the calls persist over a long period of time, I start to lean toward the receiver being a potential victim themselves, rather than just someone whom the rapist is trying to avoid when he hops fences. The particular woman and her two daughters who received calls in this case fit the victim profile well, right down to the woman's job at a construction company (at this point, connections to the construction industry had started to emerge as a commonality among some victims and circumstances of the attacks).

Finding the cloth bag full of tools was huge, not just for the wealth of physical evidence it could've provided if it hadn't been discarded, but because of what it possibly tells us about the way that the perpetrator would move through neighborhoods and plan attacks. A similar bag was found in December of 1976, unconnected to any attack of that era (but possibly connected to a later one). It's very unfortunate that the dispatcher instructed the caller to throw out the evidence—the dispatcher clearly didn't understand the significance of what had been found. Granted, the area of Attack #14 was pretty far to the northwest of where the EAR had operated up until then, so a connection wasn't immediately obvious to anyone.

The flashlight was kept by the witness however, and police were able to analyze it. Unfortunately, it yielded no fingerprints and it had no identifying marks (not even a manufacturer), but it looked exactly as Victim #9 had described. Because it was a fairly unique flashlight, the local military angle was investigated, but a flashlight of that type wasn't used by any groups housed at Mather Air Force Base. It was kept in evidence for awhile, but probably tossed out when the statute of limitations lapsed and physical evidence was tragically disposed of.

The big takeaway from that incident was the new knowledge that the EAR was likely stashing tools around the city to come back to and use later on. If he got pulled over, he would've had nothing incriminating on him. Stashing things in the bushes might explain the terrible smell that the EAR had on him in Attack #12 and occasionally in other attacks—his clothes could've been in the "kit" and could've been out in the elements, been rained on, and become musty and moldy. I find it interesting that he didn't stash the bag at the residence that he hit, but he stashed it at a place where he seemed to be doing some reconnaissance. The footprints and cigarette butts under that fluffy tree were probably his, and this tree was in the same yard as the hedges where he had hidden his bag. All of this ties together to paint an interesting picture of how the EAR was operating at this point in the crime spree.

Victim selection is always a tricky thing, but it's something I like to think about in each attack. In this one, I'm almost sure that voyeurism is at play. Analyzing the victim's daily life for connections probably wouldn't do much good. It was noted that from the backyard, anyone standing at the window could see into the victim's bathtub and into the master bedroom. There were many, many footprints in the backyard, and the police estimated that someone had been spending time back there for days, possibly weeks. If there were instances where EAR selected neighborhoods that met his tactical criteria first, and then went cruising backyards for victims, this situation might have appealed to him. Studies show that many sex offenders begin their "careers" as peepers, and if the EAR got his start this way, it was probably something that he continued to do from time to time. As the years went by and the East Area Rapist morphed into a killer, there's *still* evidence that he selected some of his victims by peeping in on them and witnessing something sexual. With some of his victims being selected this way, it muddies the waters and make it difficult to find any common links with other victims, and those common links must exist somehow because he probably didn't select *all* of his victims through peeping. Or did he?

Because of the assailant's prolific years as a burglar and rapist, much is made about how he "must've been an expert" at breaking and entering. I personally don't see a lot of evidence that the offender ever did much more than hack away at things and try to pry things open with screwdrivers, and I feel that his skill set was rather crude and limited in this regard. Chipping away at a deadbolt, prying open a sliding door or sliding window... that sort of thing was about the extent of his talents. That's not to say that he wasn't "successful," because he was. But his ability never seemed to evolve. It didn't have to—he could get in where he wanted to without becoming an expert at locks and windows. With all of that said though, every once in awhile (probably less than 2% of his illegal entries) he got in somewhere or did something that left investigators scratching their heads. This attack was one of those instances. He was able to break a small corner of the glass on a window and pry it back without shattering the pane or breaking more of the window. I haven't taken examined the window myself, but I've done my fair share of locking my keys out of the house and finding creative ways back inside and I understand some of the puzzlement regarding this. It's hard to say if this was simply luck being on his side, the window panes having a lot structural integrity by being spaced together so closely, or what. I lean toward the glass just being a little thick and him being a little extra careful. If he had special burglary skills, I think we would've seen them on display a lot more often.

Just as with Victim #12, he used a lot of vulgar language, and the victim felt that he had very little interest in the sex acts themselves. He seemed to be aroused by speaking in a demeaning way and by issuing threats, and even by the sadistic manner in which he tied her hands. Several studies have concluded that a lot of rapists are motivated by something other than sex, and someone as prolific as EAR would probably fit that criteria.

Not having the analysis of the blood samples anymore is very unfortunate. We have two potential samples and a potential saliva sample, all of them coming back as type A or A+, but in a crime spree where the offender evolved and changed jurisdictions so often, we obviously want as much physical evidence as possible to link them up. Before DNA, blood type was used as a basis to rule out suspects, so it helped to have as many samples as possible and to be sure of the findings.

A tracking dog was used in this attack. While the same bloodhound had been used in Attack #7 and Attack #12, this time, the police got to use a new bloodhound. This dog was a young German Shepherd with special training. Bloodhounds were used fairly extensively in the EAR case (utilized in sixteen or so of the rape attacks), and the dogs often gave unique insights into how the assailant traveled to and from the attack. And if you remember, in Attack #7, a dog was even used to rule out a promising suspect. Much later, in the attacks at Walnut Creek, a dog was actually used to link two attack together because it was able to remember the scent over a period of time.

Did you see the call that the victim got in 2001? That's nearly twenty-five years after this attack took place. The 2001 call is considered a genuine communication from the EAR, and it's further proof that he might still walk among us. The offender was clearly inspired to call this victim after a series of reports and articles that were released with the major announcement that DNA had connected his rape crimes to his murder crimes. The San Francisco Chronicle and the Orange County Register ran the news on April 4th, the Sacramento Bee ran it on April 5th, and the call occurred on April 6th. When another major announcement was made regarding the case a few years later, the sister of the final murder victim received five hang-up phone calls a day for roughly a two-week period. A call in 1982 during a "quiet period" came about twenty-one days after a major article about him was printed in the Contra Costa Times. It seems a pattern exists here. With all of the current media attention being given to the case at the moment, all eyes are peeled for any sign of the offender's continued existence.

First Phone Calls

The afternoon and night of March 18th, 1977, was a game-changer in the EAR case for several reasons. It was the rapist's last attack in the Rancho Cordova/Carmichael/Citrus Heights area before starting to expand to an entirely new part of the city. It was the last attack before he launched a campaign of terror against couples in their homes. It was the first night that anyone got a confirmed look at his actual face. And it was the first night that he apparently made contact with the police.

Three calls came in that evening—highly suspicious calls, because the rapist did indeed attack a few hours afterwards. If they were pranks, their timing was nothing short of miraculous. Was he psyching himself up before an attack?

All three calls came in to the Sacramento County Sheriff's office. All three calls were the same voice. None of them were recorded.

March 18th, 1977, 4:15 PM
The phone rang at the Sheriff's office. A dispatcher picked it up.

"I'm the East Side Rapist," the male voice said, and then he laughed and hung up.

March 18th, 1977, 4:30 PM
The phone rang again.

"I'm the East Side Rapist," the same male voice said. Again he laughed and hung up.

March 18th, 1977, 5:00 PM

Once more, the phone rang at the Sacramento County Sheriff's office.

"I'm the East Side Rapist and I have my next victim already stalked and you guys can't catch me." He laughed and hung up.

They were certain that the voice was the same in all three calls. There didn't appear to be any accent, stutter, or anything particularly identifying. It sounded as if the phone was being held far away from the caller's mouth.

Attack #15

Date: March 18th, 1977 10:45 PM to 11:40 PM
Victim: 16-year-old girl
Location: Benny Way, Rancho Cordova

Pre-Attack Events

February 1977 through early March 1977
For several weeks leading up to the attack, the victim's family received frequent hang-up phone calls. The calls were coming in at different times of the day. When a family member would pick up, there'd be nothing on the other end of the line except silence. There was one call where it sounded like a female was in the background coughing. The calls began to become so frequent and annoying that the victim's mother began blowing a whistle loudly into the phone. The calls stopped a week before the attack.

February 1977
A neighbor living nearby received hang-up phone calls also. The calls came at all hours of the day and night. They stopped a couple of weeks before the attack.

February 21st, 1977
A neighbor living next-door to the victim saw a prowler looking at her through her front window. The neighbor could make out blonde hair, but his other features were disguised by the nylon stocking he was wearing over his head.

Mid-February 1977 through Mid-March 1977

Neighbors living on Ellenbrook Drive, a street nearby, began seeing a 1966 or 1967 gray Chevrolet Bel Air station wagon parked on the street. It was spotted on numerous occasions all throughout the month before the attack. No one took down the license plate, but several people noticed that the car had a decal of some kind.

March 13th, 1977

A nearby family with two teenage daughters in the house had left their residence for about two hours. When they returned home, they found that one of their bedroom windows had been pried open. Nothing in the house appeared to be disturbed.

March 18th, 1977 12:00 PM

A yellow pickup was seen on Malaga Way, a street near Benny Way, and the site of Attack #3. The driver, a male in his early twenties, appeared to be writing something on a notepad.

March 18th, 1977

A call came in to the victim's home. It was a man who identified himself as a roofer. He asked to speak with victim's father, but one of the kids told him that her parents were out of town for the weekend.

March 18th, 1977 between 8:30 PM and 9:00 PM

The next-door neighbor's dog began growling at the fence near the victim's house.

March 18th, 1977 9:30 PM

A fifteen-year-old girl living across the street from the victim looked out her window and saw a man come from a dark area of the street. She watched him walk down the sidewalk. The man stopped in front of the victim's home, then walked toward the front door. He stopped short of the front door, turned, and walked to the side of the house. He opened the side gate and disappeared into the victim's backyard. Unfortunately, the girl couldn't make out any of the man's features because of the distance and the darkness. All she could note was his height, which seemed to be average.

The Attack

It was 10:30 PM, and the victim had just finished her shift at Kentucky Fried Chicken. She pulled into her driveway with plans to eat the chicken she'd brought home and then call the friend she'd planned to spend the night with. The friend was expecting her call.

When the victim arrived, she noticed that the front porch light was off, which was out of the ordinary. She figured that her parents had forgotten to turn it on when they left for their weekend trip. She unlocked the front door, entered, and walked into the kitchen. She placed her chicken dinner on the counter, and then reached for the phone and dialed her friend's number. It rang once, and then she heard a noise behind her. She turned to see what it was.

It was the last thing she'd expected to see—a man with an ax above his head. She tried to scream.

"Don't scream or I'll kill you," the man snarled. "Don't look at me or I'll kill you."

He grabbed the phone cord and ripped it out of the wall. He snatched the phone out of her hand and started to violently push her toward the family room.

"Get on the floor." She went to the floor. "On your stomach." He pulled her hands behind her back and tied her very tightly with brown shoelaces.

With his victim secure, he began moving about the house. He opened the back door, stopped for a moment, then opened and closed the living room drapes.

The phone in the bedroom started ringing and the assailant stood motionless. After the ringing stopped he went and stood beside the victim.

"My car is just a block away. If you don't do as I say, I'll kill you."

He cut a towel into strips with scissors, then he walked across the room and stared at her intently. She had a feeling that he was going to gag her because he'd been concerned about her screaming, so she spit out the piece of gum she'd been chewing.

"Please don't hurt me," she pleaded.

"I'm not going to hurt you. I just want your money."

"Really?" she asked.

"Just do as I tell you."

He tied a strip of towel around her mouth and a second strip around her eyes, and then began rummaging through the house. Occasionally he'd return to her, and each time he did he clicked scissors near her ear or pressed the ax against her neck.

The phone in the other room began ringing again. It rang a over a dozen times and then stopped. He took the gag out of her mouth.

"When's your family coming home?"

"My sister's at a friend's house and my parents are in Lake Tahoe. Please don't hurt me."

"Shut up." He loosened the bindings on her legs.

"Have you ever fucked?" And then he called her by name.

"No, please," she begged.

He pulled her pants off, and then her underpants.

"You have a beautiful body, don't you?" And then he called her by name again.

When she didn't answer, he shouted "Don't you!"

"Yes."

He covered the lamp with her pants to dim the light, then forced her legs apart. He worked his way down and then put his tongue inside of her.

A moment later, she heard him apply lotion to himself. He made her lie on her stomach and "play with it." He asked her questions, and would tell her to "shut up" when she tried to answer.

He raped her. He made a vulgar remark about his "eight-inch dick" while he did. After the assault, he wandered the house some more. He ate in the kitchen. Then he returned and raped her again. After that, he made her sit on his lap, facing forward, while he raped her. He sexually assaulted her several times during the hour or so that he was in the house.

As this was going on, the victim's friend was getting worried. It was nearly midnight, and the victim was supposed to have been at her house before eleven. To add to her worries, the victim wasn't answering the phone. She and her dad went to check on her. When the dad knocked on the door, the assailant hurried out the back door and made his escape.

Immediate Aftermath

March 18th, 1977 11:05 PM
A sixteen year-old boy who lived on Garrett Way, a nearby street, arrived home. He sat in his vehicle for awhile. At close to 11:15 PM, he saw a Chevy station wagon with brown wood trim start up and pull away from a house on Ellenbrook Way. The boy didn't see the driver, and he didn't see anyone get in it. It drove away slowly. The boy had never seen the vehicle before. The timing on this sighting doesn't really work out for it to be the assailant, assuming he acted alone, but it might be significant somehow.

March 18th, 1977
Around the time of the attack, another neighbor saw an older model gray sedan parked on Benny Way for several hours.

The police got the call shortly before midnight. The victim was taken to Sacramento Medical Center while responding officers worked the scene.

They found the assailant's ax abandoned on the back fence. Shoe impressions of a herringbone/zigzag pattern were located in some mud in the backyard. A pen or pencil bearing the name of a real estate company was found sticking up in the ground near one of the footprints, and one bearing the name of a bicycle shop was nearby as well. Two empty Dr. Pepper cans were found by the garage—they didn't belong to the house, so it was assumed that the assailant had brought them with him and possibly had even consumed them at the scene. A bottle of Vaseline Intensive Care hand lotion not belonging to the household was found on the victim's roof in the backyard.

Multiple doors and windows had been pried at and opened.

The victim's driver's license and two of her rings were stolen. Her sister's school identification card was also taken.

The bloodhound used in the previous attack was brought to the scene. He immediately picked up a scent in the backyard, and then followed it to the side gate and across several front yards to curb of 2626 Ellenbrook Drive. The scent ended there. Interestingly enough, this was the exact spot that neighbors had been seeing the 1966 or 1967 gray Chevrolet Bel Air station wagon all throughout the month before the attack.

At 3:00 AM, the victim underwent a rape examination at Sacramento Medical Center. She was experiencing bleeding from the assault, but medical staff were able to stop it. At 3:30 AM, her parents arrived from Lake Tahoe and were able to take her home.

Suspect Description

The victim got a decent look at the assailant. She described him as a white male, twenties, 5'9" or 5'10". She actually saw his face, as well. She described it as a young, round face, and while no solid descriptors came out of it, she was able to pinpoint a face in an early 1970s yearbook that looked exactly like the one she had seen.

The assailant wore a dark green nylon jacket, gloves, and dark shoes with no heels. He attacked her with a green-handled ax. His mask appeared to be a balaclava-type of ski mask, very similar to the ones firefighters wear (or in the shape of the type that scuba divers wear).

Despite the assailant's remark about his "eight inch dick," the victim said it felt about the size of a "hot dog."

He spoke in a harsh whisper, and he'd bound her with brown shoelaces and an electrical cord he'd cut from an iron in the house.

Context and Analysis

It's been awhile since we've been back to the area of Dawes and Dolecetto, but here were are on Benny Way, a street that connects to the area of that intersection and ends up right in the thick of the early

EAR attacks (as well as the 1974 dog-beating incident, the 1975 attack, and other important events including a 1978 double-homicide commonly attributed to the EAR).

The mask he wore appeared to be essentially a basic ski mask but instead of two eye holes, it had one big round hole for the entire face. Several of the police reports and documentation created for the case, even the ones created as late as 2003, used the glimpse that this victim caught of his face as the gold standard for how the East Area Rapist looked at the time.

While her description of his face didn't include anything *particularly* identifying, she noted wide eyes and a wide mouth. She saw enough detail to pore through various mugshots and yearbooks and make an identification. Naturally, they brought the victim to a place where she could observe the man that she had pointed out. She felt that the person she'd identified wasn't her attacker after all, and years later, this suspect was cleared by DNA. While it wasn't the person they were looking for, at least she'd given the police a template of what kind of face to find.

The attacker appeared to be lighting up the phone lines before this attack. In addition to the plethora of hang-up calls he made, he apparently called the Sheriff's office three times just hours before the attack and he might've even called the victim posing as a roofer. At this juncture, it seemed that the EAR had rarely spoken to his targets on the phone, even under pretense. The victim later asked her father if he'd been expecting a call from a roofer, and he confirmed that he had not.

The attack itself, with him surprising her in the dark, is terrifying—as they all were. Did you notice the continued use of the "I just want your money" ruse? Trying to lull his victims into a false sense of security by making them think he was simply there to rob them is a trick that he refined and perfected as time went on.

Clicking the scissors near her ears while she was blindfolded was particularly cruel. He ate at the scene, something that by now had become an unmistakable calling card. Apparently he'd brought some Dr. Pepper along as well, and he'd taken the time to throw his lotion onto the roof. The shoe impressions found in the yard were the same as those found at a few of the attacks immediately preceding this one.

The pre-attack timeline immediately before the assault began can get a little confusing, so let's walk through it. Sometime before 9:00 PM, the neighbor's dog was growling at the fence near the victim's house. Then at around 9:30 PM, a suspicious man was seen basically coming off the street and going through the side gate into the victim's backyard. What exactly happened there? Did the assailant come through the backyard, do some things, then leave and come back through the front? I find it hard to believe that the dog was growling at nothing. Was the assailant depositing his attack materials, and then leaving and coming back? Was he confirming that the victim was gone? The tracking dog offers a little insight, but it seemed to me that the tracking dog was marking his *approach* to the scene and not his escape. Some of these odd little details could mean something, but I'm not sure what.

Like with most of the attacks, he took some risks, but he also seemed to work hard to mitigate them. Opening the back door and standing there in silence for a few minutes was probably him listening for cars, or listening for some other sign that the person on the other end of the phone had or hadn't been alerted to what was going on.

One of the things I haven't discussed much is the lotion that the assailant used in the attacks, or where it came from. Usually the assailant used lotion that was found in the house. In this case he actually brought the lotion with him, which was somewhat rare for him to do. It was a bottle of Vaseline Intensive Care hand lotion. As I mentioned earlier, it was found on the roof. In other attacks, typically when he brought something like that to the scene, it could often be found nearby, just like in this one.

A yellow pickup shows up here for a bit. Given the huge amount of sightings of yellow pickups in the previous attack, this pops out for me, even though there are a lot of other vehicles associated with this attack as well. Most of them, if not all of them, probably don't have anything to do with the EAR, though the gray station wagon with the decal might be important since it had been seen several times parked right where the tracking dog lost the scent.

The pen or pencil found sticking up in the grass was from a real estate company might be important, given the fact that there were also two real estate signs in the yard related to her father's second job as a real estate agent (his main job was with the school system, as was his wife's). The housing market connection is one that we haven't fully explored yet, though. As the attacks progressed, it seemed that more and more connections to the real estate world were becoming apparent. Granted, it was California in the mid/late 1970s, so it's impossible to know how much to read into it.

Attack #16

Date: April 2nd, 1977 3:20 AM to 5:00 AM
Victims: A woman and her boyfriend. The woman's two children (an eight-year-old son and seven-year-old daughter) were also in the house.
Location: Richdale Way, Orangevale

Pre-Attack Events

Early January 1977

A neighbor looking out his back window spotted a man he didn't recognize. The man was standing in the backyard of a house that belonged to a single woman living alone. The neighbor decided to confront the stranger, and as he made his way over, the prowler saw him and took off. He was described as a white male, late twenties, 5'9" or 5'10", with a stocky build. He had collar-length, light brown hair and was wearing a white or tan shirt with dark pants. He was very quick and agile.

Early February 1977

A house near the victim's residence was burglarized. The upstairs window was the point of entry.

Spring 1977

A family living near the victims (a woman and her two daughters) received hang-up phone calls for several weeks before the attack. In most of the calls, only breathing could be heard.

March 1977
The victim received hang-up phone calls all throughout the month.

Early/Mid-March 1977
The house next door to the victim's had been put up for sale, and two different people matching the description of the EAR came by to look at it. The first one came on the very first day the house was put up for sale, and he had a young woman along with him. He was described as white, blonde, and slender, and he drove a 1976 Chevrolet station wagon. A day or so later, a different man stopped by who was described as "thin" and "strange." He had blonde hair (cut short) and blue eyes. While looking at the house, he mentioned that he was transferring from Las Vegas to work as a civilian employee at McClellan Air Force Base.

Mid-March 1977
Three weeks before the attack, a neighbor saw what she thought was a police officer near the victim's home late at night. The victim didn't know anything about a police officer being near the property. The neighbor who spotted this man was the neighbor whose house was burglarized in early February.

March 23rd, 1977
Phony "meter readers" had been spotted in the area a number of times throughout the two or three months leading up to the attack. The last one was seen on this date, and seen fairly clearly by a witness. The witness described him as clean-shaven and wearing a blue nylon windbreaker and dark pants. He didn't have any equipment with him or anything to mark down meter numbers.

Late March 1977
A week before the assault, a man who kept his dog in the backyard found an empty meat wrapper near the patio. He also found a tennis shoe print on the top of one of his fence beams.

Late March 1977

A neighbor on Richdale Way was gardening in her front yard when she spotted a strange jogger. He was crossing the street back and forth, staring intently at a couple different houses (one of which was the victim's house) as he went. He didn't seem to know that he was being watched until he approached her yard. "Good evening," he said quickly upon spotting her, and then he turned away and ran across the street. He turned left onto Bullion Way, and just seconds later, the neighbor heard tires peeling out loudly and saw a light-colored sedan (possibly blue or possibly gray) driving away quickly. She described the man as white, probably twenty years old or a little younger, 5'10", 165 lbs, with a slender but fairly muscular build. He was "average-looking." He wore jogging clothes that were described as a blue-gray, two-piece sweatsuit that had a hood. His tennis shoes had several white stripes (probably Adidas, used by EAR on several occasions).

April 1st, 1977 Afternoon

A neighbor saw a primer-gray station wagon passing back and forth on Winterbrook Way nearly a dozen times. Winterbrook Way was a street just to the south of the attack house. The car passed by the house that would be hit in Attack #19.

April 1st, 1977 Evening

A neighbor's dog barked in a nearby backyard.

April 1st, 1977 10:00 PM

A loud car was heard.

April 2nd, 1977 12:00 AM

The same dog began barking again. Other neighborhood dogs were also barking, and they continued to sound the alarm for roughly thirty minutes.

The Attack

The victim, her two young children, and her boyfriend pulled into the driveway of her home after a late movie. The kids were already asleep in the backseat and the woman's boyfriend decided to stay the night. Everyone was in bed and asleep by 2:00 AM.

About an hour and a half later, the victim awoke to a bright light shining in her eyes. A masked man stood in the doorway.

"Don't make a sound. Do you see this gun in my hand?"

"Yes," she replied, although she actually couldn't see the gun.

"Wake him up."

As she woke her boyfriend up, the intruder trained his flashlight on the man's eyes. The man started to get out of the bed, but the intruder hissed orders at him.

"Stop. Don't move. Lay on your stomachs. I have a forty-five with fourteen shots and two clips. I want your money. Exactly where is your wallet? If you don't tell me the truth I'll kill you. Don't make any sudden moves. Lay still or I'll kill you like I did some people in Bakersfield."

"It's in my pants on the floor."

"All I want is your money. If you cooperate I'll be out of here in a couple of minutes. Get on your stomach and put your hands behind your back."

They complied.

"You! Tie your husband up."

"With what?" she asked.

"With the rope on the bed." He moved the light downward, illuminating some white shoelaces on the bed that he had placed there at some point.

"Do exactly as he says," her boyfriend said.

"Shut up. Don't talk. Point your hands apart. Tie up your husband. Tie the rope tight."

As the woman complied with his demands, the intruder went to the boyfriend's pants, picked them up, and walked up to the boyfriend. He put the gun against the man's head.

"Don't look up. If you see me I'll have to kill both of you." He backed away and they heard him digging through the pants.

"After I take the money I'm going down to my camp by the American River."

The boyfriend then felt his ankles being tied together, and then the assailant retied his wrists—much more tightly than his girlfriend had. The assailant tied the woman's wrists as well.

He then began going from room to room, ransacking drawers and closets. He returned to the bedroom and stacked dishes on the man's back, saying "If I hear the dishes rattle or the bed squeak, I'll kill everyone in the house. I don't want to hear bed springs."

He pulled the woman off of the bed. "I'm going to tie you up in the hallway so you can't untie each other."

She was guided out into the hall and felt something sharp against her back as they moved through the house toward the living room.

"Lie down. On your stomach."

Her feet were tied, and she was blindfolded by a towel. Dishes were rattling in the kitchen, and then he returned.

"Where's your matches?" he asked.

"I don't know. I don't smoke."

"You better not lie to me or I'll have to kill you." A cup and saucer were placed on her back.

"If you move I'll hear you and I'll have to come back and kill you."

He went back to the kitchen, and she could hear him eating. He then went to make sure that the boyfriend was still bound. When he returned, she could see the glow of a candle through her blindfold.

"I'm going to go get your purse out of the car." She wondered how he knew that her purse was in the car.

When he returned a short time later, she felt the cup and saucer being removed from her back.

"Hold my cock," he told her. "Be gentle with it." She felt his penis in her hand and felt him start to rock back and forth. He rolled her onto her back, untied her ankles, and pulled her underwear off.

"You have to tell me the truth and if you don't, I'll find out and kill you both. Did you fuck tonight?"

"No," she replied. She was lying—they'd had sex that night. The assailant's mouth went between her legs and he orally copulated her.

He stopped, left the room, returned, and the next thing she felt was him placing a pair of high-heeled shoes onto her feet. After that, he raped her.

"Make it good and I'll leave you alone," he said. He climaxed, then went to the kitchen to eat again. He went to check on the boyfriend, and when he came back he told her "I was in the Army and I fucked a lot while I was there." Then he raped her again and went to check on the boyfriend once more.

He ordered the woman to get up and pulled her arm. He led her to a chair, pulled her onto his lap facing away from him, and penetrated her yet again. After he was done, he pushed her down to the floor, retied her ankles, checked on the boyfriend again, and went to the kitchen to eat some more.

After he was finished eating, he went back to check on the boyfriend one final time. "Next place, next town," he told him.

The house went quiet. The victim's dog, which apparently had been hiding or had been locked up by the assailant, was now free in the house and nudging the victim. The boyfriend was able to slide out from under the cup and saucer. They summoned the police.

Immediate Aftermath

April 2nd, 1977 4:30 AM or 5:00 AM

A neighbor saw a small foreign vehicle circling the block several times during the timeframe that the EAR was leaving the victim's house.

April 2nd, 1977 6:00 AM

The neighbor living next door heard her dog barking, so she looked out the window. She saw a dark-colored vehicle, possibly brown or purple, full-size, with a loud exhaust, backing out of the victim's driveway. She couldn't see the driver. The timing of this sighting is strange—a detail we'll explore in a moment.

The police arrived a little after 5:00 AM, five minutes after they had received the call. After examining the scene, they learned that the EAR had pulled the furnace plug out of the socket and had cut the cord to the television. He'd taken money out of the man's wallet and the woman's purse, but he'd abandoned some of the money on the kitchen counter before leaving.

At 7:30 AM, the bloodhound arrived. The dog followed the scent out of the house and onto the sidewalk, then around the corner. It followed the trail about fifty yards to the northwest and stopped where it ended, which was near the intersection of Bullion Way and Main Avenue. The exact location the dog stopped at was such that it wasn't directly in front of anyone's house. It was very close to the main thoroughfare. There were thick shrubs at that location, so if the EAR hadn't used a car and had used a bicycle instead, the bicycle could've been completely hidden in the greenery.

Some physical evidence was found at the scene. There was a fingerprint from the assailant on the woman's wrist, but unfortunately the technicians were unable to lift it. There were some spoons possibly used by the EAR, and also some bubble gum that he had probably used. These were sent to the crime lab.

Suspect Description

The suspect was described as a white male, mid twenties, 5'10", medium build, no pot belly, with a light complexion. His thighs were larger than they should have been for his frame and they had a lot of abrasive hair, as if they'd been shaved. His penis was described as about 5 inches long and thin.

He wore a white mask, possibly a ski mask, with skin-tight leather gloves and a dark-colored nylon windbreaker.

He'd brought a flashlight with him and was armed with a .45 automatic.

He talked with his teeth clenched, always in a "controlled" manner, and in a whisper. The male victim was sure that the assailant had consistently spoken with a hint of a German accent.

Post-Attack Events

Late Spring 1977

A strange event with a masked bicyclist happened in Orangevale near this attack, though it may or may not be related to the EAR. On a street called Pershing Avenue (located just north of Madison Avenue), a woman was coming to a stop at a stop sign. She intended to turn from Pershing Avenue onto Madison Avenue. A bicyclist wearing a ski mask rode up quickly behind her and stopped very close, so close that he was virtually against her bumper. She turned onto Madison, and the masked rider followed her, still keeping very close to her vehicle. She picked up a little speed, and he kept pace. Finally, she sped up so much that he couldn't keep up, and he turned off onto another street.

August 18th, 1977

The crime lab finished processing the trace amounts of saliva left on the spoons and bubble gum. The results were positive for someone who had a blood type in the A group.

Context and Analysis

This was his first attack with a man in the house—apparently the rapist was now confident enough to attack couples in their own home. His "script" that he followed during this attack had been perfected over several months of targeting more vulnerable victims, and you'll quickly see that the rapist starts to follow more of a routine and that the attacks start to look a lot alike for awhile. In fact, attacks in 1977 and 1978 that *don't* fit the template of this attack (for instance, the ones where he devolves into attacking singles or teenagers again) are just as important for finding clues as any other significant attack.

Some felt that the media had "dared" the rapist to begin attacking couples. In a few of their articles, particularly the one released right after Attack #15, reporters emphasized that he had only attacked women alone or women with their children and pointed out that there had never been a man present during the attacks. Whether the assailant actually took this is a challenge, or whether he was looking to up the ante already, it's impossible to know. It's likely that he had come across some victims he didn't want to pass up, but had felt like he couldn't risk the attack because there was a man present. Attacks #5 and #13 are probably good candidates for that, because he had to attack them in the very risky morning hours. He probably planned and schemed to the point where he felt he could successfully carry out an attack with a man present, and the other attacks had given him the confidence to do so. Profiles generated by Law Enforcement describe a man who meticulously plans and fantasizes different aspects of the attacks and tries to find "efficiencies." If he had continued to attack houses where the woman had to be alone, it would greatly restrict his pool of potential victims. He wouldn't have to be as "choosy" if he could build up enough confidence to attack a couple. Perhaps he felt that attacking sleeping couples was possibly "safer" than blitzing people in their houses, which was his primary method of attack for awhile. There's likely a psychological component to it as well, because for a period of time he began to *exclusively* target couples, so obviously it satisfied him on some level to do that. This is more support for the idea that power and control and the infliction of fear, pain, and humiliation were huge motivating factors for these crimes.

It was clear that he'd picked up a few new tricks somewhere before attacking this couple. One of them is the "dishes trick"—he started stacking plates, cups, or some perfume bottles on the man's back after he took the woman into another room. If the man began to stir or tried to get free, the assailant was able to be warned of it well in advance. He often placed dishes on the woman's back as well, which allowed him to roam the house freely and rummage through things without having to keep an eye on both of them. As the attacks continued, every once in awhile he locked an errant child in the bathroom or a closet and put a dish or two on the doorknob. This particular maneuver was also used by the Visalia Ransacker and a few other criminals, usually on a front or back door during a burglary.

The idea of having the woman tie the man up is actually an interesting one. What made him think of doing this? Was it practical, or did it gratify him? The fact that this part of the attack went so smoothly makes me wonder how much time and planning he really did spend on this assault. It could've been quite a bit. Orangevale, a new area for him, was being stalked quite a bit it seemed, and the gears appeared to be in motion before Attack #15 was even committed. Was Orangevale (a fairly out-of-the-way place compared to his usual haunts) chosen so that if things *did* go poorly during the attack, it wouldn't be so close to his home base? Orangevale is fairly far from his other assaults, and this one would not be easily connected. Was this a factor in his new M.O.? Did going to a new location inspire him to change his M.O., or was it the other way around?

A study of bike trails in the area shows that a lot of them connect Orangevale to his previous attack areas, but further research has revealed that the bike trails near Orangevale didn't connect to the other attack locations at the time of this incident. This kills any theory that has him biking all the way from Rancho Cordova to stalk or commit this assault. There's dense foliage in the area now, great for cover, but old photos show that the area wasn't nearly as dense back then. At the time of the attack, the houses in the area were only about five years old.

If the rapist had grown up in or spent some time in Rancho Cordova, Carmichael, and/or Citrus Heights before the attacks started to occur, then this was very likely the first "new territory" that he had stalked since the beginning of the attacks. That might explain the clumsy and visible prowling that went on. Unfamiliarity might not be the only explanation—some of the extra reconnaissance put into this attack was probably in preparation for his big move from single victims to couples.

A few of the sightings of suspicious men were quite notable. The couple who stopped by the house for sale on the first day had a vehicle (they were driving a 1976 Chevrolet station wagon) that matched a suspicious vehicle sighting at one of the recent attacks.

And then on April 1st, a neighbor saw a primer-gray station wagon passing back and forth several times on Winterbrook Way. A gray Chevrolet station wagon was sighted at the previous attack. The woman working in her flower bed on Richdale Way had a fantastic encounter, and we did our best to find out if there was a composite made of this man, but we came up empty-handed.

Much is said about the EAR's "way with dogs." Questions about whether they appeared to be afraid of him or not, whether they liked him and didn't attack or alert their owners, and whether or not he befriended the neighborhood dogs while he was out stalking a victim are often asked. The accounts vary and his luck with dogs seemed to be hit or miss—some barked and some growled but indeed, very few attacked. Some of the more interesting theories involve him maneuvering past dogs by covering himself in bear urine or some kind of scent that would disgust the animals, and some theories involve him being an experienced dog handler who knew how to control animals easily, but a simpler explanation presented itself in this attack: an empty meat wrapper was found in one of the backyards where a dog was kept, along with an EAR footprint on the fence. This wasn't a common finding in the attacks and it could mean nothing, but it's something to ponder. If you're stalking an area and you want a dog to leave you alone, perhaps he tried feeding it.

Did you notice how the intruder ordered the woman to tie her "husband" up during the attack? The man wasn't her husband, but the victim *was* married—just not to that man. She had recently separated from her husband. Did the EAR have good intel about her being married, and assumed that the boyfriend was the husband? The boyfriend had stayed at her house before. Did he not have any intel at all, and just made the assumption because of the kids in the house? It's always difficult to tell how much he knew about his victims. Most of the time, it seemed like he didn't know very much. In this case it's impossible to tell, because the mistake could be made either way. Interestingly enough, he generally refrained from calling anyone "husband" or "wife" in the future—it became "the man" or "the woman." Was this done to mask who'd been stalked and who hadn't?

Was one of his goals to seem scarier and more omnipotent than he really was? He did seem to like to call people by their first name and make it seem like he knew them, so if that was the goal, making a fundamental mistake about marital status would be detrimental. I did a close search for newspaper articles of the time period, wondering if the Sacramento Bee, Sacramento Union, or some other publication indicated that the woman and man weren't married—which would've allowed the EAR to realize his mistake after the fact and would've accounted for the change in behavior, but since this was an attack on couples and the EAR had never done that before, it wasn't tied to the rapist immediately. An article about it finally appeared in mid-May, and in it the writer insinuates that the victim in this case was the woman's husband, so if EAR ever realized his mistake, it wasn't from the papers. Most likely it was from going through a purse and wallet during the attack itself.

"After I take the money I'm going down to my camp by the American River," he said. Intentional misdirection? "Like I killed some people in Bakersfield." More intentional misdirection? Regardless, it's incredibly interesting, especially since he mentioned Bakersfield in Attack #4. That's a really small, random place for the assailant to name-drop *twice*. A prolific rapist from near that area was arrested in July, 1976. Was the first mention (and possibly second) inspired by the news of that arrest? Or was the EAR a Johnny Carson fan and liked the "Bakersfield" jokes that he would sometimes slip into the monologues? Who knows.

He asked for matches in this attack, which was an important consideration because of the fact that a few years later, spent matches were found at two of the murder scenes. In this case it seemed he used them to light a candle for some low-level light. Cigarette butts were sometimes found at the scenes—perhaps he wanted a match to light a cigarette.

In one of the strangest turns that an attack took, the EAR went and placed high-heels on the female victim before raping her. That's definitely a new one, and not one that he would repeat. He would, however, grab Victim #30's foot and rub it all over his genitals. Not quite enough evidence to accuse him of having a foot fetish, but perhaps this type of behavior is something that someone might recognize in another offender or in someone they once knew. Supposedly, the victim had engaged in this behavior with consensual partners before, which adds an interesting clue as to how much stalking he might have done with this victim.

He forced the victim to sit in his lap, just as he had done with Victim #15. This wasn't something that the EAR did very often at all, but it's an important M.O. link (along with so many other details) from the man who attacked teenage girls in Rancho Cordova to the man who attacked adult couples elsewhere in Sacramento. Another parallel: despite multiple sexual assaults, the assailant never touched her breasts with his hand or mouth. That was pretty much par for the course.

There's that pesky inkling of an accomplice again, where a car circled the block several times in the time frame that the EAR left the victim's house. And let's talk about the other vehicle sighting—the weird one where *after* the attack had occurred, the neighbor saw a dark-colored vehicle backing out of the victim's driveway. This sighting is strange for a few reasons. For one, according to source material, the police were there at that time. It's possible that the neighbor saw a police vehicle, but according to a detective on the scene, no police vehicle matched this description. Later in the morning the bloodhound followed the EAR's trail to a location three blocks away, so it takes some mental gymnastics to bring this sighting into the fold if the EAR had parked a vehicle in the victims' driveway. I'm not discounting what the witness saw or her description of events of course, just addressing the question of whether this was related to the attack or not. Perhaps the time was noted incorrectly somewhere.

Inside the house, the children had slept through the entire assault. The EAR hadn't engaged them or bothered them in any way. The victim had a poodle which was usually quite noisy, but for some reason it didn't make a sound the entire time that EAR was there.

More evidence of type A blood was found at this attack. Sadly, this was the last time that evidence related to EAR's blood type would be found. Nothing else substantial was ever located and tested, though hindsight eventually gave us a few more places where it could've been retrieved. Once he moves down to Southern California, evidence is retained that later gets analyzed for DNA, which ended up being more useful than blood type, anyway.

As far as connections to other victims, both the female victim and her boyfriend worked as clerks at a Kaiser Pharmacy. This serves as our requisite connection to the medical field in this attack.

The bicycle incident in late Spring is very reminiscent of a previous incident already covered. The ski mask, more than the behavior, is what throws me. I've spoken with a *lot* of residents who lived in Sacramento at the time, and a ski mask wasn't a common thing to wear at all, *ever*. Bike or no bike. Maybe these sightings were indeed the EAR behaving very strangely in public. If not, then they were still probably sightings of people who were up to no good.

Attack #17

Date: April 15th, 1977 2:40 AM to 4:05 AM
Victims: Woman and her boyfriend
Location: Cherrelyn Way, Carmichael

Pre-Attack Events

Late February 1977
Around 6:30 PM on a day in late February, a twelve-year-old girl and her mother were inside of their home when they spotted a man jumping the back fence and landing in their backyard. They watched the man walk onto the patio and stand there for a few moments while he examined the exterior of their house. He then began walking the back perimeter of the residence. He left without doing any damage or trying to break in. The police were called and they intended to make a composite of this prowler, but it's unknown if one was made.

March 24th, 1977
A prowler was spotted in a nearby backyard. He was about twenty-five years old, 5'9", and 150 lbs.

Late March through April 1977
The victim begin receiving hang-up phone calls in the morning, at midday, and in the evening. The caller did not speak—all that was heard on the other end of the phone was quiet breathing.

<u>Early April 1977</u>
A house nearby was burglarized.

<u>April 11th, 1977 9:30 AM</u>
An eighteen-year-old woman and her nineteen-year-old boyfriend heard a sound at the back of the house. The young lady went to the window to investigate, and through the curtains she saw a man standing outside the window. He was examining one of her locks. He didn't notice her until she called out for her boyfriend. Alerted by the proximity of her voice, he took off running and disappeared over the fence. Despite several neighbors being outside, none of them saw or heard the man escape. He was described as a white male, 5'10", with dark blonde collar-length hair.

<u>April 14th, 1977 1:30 AM or so</u>
A dog inside a residence barked at something outside. It barked again at the same time on the night of the attack.

<u>April 15th, 1977</u>
A strange event that occurred on the day leading up to the attack (it was recalled by the victim at a hypnosis session followed the attack). On April 15th, she'd seen a car being driven by a suspicious man. He'd gone past her very slowly, staring at her intently as he did so. She described the car as a light-colored Valiant, and remembered a license plate. Police ran the license plate but it was unregistered. It's unknown if the license plate was fake or if the victim perhaps misremembered one of the letters or numbers.

The Attack
The victims (a woman and her boyfriend) were asleep in bed. The beam of a flashlight brought them out of a deep slumber.

"Don't look over this way or I'll kill you. Roll over on your stomach. I'll blow your brains all over the room with it if you don't do what I tell you. Do you know what a forty-five Magnum is?"

The boyfriend could see the gun. The woman could feel a knife at her neck.

"All I want is your money and nobody will get hurt." He threw black shoelaces at the woman. "Tie him up."

She tied her boyfriend's wrists, then the intruder tied hers, then he leaned over her and retied the boyfriend's wrists.

"Don't move or I'll kill you." He left them and wandered the house, rummaging as he went. He was gone for a several minutes before he reappeared.

"Come with me. I can't find your purse." Then he addressed the man: "If you move one inch, I'll cut her throat."

He took her out of the room, but he quickly came back, bringing the woman with him. He retied the man's wrists again, then took some electrical cord and tied it around his ankles. "Don't move or I'll kill her." He turned to the woman. "Do what I say or I'll kill him."

They left the room again, went down the hall, and went into the living room. The first thing she noticed was that the lamp had been covered with a towel. He quickly blindfolded her and tied her ankles together. He didn't gag her.

He left her side for a moment to put dishes on the boyfriend's back. "If I hear the dishes fall, I'll kill her first," the intruder warned him. Several minutes later, the dishes did fall. He was at the boyfriend's side instantly, cocking the gun and placing it against his head. "You do that again and I'll kill you." He replaced the dishes and left.

He went back to the woman, held a knife against her throat, and forced his penis into her hands. "Touch it," he commanded. It wasn't lubricated (which was odd because the EAR usually lubricated it before getting to this step), but after he withdrew from her hands, she heard him pumping a bottle of lotion. He put the gun against her head, used foul language, and made her repeat sexual phrases. He specifically made her talk about his "cock," and the more he talked to her, the angrier he started to sound. He breathed emphatically, making loud noises by sucking in through clenched teeth and breathing in a gasp. He did that at various times throughout the attack. The victim felt that he enjoyed making her speak vulgar phrases more than he enjoyed any of the sexual acts.

He forced his lubricated penis into her mouth (he'd probably planned on doing this, which was why he hadn't gagged her). When he pulled out, he pumped the lotion again, and then he raped her. During the rape, she could feel the gun in his jacket pocket.

After he raped her, he went to the kitchen and began to eat. He also rummaged through a few drawers, stepped outside onto the patio for a few minutes, came in, and raped her again.

At one point, the dishes fell in the master bedroom once more. The assailant raced back to the room. He pulled sheets over the man's head and restacked the dishes. "Kill the girl," he whispered menacingly.

Again he stepped out onto the patio, came in, raped the woman. Then he rummaged through the refrigerator, ate in the kitchen, and rummaged through drawers.

When he went through her purse, he found two bottles of codeine. They weren't labeled as such—only the generic names were on the bottles. The victim had recently received them after going through dental procedures. After discovering them, the assailant left them in her purse, then went back to her and began gasping strangely. He told her that he was "in real need of a fix," and he asked her where she kept her "codeine." After that he went and retrieved the pills, then he disappeared into the kitchen. She heard him running the water in the sink. Two empty pill bottles were found near the faucet.

Immediate Aftermath

The phone cords in the bedroom and in the kitchen had been cut, so the victims had to summon neighbors for help. The woman was taken to Sacramento Medical Center for treatment and an examination.

Entry had been gained by prying the lock at a sliding glass door. Two empty Miller beer cans were found just outside the back door. The assailant had used Rose Milk lotion, and he had cut the cords from several electrical appliances in the house to use as ligatures. He'd brought several black shoelaces with him and had torn towels into strips. The thermostat had been turned down to sixty-eight degrees. In addition to the codeine, he'd found some recreational drugs in a couple places in the house, including the refrigerator, and had stolen them. A day later, a plastic bag with wet pills was found in the backyard of a neighbor's house.

Suspect Description

He was about 5'9" to 5'10", had brown eyes, and had collar-length dark-blonde hair. His hair was straight, but it had a full-bodied texture. He didn't have much hair on his arms or his legs, and it was light brown and medium in texture, not coarse. The victims didn't feel that he had facial hair. His penis was approximately five inches long and about the diameter of a quarter.

He wore a ski mask, which the victims didn't see clearly. He wore an olive-green to light-green nylon jacket with straps in the front, dark pants which may have been corduroy, weathered gloves made out of black leather (with stitching on the sides of them), and laced-up combat boots that were worn and dull. His pants were tucked into his boots.

The knife used in the attack was seven to eight inches long. The blade was very thin and sharp. The beam from the flashlight was large and bright.

The assailant whispered through clenched teeth. The female victim felt that he had a slight Asian accent, and that it was probably genuine.

The shoelaces were black, and he'd used electrical cord as ligatures.

Context and Analysis

There are some fascinating things to discuss with this case, but I want to supplement it with a little bit of additional information. It's not always very interesting to read the exact timeline of events as they unfold immediately following an attack, but in order to help paint a picture of what usually happened after the police were called, let's walk through it:

The assailant left sometime around 4:00 AM. When the female victim was fairly sure that he was gone, she was able to make her way to the master bedroom, where she and her boyfriend were able to untie a few of the ligatures.

A little past 4:10 AM, the boyfriend made his way to a neighbor's house to call for help (their own phone lines had been cut).

By 4:16 AM, the dispatcher had sent word out to everyone on patrol.

By 4:25 AM, responding deputies were at the house. Another unit was positioned on a bridge near Sunrise Blvd and was looking for any vehicle or driver who matched the EAR's description. They began writing down license plate numbers and pulling people over at 4:27 AM.

By 5:15 AM, all Law Enforcement tasked with investigating EAR scenes had arrived at the residence. The female victim was transported to Sacramento Medical Center sometime between 5:00 AM and 5:30 AM. Police spoke with the male victim at the residence.

The female victim had a rape examination at 6:47 AM and was discharged at 7:30 AM.

At 8:45 AM, the female victim was interviewed by police.

During the interview and subsequent hypnosis session, the female victim was able to describe many details of the attack. A possible additional detail came to light many years later, when a detective who'd worked the case (Detective Richard Shelby) had a conversation with a former sister-in-law of the victim. The former sister-in-law claimed that the victim had confided in her that there were actually two assailants, one with a small penis who didn't put his full weight on her, and one who was heavier, with a normal-sized penis, who *did* put his full weight on her. She claimed that the victim never saw the two rapists together in the same room, but that they appeared to trade places when one would go out to the patio and the other one would come back in. Since this information came many years later, and there was no mention of it at the time of the attack by the victim, it's difficult to know what to make of this. I've included it here because it's discussed so frequently (and usually out of context). It's important to note that this information wasn't given from a primary source at the time of the attack, but it's still a fascinating detail.

Other than that situation and a few minor variances, the attack itself was remarkably consistent with the Orangevale assault two weeks prior. It was apparent that the East Area Rapist had evolved. He'd refined his M.O. and modified his victim profile, and he'd begun attacking outside of his normal areas (victim-wise and geographically), which meant that the officers responsible for catching him had to change their approach on a few things.

The assailant apparently knew the generic name of codeine. That could be an important clue. It's easy for him to mislead police by pretending that he *doesn't* know something, but it's impossible to conjure up knowledge like that out of thin air. Investigators noted that the previous victims were both clerks at a Kaiser Pharmacy, which made for a slight chance that he'd learned this information while stalking them. Of course, other medical links had been established throughout the crime spree as well. If the assailant did indeed know this information, it seems to indicate that his connection to the medical profession went deeper than coincidence or deeper than having a way of selecting victims from it.

The location of the attack was very close to Madison Avenue, a major street in the neighborhood going east and west. It was about two miles southeast of Interstate 80. There were several main thoroughfares other than Madison Avenue that the assailant could've taken to leave the attack site—if indeed he had to take a car and travel out of it. Taking Manzanita Avenue north or south could've also been a likely escape route.

One of the unique features of this attack site was the house across the street. It was vacant and listed for sale by R.R.W. Real Estate.

Police examined the interior of the house and found evidence that a prowler had been in the laundry room. This room was in the southeast corner of the house and provided an unobstructed view of the victim's residence. There were shoe prints in the dust made by tennis shoes, and there were several filter-tipped cigarette butts. It appeared to them that the EAR had used the location to surveil the victims' house, possibly watching it for several days or weeks before the assault.

The female victim in this attack worked in downtown Sacramento on S Street as a typist for the State of California. This occupation was very similar to other victims. She played softball for the American River Construction Company—a construction link. The victim's sister was employed downtown as well, working for the Pacific Bell Telephone company on J Street.

Attack #18

Date: May 3rd, 1977 3:00 AM to 4:30 AM
Victims: Wife and husband. Their two young boys were also in the house.
Location: La Riviera Drive, Sacramento

Pre-Attack Events

Mid-April 1977
Neighbors started receiving hang-up phone calls. As the month progressed, two of them had burglaries at their house.

Late April 1977
The victim started getting hang-up phone calls every day. They occurred right as she would return home from school.

May 3rd, 12:30 AM
On the night of the attack, the victim heard a loud sound near the fence in the backyard. She quickly checked the locks on all of the doors and windows and then looked outside, but she didn't see anything wrong. She went to bed.

May 3rd, 1977 1:00 AM
A neighbor heard someone walking on the gravel in her yard. The next day she found that the prowler had left her side gate open.

The Attack

The couple's young children went to bed at 10:00 PM, and the husband went to bed at midnight. The wife went upstairs to exercise. Some of the blinds and curtains were open while she did this. As noted above, shortly after starting, she heard a "thump" in the yard. It sounded like someone jumping the fence. She checked the locks and closed the curtains, then went to bed. By this time it was 1:00 AM.

Two hours later, she was awakened by a man standing in the doorway of the bedroom shining a flashlight on her. She quickly woke up her husband. The man in the doorway told them not to move. "All I want is your money. I got a forty-five caliber military automatic. I'll kill you if you move." He shined his flashlight on the gun for emphasis. He told them that he could kill them and then "quickly get across the levee" to his "camp."

He approached the husband, put the gun against his temple, and repeated the threats. He tossed a shoelace to the wife and ordered her to "tie the man up tightly" or he'd "kill everybody in the house." He threatened the husband yet again, saying that if he moved he'd be killed, and if he looked at him then he'd kill the woman.

The intruder then forced the wife onto her stomach, and he bound her hands tightly. "If you try to grab me, I'll kill everybody in the house, and then I'll be gone to my camp on the river." He retied the husband's hands and then tied his ankles.

The intruder mentioned cocaine. "I need big money for a fix," he added.

"My wallet's on the dresser," the husband said. The EAR grabbed the wallet.

"This can't be all your money. You better have more money or I'll kill you both."

"My purse is upstairs," the wife told him.

The intruder began to tremble and shake, a performance that the victims felt was an imitation of something the attacker thought an addict might do. Then he stopped. He covered the husband's head with a sheet, put a box of jewelry on the husband's back, and told him that if it made a noise he'd "kill everybody in the house." Then he ordered the wife to get up. He grabbed her arm, pulled at her, shoved the gun into her back, and led her out of the room. They went upstairs. He asked her to show him where her purse was.

She was forced onto the floor near the bathroom, and he bound her ankles together. Again he shivered like an addict needing a "fix," and then suddenly stopped. He went into the bathroom, retrieved a shower cap, and placed it over her face. She heard him disappear down the stairs for a few minutes. While he was down there, he placed a cup and saucer on the husband's back to supplement the jewelry box. She heard him return, and he began ransacking the kitchen and family room. As he did, she heard him opening and closing what sounded like the zipper to a large bag.

She soon felt her ankles being untied, and the intruder told her that he was going to tie her to a table leg. He stepped out of the room, she heard him open and close the refrigerator, and then he was back. He ordered her to "sit up."

At this point she could hear a wet, slurping sound. She realized that he was masturbating.

"Do you know what this sound is? If you don't tell me, I'll kill you." He placed his penis into her bound hands. "Do it like you're doing it to your husband." Then he raped her.

"You know, you're big," he said (the victim was six feet tall). "Bet you like big cocks, too." He called her a "bitch," and called her more vulgar phrases. Whenever he said something or asked her a question, it seemed to the victim that he expected an answer, and if she didn't reply, he seemed to get very angry. He called her a "bitch" multiple times. He fondled her breasts and stomach through her pajama top.

When he finished, he positioned her on her stomach. He tied her ankles together again, and then placed some dishes on her back and told her that if he heard them move or fall, he'd kill her. Then he left the room and went downstairs.

The assailant began rummaging through the closet in the master bedroom while the husband lay helpless. The offender asked the husband if he was in the Service. "Yes," the man responded. "Which one?" the assailant asked. "Air Force," the husband replied.

"I got kicked out," the assailant told him.

The EAR then went back to the kitchen and started eating. He made another trip down to the master bedroom to check on the husband and told him that if he moved while he was eating, he'd "hear him and kill everybody in the house." His mouth was full with food while he told him this.

He returned to the woman and pressed his gun against her neck. "You don't want to die, do you?" he asked. She started to answer, but he cut her off by saying "Shut up!" She started to cry, and he told her to "shut up" again and started breathing heavily like he was very angry.

The next thing she knew, the house was silent. He appeared to be gone.

Immediate Aftermath

The victim was taken to Sacramento Medical Center at 7:00 AM.

Responding officers found that entry had been made by prying a sliding glass door. A bloodhound was brought in, and the dog tracked the assailant's scent to the levee behind the victims' house. A knife was found at the base of the levee, and it was identified as belonging to the victims. Two empty beer cans were found at the levee, and despite it being a common feature of EAR attacks, the cans couldn't be confirmed as having been left there by the assailant. There was a suspicious shoe impression and a suspicious tire track found.

Suspect Description

The attacker was a white male, 5'8" or 5'9", 165 lbs, with a slender build. The victim described his penis as very small and short.

He wore a light-brown mask, probably a ski mask but possibly a stocking. He had on a dark, puffy jacket (probably a ski jacket). The husband and wife each gave different descriptions of the gloves, with the wife saying that they were form-fitting leather and very smooth, and the husband saying that they were made of heavy canvas.

The assailant carried a .45 automatic.

His voice was described as calm, soft, clear, articulate, and quiet.

There was some heavy breathing but the "harsh whisper" usually described in other attacks had been dialed back.

Post-Attack Event

January 20th, 1978 5:30 AM

The female victim in this case had just gotten out of bed for work when the phone rang. At the other end of the line was a man:

"I have not struck in awhile. You will be my next victim. I'm going to fuck you in the butt. See you soon."

Then the phone went dead.

The exact same call was received ten minutes earlier at the house of Victim #27. These two victims lived very close to each other.

Context and Analysis

This attack connects very cleanly with the victim attacked on November 10th, 1977 (Attack #27) because of that identical call that they received on January 20th, 1978. There are a few notable things about this phone call. The first is that the caller tells the victims that they will be "next," yet he's *already* attacked them. Another notable thing is that, as mentioned above, these victims lived very close to each other. It makes me wonder about how the EAR organized his notes, or how he categorized things in his mind. Was he up early/late, and trying to get back into that attacking mindset, or getting antsy, and going through his notations from the La Riviera Drive area? If it was him that called them, since he called them both ten minutes apart, does that mean that those notes on the victim were kept together? Would that mean that he possibly spotted or noticed both of these victims around the same time, even though their attacks happened months apart? Did he keep his notes in order of chronology or in order of geography? Since the common factor between these two victims is geography, I have to think that he was not just sitting there thinking of these two victims who had very little else in common other than basically the street they lived on. He must've been looking at or thumbing through the *area*, and the phone calls came about *that* way. It's a seemingly minor detail but it's a significant one, because very rarely do we get a peek at what's going on inside his head or at his house. The chance that this was a prank caller trolling an area is slim, because the main Bell Telephone directory was listed by name, not street.

Speaking of the phone, in the weeks leading up to this attack, multiple people were receiving calls. It seemed that several potential victims were in his crosshairs, so what made him choose this victim over the others? Did he see her exercising in the middle of the night while he was prowling a familiar area, and that's why he decided to attack that particular family?

The victims lived in a two story house, and this was the first time that an EAR assault had happened in a two-story home. The neighborhood was considered upper-middle income. Tactically, it was situated close to the American River levee. The levee would've been the perfect spot for him to prowl unseen at night, especially houses that had a second story. Attacks near the levee (and topography *like* the levee) would start to become more frequent for the assailant.

Again he mentioned his "camp by the river." And this time, he mentioned needing money for cocaine. He "shivered like an addict" but the victim thought it was fake. He'd mentioned needing a "fix" in Attack #6, so this wasn't exactly new, but it wasn't something that he did commonly, either. And he'd just handled drugs and put on some theatrics regarding them in the previous attack, so this was kind of a repeat performance.

One of his more plausible confessions was when he told the husband that he'd been kicked out of the military. Looking for suspects among the "dishonorable discharge" pile has yielded some interesting persons of interest, but so far it hasn't yielded the EAR.

The female victim heard him zipping and unzipping a large bag as he made his way through the house. Bags of all types were frequently described, but strangely, almost none of suspicious men sighted prowling any of the areas related to the entire case have had bags with them. The bag found under a window in December 1976, and the bag found in early February 1977 near Attack #14 might explain why—he probably didn't walk around with them. He stashed them nearby.

The assailant didn't cut the phone cords, he didn't gag the woman, and he only used shoelaces belonging to the victims. He fondled her breasts and rubbed her stomach. He didn't whisper through clenched teeth. In fact, he spoke rather clearly. These things, along with the house being a two-story, are definitely anomalies. Separately, they happen from time to time but together, it's almost unheard of.

There was another anomaly, but it's difficult to explain. The assailant was described as treating the victim "gently." I know that's a laughable phrase on the surface, and to be honest I'm not entirely sure what it means. Perhaps he wasn't excessively violent or sadistic with her compared to other attacks. Obviously it's all relative because every second he was in that house, he was doing something tortuous to them on several levels. He handled this victim with a bit more care than the others. This wasn't the only time the assailant did this, so it's worth noting, despite how insensitive it sounds.

The victims described the assailant's demeanor as "bored" (like he'd done this a few times and was tired of it), and as if he were acting from a "script." There were times where they felt he appeared nervous, but the victims didn't feel that it was genuine nervousness. There were times where it seemed that he had to stop and take deep breaths to keep himself together, and times where he'd breathe heavily, especially when emphasizing threats, but again, the victims didn't feel that he was actually nervous.

The discrepancy about the gloves is interesting. Since the wife described smooth ones and the husband heavy, is it possible that the assailant removed his gloves when he was with the female victim and she wasn't actually feeling "smooth gloves" but was feeling his actual hands? Was he wearing two different types of gloves? This could also just be an example of how eyewitness testimony is not always accurate, even though the witnesses try their best.

The victim and her husband both worked at Mather Air Force Base. She was also taking a real estate course at Sacramento City

College. Her husband was an Air Force Major. These things come up over and over again.

Attack #19

Date: May 5th, 1977, 12:15 AM to 2:40 AM
Victims: 25-year-old woman and 34-year-old man
Location: Winterbrook Way, Orangevale

Pre-Attack Events

Late April, Early May 1977
A teenage girl on Dredger Way (which connected to Winterbrook Way) saw a man driving around the neighborhood in an older four-door Chevrolet. The car looked rusty, and as if it had no paint at all. The car reappeared again on a different day, and this time the driver stopped at her house and told that her he worked for "Stone Plumbing" and that he'd been sent to make a repair at her residence. She wasn't aware of any problem or aware of her parents having called a plumber, so she turned him away. The driver and vehicle reappeared a third time, this time parked very close to her house. She noticed him when she walked outside, and upon seeing her, he drove away. He was described as a white male, early twenties, 5'1", very muscular, with short, curly, hair (brown) and a pock-marked face.

May 2nd, 1977
A neighbor was opening the garage door for her husband, and as she did, she spotted a car parked across the street with a suspicious man inside. She attempted to get his license plate number but as she did, the man drove off.

174

May 3rd, 1977 Evening

A neighbor who lived three doors down from the victim spotted a suspicious man sitting in a vehicle outside of her house. She described the vehicle as a metallic-gray Plymouth. The first letter of the license plate was a "D." She reported it, but by the time the police arrived, the vehicle was gone.

The Attack

The female victim was visiting her male friend for the first time. She'd never been to his house before, and they looked forward to having a friendly evening and discussing a job interview that she'd been on earlier that day. She arrived at 10:30 PM with her two dogs in tow.

The dogs were let into the house and then guided out the back door. Once they entered the backyard, they zeroed in on a large oak tree at the house next door and began barking wildly at it. A dog on the other side of the fence was doing the same. She and her friend looked outside to see what the commotion was about, but they didn't see anything out of the ordinary.

They discussed her job interview, watched some television, and ended up having sex on the living room floor in front of the window. The window was uncovered—the man had just moved in and he hadn't yet hung any curtains or blinds.

At 12:15 AM, she gathered her things to leave. The dogs went out the front door ahead of her, and they immediately turned to the right and began barking. They seemed very agitated, and the hair on their backs stood straight up. It was then that the attacker appeared from around the corner of the garage.

He ordered the man and woman to turn around and go back into the house, and if they didn't, he'd "blow their brains all over the house." Once inside, he ordered them to lie on their stomachs. He tossed shoelaces at the woman and told her to "tie the man" up or he'd shoot her and "blow [her] brains out." He repeated his threats a few times, adding that if she wasn't able to keep her dogs quiet that he'd "kill all of them." The dogs were barking and even snarling, but they didn't attack.

After she was finished tying the man's wrists and ankles, the intruder forced her to deposit the dogs into a spare bedroom. As she did, he told her that he'd kill her if she looked at him.

When she returned, he made her lie on her stomach again and had her cross her ankles. He didn't bind her feet, but he tied her wrists very tightly. She closed her eyes out of fear and sensed that the assailant had begun turning out all of the lights.

He went to the kitchen and returned with some dishes, which he stacked on their backs. He told them that if he heard them "click" that he'd kill them. He claimed that he just wanted their money, and once he got it, he'd leave. The male victim told him to take whatever he wanted, and the assailant immediately put a knife to his neck and told him to "shut up."

At this point, he separated them. He pulled the female to her feet and led her into a back bedroom. He held his gun close to her, put the knife against her throat, and told her not to move.

Then he unbuttoned her blouse and cut her bra open with a knife. At that point he blindfolded her.

The room was quiet. She heard him begin to masturbate himself with lotion.

Then the sexual assault began. He orally copulated her and raped her three times. While raping her, he never removed his gloves. He seemed to be having difficulties maintaining an erection, and it seemed to make him angry. In between the assaults, he rummaged through the house, ransacked closets and drawers, and occasionally went into the kitchen. While he was rummaging, she heard the sound of a zipper being opened and closed several times. At one point, he told her that if she made a sound while he was eating and drinking, he'd kill her.

During one of the final visits to the bedroom, he told her "You better swear to God you didn't see a van down the street." He said it multiple times and made her repeat it.

Eventually, the house fell silent. Once the victim was fairly certain that he was gone, she made her way to the man and freed his feet. He went to a neighbor's house called the police.

Immediate Aftermath

Officers arrived a little after 3:00 AM. They surveyed the scene, starting with a perimeter sweep, and then they took a look at the oak tree that the dogs had been so interested in. There were fresh scuff marks on it, as if someone had been climbing it, and some tennis shoe prints nearby. Officers noted that the tree overlooked the living room window, and determined that someone hiding in it would've had a direct view of the couple having sex.

Inside, they found the phone lines severed. An empty Coors beer can was found near the back door. Also, the assailant had apparently dropped a few things at the scene that weren't typical of him: there was a zippo lighter on the floor in the master bedroom, a knife behind the couch, a piece of chewed gum with hair stuck in it on a clothing hamper, and a small piece of plastic under the couch with "075" typed on paper that was attached to it.

The victims were taken to Sacramento Medical Center and the woman's clothes were sent to the crime lab. The male victim needed medical attention because his hands had been bound so tightly that they'd turned black and lost all feeling.

Suspect Description

The assailant was a white male, twenty-five to thirty-five years old, 160 lbs, with a slender build. The male victim felt that he was 5'10" to 6' tall, and the female victim felt that he was no more than 5'9". The assailant didn't have facial hair, or at least the victim didn't think so, based on how his face felt when he orally copulated her.

He wore a knitted mask which had holes for the eyes, nose, and mouth. He wore light brown gloves with tiny air holes, a dark-blue navy jacket, and a brown pullover sweater.

He carried a .45 caliber handgun.

The assailant spoke in whispers through clenched teeth. The female victim thought she might've detected a hint of a Spanish accent, but she wasn't sure. He went through spells where he'd take several deep breaths. The male victim described the assailant's voice as higher-pitched, and felt that the assailant spoke through clenched teeth in an effort to sound threatening. He described the voice as quiet, but not a definite whisper.

The assailant's penis was described as five inches long, with the circumference of a quarter.

Black, blue, and white shoelaces were used to tie the victims. They were all brought to the scene by the attacker.

Post-Attack Event

November 29th, 1977

Two semen stains were found on the female victim's sweater at the crime lab. They were tested for blood type, but it couldn't be determined, meaning that the sample came from a non-secretor (just like other EAR semen samples).

Context and Analysis

On the surface, this is what appears to have happened: the EAR was prowling around Orangevale, very close to the area he'd previously attacked, and he noticed the pair coming home. He hid up in a tree, or was already up there for some other reason... perhaps scoping out the victim's house, which had recently been vacant. He'd entered vacant houses before, and one of the reasons could've been to learn the layout. Regardless of why he was there, he most likely witnessed the couple having sex. Voyeurism, at various times, seemed to be a big component of his selection methods, and this one is a good candidate for that. Perhaps what he saw "excited" him (or, perhaps, "angered" him) enough to attack. It seems logical enough, given the dogs and the open window and how quickly he attacked after the couple had finished having sex. As likely as this narrative is, there are a few problems with it.

The first relates to timing. He was in the tree as early as 10:30 PM, and the couple didn't have sex until about an hour later. We know the EAR was patient, sometimes approaching a target house *hours* before the attack occurred, so this is a minor issue, but that's still a long time. Perhaps he was more of a voyeur than we realize, and he simply enjoyed watching the pair with the hope that something would develop. She'd never been there before, but apparently he knew she was in there or he wouldn't have been at the ready. He must've spotted them through the window or seen her entering the house at *some* point, and then waited around for awhile to accost her when she left. I suppose it's possible that he stalked her ahead of time and followed her to this location. Confronting them while she was leaving was an interesting move, seeing as how at this point in his crime spree he was usually surprising couples while they slept. He could've been waiting for them to go to bed and go to sleep together, but decided to blitz when they didn't.

The next potential issue with the idea that he saw them having sex is the fact that he orally copulated the female. That's really not something the offender seemed to want to do to a victim who'd just had sex with another man when he knew that they'd had sex. Of course, I can't speak for what goes on in the offender's brain, but in the past, he'd asked a female victim if she'd had sex *before* he did that to her. So did he really witness them having sex? Because of the scuff marks, footprints, and dogs it sure seems like he was in that tree. If so, it makes this action puzzling.

With the extent that he'd stalked the neighborhood already, it's interesting that he seemingly chose a random victim. Were there no other victims that met his criteria, or who seemed vulnerable enough to assault?

"You better swear to God you didn't see a van down the street," he told her three times, even making her repeat it. She *didn't* see a van down the street. The EAR talked about vans a lot throughout the series, but at this point, there wasn't really any particular van associated with any of the attacks. It's commonly thought that his frequent mention of vans was an intentional misdirection. However, vans *were* sighted in connection with some of his attacks, especially later.

Here's some odd trivia for you: chewed gum was found at this scene and at the other Orangevale scene (Attack #16) as well, but not at any other EAR scene that I'm aware of.

The fact that the assailant didn't remove his gloves for a most of the attacks around this time period is frequently discussed in relation to a new technique that had just been developed for lifting fingerprints off of a victim's bare skin. Since the assailant didn't remove his gloves as much after this new technique came into practice, some Law Enforcement officers wondered if he'd somehow found out about it. It's certainly possible (and there was an article published about this technique at the time, which he could've read), but it's just as likely that he was being extra careful while he upped the ante to attacking couples and expanding his perimeter. It's possible that the sexual component of the attacks was losing some of its luster and he didn't feel the need to touch the female with his bare hands as much as he had, which wasn't a lot to begin with. This victim (in agreement with several previous victims) noted that the assailant didn't seem to be deriving pleasure from the sexual component of the attack, and that he wasn't able to maintain an erection. He does remove his gloves a few times to touch the woman's skin after this technique came out, which leads us to believe that he was ignorant of it.

An accent was detected again at this scene. So far we have three different nationalities possibly associated with the assailant based on accents. Many of the victims felt the accents were fake, and there were many attacks where no accent, stutter, or anything distinctive about the voice was noted whatsoever. Perhaps he didn't have one, or perhaps the varied opinions on his accent could be explained by someone trying to disguise a *real* accent. If you've ever heard someone try to do that, the results can be quite uneven and hard to place. Someone trying to suppress a southern accent might sound British, and someone trying to suppress a French accent might sound German, or any number of combinations.

Again, a large bag was heard being opened and shut. In earlier attacks, it was usually the sound of a paper bag. Money and a few trinkets were usually missing from the scenes, so that was probably what the bags were used for. He also seemed to bring beverages and cigarettes with him from time to time. He might've been taking some of the victims' food along with him, too. And while those are some good guesses about what went *into* the bag, at this scene it seems a few things came *out* of the bag, such as the zippo lighter and a small piece of plastic with "075" typed on some attached paper. A lighter is a fairly common thing, and remember that in the other Orangevale attack, he'd asked for matches. So that's the gum *and* the matches/lighter that were exclusive to the Orangevale attacks, at least in Northern California. The plastic with the small tag on it was a lead that didn't seem to go anywhere.

Attack #20

Date: May 14th, 1977 3:45 AM to 5:15 AM
Victims: Wife and husband
Location: Merlindale Drive, Citrus Heights

Pre-Attack Events

Late December 1976
About six months before this attack happened, a neighbor in the area found a plastic bag containing cotton gloves and a flashlight hidden in the bushes under her window.

Late January, Early February 1977
Before the victims moved into their house, the woman who had lived there before them received hang-up phone calls. The calls started a few weeks before she sold the property and lasted until she moved out. While she was selling the house, she had a strange encounter with a man who came to see the property. The company that he claimed he had been sent by had already sent someone out to look at the property, and that person had toured the property twice. The suspicious man was very interested in the outside of the house (not the inside), and he asked a lot of probing questions about the woman's schedule. He also asked about the whereabouts of her family at certain times of the day, and she felt that he looked at her with thinly-veiled "hatred." She described him as a white male with a dark complexion, in his mid-twenties, 5'10", medium build, with salon-styled, light brown hair. He was very well-dressed, but drove

an old, broken-down brown car that was in terrible shape. Police followed up on this story, and found that neither man worked for the real estate company that they'd claimed to work for. The police thought that they had eventually tracked down the second man (the one who had raised the most suspicion), thinking that he was wanted in the Lake Tahoe area for a series of burglaries and attempted rapes that had occurred in 1975. That individual was cleared of being the East Area Rapist when the police found that he had an alibi for one of the assaults. Later on, it appeared that the police had possibly identified the wrong man, and this lead might still be open.

February 7th, 1977
The owner of the house had moved out, and the victims had begun the process of getting ready to move in. The previous owner didn't move very far away, the hang-up phone calls that she'd been receiving followed her to her new address.

Mid/Late February 1977
The victims began getting hang-up phone calls almost right after moving in. These started a full three months before the attack.

Early March 1977
A woman living on Viceroy Way, a street that both ran parallel to and intersected with Merlindale Drive, heard a knock at her door. She opened it to see a white male in his thirties, and he told her that he was with the "American Pet Association." He asked her if she had any pets that needed to be "registered." She told him that she didn't and he began walking away, but a moment later, she saw that he had stopped in front of her garage. He appeared to be studying the lock on one of her doors. She turned her back for a moment and he disappeared. She looked out a few different windows but couldn't locate the man again. The experience made her uneasy so she checked with some neighbors, and apparently her house was the only one that this man had gone to. On top of that, there was no such thing as the "American Pet Association." She contacted the police,

who scheduled her to make a composite of this man, but it's not known if one was made.

Late April or Early May 1977

Young children were playing in a nearby yard. A boy was holding his sister up on his shoulders, and from the elevated vantage point, she spotted something. It was a short, stocky man dressed in dark clothing, and he was hiding behind some bushes in the backyard of the victims' house. She pointed at him, which caused him to take off. He ran quickly and climbed over several fences with ease.

Early May 1977

A few days before the attack, the victims had a prowler in their backyard.

May 10th, 1977 2:00 AM

The woman who'd been visited by the man from the "American Pet Association" was awakened by a light flashing into her room.

May 12th, 1977 Late at Night

Sometime during the night, a woman living nearby thought that she heard noises in her garage. The next day, neighbors confirmed that there had indeed been a lot of noises coming from her garage, but they'd assumed that it was her husband doing some work out there. It wasn't. This event concerned the woman greatly, because she and her husband had been victims of a burglary in December 1976 at the house they'd lived in previously.

May 13th, 1977, shortly after 12:00 AM

Two blocks south from the victims' house, a couple was awakened in the middle of the night by the sound of someone walking around on their roof. Dogs began barking in the neighborhood. The footsteps stopped.

May 13th, 1977 1:00 AM

An hour later, on the victims' street, another couple heard someone on their roof. Their fourteen-year-old son slept through the noises. The couple touched base with another neighbor on the phone, and that neighbor told them that there had been someone on *their* roof, too. They called the police, and a deputy responded to the scene just a couple of minutes later. He checked the residences but couldn't find any sign of a prowler, despite the fact that one of the neighbors had heard the noises just seconds before he'd pulled up.

May 13th, 1977 2:00 AM

The third family who'd heard noises on their roof (and who actually lived next door to the victims) woke up to hear someone prying at their rear sliding glass door. They turned on the back porch light and looked outside, but they didn't see anything out of the ordinary. No dogs were barking. Not only did these neighbors live next door to the victims in this case, but by strange coincidence, they shared a last name with a family that would be victimized much later by the EAR outside of Sacramento.

May 13th,1977 6:30 AM

A neighbor on Merlindale Drive saw a suspicious white male on the street. She called the police, but by the time they arrived, he was gone. This neighbor, too, had been receiving hang-up phone calls for quite awhile. She described the man she'd seen as a white male, 5'8" to 5'10", 165 lbs, with short, light brown hair. He had on a blue shirt and pants.

May 13th, 1977 6:30 PM

About twelve hours later, another woman on Merlindale spotted an old, dark car parked on the street for about two hours. The man who drove it stayed inside the vehicle. When he finally left, the car roared to life with a very loud engine. She couldn't describe the man very well but noted that he was wearing what appeared to be a wrinkled, stained, brown uniform. The car's paint was uneven and peeling.

The Attack

The victims went to bed around 3:00 AM. Shortly after retiring for the night, the wife heard something at the side of the house. She sat up with a start. Her husband told her that it was probably a cat or a tree branch scraping the house. It was actually the EAR.

The couple had fallen back asleep, but they were awakened when the intruder stood in the doorway and shined a flashlight into their eyes.

"You make a sound and I'll kill you. I have a .45 and I'll kill you if you move. I'm going to take your money and I want some food and then I'll leave in my van."

They were both awake. The gun was visible.

"Get on your stomachs. I'm just going to tie your hands and legs." He removed shoelaces from his jacket pocket and threw them on the bed beside the woman. "Tie his hands."

She moved slowly and tied his wrists in bowties. The intruder got angry. "Do it over. Tie them tighter. In a knot, or I'll kill you."

She tied him again. He pushed her to the bed, pulled her arms back behind her, and violently began tying her up.

"Don't hurt her!" the husband shouted.

"Shut up or I'll kill you."

The woman cried out in protest.

"Shut up!" he commanded.

He lifted the blankets up near their feet and ordered them to cross their ankles. He tied the woman's feet, then went over to the husband and retied his hands tightly, then tied his feet.

"Where's the money?" He pressed the gun against the man's neck. The husband told him it was on the dresser.

The intruder went to look and found a bottle filled with pennies. He smashed it by hitting it with his gun, then began rummaging through the closet. He picked up the dog, who was very docile despite the dangerous situation, and moved him to another bedroom.

He returned to the couple. "Is there any money in the green box?"

"No, there's just insurance papers," the husband answered.

"You better not be lying or I'll kill you." The intruder pried it

186

open with his knife and threw the insurance papers onto the floor. He found a glass coffee mug on the dresser that contained Canadian coins, and he put them in his jacket pocket.

"I have to take a break now." He opened their sliding glass door and stepped out into the backyard.

After a few moments, he returned and closed the door behind him. He asked the woman if she had a purse.

"It's in the family room," the man answered. The intruder disappeared, and when he came back, he was holding a cup and saucer that he'd taken from the kitchen counter. He placed the items on the man's back.

"I can't find your purse. If I hear this move, I'll slit her throat, cut off her ear, and bring it to you." He untied her feet with one quick motion and pulled her off of the bed. "Walk and don't look at me. If you don't do as I tell you I'll kill you both." His gun was digging into her back as he pushed her toward the living room.

When they arrived, he ordered her onto her stomach and crossed her legs. He tied her ankles, then grabbed her purse from the bookshelf and dumped it out onto the couch. He sifted through it, put the money in his pocket, and then went to the kitchen. He removed a beer from the refrigerator and returned to the victim.

"Please God, don't kill me. Please!" she whispered softly.

"Shut up. You better cooperate or I'll kill you."

He went back to the bedroom to check on the male. He put the gun against the man's head. "You move and I'll kill you." He took his knife and pressed it against the man's neck. "I'm going to rest now and have a beer." He left the room.

They heard the intruder wander the house, and he eventually returned to the woman's side. He was holding a bottle of Vaseline Intensive Care lotion that he'd taken from the medicine cabinet in the bathroom, and he'd removed a towel from there as well. He stood over the woman and tore the towel in half. One of the halves went over the front of the television set, held in place by a candleholder. He turned the television on for light and turned the sound off.

"If you move I'll kill you," he told her as he placed a cup and saucer on her back. Then he took the other half of the towel and blindfolded her with it.

He took off his pants. She began pleading again, crying and sobbing. "No… just leave me alone and go."

"Be quiet or I'll kill you. I'll slit your throat."

He opened the Vaseline jar, lubricated himself, and began masturbating. He placed his penis into her bound hands and began moving back and forth. "Massage it. Play with it."

After a few moments of that, he rolled her over, untied her feet, removed her pajama bottoms, and removed her underwear. He then lifted part of his mask and orally copulated her.

"You're beautiful," he hissed. "I'm going to take you in the van with me. How would you like to be in the river?"

Her sobbing grew louder.

"Shut up. Don't make a sound or I'll kill you."

He raped her. When he was finished, he rolled her onto her stomach and put the cup and saucer on her back again. As he was getting ready to leave, he reached down and grabbed her left hand. He started to pull her rings off, and she instinctively made a fist.

"No, please don't take them. Please don't take them off," she begged.

"Shut up or I'll kill you." He pointed the gun to her head. She relinquished the rings, and he escaped through the back door.

Immediate Aftermath

The assailant had left around 5:15 AM. At 5:20 AM, the paperboy, who at the time was positioned just north of Greenback Lane, saw a van with wide wheels speeding north on Birdcage Walk. When it reached Greenback Lane, it turned left, heading west. The van was blue, and it looked like it had been sanded. Law Enforcement felt that it was probably the assailant, and that he had probably parked at a nearby apartment complex about three minutes away.

The responding officers determined that entry had been made by prying open the window to an empty bedroom on the other side of the house.

At the scene, they tried a new technique (mentioned in the previous attack summary) to look for fingerprints on the victim's body, but they didn't come up with anything. About an hour after the police arrived, the female victim was transported to Sacramento Medical Center.

Suspect Description
White male, 5'9" to 5'10", stocky build, with dark brown collar-length hair. He had very hairy legs and no facial hair.

He wore a tight nylon stocking over his head as a mask. He carried a black zippered gym bag, a flashlight, a knife, and a blue steel .45 automatic.

He bound his victims with brown shoelaces.

Post-Attack Events

May 14th, 1977
Several hours after this assault, a suspicious event happened in Rancho Cordova. A young woman was riding her bicycle when she noticed a suspicious man in a white compact station wagon. He had shoulder-length dark brown hair and a beard (but no mustache). Later that afternoon, she saw him again, this time closer to where she lived. And strangely, he didn't have the beard. Then, a third time that day, she spotted the same man in the same white compact station wagon. She was in a car traveling with two other girls when the man pulled up beside them and stopped his car. They moved forward, and he kept pace. Each time they moved forward or backward, he'd do the same. They made it obvious that they were writing down his license plate number, but he didn't seem to care. After awhile he simply drove off. The police were contacted, and the car was traced. The vehicle was registered to a Coast Guard base on San Mateo Street in San Clemente, CA, four hundred and fifty miles south of the incidents. The owner lived in Imperial Beach, CA, which was in the same general area but about fifty miles more to the south. His registration information listed him as 5'9" and 130 lbs. A second

name for the car belonged to a person living in Paramount, CA, an area near Los Angeles (four hundred miles south of the incidents). We do have some information that we're not able to publish about this lead, but unfortunately not any information on whether either of these individuals were ever cleared of anything related to the East Area Rapist.

Context and Analysis

It seemed this house was haunted by EAR for a long time before he finally invaded it. Hang-up calls were coming in for the previous owner, and then for the new ones, over quite a long period of time. The fact that the calls started up almost immediately for the new owners makes one wonder about the details related to phone service... when it was changed, how soon after being changed over that the calls began coming in, and if the previous owner changed her number when she moved or kept the old one. These seemingly unimportant details could mean a lot when it comes to the technical prowess, burglary patterns, or even the occupation of the offender. It could help determine how he was actually getting the phone numbers (if he had some way of looking up current numbers by address rather than name, for instance). Perhaps he broke in or simply saw the new numbers written down from a window.

This area was stalked extensively for a *long* time, starting with the bag being found around the holidays in 1976. The lengthy history of hang-up calls makes me wonder if the EAR could not keep tabs on them by sight or by exploring their backyards every day or week, like it seemed he could do in Rancho Cordova and Carmichael. Because so many more hang-up calls seemed to happen in several of the Citrus Heights attacks, it makes me think that he didn't live in Citrus Heights, or that he didn't live in a part that was near the addresses that he hit. Regardless of where he lived, this area had more than its fair share of EAR activity—Merlindale Drive was close to Primrose, where another EAR assault took place later on.

Have you noticed how busy this month was for the assailant? We're only in the middle of May, but already it's shaping up to be the busiest month in the entire East Area Rapist crime spree. For some reason, it seemed he'd begun acting on all of the intel that he'd clearly been gathering for months. Perhaps he was empowered by his "success" and the thrill of overpowering couples, or perhaps there was something scheduled for the summer that would take him away from the area or keep him otherwise occupied and he didn't want all of his "hard work" to go to waste. He wouldn't offend for the entirety of June, July, or August of 1977, so the latter theory is somewhat likely.

There was a *lot* of activity in the early morning hours of May 13th, so much that it's possible that this was actually going to be the morning that EAR attacked. He didn't for some reason. The prowling on the rooftops was new and seemingly rare for the offender. For some reason, this detail has taken on mythical proportions among some who follow the case, with many people claiming that the EAR used to jump from "roof to roof." Indeed, that was probably him on the roof, but again, this wasn't a common occurrence that we know of, and it certainly didn't seem like he was leaping from house to house. If that *was* him, why was he up there in the first place? Was he hiding? Listening to the family through the chimney? It reminds us of the dog incident in 1974 where the subject hid on the roof after beating the dog to death.

Speaking of dogs, the couple had a German Shepherd puppy that didn't seem bothered by the EAR at all. A lot of dogs didn't react to him. Given the 1974 dog incident just mentioned (which again, may or may not have been the assailant), the later dog stabbings, and a dog beating that seem to be EAR-related, maybe the animals had an innate sense that the assailant could and would hurt them, and they didn't want to challenge him.

During the attack, he took a "break" and went outside. Was he listening for neighbors or cops? Doing something else, like peeing in the yard? Was he telling the truth and actually catching his breath in the May heat? Was he hobnobbing with this elusive accomplice that he may or may not have had?

Again he mentioned a van, and he mentioned the river again. This time, a van was actually spotted. It doesn't entirely give credence to his earlier mentions of a van, but it opens the door to the question of how many of his words were truth and how many were deception.

He took the female victim's rings, something he seemed quite fond of doing. It's hard to say what the motivation was behind this. It's clearly very important to him because sometimes he goes to great lengths to make sure that he does it. Other times he leaves them alone. Is he fencing them for money? Is it to have a personal memento of the attack? Is it to hurt the victims emotionally by taking something of importance? Is it symbolic in nature, a statement about how he had broken in and hurt their marriage by raping the wife? This is one of the psychological questions that I hope we can answer once the offender is unmasked.

Even in this relatively early portion in the crime spree, the detectives assigned to the case were starting to be able to predict what the assailant would do, where he would do it, and when. Some of them took a proactive approach rather than a reactive one, and predicted that the EAR would strike the weekend of the 14th near the Birdcage Mall area. The specific streets they'd "earmarked" were Farmgate, Merlindale, Guinevere, or Thornwood Drive. Extra manpower and even military-style alarm traps were set up in the area of Thornwood Drive but unfortunately, Merlindale Drive was hit instead. Still, they were getting closer.

Speaking of traps, Law Enforcement set up a series of traps after the assault ended. At 6:00 AM, they took up positions along certain roads and began copying the license plate numbers of cars passing by. If they noted a suspicious man driving, they pulled him over. At this attack, the exercise was futile because most likely, the assailant had left about forty-five minutes before they were able to set up position.

At the time of the attack, the victims had lived at their current address for approximately three months. The husband was the manager of a restaurant, and the wife worked as a waitress (but at a different restaurant). They weren't from Sacramento—they'd come from out of town. As usual, no solid connections between them or any other victims could be found.

Attack #21

Date: May 17th, 1977 1:30 AM to 3:15 AM
Victims: Wife (26 years old) and husband. Two small boys were
in the house, as well as the husband's father.
Location: Sandbar Circle, Carmichael

Pre-Attack Events

Late 1976 or Early 1977
The man who would become the male victim in this attack stood up
during a public forum at a school in Del Dayo and began berating the
police for not catching the East Area Rapist. This event occurred
about five months before the EAR attacked his home.

January 1977 to April 1977
One of the victims' neighbors began getting hang-up phone calls.
These calls went on for several months.

February 9th, 1977
A prowler was seen in a nearby backyard.

April and May, 1977
A neighbor was approached twice by groups of people trying to pass
themselves off as Census workers. Since it was only 1977 (the next
Census would be taken in 1980), it seemed odd. Also suspicious was
the fact that Census workers usually didn't travel in groups, and they
didn't ever visit the same house twice. The neighbor and his wife

never saw more than two people at once acting as Census workers, but there seemed to be multiple different folks. Around this time, harassing phone calls were received by these neighbors both at home and at work, and at one point they arrived home to find their sliding glass door open. On high alert after all of these incidents, when they saw a suspicious Plymouth car in the neighborhood with a CA license plate, they wrote it down. It came back to a man who fit the EAR's description, and it's unknown whether this man was eventually cleared or not.

April and May 1977
Over the six week period leading up to the attack, the victims received a few hang-up phone calls.

Early May 1977
A neighbor heard noises in his backyard, and upon investigating, found that his window screen had been pried off. This neighbor's dog had been barking for a few weeks at different times of the night.

Early May 1977
Two weeks before the attack, someone shot two BBs through the windows of the victims' house.

Early May 1977
Sometime between the BB incident and the attack, the victims noticed that someone had pried the top of their garage door. The door was damaged by the prying and it was stuck shut. This incident, as well as the BB incident, were reported to the police but by the time the police arrived to inspect the damage, the victims had already repaired everything.

May 15th, 1977
The female victim saw a strange man walking across her neighbor's lawn. He disappeared behind the neighbor's house with something in his hand. She didn't think much about it, even though she didn't

recognize him, because the man living at that house had recently lost his wife and several people had been checking in on him.

May 15th, 1977 Night

A neighbor spotted a prowler on the street. He was shining a flashlight into all of the cars parked on Sandbar Circle. Around that time, all of the neighborhood dogs began to bark.

May 16th, 1977 Day

A vehicle was seen parked on the river levee behind the victims' house. It was a late model brown El Camino with California license plate 366-T??. The driver was a white male, late twenties, with collar-length brown hair and deep-set eyes. In order to recall more information about this sighting, the witness underwent hypnosis. While under hypnosis, she recalled details about a decal that she had seen on the car: it had a parachute with a missile carried underneath, set on a diamond pattern, with possibly the letters "AFC" on the bottom. This decal, seemingly military in origin, has never been positively identified.

May 16th, 1977 1:00 PM

A woman walking on the American River levee spotted a man peering into backyards. One of the backyards he was looking into was the victims'. She later described the man as looking exactly like the composite sketch that the police released in the newspapers right after this attack occurred.

May 16th, 1977 Evening

A neighborhood couple saw a brown 1960s or 1970s Dodge Charger on the street in front of their house. It looked out of place. These were the same neighbors that had been approached by the "Census workers."

May 16th, 1977 9:00 PM or 9:30 PM

A neighbor saw someone with a flashlight near the victims' house. Around this time, the neighborhood dogs began to bark furiously.

May 16th, 1977 10:25 PM

A couple walking down the street observed a man looking intently at houses. They kept an eye on him, but lost track of the subject around Sandbar Circle and McClaren Drive. He was about 6' and walked with a slight slouch.

May 16th, 11:30 PM

A neighbor's dog began barking very intensely and running from one side of the yard to the other.

The Attack

The children and the grandfather went to bed around 10:00 PM, and the husband and wife retired between 11:00 PM and midnight.

Around 1:30 AM, the wife woke up to a light shining in her eyes. All she could see was the silhouette of a masked man standing by their sliding glass door. He was holding a flashlight in his left hand and a gun in his right hand.

"L-l-look at me. L-look at me. Do you hear me?" the man whispered, stuttering a bit.

She pulled the covers over her head. He told her that he had a .45 Magnum and ordered her to bring the covers back down. He began banging on the door and telling them to wake up. The wife shook her husband and told him what was going on. Her husband started to get out of bed, but the intruder focused his flashlight on him and told him to lie back down. He ordered them to roll onto their stomachs.

"I'm going to tie you up. I'm going to take all your money and jewels." He threw some shoelaces onto the man's back and told the woman to tie him up. As she did, he kept telling her "tighter, tighter!" He told them that he'd "kill everyone in the house" if they didn't do what he told them to do.

After the woman had finished tying her husband, the intruder retied his hands and bound his feet. He put the gun against the man's head and issued more threats. Then he tied the wife.

The husband started to say something, but the intruder became very angry and told him to "shut up," and said that if they spoke one more word that he'd "kill everybody." "She's dead, she's dead," he said, referring to the wife.

The intruder opened the sliding door and went outside, and it sounded like he was putting something into a tool box. He came back in and put a something on the husband's back that sounded like a glass or ceramic dish. He started rummaging through all of the drawers in the bedroom, and he ransacked the closet as well. After looking at everything, he told the victims that he was going to "get something to eat" and if he heard anything, he'd "kill everything in the house."

He was out of the room and rummaging elsewhere in the house for as long as thirty minutes. There were times when the couple thought he was gone, but then they'd hear him again. When he finally came back to the bedroom, he seemed very angry. He asked the wife where she kept her purse, and she replied that it was on the refrigerator. He threatened her, saying that if she was lying, he'd kill her, then he said that she needed to go with him to find it. He untied her feet and pulled her off of the bed. As they left the room, he reminded the husband that he'd "kill her" if there was any movement. "She's dead. The first thing you'll hear is two shots."

He led the woman into the kitchen, and she showed him where her purse was. They continued into the living room and she was forced onto her stomach. He tied her feet again. As she was being blindfolded, she noticed that her afghan had been draped over the lamp and the scene had been prepared for her arrival.

The intruder went to the kitchen, and she heard him opening the knife drawer. He went back to the bedroom where the husband was bound, placed a saucer and bowl onto his back, and told him that if the dishes fell or any noise came from the bedroom, he'd kill the wife. The husband felt the gun on his head once again.

Soon the intruder was back, and he was holding a knife against the woman's throat and telling her that he wouldn't hurt her if she obeyed him and did everything that he asked. Then he went back to the kitchen again, and she could hear him eating. When he returned, he told her that he needed more money and he "knew that they had more." She told him about some coins in the study. He answered very angrily that if they weren't there, he'd kill her.

He was gone for awhile, and then he was back. He quite suddenly straddled her and placed his penis into her hands. It was slick with lotion. "Rub me," he told her. He began calling her by name.

After a few moments, he ordered her to sit up, and then he put his penis in her mouth and told her to "suck it," or he'd "kill everyone in the house." She complied, and as he moved back and forth he kept using her name and saying "It feels so good. I like that."

He then untied her feet and raped her. He took his gloves off briefly while he was caressing her legs.

When he was finished, he went back into the kitchen and started eating again.

The assailant went back and checked on the husband several times. Each time that he did, he rummaged through drawers and closets and threatened to kill him if he made a noise. At one point he told him "I'll kill everything in the house and then I'll leave in the night."

When he returned to the woman, he tied her feet together tightly. He placed dishes on her back and told her "I'm gonna get some beer and food and go into the backyard and eat and drink for about an hour." He said that if he heard the dishes rattle, he'd "come back and kill for the first time." When he began talking about "killing for the first time," the woman noticed his excitement, and his voice became intense and he began to stutter. She felt that it was genuine and not a put-on.

He continued talking, getting more excited as he went. "Those fuckers, those fuckers, those pigs. I've never killed before, but I'm going to now. Listen, do you hear me? I want you to tell those fuckers, those pigs. I'm going to go home to my apartment and I have bunches of televisions. I'm going to listen to the radio and watch television and if I hear about this, I'm going to go out tomorrow night and kill two people. People are going to die."

Then the assailant went back to the bedroom to check on the husband again. The attacker seemed very angry. He told him "You tell those fucking pigs that I could have killed two people tonight. If I don't see that all over the papers and television, I'll kill two people tomorrow night." He stuttered while he talked. He then told him that he was going into the kitchen to "cook and eat something," and that if he heard any noise, he'd kill the wife.

Meanwhile, the woman was listening closely. She hadn't heard anything for about ten minutes, so she started to try to wiggle free. All of a sudden the assailant was back. She heard him breathing loudly through his mouth as he paced around the room, walking all around her. He didn't speak. Then he leaned down close to her face and said "Those fuckers, those fuckers, those pigs. I'm going to kill them, too."

"I'll tell them tomorrow," she replied, thinking that he wanted her to say something.

"Okay," he whispered. "Tell them I'm going to kill those fuckers."

Then it was quiet again. A bit of time passed. The husband, not having any idea what was going on but thinking that the assailant was probably gone, started yelling in Italian to his father. The father responded, checked on the two boys, and then cut the victims free.

Immediate Aftermath

When officers arrived, the female victim was transported to Sacramento Medical Center while the police examined the scene. There were several white shoelaces on the floor in front of the couch. Two plates and a cup were nearby. In the master bedroom, there were more white shoelaces, along with a saucer and broken plate. The plate had been broken by the victim's father so that he could cut the shoelaces off from around the victim's wrists. In the backyard, they found partially-empty containers of three types of cheese crackers and some empty beer cans. A Saint Christopher's medal was later found in the victim's jewelry box that didn't belong to them and had most likely been placed there by the offender.

A tracking dog was brought in. The dog entered the house, became excited immediately, and went out through the rear sliding glass door. The dog followed the assailant's scent all through the backyard, finally stopping for a moment at the area where the assailant had eaten. Then it followed the scent into the garage and to the victim's vehicle and then returned to the backyard. The dog then went through the gate and to the corner of Sandbar Circle / Canebreak Court. He lost the scent at the curb, having only gone a short distance from the victims' home.

Suspect Description

The assailant was described as 5'8" or 5'9". He had very hairy legs. In one statement his penis was described as 5 inches, and in another it was described as "very small."

He wore a grey or beige ski mask with knitted ribbing that ran down from side to side. His gloves were a light brown leather with rough seams. His shoes made a squeaking sound when he walked, indicating that they were probably hard-soled.

He had used a knife taken from the kitchen. His gun was big and square, and the assailant claimed that it was a .45 Magnum. The male victim said it felt like a large caliber. When he first appeared, the attacker had the gun in his right hand and the flashlight in his left. The flashlight was over a foot long and had a very bright, round beam.

He stuttered when he became excited, and the victims felt it was genuine. He took deep breaths almost constantly and seemed to talk in a whisper with clenched teeth. His voice was young-sounding and he frequently sounded nervous.

Post-Attack Events

May 17th, 1977
Due to the threats that the EAR had issued about killing, the Sheriff's department initially asked the press to refrain from reporting the

attack. But because the threats had been contradictory, the ban was lifted and a press conference was called. They released a composite sketch and some information from a psychological profile. They called him a "paranoid schizophrenic" of "above average intelligence," most likely from a middle-class or upper-middle-class home, "raised by a domineering mother and a weak father." This was also one of the occasions where they talked about him being in a "homosexual panic" because of "his inadequate endowment." The phrase "homosexual panic" apparently meant that the offender was not an overt homosexual, but he supposedly had an unconscious fear of *being* homosexual. The "panic" supposedly set in when that fear would come "close to consciousness." Obviously, this odd notion is not something that is officially recognized in the field of psychology, and it wasn't even an opinion shared by of most members of the police department. But that's what they reported at the time.

May 23rd, 1977 2:15 PM
A woman fitting the profile of a typical EAR victim found that someone had opened her side gate. She examined the perimeter of her house and found a towel in her bushes with what appeared to be semen stains on it. She contacted the police, who felt that the incident was EAR-related. They left the towel in the bushes and set up stakeouts nearby in case the EAR showed up to attack her. Apparently he never came back. This incident happened on Madison Avenue in Carmichael.

December 9th, 1977 5:40 PM
The phone rang at the victims' house. The wife answered it. "Merry Christmas. It's me again," whispered the caller. The phone clicked several times (most likely the caller pushing the hook switch rapidly) and then the line went dead. The victim confirmed that it was the voice of the man who had attacked her.

Context and Analysis

There's a fascinating possibility at play in this attack, considering what had happened at the community forum the previous winter. At that meeting, where information about the rapist was discussed with the public, the future male victim stood up and began berating the police, saying that in his home country (Italy), the police and the public wouldn't stand for such a criminal to remain at large. The unlikely but tantalizing possibility exists that the offender himself was at that forum and targeted this man because he'd made a spectacle of himself.

Side note on this—there's a picture floating around the internet of a community forum, and many people have spent time examining the photo and looking for the offender. This photo, however, is *not* from the public forum at Del Dayo where the man stood up and berated the police. The photo is actually from another public forum, which was held a year later at Mira Loma. Folks are more than welcome to examine the photo for clues, as long as they keep in mind that it's a photo of an entirely different meeting.

It *is* possible that the offender was at the Del Dayo meeting, that he followed the victim home, and that he went back and attacked much later. It *is* quite coincidental that this man would become a victim. Another possibility exists, however. The husband who would become the *next* East Area Rapist victim after this one actually worked at the water treatment facility right behind *this* victim's house. It's possible that EAR found Victim #21 while stalking Victim #22, or vice versa. If this victim's selection is tied in with Victim #22's somehow, then it sheds an interesting light on the totality of EAR's stalking. Would he really go so far as to stalk the husband of a potential target couple all the way to his place of employment? The victims in Attack #22 lived all the way down in South Sacramento, so why stalk him at the water treatment plant? If he planned on attacking them as a couple, and thus didn't plan on attacking the woman while the husband was at the office, why would it matter where he worked or if EAR tracked him there? Regardless of whether the chicken or the egg came first on this, the geographical clues are quite amazing (even more coincidental than the male victim from Attack #21 standing up at a meeting and later being attacked), and certainly seem to be indicative of *something* important.

There's one more factor that could've influenced the selection of the victims in this attack, and that's the geography and obvious tactical advantages EAR would've spotted while trying to decide which house to attack. They backed up to the river levee, and it offered the perfect place to hide, stalk, watch, and even park a vehicle. The river came into play in Attack #18 and in many other incidents. Hang-up calls were in the area for a long time, prowlers were seen, and it doesn't *seem* like this couple was targeted from the beginning of the EAR's presence in the area or that he zeroed in on them right away. I would think that the stalking of this couple would've been far more focused if the male victim was targeted based on that community meeting. I suppose it's possible that while stalking the area, the EAR recognized the man from the meeting, and thought it would be a kick to attack him since he and his wife met his general victim profile. If the EAR *did* know him from the meeting, there was no indication during the attack that he did, and he showed considerable restraint in not inflicting that extra jab into the victim by letting him know that his outburst had caused his family to be attacked. Still... there's no denying that it's an incredible coincidence.

The stuttering is back in this attack, particularly on the letter "L." And he said female victim's name several times, but she didn't feel like he actually knew her (she assumed he'd gotten her name from her purse).

Some interesting and tell-tale phraseology was used here, particularly the part where he said "I'll kill everything in the house and then I'll leave in the night." One of the more curious things he said was "Rub me." That's some different lexicon from the usual "Play with it" or even "Massage it." Another phrase that struck us was when he mentioned having "bunches of televisions."

He mentioned something about having never killed before, but in Attack #16 he told his victims "Lay still or I'll kill you like I did some people in Bakersfield." So here we have a verifiable example of the assailant lying or throwing a red herring. One or the other is true, but not both.

Talking about killing seemed to excite him. He was very, very chatty in this attack, and he seemed to issue contradictory demands about telling or not telling the police. It's hard to figure out if he *meant* for his demands to be contradictory or if he was just nervous and flubbing what he was trying to say. If this man had a genuine stutter, then the heightened tension of issuing an ultimatum sure brought it out, and not just during the threats, but even when he was simply waking up the couple. It could've been that the additional people in the house (father-in-law, children) added to his tension (though they never woke up during the attack). The fact that talking about killing seemed to excite him was definitely a bad sign, and surely it was taken seriously. As history shows, he did indeed start to murder his victims later on.

A few things were noted from the interviews with the couple. They both felt like he wanted to kill them, and the wife in particular felt that he was crazy. She also felt that he had an "eating obsession."

Again, it was noted that that the assailant wasn't particularly "rough" with the female victim, but he seemed to feel an incredible amount of rage toward the male victim. Their dog (who lived outside) didn't bark at the assailant or mess with him at all, which was odd for the animal. Is it possible the assailant befriended or "bribed" the dog that night, or even over a period of time, to elicit such calm behavior?

Information came out just a few years ago that's unsubstantiated, but it adds a few details to the mix. The source claimed that the couple had a lot of money in the house and that EAR took it all (we *were* able to confirm this), and that the EAR tore the cover off of the couple's copy of "Helter Skelter" and set it on the husband's back. This is an interesting thing, considering that a newspaper article that came out shortly after this called the "EAR Citizen Patrol" group a bunch of "helter-skelter vigilantes." (The EAR Citizen Patrol group was an organized team of volunteers from the community who rode around at night with CB radios looking for signs of the East Area Rapist). Was that description of them a common one before the article came out, and was the placing of this cover on the male victim a reference to it? Evidence that the assailant read all of the articles about himself? Either way, the Manson thing was very popular at the time. There was a 1976 television movie about called, of course, "Helter Skelter."

Before we move on to the next incident, I want to go over the decal seen on a suspicious vehicle in the vicinity of the attack just one more time, because this is possibly an important clue. The vehicle was a new model brown El Camino, with a California license plate 366-T??. The driver was a white male, late twenties, with collar-length brown hair and deep-set eyes. Under hypnosis, the witness recalled details about a decal that she had seen on the car: it had a parachute with a missile carried underneath, and was set on a diamond pattern, with possibly the letters "AFC" on the bottom. This decal, seemingly military in origin, has never been positively identified.

Attack #22

Date: May 28th, 1977 2:20 AM to 4:00 AM
Victims: Wife and husband. Their young son was also
in the house.
Location: 4th Parkway, South Sacramento

Pre-Attack Events

April and May 1977
A lot of suspicious phone calls took place in the area during this time
period.

Early May 1977
While on patrol, police noticed a "pencil-necked" blonde male in his
early twenties driving a light-colored square-shaped car (possibly a
Datsun or a small Chevrolet) through a park located about a mile
away from where the attack would be. The suspicious male seemed to
be staring intently at a young woman participating in a football game.
The police ran the license plate and it didn't exist.

May 1977
There were a lot of suspicious solicitors in the attack area. In addition
to a lot of Mormon missionaries, there were strange men selling
vacuum cleaners and children's books.

May 1977

A suspicious man was seen in a white station wagon on Sky Parkway, a street that connected to the victims' street. This man stuck out because it appeared he was living in his car.

Late May 1977

For several days, different cars were seen parked at a fenced-off utility building near the victims' house. There would be a different car every day, and whichever car was going to be there for the day would usually show up around noon. A driver was never spotted, nor was a license plate ever copied down.

The Attack

The wife was home alone with her son. She was doing laundry, making trips back and forth from the house to the garage (where the washing machine was located). On one of the trips, she noticed that the side garage door was open. She thought that maybe the wind had blown it open, so she closed and locked it.

Later that night, the couple's young son fell asleep on the couch. She took him to bed and then watched television until 11:30 PM. At that point, she went to bed.

Her husband got home from work a little after midnight. He watched a movie and went to bed around 2:00 AM. He dozed off but was awakened by his wife. The couple began to be intimate with each other. The man had his back to the sliding glass door while they did this, and he heard the door rattling so he turned around to look at it. When he did, he saw a man coming into their room from the outside. The man had a small flashlight in his left hand and a .45 automatic in his right hand. He trained the flashlight on them.

"Lay perfectly still or I will kill all of you. I will kill you, I will kill her, and I will kill your little boy. Don't make a move and don't look at me. Put your hands where I can see them in front and don't move a muscle." He told them that all wanted was "food and money."

He threw some shoelaces at the woman and told her to "tie the man up." He told her to "do it right," and kept telling her to "tie him tighter." The woman made an effort to tie her husband loosely so that he might be able to escape. After the man was bound, the intruder tied the woman. He told them that he was "hungry" and that he was going to "find food and money and then leave." He began rummaging through drawers and closets. He went in and out of the bedroom a few times. He kept shining his flashlight on the husband and telling him "I'll kill her and your son if you don't keep your face down." The intruder took laces out of some of their shoes, put his gun to the man's head, and told him to "lay still." He retied the man's hands and then tied his feet.

They heard him leave the room. He went to the bathroom, pumped lotion a few times, returned to the bedroom, and put some glass objects on the man's back. "Don't move," he said. "If I hear that sound, I'll kill everyone in the house."

He tied the woman's feet, then he left the bedroom again. They heard him rummaging in the kitchen. When he returned, he placed dishes on the man's back to supplement the other objects he'd already placed there. He put a knife to the man's neck and said "Don't make a move or I'll kill everyone in the house. As I promised, I'm only gonna get food and money and then go to my van and eat it. If I hear that sound I'll come back and kill everyone in the house."

He then untied the woman's feet, pulled her off of the bed, and took her into the living room. She saw that he'd taken some of her towels and torn them into strips, and he'd laid them out in a row on the floor. He forced her to the ground and used one of the strips to blindfold her. Then he went to check on the husband. The intruder scanned the bedroom with his flashlight, then left it and closed the door behind him.

The woman heard a zipper and then what she later described as snapping or sloshing noises. While she was still on her stomach, he got on top of her and penetrated her. He was in for only a moment, and then he rolled her onto her side and did it again. Then he sodomized her. He touched her breasts but he didn't fondle them. She didn't think that he climaxed. After he pulled out, he leaned down close to her ear and said "They got it wrong last time. I said I would kill two people. If this is on the TV or in the papers tomorrow, I'll kill two people. Are you listening?" Then he made her repeat it.

After about five minutes, the assailant checked on the husband briefly, then returned to the woman to deliver his message again.

"I have something for you to tell the fucking pigs. They got it mixed up last time. I said I would kill two people. I'm not going to kill you. If this is on the TV or in the papers tomorrow, I'll kill two people. Are you l-l-l-l-listening? Do you hear me? I have TVs in my apartment and I'll be watching them. If this is on the news, I'll kill two people." She noticed that he seemed very angry when he used the word "pigs."

Then, to her surprise, he started sobbing a little bit. "It scares my mommy when it's on the news," he cried. He appeared to hold back more sobs, and then he repeated it. "It scares my mommy when it's on the news." It sounded to the victim like he cried harder when he said the word "mommy."

The husband didn't hear anything for awhile, and then he heard the other sliding glass door in the house open. He waited a few minutes and then moved, which knocked the dishes off of his back. When the assailant didn't respond, he figured that the coast was clear. He managed to dial the police.

Immediate Aftermath

May 28th, 1977 5:00 AM

A member of Law Enforcement noticed a white sports car stopped at the intersection of Fruitridge Road and Stockton Blvd. The driver of the car and the officer were both stopped, waiting for one or the other to move forward. The driver would not look at the officer, and instead stared straight ahead. He was wearing a sports coat and tie, which was out of place for the area at that time of day. They eventually both moved through the intersection. This incident happened about three miles north of the attack, so it might or might not have been related. The officer didn't know of the attack at the time, or he would've investigated the driver.

Police arrived at the scene. They used a special technique on the female victim to see if the assailant had touched her with his bare hands. He hadn't, so no fingerprints were found. The victim was taken to Sacramento Medical Center.

Torn strips of towel and brown shoelaces were found inside the residence. Outside on the patio, two packages of sausage and a green wine bottle were found.

Sometime around 5:00 AM, the tracking dog arrived. The dog led police across a small lot and then to a low fence bordering Highway 99. Beyond the fence, the dog traveled for a short distance and then lost the scent in a group of tall trees bordering the northbound lanes of Highway 99. The scent was lost in *front* of the trees, not among them. There were tire tracks where the bloodhound stopped. The tire tracks belonged to a small car, like a Volkswagen or even a Porsche. It's unknown if the sighting at 5:00 AM in the area was related, but the finding of these tire tracks opens the possibility.

Suspect Description

The assailant was described as 5'9" or 5'10", 165 lbs, with a slender build. His penis was described as "short."

He was wearing a red knit ski mask with eye holes and an oval mouth hole. He had a bulky dark-colored jacket and black pants with black leather gloves.

He had a small two-cell flashlight that had a bright beam, and he carried a .45 automatic in his right hand. It was a blue steel military type, and the male victim recognized it as military because of his own experience in the Marine Reserves.

The assailant spoke in a whisper through clenched teeth. Harsh, raspy, and with loud breaths. He generally sounded "hyper" and high-pitched, especially when excited. He kept breathing in and out very loudly. He stuttered, especially on the letter "L."

He used brown shoelaces to bind them, some of which came from the husband's shoes.

Post-Attack Event

May 28th, 1977 1:50 PM
Some odd writing was noticed on the stall at one of the restrooms at a gas station on the corner of Florin Rd and Riverside Blvd. This gas station was located about six and a half miles west of the attack site, between the Sacramento River and Lake Greenhaven. An Alpha Beta Market (a chain that would possibly become important later) was nearby.

The writing read:

This is a fucked part of town
Next month I start this area
EAR

While this was some distance away from the attack site, it was still the same general part of town. This incident and Attack #22, were further south than almost all of the other Sacramento EAR crimes.

Context and Analysis
This attack raises some important questions about the motivation of the assailant and the specifics of what he "liked" and "didn't like" in his attacks. It was becoming clear that the sexual part of the attacks probably wasn't the main aspect that fueled his compulsion. Perhaps it was the power he felt when he terrorized the victims, or a feeling of domination, or perhaps something else entirely. It's not possible to say for sure, but this attack offers a clue as to what his preferences were as far as his attack style.

What I'm getting at is that the EAR potentially had an opportunity to blitz the female while she was alone, like he had done in so many of his early attacks. She was doing laundry, and then in a really creepy turn of events, she noticed that the door was open in the garage. Was the assailant with her from that moment on? Hiding in the garage, or in the house? It's very possible, given that we couldn't find anything about forced entry in this attack (that doesn't mean that it didn't happen, it just means that we didn't find anything about it). True, he entered through the sliding glass door to the bedroom, but he could've gone through the house and unlocked it. The dog seemingly traced the EAR's escape route, but not the route where he came to the house (if it was indeed a different route). Perhaps, of course, it really was just the wind that blew that door open. We don't know if they had the dog follow the assailant's pathways through the house or not, which was usually a hard thing to do because of the length of time he usually stayed at a scene.

If the EAR *was* in her house while she was there without her husband, why didn't he attack her then? Did he know the family's schedule well enough? He apparently knew that they had a little boy, which meant that he'd been around the house before (at least a few hours before, if not days or weeks). She was alone at night for quite awhile, and he could've attacked and been gone. Did he prefer to wait for the husband to be there, because that was how he wanted his attack to play out? It seems he was targeting couples exclusively at this point in the series. It's very unlikely that he was just passing through their yards and happened to see them being intimate with each other, got aroused, and attacked, because he *did* know about their son.

In the last attack, we mentioned the possibility that he could've stalked the husband at his workplace, since his workplace was right behind the house from Attack #21. That's a big coincidence. Because of this detail, it's possible that EAR knew the husband's work schedule, which would lend credence to the idea that he wanted to attack them as a couple. So perhaps dominating and humiliating the man was an important part of these attacks, at least during this particular phase.

To explore the idea further, it's certainly interesting that after attacking women alone or with their children, that he suddenly switched almost exclusively to couples for quite a long time period. Surely he had come across lone women that he could've victimized in the meantime. A more balanced distribution between singles and couples would be expected unless he was *intentionally* targeting couples exclusively. This proves that these were not just crimes of opportunity—there was something very psychological going on here. This couple wasn't asleep when they were attacked, even though he probably could've waited a little bit longer and they would've been. Apparently the couple being asleep when he encountered them wasn't part of the fantasy (and remember, he confronted the couple in Attack #19 in the driveway). Maybe he wanted to stop them before too much sexual activity occurred, or maybe their foreplay was enough to get him "excited" to the point of needing to attack.

The assault played out in a familiar fashion, but there are a few things to point out. He told the woman to "tie the man up." He didn't venture to say "husband." He mentioned a van again. At one point before the sexual assault, the female victim heard a zipper, but she wasn't sure if it was his pants being undone or some kind of bag that he had with him. In this attack, he sodomized the female victim, which was something he hadn't done in awhile.

This is the first of nearly a dozen crying fits that the offender engaged in. It was certainly one of the more bizarre things that he did, considering that a lot of his other dialogue seemed to be overtly aggressive, masculine, and tough-sounding. "It scares my mommy when it's on the news." He said it twice, making sure that the victim heard it and would repeat it correctly, in our opinion. Honestly, several of his sobbing episodes seem genuine, but this one doesn't. And if this one isn't, then it calls into question the ones that would come later. Folks theorize that he began crying at the scene in order to seem mentally unstable or crazy, perhaps hoping to cop an insanity plea if he were ever caught.

He also stuttered again at this attack. If this, too, was fake, then he was putting on quite a show. His threats and rant about the "pigs" was very reminiscent of Attack #21, linking the two of these together rather nicely even without a lot of physical evidence.

Some other details, like using shoelaces from the scene instead of ones that he brought, are interesting. Did not having the proper ligatures with him indicate that perhaps he didn't intend on attacking that night? Could it point to a more spontaneous attack compared to ones where he *did* have the proper bindings with him? Another thing to point out is his mask, which had a hole for the mouth this time. Usually it didn't. Would this be more of a "prowling" mask or more of an "attack" mask?

The water treatment plant isn't the only place that the EAR could've encountered the husband, if indeed he encountered him at some point before this attack took place. The husband was also a Marine Reserve (and assigned to an Army depot on Fruitridge Road). There are some ties to Fruitridge Road in other attacks, like #15, which we can only allude to vaguely because of victim privacy. Something else worth mentioning is that the victims had only lived in this house for about three weeks. There was still a "For Sale" sign in their front yard. The real estate company was AIM Realty. Lots of similarities to other victims aside from these things too, but nothing concrete. The EAR remained enigmatic and elusive.

With the conclusion of this attack, May 1977 was finally over as far as the EAR was concerned. A few months of relative quiet would follow, but things weren't *all* quiet on the EAR front. Next, we explore some incidents that seem to indicate that the EAR began prepping for an attack that thankfully never came.

Carmichael: June 1977

<u>Late May 1977</u>
The next uptick in activity that seemed to be related to the EAR began to occur on Cedarhurst Way, a street in Carmichael very close to the location of Attack #17. Around the time of Attack #22, a single young mother who lived near the intersection of Cedarhurst Way and Templeton Drive started receiving hang-up phone calls. Around the time they started, she began returning home to find her front door unlocked. Sometimes the door wasn't just unlocked, it was actually ajar. There was never anything stolen or particularly out of place, but she began noticing that small things had been moved around inside the residence. One day, she noticed that a large floor plant had been moved a few feet. She kept a spare key under the doormat, and it appeared someone was using it to make themselves at home while she was away. She called the police and they examined the area. Across the street, they found something very incriminating—apparently someone had been spending quite a lot of time under a short, thick tree in direct sight of the woman's house. There were tennis shoe prints and cigarette butts (filters with a double yellow stripe around them) scattered around the tree.

<u>Early June 1977</u>
A neighbor on Cedarhurst Way discovered that someone had broken into his house and unloaded a handgun that he kept in his nightstand. A sheet of paper with a copy of his work schedule was also missing. Police found tennis shoe prints (similar in size and design to ones

found at EAR locations) on a path behind his house. Local children had seen a man with thick black curly hair on that path.

Early June 1977 10:00 PM

A neighbor living on Templeton Drive (in a house very near the single young mother mentioned earlier) spotted a a suspicious man walking through his neighbor's gate and onto Cedarhurst Way. He described the man as about 5'9" and blonde.

Early June 1977

A house on Templeton Drive close to Cedarhurst Way was broken into. Nothing was stolen, but the house had been rummaged through. A herringbone-pattern shoe print, the same size as the ones found at EAR crime scenes, was found on the wall several feet up from the ground (just below a window).

Context and Analysis

Even after a busy May, it appeared that the EAR was not quite done. This small pocket of activity, occurring on the other side of Madison Avenue from Attack #17, had all the hallmarks of the EAR preparing to attack. For whatever reason, that attack never came. Maybe there wasn't a suitable victim or timeframe for an attack, or maybe the police were just getting too close. They'd been out to examine the burglaries and odd happenings several times, and in a town where people hadn't been calling the police on him very often, this probably wasn't a welcome change of procedure.

Did he know that the police had been out, though? If so, how? Could it be as simple as there not being any suitable couples for him to attack in this area? One of the first people he seemed to be stalking was a single mother. She fit his profile in every way, except she didn't have an adult male living in the house.

This might be the first, and perhaps only, clear indication that the EAR had entered a home in advance and unloaded a gun. There were a couple cases where it seemed that he might've, but it can't be known for sure. In this one, we can be pretty sure.

Thankfully, this area was spared any known terror from the EAR. There's always the unfortunate chance that a victim was attacked but the assault was never reported, though. "Quiet" periods from the assailant, or those where he seemed to be going back and forth (like he did with Rancho Cordova and Carmichael, and would later do with Modesto and Davis) with a "partner" that seems to be missing are good candidates for unreported attacks (for instance, the two Davis attacks in a row without a "Modesto-in-the-middle"). The fact that EAR bound his victims and rendered them so helpless (ligatures that wouldn't come undone, phone lines that had been cut) meant that most of his victims had to seek the assistance of a neighbor or summon help in order to be set free, so *most* of them were probably reported simply because of that. With such a long crime spree though, and with these assaults being so horrific and personal, it's certainly possible that there are several unknown victims out there.

Speaking of "quiet periods"—the summer of 1977 is among the quietest. There were no known East Area Rapist attacks for the entire months of June, July, and August in 1977. Where he went or why he stopped attacking is anyone's guess. American River College was out for the summer starting July 17th, and perhaps that was relevant somehow... maybe he was a student or he worked for the college in some way. The weather was hotter, the daylight hours were longer, and people's schedules were far more unpredictable than they were during the school year. The cops were getting closer to him, and neighbors had begun forming small vigilante squads and patrolling the streets for him. Maybe the offender decided to quit while he was ahead or at least take a break for awhile. Indeed, the next time he surfaced, he wasn't even in Sacramento at all—he attacked in Stockton, a town nearly fifty miles to the south. He still came back to Sacramento, but going down to Stockton was a much bigger move than simply going from Rancho Cordova to Orangevale. It's possible that during the summer months, he was simply experimenting with moving his base of operations to a completely different area. Learning and stalking a new town probably took time.

The "Afraid" Letter

Much has been made about a mysterious letter that arrived at the police station in mid-August 1977. The Sacramento Bee (a local paper) published a story called "Clue to Rapist at Last?" which provided a few generalities about this mysterious letter. They appealed to the letter-writer to come forward. Rather than summarize what was reported about it, I'll just print the relevant portions from the Sacramento Bee article below:

The Sacramento County Sheriff's Department is asking a letter-writer who signed himself "Afraid" to call the detective bureau to elaborate on inside information about the East Area Rapist.

It could prove to be the first break in a case that has stumped dozens of investigators since the ski-masked rapist began his attacks nearly two years ago.

"We've been given information, possibly valuable information," said sheriff's spokesperson Bill Miller, "in a well-written, typed letter. It's not from a kook."

The information, which Miller indicated could only be known by someone familiar with details of the case that are not generally known to the public, "gives no clue to the identity of the suspect. We assumed the letter-writer knows the person he or she is writing about. Our detectives want to talk to 'Afraid,'" Miller said, adding that "Afraid" wrote that if detectives wanted more information, "you should indicate you do in The Sacramento Union or other local media."

Miller explained that the information may not necessarily mean a break in the case. "We're not sure of the information. It requires contacting all of the victims and taking time to check things out. But there is a statement in the letter of something that the letter-writer is aware of that is very, very interesting," Miller said.

Miller said that informants can be guaranteed anonymity and urged "Afraid" to call the detective bureau.

We don't know much apparently, but at least we know it's not a "kook."

A few things can be gleaned about the letter from the details provided. They call the author of it a "him," but admit that it could be a "her." They say that it was "well-written" and "typed." The author didn't give any clues about the identity, but clearly felt they knew something that only the assailant (or someone who knew the assailant) would know. What that thing might be though is hard to say. "We're not sure of the information. It requires contacting all of the victims and taking time to check things out." He called the information "very, very interesting."

Sadly, the letter that "Afraid" wrote to the police has been lost. For many years, there was speculation about this letter, and theories abounded that perhaps it was a trap for the EAR, or perhaps the offender wrote it himself. But recently, investigators have gotten to the bottom of this mystery and announced that the information contained in the "Afraid" letter was analyzed, acted on, and it ended up being a dead-end. A person of interest related to this letter was discovered and cleared.

So with that, one mystery related to the EAR has been solved... but there are many more left!

Attack #23

Date: September 6th, 1977 1:30 AM to 2:45 AM
Victims: Wife (27 years old) and her husband. Their daughter
(6 years old) and another child were in the house as well.
Location: North Portage Circle, Stockton

Pre-Attack Events

Mid-August 1977
Starting a few weeks before the attack, there was evidence of
prowling in the neighborhood. Footprints in people's yards, dogs
barking during the night, and noises at fences between 10:00 PM and
midnight. Hang-up and obscene phone calls began to occur in
various parts of the city.

August 23rd or 24th, 1977
Starting around these dates, a woman began regularly seeing a white
station wagon parked at what is now Fritz Grupe Park on
Cumberland Place, an area very close to the victims' house. The first
time that she saw the car, it was driving around a cul-de-sac very
slowly (and then it came back around and drove around it again).
There were two houses with "For Sale" signs in the cul-de-sac. The
driver was a white male, twenties, with brown hair over his ears and
a rough/ruddy complexion.

August 30th or 31st, 1977
The same woman saw the same white station wagon go around the cul-de-sac again very slowly. The same suspicious man was driving it.

Early September 1977
A lot of dogs barked at night in the week leading up to the attack. The hang-up and obscene phone calls increased.

September 4th or 5th, 1977 Evening
A suspicious man was seen in the neighborhood. When he realized that he'd been spotted, he started jogging. It made him look even more out of place, because he wasn't dressed for jogging.

September 4th or 5th, 1977 10:30 PM
A light-blue or green two-door Datsun (or possibly a Toyota) was seen driving slowly around North Portage Circle (the street where the attack would happen). That night, several neighbors received an identical phone call. The caller said "Go to hell, babe."

September 4th or 5th, 1977 Night
A woman was on the phone when she suddenly heard someone trying to open her back door. This was the same woman who had seen the white station wagon parked on Cumberland Place and driving down her street. She immediately hung up, fetched her handgun, and waited in the dark for a possible intruder. Whoever had been trying to break in ended up leaving without gaining entry.

September 6th, 1977 1:00 AM
The neighbors heard what sounded like a small older-model vehicle driving around the cul-de-sac. Fifteen minutes later, dogs started barking.

September 6th, 1977 Early Morning
Sometime between 1:00 AM and 3:00 AM, a neighbor heard a car with a big engine drive around North Portage Circle. It drove

through so fast that the tires squealed.

The Attack

The wife woke up to the sound of her drapery hooks knocking into each other. She looked at the sliding glass door and saw a masked man coming through it. He stepped inside, then reached back through the door and picked up an old-style medical bag. He realized that she was awake and instructed her not to speak. She reached over and woke her husband up. The intruder swung the bag inside and let it hit the ground with a solid thud. From the sound it made, the couple had the impression that the bag had cans in it.

The intruder aimed his flashlight beam into the husband's eyes and told him that if he moved, he'd be killed. The threat was repeated several times. The intruder told the man to roll over onto his stomach, and he ordered the woman to tie the man's hands behind his back. He took shoelaces from the husband's shoes, gave them to her, and she complied. The intruder retied him and then tied his feet. Then he tied the wife up.

He told them he only wanted money and food "for his apartment." He asked about the husband's wallet, and he asked if there was anyone else in the house. There were two kids. The intruder told them that if there was any trouble, he'd "chop up the kids" and bring the victims "their ears."

The intruder left the room for awhile. He came back, held a knife to the husband's throat, and told the couple to "shut up." He once again threatened to kill the man. He took the woman out of the room and he held a knife to her throat as he walked her down the hall. Like most of EAR's victims, she'd been sleeping naked (we haven't emphasized that detail until now), so she asked for a robe. He retrieved one and draped it over her shoulders. They made their way through the house, and he carried his medicine bag with him as they did.

When they arrived at the living room, there was a blanket draped over a lamp. Still carrying his medicine bag around with him, he retrieved some dishes from the kitchen, went back to the male victim, and placed the dishes on his back. He put his gun against the husband's head and cocked it, then told him that if he heard them "rattle," he'd kill him.

He returned to the wife, and she heard him masturbating with lotion. He told her that he had "seen her in the store and wanted to fuck her." Then he raped her. In the middle of the rape, he stopped for a minute, and when he entered her again, his penis felt different. The victim thought that it felt artificial and much bigger and firmer than his real penis. He withdrew again, and then it seemed his real penis entered her. He climaxed.

After finishing the assault, he went to check on the husband. Again he threatened the man with a knife.

He went to the kitchen to eat. When he was finished, he checked on both of them and began talking to them. He told them that he only lived "a few blocks away," and that he needed "a few things for his apartment," like "towels, soap, and a portable television."

The couple's six-year-old daughter woke up to use the bathroom, and as she made her way down the hall, she saw the assailant standing in the kitchen doorway eating. She didn't react, and was wondering if what she was seeing was even real. "I'm playing a game with your parents. Do you want to watch?" he asked her. The child ignored him, went to the bathroom, and went back to bed.

The attacker went back to the woman, and he began masturbating again. He raped the woman a second time. Again, she felt that at times he was using an artificial penis (possibly a rubber penis strapped to his waist). Toward the end, she felt his real penis, and again he climaxed in her.

Eventually the house fell quiet. The victims felt that he had left. A couple minutes later the victims, several neighbors, and the six-year-old daughter heard a Volkswagen start up and leave the area.

Immediate Aftermath

Entry had been made through the sliding glass door in the bedroom, which had probably been left unlocked. There were pry marks on the screen door, but not on the sliding door itself. There were footprints in nearby backyards, indicating that the suspect had traveled through several yards to get to the victims' house. Impressions from some of those prints were taken to a local shoe dealer, who positively identified them as coming from a Converse All-Star tennis shoe. They were size nine and a half.

There was a Pepsi can in the backyard, and the assailant had removed a peanut butter jar from the fridge and left it on the kitchen counter. There was a bottle of Fuller Brush lotion on the bathroom sink that the assailant had removed from the medicine cabinet.

Strangely, a pair of pantyhose had been taken out of a drawer, one of the legs had been knotted, a finger-sized hole had been poked in the crotch area, and then it had been placed back into the drawer.

A knife was found at the foot of the bed. Initially the husband thought it was his, but later he located his own knife under the bed and realized that the knife had been left there by the assailant.

The victims' wedding and engagement rings, some cufflinks, a tie pin, and man's onyx ring were stolen. Cash from the man's wallet was left alone.

Suspect Description
White male, 5'9", between 150 and 160 lbs. He had a slender build.

The victims thought he was wearing a hat or a mask. During the sexual assault, the woman felt a small holster, or something similar, on his belt. She described it as something that "a beeper might fit into." The material of the entire belt was firm, like "rough plastic."

The offender spoke in a low, raspy whisper, seemingly in an effort to disguise his voice. His tone became higher-pitched when he was excited. The victims didn't notice the stutter that had been showing up in previous attacks.

He had a very bad, unpleasant odor, like he hadn't been bathing. He seemed very nervous, and his actions didn't feel "genuine." The victims felt like he was playing a "role."

The daughter, who got a good look at him, was able to provide more detail. She described him as a white adult male wearing a brown ski mask, a short-sleeved purple t-shirt with a pocket and a zipper (instead of buttons), and wearing black knit mittens on his hands. He wore a belt with a "sword" in it (most likely on his right side) and a holster with a gun in it (most likely on his left side). He had on no pants or underwear when she saw him. He wore a metal-banded wristwatch on his right wrist.

A hypnosis session done with the daughter nearly two months later (on November 27th, 1977) revealed a few more details. She remembered a tattoo, similar to the Schlitz Malt Liquor bull, on his left forearm. The bull was black with white horns. She recalled a belt buckle with two revolvers imprinted on it, and the guns were depicted with their barrels crossed over each other. He might've had a large black ring on his right hand.

Post-Attack Events

September 7th-12th, 1977

During this time period, the victims' phone would ring in the middle of the morning, but there was no one on the other line. Other calls seemed unable to connect. The police tried to call them, but they couldn't get through, so they notified the telephone company. Later, the police called to let the victim know that it had been repaired. Right after that conversation, the victim's mother used the phone, only to have it go dead in the middle of the conversation. The victim called the phone company and got ahold of an "older man," who assured her that her phone had been repaired. It continued to act up. Every time they made a call there would be a click in the middle of it, followed by a disconnect, then a moment, then a reconnect. They felt that someone was listening in on their conversations or hijacking their line. Toward the end of this ordeal, the police happened to be at their house just as they received a phone call. A young-sounding man was on the other line, and he asked her to tell him her phone number. She was wary of doing so. He told her something about how his "office" had recently been tasked with fixing her phone. The police officer took the phone from the victim and asked the man to repeat what he'd said, but the young man hung up. On September 13th, a trap was put on the phone, but there was no more strange activity.

December 1977
The female victim received an obscene call. She identified the voice as that of her attacker.

January 1978
The police got in contact with this victim, and they played a tape of an obscene phone call that Victim #1 had received. She listened to the tape a few times and confirmed that the voice on the tape was the voice of the person that had attacked her (and also the voice of the person who had called her in December).

Context and Analysis
The "Summer Break of 1977" that the EAR took wasn't nearly as long as it appeared to be when you count the strange activity in Cedarhurst and Templeton, and then notice that the stalking and prowling began in Stockton as early as mid-August. It's certainly interesting that things had started to quiet down after such a flurry of attacks in May, but the lull could be explained by so many factors (most of which we've already covered, such as heat, the extended daylight hours making it difficult to prowl as often, more people outside enjoying the season, people having unpredictable schedules due to school being out of session, increased police pressure and citizen patrols, and many other reasons).

This was brand new territory for the assailant. Stockton is situated forty to fifty miles south of Sacramento (going straight down I-5). The decision for the assailant to lay low and then skip town for a little while was a good one on his part. Police were beginning to be able to predict with reasonable certainty when and where he would strike, and in areas like Cedarhurst, they were even starting to find his calling cards before he struck. Taking the show on the road so to speak was one of the offender's only viable options if he wanted to keep doing what he was doing. The fact that he actually did this shows that he had at least a basic intelligence and awareness of his predicament, and it tells us a few things about the how risk-averse the assailant probably was.

This attack is significant in ways other than the change in scenery: we have have a star witness. The six-year-old daughter, who got a good look at the assailant while he was in the kitchen, was able to provide perhaps the most detailed visual survey of the East Area Rapist that the police would have for quite a while. Sources describe how intelligent, astute, and reliable this child was in her manner and in her descriptions. Most of the details gleaned about his appearance were from simply questioning her, and some interesting police sketches were made based on her observations. A hypnosis session was able to suss out a few more details, such as the belt buckle and the tattoo, and while we wish those details had come out in regular questioning rather than during the hypnosis session (since those are the most distinctive details), they're still worth pursuing as leads. The fact that the offender rarely, if ever, showed bare arm after this means that the girl's description of his tattoo can't be confirmed, but it can't be disproved either. The belt buckle (and its western-wear connotations) is interesting, especially since a few suspects have sprung up over the decades who have had a penchant for wearing such items. The buckle, the shoulder holsters, and the occasional phrases like "Give me a good drop" commonly found in old cowboy movies can make one wonder if part of the "character" that some of the victims felt he was playing had its roots in old Western films. A poem purportedly from the assailant mailed in December 1977 makes reference to Jesse James, which furthers the tenuous "cowboy" motif.

This attack featured not just hang-up phone calls, but obscene calls as well. This was not something that was typically experienced in the Sacramento attacks, but he seemed to do this more often when he offended outside of Sacramento.

In this attack and in the next, the assailant was described as having a really bad, unpleasant body odor. He was wearing a belt that may be similar to the "lineman's belt" observed in Attack #3. The phrase he used about "chopping up the kids and bringing the victims their ears" is a pretty distinctive threat, and one that the EAR made in a few different attacks (#13, #26, #27, #37, to name the main ones). The bag that he carried in this attack was a satchel-type that was opened by pulling the handles apart. It wasn't a very common type of bag.

In this attack, there was no mention of the victim being forced to masturbate him with her bound hands. Perhaps it happened and we don't have that detail available to us, or perhaps it didn't, which would make it an odd variation.

One of the weirdest things in this attack was the knotted pantyhose with the hole in the crotch. Apparently the assailant had tied a knot in the leg of it and punched a finger-sized hole right in the middle. Is this symbolic, or sexual, or... what? What's even stranger is that he did this in Attack #30 as well, and Attack #30 was the only other attack that happened in Stockton. Theories about this have ranged from the logical to the absurd, with one of our favorites being "well the town is called 'stockton' so he's poking a hole in a 'stocking'... see?" Whatever the reason, it's odd that he only felt the need to do this in one particular town.

There's that strange pseudo-evidence of an accomplice being involved again, with a large car driving around North Portage Circle with squealing tires, and then sometime later the assailant leaving and everyone hearing a VW engine starting up. A strange vehicle on the block while the EAR was in the house could mean absolutely nothing, but it's interesting how many times it seemed to happen.

The assailant mentioned his "apartment" in this attack. What stands out to me is that almost every time he takes a fairly lengthy break, he either mentions an apartment (the next time he mentions it, it's a "new" apartment), or he steals a lot more than usual (one time after a break he even took a lot of practical household items). Is it possible that he's moving to a different area or relocating when he takes a break? You'll notice as we get further along that usually his breaks are followed up by the assailant offending in a brand new jurisdiction. Either he's living in the same place and he's commuting to all of these attacks from somewhere, or he's actually moving around as he changes attack locations. He told these victims that he needed things like "soap, towels, and a portable television" almost as if he were moving in somewhere new. Of course, with an offender this tricky, you can never be sure if anything he says is even remotely true. Some things probably are, and some probably aren't. It's usually more telling to look at what he *does* rather than what he *says*.

The strange business with the phone not working right and perhaps even being hijacked is a little hard to follow, but the timing of it makes it seem related. This is the most evidence we have of the EAR possibly being a "phone phreaker" or having some kind of technical know-how when it came to tapping or rerouting phone lines. Maybe he did, and maybe he didn't. Something very strange was going on with the victims' phone, but whether it was EAR-related or not is impossible to know. Events like this were a very rare occurrence. Nothing this extensive happened to any other victim, and if it did, he was much better at it and the victim was unaware.

Attack #24

Date: October 1st, 1977, 1:00 AM to 2:45 AM
Victims: 17-year-old girl and her 21-year-old boyfriend
Location: Tuolumne Drive, Rancho Cordova

The Attack
On the night of the attack, the couple had been fighting, so the boyfriend had driven the victim back to her apartment. However, she was feeling quite ill from a recent medical procedure, so around 11:30 PM, he took her back to his residence. They went to bed.

At 1:00 AM, a flashlight woke them up. An intruder was standing by the bedroom door with a handgun is his right hand and a flashlight in his left.

"Shut up. Don't make a move or I'll kill you. I want your dope. I know you have some and I'll look until I find it."

The boyfriend's shotgun was leaning against the bedroom wall, and the young man considered making a move for it. The intruder stood in the doorway and stared at him. He moved the flashlight beam from the boyfriend's eyes over to the shotgun, and then back again. By now the girlfriend was awake too, and the flashlight was shining in her eyes as well. Both victims felt that the intruder was afraid that the boyfriend would go for the gun, but as the moments passed and he didn't, they felt the intruder's relief. He took a step toward them.

"Roll over. Get on your stomachs." He threw shoelaces at the girl and ordered her to "tie the man up." EAR retied him when she was done, and then he tied the girl's wrists. He placed the gun against each of their temples, cocked it, and threatened to kill them.

With his victims secured, he rummaged through the residence. The boyfriend's pitbull puppy jumped up on the bed and growled at the intruder, but he didn't bark or attack. EAR picked the dog up and took him to another part of the house.

He moved the girlfriend to another room, tied her ankles, and blindfolded her. Then he retrieved a tray and a salt shaker and placed it on the boyfriend, who immediately began working on getting out from under it without making a sound. He placed the gun against the boyfriend's head and cocked it again, issuing threats.

The EAR moved to the other room, where he held a knife to the girl's neck and told her that he'd "slit [her] throat" if she didn't cooperate with him.

She heard him masturbating himself with lotion, and then felt his penis in her bound hands. "Play with it," he commanded. Then he raped her.

When he was finished, he checked on the boyfriend, and then began roaming the house. He checked on the boyfriend several more times.

Suddenly, the doorbell rang. Both of the victims heard the intruder go outside. He was gone for several minutes.

He came back in, returned to the girl, held the knife to her throat again, issued more threats, and raped her again. At one point during the rape, he put the gun against her head and cocked it.

He went to the kitchen right after sexually assaulting her. A car horn honked twice. Several seconds passed, and then it honked twice more. A few more minutes went by. The doorbell rang five times, and then there was a knock on a window (not on a door). The female victim heard muffled voices. One sounded like a woman's voice. Right after the voices were heard, the assailant left through the rear sliding glass door.

Around the time that the doorbell was ringing, the boyfriend had finished wiggling free from the tray and salt shaker. He rolled onto the floor, rummaged through his pants, retrieved a pocket knife from them, and was able to cut himself free from the shoelaces. He pulled a revolver out from between the mattresses and ran into the hall, looking for the assailant. Unfortunately, EAR had just left. The boyfriend cut the girl free, then ran into the backyard and fired a shot into the air out of frustration.

Immediate Aftermath

After the police arrived, the girl was taken to Sacramento Medical Center.

The loaded shotgun that had been leaning against the bedroom wall was found underneath the living room sofa. The assailant had moved it there, and at some point he'd unloaded it. The shells were found lined up in a row.

Pry marks were found on the window, even though the window had been left unlocked.

Suspect Description

The assailant was described as a white male, twenties or early thirties, 5'9", and 170 lbs.

His mask was a nylon stocking, and he wore a dark knit-type cap on top of it. He wore a black vinyl or leather jacket that ended below the waist. The jacket had four pockets. His shirt was either dark blue or dark brown, and his gloves were black and made of leather.

His weapons were a knife and a .357 revolver. He also had a flashlight with him.

He spoke through forced whispers and clenched teeth.

He had bad breath, and a very, very bad odor.

Post-Attack Event

October 21st, 1982

The victim in this case received a call while she was at work (waitressing at a Denny's restaurant). She identified her caller as the EAR.

Caller: "Hi, it's me again. Remember me? I'm going to come over and fuck you again. You're going to suck my cock again."

Context and Analysis

After going four months without attacking in Sacramento, the EAR reappeared in Rancho Cordova. In this attack he made two notable changes, perhaps in an effort to throw Law Enforcement off his trail or perhaps for reasons we're unaware of. The first change was to attack a duplex—this was the first time that the assailant ever done that. There were still some tactical advantages for him at this location, but it was definitely different scenery. Another change was that the socioeconomic profile of the victims was different—they were described by an investigator as "not his usual clean-cut upper middle-class type." He had typically attacked older couples, as well.

There were a few other minor variations. Asking for "dope" took the place of asking for food and money, for instance, but he'd done that before. Like the previous attack, the assailant had a very bad odor and terrible breath.

We've flirted with the idea of an accomplice, lookout, or getaway driver before but up until now we were just trying to make a few stray pieces of evidence fit into a puzzle that didn't necessarily need them. This is the attack where it becomes difficult to ignore the possibility that someone else was with the attacker that night. There's the doorbell, the car honking, the doorbell again, the knock at the window, and then what sounded like a woman's voice. All the while, both victims were fairly certain that the assailant was still inside the house with them. Maybe it was a complex performance that he was putting on for the benefit of his victims, or maybe this was the one and only time that he had a lookout or someone with him for some reason. He didn't *mention* having someone with him to the victims, which we found kind of odd if he truly *was* putting on a show for them.

If he did have an accomplice for this one, the timeline might tell us what was going on. The offender had possibly been out of the area for a few months, and we have no idea what he was doing during that time. Without knowing what he was doing or even much about him, how are we to know that he didn't have a new wife or girlfriend that he manipulated into helping him? Or a family member? When

233

thinking about an accomplice, one of the biggest questions is always *motivation*. What would a partner or accomplice have to *gain* by his or her involvement in these crimes? Would the EAR have a burglar buddy who didn't care about the rapes? Was there enough in stolen goods to make a partner happy? These types of robberies weren't nearly as lucrative as other types of crimes, and the risk goes way up when more than one person is involved. A partnership would almost have to have a basis in loyalty, intimidation, or manipulation of some kind.

There's some confusion about the shotgun from the bedroom, and I've done my best to untangle everything. The boyfriend had a loaded shotgun leaning against the bedroom wall. When police arrived, it was found under the couch, and it was unloaded. What seems to have happened was that at some point, the assailant unloaded the gun, lined up the shells neatly, and then stashed the gun under the couch. The big question is related to when the gun was actually unloaded. There's speculation that the EAR broke in while they were away and unloaded it before they returned, which is why perhaps he seemed to feel confident enough to attack the man while his shotgun was in the room with them. But the way the information reads, it actually seems more likely that it was unloaded after the attack began and the man was tied up. It's possible that the EAR didn't know it was there until he ended up in their bedroom that night. Why did he move it under the couch? Was he separating the ammo and the gun or trying to hide it from the victims in case they got loose? He did this in a later attack, but the ammo was actually found in a nearby backyard in that one. Did EAR unload it before he woke them up? After the boyfriend was bound? Before the rapes? After the rapes? It's not a closed issue and we can't make assumptions. If he broke in beforehand to unload weapons, then he obviously did a bad job of it because he missed the gun between the mattresses.

Folks might ask how he could take the shotgun away while the boyfriend was in the room, and the boyfriend not know about it. The EAR often pulled the covers over the head of the male victims, sometimes even putting a pillow over their head, so that they couldn't see or hear what was going on very well. This kept them from knowing what was going on in the house, and gave the EAR more of a tactical advantage.

It's difficult to figure out how the East Area Rapist arrived at their duplex that night. There's not much evidence, if any, to suggest that any kind of stalking went on for this particular attack. Even if there was, how would the assailant even know that the girl would be there that night? It wasn't planned. She'd actually moved out and had been living elsewhere with a roommate. If he *did* stalk her, two places come to mind where the assailant could have encountered her. One is her job—she worked as a maid for the Six Pence Motel in Sacramento at the time of the attack. If he'd moved out of the area and needed to come back for a bit, it's possible that he stayed there and spotted her. The other possible place is the hospital in North Sacramento where she'd had a medical procedure two days before the attack.

Attack #25

Date: October 21st, 1977 3:00 AM to 4:15 AM
Victims: Wife (32 years old) and husband. There were two
other children in the house, a 13-year-old daughter and a
10-year-old daughter.
Location: Golden Run Avenue, Foothill Farms

Pre-Attack Events

October 1st, 1977 through Late October 1977
Hang-up phone calls began in the neighborhood. Some of the usual
minor prowling incidents began to occur.

October 7th, 1977 through October 21st, 1977
Hang-up phone calls started at the victims' residence.

October 18th, 1977
The victims' thirteen-year-old daughter returned home from school
to find a door slightly open. The door led from the garage to the
kitchen. She assumed that someone else in the family had left it that
way by mistake. She returned home on another day and found the
door ajar once more.

The Attack
The couple was intimate with each other before going to sleep for the
night.

Sometime in the early morning hours, their ten-year-old daughter woke up and used the bathroom. She heard someone moving around in the hallway and simply assumed that another family member was awake.

The wife woke up to a bright light in her eyes. When her vision focused, she saw that there was a masked intruder in the bedroom. He held a flashlight in his left hand and a gun in his right hand. He also had a knife. She nudged her husband awake.

"I have a .357 Magnum. If you don't do as I say, I'm going to blow your fucking head off." He threw shoelaces at the woman.

"Tie him up. If you don't tie him up tight I'm going to blow your fucking head off. Put his hands behind his back and be sure that you tie him tight."

She complied. After she finished tying her husband, the intruder did the same to her, and then he began rummaging through the house. He returned a little while later and stacked dishes on the husband's back.

He rummaged through the house some more. He husband moved slightly, making the dishes on his back rattle. The intruder was back in a flash, threatening them and using profanity.

He pulled the woman up from the bed and took her to another room. He put a knife against her throat, threatened her, and then raped her. In this attack, he didn't force her to touch his penis with her bound hands and he didn't climax. When he was finished assaulting her, he immediately went to the kitchen. The victim could hear him crying. Then he began eating.

A few minutes later, the assailant checked on the husband. He put a gun against the man's head and repeated some of the earlier threats. Then he returned to the wife, put a knife to her throat, threatened her, and raped her once more. Again, he didn't force her to masturbate him, and during the rape, he didn't climax. He began crying again immediately after pulling out. He walked away, and she heard him settle elsewhere in the house and sob for awhile.

When he came back, he told her "My buddy is in the car waiting. Tell the p-p-p-p-pigs I'll be back New Year's Eve."

And then the house was quiet. Once the couple was sure that he was gone, they woke up their children. The kids untied them, and the husband called the police.

Immediate Aftermath

The police determined that entry had been made through a side door on the garage, and then the assailant had broken through the kitchen door to enter the home (the same door that the daughter had found open twice). Neither of the doors were secured with deadbolts. The press noted that this was one of the few forced entries in the series, explaining that the East Area Rapist usually entered by snapping open sliding glass doors or finding an unlocked window.

Police found three empty Miller beer cans outside the residence. They didn't belong to the victims.

Traces of blue paint were found on boots in the master bedroom, on shoelaces, and in vacuum sweepings done by scene technicians. These could not be conclusively tied to the offender.

Suspect Description

White male, twenties, 5'10", fit and muscular, with no fat. His penis was described as fairly large around with a very small head. The female victim was positive that he was circumcised.

He wore a dark-colored ski mask with a plastic trim on it. His gloves were a thin leather or a smooth plastic, perhaps surgical gloves.

He spoke in a whisper through clenched teeth. They thought that he spoke with a slight accent.

Both of the victims felt that the assailant was nervous and very "hyper-active."

Context and Analysis

The attacks are starting to look alike, aren't they? The East Area Rapist developed a plan of attack and he stuck with what worked. Perhaps the monotony was starting to affect him, because apparently he was unable to climax during this assault. Is that why he was crying? Because he couldn't perform? We prefer to think that he was having a semi-lucid moment and he realized that what he was doing was wrong, but if that were the case he wouldn't have come right back and tried to do it again.

This was the first time that the rapist had struck in the Foothill Farms area, which was located a little further to the north of where he usually attacked. Geographically, it's just above American River College and it's situated off of Interstate 80. It's hard to say what led him to this area, other than perhaps a desire to avoid the East Area where people were still on the lookout for him. Foothill Farms didn't have the same "feel" as some of the other areas he attacked, having a noticeable lack of cement-lined canals and a lack of the usual hideaways created by dense housing. Perhaps, like with the previous attack, he was trying a different kind of residence for some reason.

One of the big differences in this incident compared to the others is that he didn't force the female victim to massage his penis, touch it, hold it, or even talk about it. It's one of the very few attacks where he didn't engage in that behavior. Also, compared to most of the other assaults, he was "gentle" with the female victim. That does sound ridiculous given the context but we gave our disclaimers and caveats about that elsewhere. Another difference in this attack was that the crank phone calls didn't stop a week or so before the assault like they often did. They actually continued right up until the day of the attack.

The assailant stuttered again. Mentioning the police seemed to be the most reliable way to get him excited enough to do that. The victim felt that the stutter was genuine and that he was struggling to bring out his words. She could be right, even though he talked quite clearly in other attacks. Even with nearly a hundred reports of the assailant speaking, we're still not sure if it was a put-on or not. He's "consistently inconsistent" with his stuttering.

The detail about the assailant being circumcised was basically new information that came out of this attack. Up until this point, investigators weren't sure, although a few victims had reported it. There would be later victims that seemed to confirm the information.

The husband of this victim worked as a cement contractor, which offered a connection to the construction industry. There were several connections to construction among the victims, but not as many as some of the other professions.

Around this time, a newspaper article published by the Sacramento Bee divulged a lot of details about the modus operandi of the East Area Rapist. Thanks to that article, investigators had to keep an eye out for more sophisticated copycat crimes. There were plenty, and it became just a tad bit more difficult to differentiate between a copycat assault and an actual East Area Rapist assault. Several copycats would emerge throughout the crime spree.

Attack #26

Date: October 29th, 1977 1:45 AM to 3:45 AM
Victims: Wife and husband
Location: Woodson Avenue, Sacramento

Before we begin this one, let's discuss some information about the street. This part of the neighborhood was still being built, and the victims had only lived in their home for little over two weeks before this attack occurred. Every house on Woodson Avenue was under construction except for the victims'. Some had barely even been started (they were just frames or foundation), and some were practically finished. It was a unique setting for an attack, but one that offered several obvious tactical advantages.

Pre-Attack Events

Mid/Late October 1977
The victims arrived home to find their garage door open on two different occasions.

October 26th, 1977 4:45 AM
A neighbor was leaving for work when he saw a suspicious man walking east on Whitney Avenue, which was the next street south of the victims' street. The suspicious man appeared to be looking at houses, and when he got in front of the neighbor's house (the one who was observing him), he stopped under a bright light and stared at the neighbor with a blank expression on his face. Then he walked

fifty feet down the street, stopped as if he were going to cross to the other side, and then looked back at the neighbor. The neighbor looked away for just a moment, and when he looked back, the man had vanished. There hadn't been enough time for the man to run across the street, and the neighbor was sure that he hadn't continued walking. He checked the area for the subject, but couldn't find him. He assumed that the man was hiding behind a large tree that was in the area. The tree was between 4507 and 4512 Whitney Avenue.

The neighbor had seen his face very clearly, and a composite was made. It seems, however, that this composite has been lost. The neighbor described the man as a white male, early twenties, 5'8" to 6', 180 lbs, medium build, with medium brown hair that was collar-length and neatly-cut. He was wearing a shirt with several brown stripes around the chest, dark pants, and soft-soled shoes which rendered his footsteps silent. The man didn't have a jacket or sweater on, despite it being a cool October morning.

October 27th, 1977 5:00 PM
The phone rang, and the female victim picked it up. There was only silence on the other end. This was the only event resembling a hang-up phone call that the victims received, and might've simply been a wrong number, given that phone service had just been installed at the residence the previous day.

October 28th, 1977 2:00 PM
A suspicious vehicle was sighted on Woodson Avenue. It was a large, dark, four-door Dodge or Plymouth. The driver was a white male in his late twenties. He appeared to be checking out houses.

October 28th, 1977 6:30 PM
The neighbors who planned to live next door to the victims spotted a 1964 two-door Ford Falcon driving slowly around the cul-de-sac on Woodson Avenue. Other neighbors spotted the vehicle on other occasions as well. No one could describe the driver.

The Attack

The victims left their home at 7:30 PM to go out to dinner. They returned at 10:00 PM and went to bed around midnight.

The male victim woke from a deep sleep to the sensation of someone steadily tapping his foot. A bright light was beamed into his eyes.

"Don't move or I'll blow your fucking brains out. I know you've got a gun in a drawer in here somewhere, and if you move I'll blow your fucking brains out. I know you've got a gun in here somewhere."

The intruder stood there for a moment without moving for three or four minutes. "I only want food and money for my van and then I'll go. I know you've got a gun in here somewhere," he repeated.

"It's in the nightstand drawer," the husband replied.

"I only want food and money for my van."

The woman said that she didn't have any money, but she offered to write him a check.

"Shut your fucking mouth," he said, throwing shoelaces at her. "Tie him."

She began tying her husband's wrist, but mistakenly only tied one of his wrists.

"Bitch, I'll blow your brains out if you try something like that again." He tossed her another shoelace. "Tie him right."

When she was done, the intruder tied her wrists, retied the male, and then began rummaging through the house. Based on some of the sounds they were hearing, the couple felt that he had a canvas duffle bag with him.

After several minutes, he returned to the bedroom and accused the wife of trying to free the male victim. He cut the ligatures off of her ankles and ordered her to get up. He held his knife to her throat, put the gun against her back, and forced her down the hallway into the living room. "If you try anything I'll kill you," he said as they walked.

Once in the living room, the victim saw that the scene had been prepared for her arrival. Strips of towel had been laid out on the floor. The attacker ordered her to lie down on her stomach, then he retied her ankles and blindfolded her with a strip of towel. He began moving through the house.

When he returned, he straddled the woman's back and placed his penis in her hands. He ordered her to "play with it" and told her that she'd "better make it good." Her hands had been bound so tightly that she'd lost feeling in them, so she tried to protest. He told her to "shut up," called her a "bitch," and warned that he'd "cut off [her] fucking ear." He forced her to orally copulate him, then tried to sodomize her.

The victim screamed in pain as he tried to enter her rectum. He gave up on his attempts, and then raped her vaginally. After a moment of that, he switched back to sodomizing her. He put it in her vagina again, but because of the angle and his apparent lack of length, he was unable to keep it inside her (despite seeming to be fully erect).

He turned her around, got on top of her, and raped her once more. Afterward, he sat her up and again forced it into her mouth.

He suddenly withdrew, stood up, and began crying. "I'm sorry. Mom. Mommy. Please help me. I don't want to do this, Mommy." The victim felt that the sobbing was genuine. He continued on, sobbing and repeating those phrases, and then she heard him start to hyperventilate and stumble around the room a bit. He walked down the hallway, and as he got close to the master bedroom the husband could hear him say "Oh Mom." Then the assailant began breathing harshly, as if angry. The husband also thought that the crying sounded genuine, like he was sobbing uncontrollably and trying to get ahold of himself.

Then the EAR made his way back to the living room. Again, he sexually assaulted the woman. And again, he began crying and sobbing afterward. He stood up and stumbled around the room some more. "Mommy, I don't want to do this. Someone please help me."

He retied the woman's feet and told her "Bitch, I'm going to watch television. You better keep your fucking mouth shut." He left her side for a moment, then returned with a cup and saucer. He placed it on her back, grabbed her fingers, and took her wedding rings.

Immediate Aftermath

When the police arrived, they processed the woman's body for fingerprints. They didn't find any. She was transported to the UC Davis Medical Center.

In the bedroom, officers found the victim's gun (a .357 Magnum Colt Trooper revolver) near the bed. It had been unloaded, and the ammo was missing.

Bloodhounds were brought in to track the assailant. The dogs led them southwest of the residence to the curb near 4400 Whitney Avenue. The man who lived there was eliminated as being the EAR.

Traces of blue architectural paint were found at the scene in vacuum sweepings done by technicians. Some of the paint was also found on shoelaces and on one of the victim's hairs. There doesn't appear to be any information on whether this paint was a match for the paint at the previous scene, but the paint *did* match samples found at the next scene.

Suspect Description

Neither of the victims got a good look at the assailant. He was described as white, with very light legs that had light-colored hair on them. His penis seemed to be large in circumference, but short in length.

He wore a nylon jacket. His pants were probably corduroy. His socks were brown and burgundy, and his tennis shoes were a medium blue with white soles and a white stripe. They were worn-out and dirty. He wore black leather gloves, and seemed to have a canvas duffle bag with him. He wore a gun holster.

The offender was described as speaking in whispers, and his voice had a "desperate" tone. The husband felt that the assailant's voice sounded feminine during the first sobbing fit.

Post-Attack Events

October 29th, 1977 6:30 AM

A woman who ran a beauty shop on Whitney Avenue had arrived at work a little after 4:00 AM. Some time later, an officer came in and asked for information about the vehicles in the parking lot, and all of them belonged to her customers (yes, she began working with customers quite early). At 6:30 AM, she saw a very peculiar sight: she spotted a man rising up from inside a parked trailer across the street (the trailer was attached to a dump truck). He was dressed in dark clothing, possibly a jump suit, and he had a hood over his head. He pulled a bicycle out of the trailer, got on the bicycle, and began riding east on Whitney Avenue very quickly. While exploring this lead, police learned that the vehicle was typically parked at that location every weeknight and occasionally all weekend. It was parked only a few feet away from the area where the bloodhound had lost the EAR's trail.

November 14th, 1977

The neighbor who lived behind the victims' house found .38 caliber bullets in his backyard. The bullets matched the ones taken from the victims' gun.

Context and Analysis

Like 1976, EAR once more had a very busy October, with three attacks occurring during the month.

The victim's gun was found on the floor, unloaded, very similar to Attack #24. The neighbor who lived behind them (where the ammo was found) was actually a State Patrol Officer. Whether that has any significance or not is hard to say. Those who feel that EAR liked to send messages might find something in that.

Again, he threatened to cut off someone's ear. That's a pretty specific threat, and it helps tie a few of the attacks together.

The sobbing here was quite a display. It's always impossible to tell if it's genuine or not. Victim after victim who witnessed it felt, for the most part, that it was real and that he wasn't acting. As we've suggested elsewhere, maybe he was having moments of clarity and remorse. If he was, he didn't turn himself in, get the help he needed, or even find some way to stop himself. His sobbing (at least as a sign of remorse) would be more convincing if he wouldn't cry and then rape someone right afterward. The phrase "Mommy, I don't want to do this. Someone please help me," sounds very contrived. But we weren't there, and the victim was. She felt it was genuine. As we see more and more of these sobbing events, you'll notice that they usually occur right after a rape, and almost exclusively in instances where the offender is unable to climax or perform. That's probably what the tears were about, to be honest.

We discussed the assailant's possible phone phreaking skills in Attack #23, but in this attack there was an event that has taken on mythical proportions among some followers of the case. The victims received a hang-up phone call a little over a day after their new phone service was installed. At this point, obviously, the number wasn't published anywhere, nor had it propagated onto bills or change-of-address forms or anything. This is the attack that people point to when they want to show proof that the EAR either worked for the phone company, was a phone hacker or phone phreaker, or somehow could manipulate the telephone system. We believe that there are more likely explanations for this solitary hang-up phone call, though. Someone might've called the number expecting someone else, but hung up when they didn't recognize the voice. It might've just been a random call that had absolutely nothing to do with this series. If it *was* EAR, maybe since the number was new, the victims wrote it down and the EAR saw it while peeping through their window or rummaging through their house in an unknown break-in. If the call could be definitively tied to the EAR (for instance, if he spoke), then that would narrow down the possibilities of how he might've obtained the number, and we could have a better discussion. Another data point to consider is that the EAR usually stopped his hang-up phone calls about a week before the attack, but not always. This call was only a day or two before the attack. A single random silent phone call on one day doesn't make much of an impression on as some of the other phone activity associated with other attacks.

Law Enforcement assumed that the assailant broke into their house a few hours before their attack (while the victims were out having dinner at Rico's Italian Pizza with the couple that bought their old house). The pry marks might support that theory. It appeared that he had pried at the sliding glass door on the patio, but was unsuccessful. He was able to break some glass near the lock in an unused bedroom and get inside that way, and then possibly unlock the back patio door for himself (and then it seemed he went and replaced the window screen to the unused bedroom). Something else that supports this theory is that he kept saying "I know you've got a gun in a drawer here somewhere." And the victim did. The removal of the ammo and its deposit in the backyard of the neighbor's house might've happened during the attack, but it also could've happened before the couple returned home.

The dump truck trailer incident is one of the most colorful anecdotes that this case has to offer. It's also one of the hardest to rationalize, but we fully believe that the witness saw everything that she claimed to have seen. Her statements, past and present, paint the picture of a woman who saw something very odd and terrifying.

As we examine the details of this sighting, it's clear that the truck was very close to the place where the dogs tracked the scent. That lends credence to the idea that the strange man seen with the bike was indeed the assailant. But where had he gone to when the dogs arrived? Could he have been hiding in it? Wouldn't the dogs have picked up on that? Surely the officers checked inside of it for him, since the dogs led to that area. Did he park there, attack, drive away, come back on bicycle, stash the bike, stalk or do something else, then retrieve the bike and leave? Sounds complicated, but there are hints every once in awhile that he stalked another potential victim for awhile after an attack. How's that for time management? That explanation is one of the only ways to make this work, given the fact that the dogs didn't lead right to the trailer. With as much as he seemed to stalk, it would make sense that he'd work on other potential victims after an attack, especially if his free time was somewhat constrained by a job or some other obligation. Maybe EAR was inside the trailer after all and the dogs and officers didn't find him. Maybe he went back to the truck, retrieved the bike, moved away too fast for the dogs to catch the scent, and then came back a little while later and stashed the bike again.

We haven't discussed the assailant's penis size very much, but generally the descriptions add up to it being on a smallish side of normal—nothing too identifying about it. Sometimes it's described as "small," or "three inches," or something like that. Some of those attacks are also ones where he doesn't appear to have achieved a full erection. Up until this attack, the media had been running stories about him being very "small" or "inadequate," and stating that the assailant was in a "homosexual panic" (a phrase which we've already addressed). After this attack, the police made a statement that the rapist was *not* "abnormally sexually endowed" and that he was *not* in a "homosexual panic because of inadequate physical endowment." The original line about him being "small" has stuck with this case, mostly because of all of the early reporting and also because it feels empowering to insult him this way. It appears he definitely *was* smaller than average, but myths about him having a "micro penis" are false.

The medical and real estate connections are strong in this particular attack (but not through employment—the husband was employed as a car salesman). The male victim had recently undergone surgery, and he'd been hospitalized at Sutter General Hospital in downtown Sacramento for two weeks afterward. At the time of the attack, he'd only been in the new home for a few days. His wife had been the one doing most of the moving and working on the house, given that he was incapacitated. She visited him twice a day in the hospital. The neighborhood was brand new, and there was real estate activity going on all over the place.

Attack #27

Date: November 10th, 1977 3:30 AM to 4:45 AM
Victims: 12-year-old girl. Her 56-year-old mother was also
accosted and bound.
Location: La Riviera Drive, Sacramento

Pre-Attack Events

April 1977
A thirty-three-year-old woman living on La Riviera Drive was
awakened in the middle of the night by a prowler. He was standing
outside her bedroom window and shining a flashlight on her while
she slept.

Late October through Early November 1977
The same woman and her husband received hang-up phone calls
throughout this time period.

November 7th, 1977
A message was found scrawled on a wall at California State
University (located less than two miles from the victims' house). The
message was written in the men's restroom on the main floor of the
library (in the middle stall on the right-hand side). It said:

The East Side Rapist was here
Will rape my first black girl tonight
Dumb cops will never find me.

250

November 9th, 1977 1:00 AM
The same woman who'd had a prowler in April was awakened by a noise on the west side of the house. The neighbor's dog began to bark ferociously. The woman's husband got up to investigate, but he didn't see anything.

November 9th, 1977 11:00 PM
A woman living on La Riviera heard something heavy hit the side of her house near the patio. She didn't hear any additional sounds.

November 10th, 1977 12:05 AM
A woman living on La Riviera heard someone try to pry her sliding glass door open. Her dog started barking and growling at the prowler, and the woman flipped on her outside lights to investigate. She didn't see anything out of the ordinary.

November 10th, 1977 3:00 AM
A man woke up to the sound of someone prying at the sliding glass door to his bedroom. He hurriedly turned on the outside light and tried to find the source of the noise, but he didn't see anything. Thirty minutes later, his mother was awakened by pounding sounds coming from outside.

The Attack
The mother of the victim woke up to the sound of her sliding glass door closing. A masked intruder blinded her with a flashlight.

"What do you want? I'm an old lady," she told him.

"I won't hurt you or harm you. All I want is your money. Lie back down."

She complied.

"No, not that way. On your stomach."

Again, she complied. He pulled her hands back and tied them together, and then he tied her feet. She complained that her hands were tied too tightly.

"Do you want me to cut off your fingers? Who else is in the house?

If you lie to me, I'll slit your throat."

She told him that her daughter was in the house. He said that he was leaving to tie her up, at which point he left the room for a moment, then came back with two plates. He placed them on her back.

"If I hear these plates jiggle you will be dead, bitch. All I want is your money and food. Do you hear me? Do you hear me? Do you hear me?"

She answered "Yes."

"I need things for my apartment. Blankets. My car is parked out front and I'm going back to L.A." He left the room and was gone for several minutes.

"I'm going upstairs and cook something to eat and if you make any sounds, your daughter will be dead," he said when he returned. "Do you hear me, bitch?"

She told him "Yes."

Next the intruder accosted the daughter. He entered her bedroom and shook her. "Leave me alone," she said, thinking that it was morning and her mother was trying to wake her up. She opened her eyes, saw the masked man, and thought it was a friend playing a joke on her. "Stop joking around and let me go back to sleep," she said.

"This isn't a joke. Get onto your stomach and put your hands behind your back."

"No," she told him.

"Do what I say or I'm going to stick you with a knife. I'll slit your throat and watch you bleed to death." He pressed the knife against her neck, and then he slid it up and down her ear. "Do you want me to cut off your ear?"

"I don't care," she replied, rolling over. The assailant stopped threatening her for a few minutes at this point.

"All I want is your money," he told her. He grabbed her hands, tied them behind her back, and tied her ankles together.

"I don't have any," she replied, although she did have a bit in her room somewhere. She didn't want the intruder to take it. He left the room, went to the mother's room, and started threatening her. "I don't care," the mother replied to his threats, echoing her daughter.

The intruder moved to the bathroom. While he was in there, the daughter worked on loosening her bindings. She was able to kick her feet free. When the intruder returned, he noticed her efforts.

"If you move again, I'll kill your mother." He retied her feet and then began rummaging through the house. He returned to her room holding strips of towel in his hands. He used one to gag her, but he wasn't terribly successful because she stuck her tongue out to ensure that it wouldn't be very tight. He blindfolded her. Then he untied her feet.

She felt his weight on the bed. He straddled her back and held his penis against her hands.

"Grab it. Squeeze it. Do you know what this is?"

"No," she replied.

"Have you ever fucked before?"

"I don't know."

"Do you know what that means?"

"No," she said.

He ordered her to roll over. She refused.

"Roll over or I'll kill you." She still refused. He ordered her to roll over a third time. She wouldn't. He grabbed her and physically flipped her over. She had a tampon in, and he took it out. His penis was fully erect, and he tried to penetrate her vaginally several times, but he couldn't. He penetrated her anally for a brief time. Then he got up and left the room.

The victim felt cold air, like a door had been opened. She still heard the assailant in the house. He returned to her room and told her that he was going to "pack some groceries." He noticed that the girl was shivering and asked her what was wrong. She told him that she was cold. He picked up a sleeping bag from the floor and placed it on top of her, and then he left.

Immediate Aftermath

For the third time in a row, traces of blue paint were found in vacuum sweepings of the scene. The small flakes at this scene (measured in microns) matched the paint evidence from the previous scene. Investigators of the era determined that the paint was architectural paint, the kind used on masonry and only used by commercial paint sprayers. The paint was never conclusively tied to the offender, nor did it generate many actionable leads.

Suspect Description

White male, mid twenties, 5'6" to 5'11" with a thin to medium build. His legs were described as "slender" and his penis was no more than five inches long.

He had a dark, tight-fitting ski mask (probably black). It had holes for the eyes and for the mouth. His shirt was plaid with long sleeves and red, green, and blue colors. His pants were dark, and his gloves were dark and tight-fitting.

His voice was a high-pitched whisper. His words came out rapidly, and he emphasized "S" sounds.

Post-Attack Event

January 20th, 1978 5:20 AM

The mother of this victim was awakened by a phone call.

"Hello?" she asked after picking up the phone.

"I have not struck in awhile. You will be my next victim. I'm going to fuck you in the butt. See you soon."

The exact same call was received by the victims in Attack #18 just ten minutes later. These attacks occured six months apart, but the victims lived very close to each other.

Context and Analysis

The victim profile in this attack was quite different in several ways. For one thing, the victim was only twelve years old, which makes her the youngest victim of record (in crimes that have officially been tied to him). This attack occurred in a condominium facing the American River, and condominiums were a rare target for the assailant. The mother was fifty-six years old, which was outside the age range for the households that he usually entered. Also, the assailant had been targeting couples for quite awhile, and he'd switched to a single target once more for this attack. It's probable that he'd planned on attacking the woman and her husband that he'd been stalking since April, but for whatever reason, he was unable to and started looking for alternate victims.

Despite the terror and the horror of this attack, in a way it's an encouraging read because of how utterly incapable the EAR was of controlling this victim. All of the terror and tragedy this killer inflicted in his lifetime, and here he is getting mentally outmaneuvered by a twelve-year-old kid. In recent discussions, the victim has revealed that one of the main reasons that she felt comfortable resisting the assailant was that she knew from the newspapers that he'd never killed anyone. Even with this knowledge, she was brave in the face of a very frightening situation, and she handled herself quite well. Also, people who follow this case closely know that this woman is involved in the advocacy work for the other victims and survivors of the EAR/GSK, so even today her fortitude looms far above the pain and terror that the offender inflicted.

It's unclear how this victim was found or selected by the EAR. The condo she lived in was an end-unit, and the victim in Attack #18 lived at the end of this complex to the east. Perhaps that was the connection. There were a few prowling incidents in the immediate area all throughout 1977. Attack #18 had happened in May. This victim was clearly an alternate—he pried at two different houses that night before settling on this one. Their personal lives were examined for clues, but there weren't many to be found. The girl went to a private school, and her mother worked for the Department of Employment Development at 800 Capitol Mall Blvd in downtown Sacramento. The area behind the victims' residence was popular with joggers. The victim said that she often played near La Riviera, a fairly busy street. She also said that she didn't always close the blinds at night when she changed clothes. If the EAR was walking in the dark near the American River, it's possible he could've spotted her. We can't really be sure how he arrived there that night. Regardless of anything that the victim did or didn't do, it's not possible for anyone to live their lives in a way that will keep them completely safe from sexual predators.

He told one of the residents that he was going "back to L.A.," though we probably shouldn't take his statement at face value. Again he threatens to cut off an ear, a threat that comes up often enough for us to wonder where he might've originally heard it. Black is a rare color of ski mask for this perpetrator, with him usually opting for a colored one or a softer neutral one. Our theory is that black ski masks would be a pretty conspicuous thing to buy, so he probably opted for other colors but stayed away from distinctive ones with designs (which might be traced to him).

Given the geography and timing, the message scrawled in the restroom seems fairly credible. A photograph of the message existed at some point, and we've always thought it would be interesting to compare the handwriting on it to the handwriting found on some papers from an attack that took place in Danville in late 1978 (Attack #42) and to compare it to the writing from Attack #22.

According to the press, the police had checked out over 5,000 suspects at this point. Some of these were flimsy eliminations due to a misunderstanding of "secretor status" (meaning that a suspect was falsely determined to be a secretor or non-secretor based on a faulty test. The assailant himself was determined to be a "non-secretor," which meant that his blood type couldn't be determined from a semen sample). There was confusion in the forensic and scientific world about how far the "secretor" status extended with saliva samples, and it eventually turned out that suspects ruled out by saliva samples were ruled out erroneously. Once this fact was discovered, records were collected and anyone who had been ruled out this way was put back on the master suspect list.

Attack #28

Date: December 2nd, 1977 11:45 PM to 2:00 AM
Victim: 36-year-old woman. Her 6-year-old daughter was also in the house.
Location: Revelstok Drive, Foothill Farms

Pre-Attack Events

May 1977
Two young women living on Brett Drive (an area very close to the victim's house) received a harassing phone call. The caller whispered "You are next" three times.

Late Summer 1977
A date on this event was impossible to pin down (two different sources and one report all had different dates), but the victim's house was burglarized sometime at the end of Summer or in the early months of Fall. One source put this as happening in October, but it seems that the date there was confused with another one (the date of the victim attending a town hall meeting). From what we can tell, the burglary probably happened in August, right around the time of the "Summer Break." Two photographs were stolen, both of them taken of the victim six years prior. A portable typewriter and an engagement ring were stolen, as well. A jar of pickles was moved from one shelf to another in the refrigerator, and the thermostat was turned off. The method of entry was the front door, which had been left unlocked. The burglar locked it on his way out.

Early and Mid-November 1977

The victim began receiving hang-up phone calls every day after 2:00 PM during this time period. They lasted for a few weeks, and then stopped a few days before the attack.

Mid-November 1977

The key to the sliding glass door, which had been hidden under a mat on the front porch, disappeared. This was two weeks before the attack.

Late November 1977

A week before the attack, various neighbors spotted a dark blue van in the area. It had a Sacramento Army Depot sticker on it. Police did a lot of investigating but couldn't find anyone in the neighborhood who was connected with that vehicle.

Late November 1977

The neighbor living next door to the victim spotted a full-size, four-door, beige-colored station wagon parked in front of the victim's house.

December 1st, 1977 Afternoon

A neighbor was working in her yard when she spotted a strange man walking from the field surrounding Woodridge Elementary School. He spotted her as well, and when he did, he stopped and stood still, then calmly watched her for several minutes. She became frightened and went inside. He was described as a white male, late twenties, 5'9", with short light-brown hair. He was wearing a multicolored print t-shirt and dark slacks.

December 1st, 1977 Night

The same two young women who'd had the harassing phone calls had moved to Kies Way, an area still very close to the victim's house. The night before the attack, they had a prowler in their yard. The prowler turned off their electricity.

December 2nd, 1977, 8:00 PM

A call was received at the police station. The voice on the other end said something to the effect of "I shall commit another rape" or "I'll commit another rape tonight." The voice sounded like a man in his twenties and it was very clear, with no accent and no background noise on the call. The words sounded like they were being read or recited.

The Attack

The husband left the house at 11:00 PM to spend time with friends. The couple's six-year-old daughter was already asleep, and their fourteen-year-old son was sleeping elsewhere. The wife went to bed at 11:30 PM.

Minutes later, there was a noise at the bedroom door. The victim assumed that it was the pet cat, and she went back to sleep. Before long, she was awakened by a louder noise. She rolled over, and as she did, a flashlight beam was trained on her eyes.

"Get up," the intruder said.

"Why?" the victim asked.

"Get up and come with me or I'll hurt your little boy." This statement puzzled the victim until she realized that the intruder thought that her young daughter, who had short hair, was a boy. She complied with the request. As she stood up, she noticed that he had black shoelaces in his left hand. He didn't have any kind of weapon drawn.

He forced her down the hall, and once they arrived at the living room, he ordered her onto her knees. He pulled her hands back behind her and tied them together tightly with the shoelaces.

He told her to lie down on her stomach, and then he removed her panties and threw them into the hallway. For a few moments he stood over her silently, and then he bent down and tied her ankles together very tightly. The victim began crying, and the assailant threatened to gag her. She begged him not to gag her, explaining that if her child happened to wake up, she'd be able to tell the girl to go back to bed. The argument must've worked, because he didn't restrict her vision *or* her mouth.

The intruder haunted the halls for a little while, frequently going to the window to observe a group of four or five kids playing in the street near the house. He walked by the victim several times without saying anything. On one of his final trips by her, he said "You think you're smarter, but I'm smarter than you are."

After awhile she stopped hearing his footsteps, and soon afterward, she heard a van start up and leave at the side of the house. A few minutes went by, and then she made her way to the phone and called a neighbor for help.

Immediate Aftermath

<u>December 3rd, 1977 12:00 AM</u>
During the time that the attack was going on, a sixteen-year-old boy living down the street on Revelstok spotted a car parked across from his house. It was a white station wagon with all-black tires. The vehicle stuck out because its windows weren't fogged up like the rest of the cars on the street.

When the police arrived, the victim was in hysterics. Her neighbor was attempting to comfort her. They didn't attempt to get fingerprints off of her skin because of her insistence that the intruder wore gloves. Her panties were taken for evidence, but nothing notable turned up from them.

Nothing was stolen. There was some evidence that the family room window had been pried at, and it was thought that it might've been the entry point. The gate on the south side of the residence was unlocked, and the victim informed them that they always kept it locked.

The children playing outside that night were questioned, but none of them saw anything out of the ordinary.

Suspect Description
White male, early twenties, shorter than 6', thin to medium build.

He was wearing dark clothing. He had on a jacket that wasn't bulky and gloves that felt like the kind used in the medical field.

The assailant didn't seem to have a weapon of any kind.

He whispered through clenched teeth, and the victim felt that his natural voice was probably higher-pitched. He sounded angry when he spoke to her.

Context and Analysis
The offender returned to Foothill Farms for this attack. Since the beginning of the crime spree, he followed a pattern where he'd attack in one area, then another area for one or two attacks, then return back to the first area. For example, he'd hit Citrus Heights and in between strikes there, he'd alternate between Rancho Cordova and Carmichael, then he'd hit Citrus Heights again. He'd hit Orangevale and South Sacramento, and then he alternated between those with a Citrus Heights and a Carmichael assault thrown in there before moving to Stockton, where he'd hit and then pulled out, went back to Rancho, began this Foothill Farms series, and then after this he went back to Stockton. There's clearly an intentional plan of attack here— we feel it's unlikely that he was simply going to where his day job took him. It seems very methodical, and it's a clearly-delineated plan of attack that seems to show that he approached some of this with a tactical mindset. Whether he really enjoyed the planning of these assaults (very possible) or he was simply hell-bent on not getting caught, who knows, but it seems very well-planned and intentional.

The burglary is notable because of the typewriter. Very soon we'll explore a poem called "Excitement's Crave" which was written on the same brand and model of typewriter that was stolen from this victim a few months prior to the attack. It was a portable model (measuring 22" x 14" x 8"), Royal brand, metal, painted blue, and stored in a blue fiberglass case. Not the easiest thing to lug around, but this model of typewriter was extremely common.

The photos that the EAR stole in the burglary were taken when the victim was a few years younger. Investigators wondered if the EAR thought that the picture was recent (having done most of his stalking by phone and through entering the home while the victims were away), and that when he arrived to the attack and found the victim looking a little different from the photos (a bit older, hair dyed), it threw him off enough to not commit the sexual assault.

Another part of the attack that throws into question how much he may or may not have stalked the victim before the attack was the fact that he mistook her little girl for a little boy. He must've seen the child after breaking in that night or at some point before or else he wouldn't have known about her, but he must not have seen her very well. Or, perhaps he was misdirecting intentionally. He'd been calling them for weeks, he'd apparently been in their home, and he might've even parked in their driveway at one point.

Aside from not sexually assaulting this victim (even though he took her underpants off), there were several other things that were weird about this attack. He didn't bind her hands in the bed. He didn't rattle off any lines from his usual "script" (he used different threats and he didn't ask for money, which was very strange). As chatty as he'd been in recent attacks, he was fairly quiet in this one. There was no visible gun or knife. He tied the victim's ankles more tightly than usual.

Did the noisy kids playing outside save this woman? Other neighbors said that the kids were quite noisy, so it's possible. He never seemed to like a lot of noise, going so far as to turn off heaters and air conditioners (and going outside from time to time to seemingly listen for any sign that he'd been spotted).

The phrase "you think you're smarter, but I'm smarter than you are," is an odd one, simply because a phrase in that spirit doesn't really show up very often and it's unclear what the assailant even meant by it. What brought it on? The victim didn't challenge his intelligence or provoke him. We tried to find something in the newspapers that he could've been responding to, but nothing jumped out at us. It could've been a sign of what might have been going on psychologically with the assailant, a hint of an inferiority complex or a tipoff to some of the rage that drove him to commit these crimes.

This victim was treated horribly by the police. Some of them accused her of making up the entire thing, and some went the opposite way and accused her of lying about not being sexually assaulted. In order to appease them, the victim subjected herself to a polygraph test. The test showed that all of her statements regarding the attack were truthful.

Obviously, given the article about the M.O. of the assailant that was released on October 1977, one has to look critically at the evidence in each attack to determine if there's a possibility of a copycat. Of course, the possibility of a copycat doesn't take anything away from the fear, terror, and trauma that a victim faced at the hands of another offender, nor does it insinuate that he or she is being untruthful about any part of the encounter. It simply means that we look at the details of the attack and trying to determine who perpetrated it. Even without the usual calling cards left by the East Area Rapist, there's enough in this particular one for it to remain part of the official canon. The angry whispers through clenched teeth, the burglary, the previous EAR activity in the area, and the shoelaces make for a pretty convincing argument.

There were two phone calls related to this attack where the caller spoke. The "you're next" call is very EAR-esque. It occurred right after a big press release about the offender, so the timing probably wasn't coincidental, either. The fact that suspicious activity followed these women even after they moved is probably more than coincidental as well, but the logistics of that are hard to figure out. There's a lot that goes into stalking someone as they move from one location to another, even if it's fairly close by. How would the EAR be able to keep track of where they moved to? What might that tell us about where the assailant lived, what his profession was, or what kind of information he might've had access to? Perhaps one of the ways that EAR was finding victims and keeping track of them as they moved was through their place of employment. One of the women living in that house worked for the State Legislature on Capital Mall Blvd, an area that seemed to have many, many ties to other victims and potential victims.

Speaking of employment, the victim's husband in this attack was in the Army. That provided another military connection, which is not so unusual given the many military bases in the area.

The other phone call, the "I shall commit another rape" one, certainly seems connected, given that the assailant *did* attempt to commit another rape just a few hours later. This phone call is important to the investigation because throughout the month of December, the EAR (or people impersonating him) began a long series of phone calls, letters, and odd sightings/communications. Up until December 1977, the assailant had been relatively "quiet." For some reason, the period after this attack seemed to be the start of a whole new career in public relations for him.

Winter 1977/1978 Sightings and Communications

One of the strangest and most unique periods of the crime spree occurred from December 1977 to January 1978. A flurry of phone calls, letters/poems, and atypical sightings took place throughout these winter months. Whether the EAR was trying to launch a media campaign similar to the Zodiac (or even the recently arrested Son of Sam), or if he was suffering from boredom or an identity crisis of sorts, it's hard to say. It's believed that most of these incidents are related to the EAR, but some of them might not be.

Late 1977
The Sacramento Sheriff's Department received a strange phone call, purportedly from the offender himself.

Caller: "You're never gonna catch me, you dumb fuckers. [unintelligible] East Area Rapist. I'm gonna fuck again tonight. Be careful."

The caller spoke at a rapid pace. The call was recorded and has been released to the public.

December 2nd, 1977 8:00 PM
This call has already been discussed, but the information is repeated here for the sake of providing a comprehensive look at the month.

When this call was received at the police station, the voice on the other end said something to the effect of "I shall commit another rape" or "I'll commit another rape tonight." The voice sounded like a man in his twenties and it was very clear, with no accent and no background noise on the call. The words sounded like they were being read or recited. Attack #28 occurred just a few hours later.

December 9th, 1977 5:40 PM
The female victim from Attack #21 received a phone call that she felt was from her attacker.

Victim: "Hello?"

Caller: "Merry Christmas. It's me again."

The phone clicked several times (most likely the caller pushing the hook button rapidly), and then the line went dead.

The victim was positive that it was her attacker. A "phone trap" was placed on her phone, as well as a tape recorder, in case the offender called again.

December 9th, 1977 6:00 PM
A Sacramento-area woman returned home to find that someone had been in her house, and that her rear sliding glass door had been unlocked. Police conducted a stakeout of her residence overnight, but nothing happened.

December 10th, 1977 9:15 PM
A masked man was spotted near the intersection of Sierra Oaks and American River Drive (directly to the west of Watt Avenue). Once he realized he'd been seen, he jumped into an older-model Chevy truck and drove off. He was described as 5'10", 170 lbs, and wearing a ski mask, dark-colored clothes, a dark coat, and gloves.

December 10th, 1977 9:50 PM
The Sheriff's Department received a phone call.

"I am going to hit tonight. Watt Avenue."

A recording was made of the call, and the voice appeared to be from the same man who had called on December 2nd, 1977.

December 10th, 1977 9:52 PM

A second call came in.

"I am going to hit tonight. Watt Avenue."

A recording was made of this call, as well. The voice was the same as the call that had come in two minutes before, and it was the same as the caller from the previous week.

The police swarmed Watt Avenue in response. Over a hundred people were questioned, but nothing concrete was developed.

December 11th, 1977 2:30 AM

A suspicious bicyclist was seen on the Watt Avenue bridge. The man was described as wearing a ski mask with a full opening for the face, similar to the mask worn at Attack #15 and a mask seen on a suspect in the Maggiore murders (which took place two months after this incident. We'll discuss those shortly).

December 11th, 1977 4:30 AM

The same bicyclist was spotted by police near an apartment complex on La Riviera Drive (near Watt Avenue). This area was very close to Attack #11 and just to the east of Attacks #18 and #27. The subject ditched the bicycle and evaded the police on foot. The bicycle, surprisingly, had been stolen from Redding, California, a town over 150 miles to the north (connected by Interstate 5). Police investigated and determined that the bicyclist was most likely not the EAR.

December 12th, 1977

Envelopes containing a poem called "Excitement's Crave" were received at the offices of the Sacramento mayor, the editor of the Sacramento Bee, and the KVIE Channel 6 PBS television station. The poems were typed on legal-size lightweight onionskin paper (a type of low-budget, durable, semi-translucent paper often used in typewriters to create duplicates). The paper and envelopes were processed for latent prints, and a palm print was found on the front of the envelope addressed to the Sacramento Bee. Police determined that they had been typed on the same common brand of typewriter that had been stolen from Victim #28 sometime earlier in the year.

All those mortals surviving birth
Upon facing maturity,
Take inventory of their worth
To prevailing society.

Choosing values becomes a task;
Oneself must seek satisfaction.
The selected route will unmask
Character when plans take action

Accepting some work to perform
At fixed pay, but promise for more,
Is a recognized social norm,
As is decorum, seeking lore.

Achieving while others lifting
Should be cause for deserving fame.
Leisure tempts excitement seeking,
What's right and expected seems tame.

"Jessie James" has been seen by all,
And "Son of Sam" has an author.
Others now feel temptations call.
Sacramento should make an offer.

To make a movie of my life
That will pay for my planned exile.
Just now I'd like to add the wife
Of a Mafia lord to my file.

Your East Area Rapist
And deserving pest
See you in the press or on T.V.

The authorship of this poem has never been verified. Apparently there are three other letters and poems that the police have not released yet, and when those are finally put out to the public, it will be interesting to see what the general consensus is on authorship.

In this poem, the "wife of a Mafia lord" is thought by some to be a reference to Victim #21.

December 1977

An event now referred to as the "7-Eleven" incident took place around this time period. It's become an interesting facet of the East Area Rapist mythos. Officers with knowledge of it are unable to discuss the details, so the story may or may not be complete and, as with other sightings of this type, the incident may or may not be related to the EAR.

Reportedly, a young man in a shiny black jacket (the jacket had a Vietnam-related image on the back) had been frequenting a 7-Eleven store at 10721 Coloma Road in Rancho Cordova at odd hours of the night. Police officers, reportedly dressed in civvies that barely concealed their true identities, attempted to stake out the store from the inside so that they could question the subject. Supposedly the store clerk received a phone call that night from a man who asked to speak with the "cops in the back." The clerk replied that there were no cops, and the caller said "Don't give me that shit." One of the officers was handed the phone, and the caller laughed and hung up. The strange man in the black jacket never returned to the store.

Again, this story might be incomplete. It's worth noting that this 7-Eleven was located quite a ways away from all of the attack areas, aside from Attack #43 (and Attack #43 is a very strange one). Looking at the map, you might even say that the other attacks and incidents form a large semi-circle *around* this incident, which is kind of interesting in and of itself.

This event is sometimes touted as myth, but we were able to confirm that it did take place. We couldn't confirm or expand on the details, however.

December 1977

Victim #8 received a phone call from someone who whispered threats. When listening to a recording that Victim #1 would later make of a threatening call, she confirmed that the voice was the same as the man who had called her, but she wasn't sure if it was her attacker or not.

December 1977

Victim #23 also received a phone call from someone whispering threats. She identified the voice as that of the East Area Rapist.

January 2nd, 1978

Victim #1 (from the June 1976 attack) had been receiving odd phone calls since around Christmas. The police gave her a tape recorder in hopes that she'd be able to catch the elusive caller's voice. On the evening of January 2nd, the phone rang.

Victim: "Hello?"
Caller: "Is Ray there?"
Victim: "Pardon?"
Caller: "Is Ray there?"
Victim: "I'm sorry, you must have the wrong number."
Caller: "Sorry."

The call was recorded. It didn't mean much at the time. Fifteen minutes later the phone rang again, but it was a friend calling. After speaking with her friend for awhile, the victim hung up the phone. Soon afterward, it began ringing once more. She picked it up. There was silence on the other end, and after a moment, the line went dead.

She received another hang-up phone call or two that night. Then, finally, she received a call where the silence stretched on—the caller didn't hang up. Deep, dramatic breathing began. And then the caller began to speak. His voice was a harsh, familiar whisper:

"Gonna kill you... Gonna killll you... Gonna killll you Bitch... Bitch... Bitch... Fuckin' whore..."

The receiver clicked several times, and then the phone went dead.

The victim immediately identified the voice as that of East Area Rapist.

Luckily, the call was recorded. At long last, investigators could listen to the terrifying voice that had been haunting California for over a year and a half.

The other victims who had received calls (#8, #18, #21, #23, and the mother of Victim #27) were given a chance to listen to the recording. Victim #8 identified the voice as the man who had called her, but wasn't sure if it was her attacker or not. The male victim of Attack #18 felt that the voice wasn't the caller or his attacker. The husband and wife from Attack #21 concluded that it was their attacker based on the way he said "kill." Victim #23 felt that it was the same man who had called her, and that it was definitely the voice of her attacker. The mother of Victim #27 couldn't identify the voice as the same man. She stated that during her attack, the assailant spoke much more rapidly and in a higher-pitched voice.

January 6th, 1978 8:30 PM

A volunteer working at a counseling service received a phone call from an adult male. He told the counselor that he wanted to stop a certain behavior, but wouldn't specify what the behavior actually was. He kept changing inflection from a normal, almost pleading voice, to an angry and accusatory one (asking multiple times "Are you tracing this call?" in a violent tone).

Finally, the caller came out with his confession: he said that he was the "East Side Rapist" and that he didn't want to hurt the "women or their husbands anymore."

He also mentioned having been to counseling throughout his life, notably at Stockton State Hospital (now the Stanislaus State Stockton Center). He angrily accused the counselor of tracing the call again and hung up.

The "East Side Rapist" was a term that the press commonly used for the offender (as opposed to "East *Area* Rapist").

January 20th, 1978 5:20 AM

This call and the next were discussed earlier in the book, but they're included here to help provide context.

The mother of Victim #27 was awakened by a phone call.

"Hello?" she asked after picking up the phone.

"I have not struck in awhile. You will be my next victim. I'm going to fuck you in the butt. See you soon."

January 20th, 1978 5:30 AM

The female victim in Attack #18 had just gotten out of bed for work. The phone rang. At the other end of the line was a man:

"I have not struck in awhile. You will be my next victim. I'm going to fuck you in the butt. See you soon."

Then the phone went dead.

As noted above, the exact same call was received ten minutes earlier at the house of Victim #27. These attacks occurred six months apart, and the victims lived very close to each other.

Attack #29

Date: January 28th, 1978 10:30 PM to 11:30 PM
Victims: Two sisters were raped. They were 14 and 15
years old.
Location: College View Way, Carmichael

Pre-Attack Events

January 14th, 1978
The victims' mother spotted a man running from their garage. After
he had disappeared, she noticed that some shelves had been
rearranged and some tools had been stolen from the toolbox.
Unfortunately, she didn't get a good look at the burglar.

Late January 1978
During the two weeks after the burglary, the sisters received phone
calls (four in total) from a man with a "funny-sounding" voice. In
every call, the man on the phone asked if the victims' mother was
there.

The Attack
The sisters spent the day skiing at Boreal Ridge. Their parents left
around 7:00 PM to see a concert, and the girls went to bed around
10:00 PM.

A thumping noise woke up the older sister. She got up and looked
out the window, but she didn't see anything. As she turned around to
go back to bed, a voice in her room startled her.

"Get all of your money or I'll kill you." She suddenly saw a masked man in the doorway. She squinted as the light of a flashlight hit her, and she could barely make out a gun in the man's right hand.

The girl complied, getting her money out from its hiding spot on her headboard. She placed sixty dollars into his gloved hand.

"Go wake up your sister," he said. "Don't make any noise or look at me."

She walked past him and headed toward her sister's room. He followed her.

"Wake up. Get your money," she said, gently shaking her sister.

"Don't look at me. You look at me and I'll kill you. Get your money," the man behind her said.

The younger sister got up and walked toward the closet.

"Don't look at me," he repeated. "Get on the bed. On your stomachs."

They obeyed. He tied their hands behind their backs tightly with shoelaces.

"If you move I'll slit your throats and slip away in the fog." He placed a pillow over the older sister's head. "What time will your parents be home?"

"Midnight," she replied.

"Don't lie or I'll kill you and when they get home I'll kill them, too." He placed a knife against the younger sister's throat. "Midnight," she said, agreeing with her sister.

He held the knife against the back of the older sister's neck for a moment, then he left the room. He roamed the house, rummaging through the drawers, opening them and slamming them shut loudly.

Some time passed, and then the returned. He climbed onto the bed, straddled the older sister, and placed his flaccid, lubricated penis into her bound hands. He moved back and forth for awhile. The penis did not become erect. He then straddled the younger sister, placing his penis into her hands and moving back and forth. He still struggled to achieve an erection.

He got off of the bed and pulled the younger sister down onto the floor. He put a sweater over her face to blindfold her, then straddled her and began pushing into her.

She winced and cried out in pain. He told her to "shut up," and then he got off of her. He focused attention on the older sister. He pulled her underwear off, removed the pillow from her head, rolled her over, and put the pillow over her face.

He tried to enter her. "Spread your legs," he hissed. He continued trying to enter her. "Relax," he barked. He was able to penetrate her, and he stayed inside for less than a minute. He wasn't fully erect and he didn't climax. He climbed off of her and then stood next to the bed. He bound their ankles with shoelaces.

"Don't talk to each other or I'll kill you," he said. Then he left the room.

It was quiet for a moment. The girls listened intently, and they heard whimpering or sobbing. The assailant was in the other room, crying and making high-pitched noises "like a child might make." Then he came back.

"Where's your parents' money?"

"On my parents' dresser," the older sister replied. The assailant left, and he quickly came back.

He was quite agitated or excited, and he began whimpering. "It's not there." He paused. "I don't want to do this anymore." He flipped from distress to anger. "She's making me do it." He left the room, seemingly upset and angry.

The girls weren't sure when the assailant left, but their parents returned around 11:30 PM. He might've left before they arrived, but it was possible that the adults scared him off.

Immediate Aftermath

The victims were taken to Sacramento Medical Center.

The officers found that the front door had been kicked in. It was the point of entry. Stolen from the house were two photographs of the younger sister, the money he had taken from the older sister, and two dimes with small holes drilled into the top to make them into earrings (taken from the older sister's jewelry box).

Suspect Description

White male, late twenties or thirties, no more than 5'9", weighing between 150 and 160 lbs. Thin to medium build. Both of them thought that his penis was small, despite the fact that they had no experience to draw from. The assailant was never fully erect.

He had a dark-colored, full-faced mask. He wore a dark, bulky coat that went below his waist. He also had ski gloves.

His weapons included a handgun and a knife.

Context and Analysis

In some lists of official EAR/GSK attacks, this one is listed as #29 *and* #30 because two victims were assaulted. That can make it hard to discuss these cases by number and even harder cross-reference information across sources. In this book, we'll always reference this event as simply "Attack #29."

After having assaulted adults and couples for quite awhile (with rare exceptions), the EAR seemed to be returning to his old pattern. This attack recalls Attack #2 in several obvious ways. One of the things that was different about this attack from all of the others was that the assailant just flat-out kicked down the front door. This wasn't his usual method of entry, that's for sure. He must've known that it was "safe" in there for him, or at least that there wasn't going to be an angry father with a loaded gun lurking around a hallway corner.

He was back to using dramatic phrases. "Slip away in the fog" was very reminiscent of being "gone in the dark." There was more crying at this attack. "I don't want to do this anymore. She's making me do it." Was the crying in this scene genuine? Was it because he couldn't "perform"? The phrase "she's making me do it" sounds like something invented for the police to mull over.

He was only in their house for about twenty minutes, making it one of the shortest assaults on record. It's unknown if the parents coming home was what chased him away—he might have planned on staying longer.

As with most victims, there are a few possibilities at play when it comes to how the assailant originally spotted them, assuming that he didn't just come across them one day while prowling the area. The father of the girls was an insurance broker, and the mother was a teacher at Sacramento City College. The girls were both students at La Sierra High School. They had spent the day skiing at Boreal Ridge, a ski resort located off of Interstate 80, close to the north side of Lake Tahoe. Several other youths who were attacked had skiing connections, including a couple of younger victims who were part of the Tioga Ski Club (an organization that picked kids up from school to go skiing).

A composite was made by a witness who saw a suspicious person related to this attack. The actual details surrounding this sighting appear to be lost. The person they saw was a white male, early twenties, 150 or 160 lbs, with brown, shoulder-length hair. He wore a maroon or purple windbreaker and jeans. He was riding a "newspaper carrier-type bike" with large tires.

The Maggiore Murders

Date: February 2nd, 1978 9:13 PM
Victims: Brian Maggiore (21), Katie Maggiore (20)
Location: 10165 La Alegria Drive, Rancho Cordova

According to several investigators, this double-homicide is not confirmed to be the work of the East Area Rapist / Golden State Killer. The FBI, however, does currently count it as an official attack.

Background
Brian and Katie Maggiore were a young couple living in an apartment on La Verta Court in Rancho Cordova. They were from Fresno and dated since high school. Brian was an Air Force Sergeant, and after their wedding on July 19th, 1976, Brian served in Alaska, Texas, and Mississippi while his wife stayed behind in California. When Brian was transferred to Mather Air Force Base to work as an administrative specialist in the 320th Security Police Squadron, it was a dream come true for the couple because they could live in an apartment and start to build their life together. In February 1978, they were busy preparing for a transfer to Germany.

A few days before their murders, they had spent time in Fresno with their families, celebrating Katie's twentieth birthday. Katie had talked to her mother on the phone for about an hour the night of February 2nd, 1978—the date she and Brian were killed.

Pre-Attack Events

For a period of time before her murder, Katie Maggiore had apparently been stalked by someone. While working her job at a Regal Gas Station, she received phone calls from an unknown male who claimed to be a person who had raped two women at another Regal Gas Station, and he told her that she'd be his next victim.

Hang-up phone calls had been happening on La Alegria (a street in Rancho Cordova) for a little while, but only at one or two houses. The main resident receiving the phone calls fit the EAR victim profile.

There was an EAR-style break-in at a house nearby sometime after 7:00 PM on the night the Maggiores were killed. The burglary was discovered when the resident returned home at 11:00 PM.

There was a vacant house up for sale across the street. This house, too, had been entered, most likely on the night of the murders. There was a what appeared to be a fresh blood stain on the carpet on the lower level and a broken window on the upper level.

The Attack

The night of February 2nd, 1978, Brian and Katie Maggiore were taking their their miniature silver-grey poodle "Thumper" for an evening walk on La Algeria Drive, just a few blocks away from their apartment. They exchanged greetings with a police officer who had just arrived home, and they continued walking. Shortly after the police officer disappeared inside his house, for some reason the couple's dog went into a nearby backyard, and they followed him into it.

What happened next is unknown. The story picks up with a ten-year-old, from the vantage point of his second-story window, watching the Maggiores being chased into a backyard by a man with a gun. The man was shooting at them. Some of the bullets missed, and one of them went into a neighbor's house and almost hit him. Two of the bullets hit Brian Maggiore as he was crossing a patio.

Katie ran for her life, screaming loudly. The killer continued firing shots, all of them missing. He chased after her, and when she made it to a gate, he fired one or two more shots. At least one of them struck her in the head. She slumped against the gate, wedging it shut in the process, and the killer callously climbed over her and jumped over the fence.

The neighbor who lived next door had come out to see what the commotion was about. He heard a man in the bushes scrambling to his feet, and then he saw the killer running toward him. The killer stopped no more than five or ten feet away from him, and then hurriedly changed direction and continued making his way through the neighborhood quickly. He zig-zagged a bit as he went, changing direction from time to time.

After some time had passed, a neighbor living a couple of streets away noticed a man moving quickly and stealthily through some front yards. When a car drove by, he flattened himself against a tree until it had completely passed. As he neared her position, he held his jacket up against his face and told her "Guess I must be trespassing." That was the last probable sighting of the killer that night. The Maggiore's dog was found in the pool, relatively unharmed. Some money possibly dropped by the killer, as well as a sighting of a suspicious vehicle, were noted. A single pre-tied shoelace with a knot EAR was known to use was found near the scene a day or two later.

Brian and Katie Maggiore were taken to the University Medical Center in Sacramento. Brian passed away at 11:14 PM, and Katie passed away twenty minutes later.

Suspect Description

The details of the ten-year-old's observations haven't been directly released, but the second witness (the man who came face-to-face with the killer) described the him as a white male, mid twenties, 6' to 6'2" tall, thin build, with dark hair. He was wearing a brown leather coat with a large stain on the back, dark pants, and dark shoes. This witness saw the killer with a ski mask on at one point, but the ski mask apparently didn't cover all of his face. The mask appeared to be similar to the one worn in Attack #15.

One of the witnesses described a man in a waist-length brown jacket. The jacket had an orange dragon embroidered on the front-left pocket.

A young girl had seen two men walking together on La Gloria Way, a nearby street, before the shooting (anywhere from a few minutes before to an hour before). She described one of them as wearing a brown jacket (possibly leather) that was tighter at the waist, had a zippered front, had a small collar, and had a dark stain on the back. He was also wearing pointed brown boots. The second man that she saw was wearing a dark jacket (zipped in the front), slash-style pockets, dark pants, black shoes or boots, and brown leather gloves.

Context and Analysis

There are enough questions and details about this double-murder to fill up a book of their own, but obviously we won't be doing that. Let's focus on what potentially makes this an East Area Rapist / Golden State Killer case.

There are a lot of witnesses to this event, but when trying to see if this case fits within what we know about the offender we've been discussing, the geography is the *best* witness. The area of Rancho Cordova where this event happened was *very* close to Attacks #1, #3, #6, #8, and #15. If the 1973 burglary, the 1974 dog-beating incident, and the 1975 attack were him as well, it's even more remarkable because each of those were very close as well. Every one of the aforementioned incidents has an element that make it important to the series in some major way. To then have this incident round out the set makes it more than suspicious.

The burglaries and hang-up phone calls in the area make for a compelling case as well. The shoelace being found at the scene also seems like damning evidence. It would be an odd thing to find if the killing *wasn't* related, right?

There are reports and even some drawings done of the killer being in a ski mask for portions of this attack, which would be another tie to the East Area Rapist / Golden State Killer. The description of the killer given by multiple witnesses during the portions of the event where he was unmasked matched the face that Victim #15 saw, as well.

While these things certainly make it seem like the East Area Rapist was the killer that night, it should be mentioned that there's a lot of evidence related to drug and gun smuggling at Mather AFB at the time of the murders. While Brian isn't suspected of being involved in anything, his position would make him a likely person to find things out that other people wouldn't want him to know. It's been theorized by some that his murder could've been related to what was going on at his workplace. It seems like quite a sloppy place for a military hit though, doesn't it? There are a lot of holes to poke in that scenario, especially the act of luring the dog into the yard and counting on the Maggiores to pass that way.

There were some reports in the media in the early days of the homicide investigation that there were two men seen running from the area. This ended up being confusing, and it took quite some time to clear it up. A little girl *did* see two men walking and talking on nearby La Gloria Way before the murders took place, but this occurred anywhere from a few minutes to an hour before the murders. It's important to note that once all of the dust settled and the witness statements were brought together, it was determined that there was only one man seen killing the Maggiores and fleeing the scene.

Several composite sketches came out of this case. Witnesses and investigators have noticed throughout the years that a couple of them look very much like Brian, the victim. It's led to a theory that perhaps the little girl had seen Brian talking with his killer sometime before the murders took place, which adds a dimension that could take the investigation in several different ways.

The stalking that Katie Maggiore was apparently dealing with could be an important clue, and it could potentially lead back to the EAR. There's also an unconfirmed incident where the stalker was watching her at the gas station and actually accosted her. Most of the details about any of this are unknown or unconfirmed, but we were able to dig up references to other crimes committed at Regal Gas

Stations in Sacramento, most of which occurred in 1977. Whether this can help lead to the Maggiore shooter, Katie's stalker, or something else, I'm not sure. We're still working with this information.

The biggest unanswered question about these murders is the motive. Did the killer know his victims? Did they catch him doing something incriminating? The killer was not acting in self-defense— he was chasing them down and then went out of his way to murder Katie. Why hadn't any of the other witnesses on this street been shot, especially second witness who encountered him after he jumped over the fence? Was the killer out of ammunition? Was killing Brian and Katie the only thing on his mind, because they saw something incriminating or they could identify him? Was he more reluctant to kill someone in a front yard as opposed to a backyard?

So many questions, and so few answers. One of the biggest questions of all, of course, is this:

Did the East Area Rapist murder the Maggiores?

Attack #30

Date: March 18th, 1978 1:05 AM to 2:15 AM
Victims: Woman (in her twenties) and her boyfriend
Location: Meadow Avenue, Stockton

Pre-Attack Events

Late December 1977 to Early January 1978
The victims received multiple phone calls during this time period. The caller always asked for someone who didn't live at their address. The calls stopped around the second week of January.

January 1st, 1978
A prowler damaged the locks on two of the victims' doors.

Early March 1978
A neighbor on Rivara Road (a street which both intersects the victims' street and runs parallel to it) began spotting a faded VW van parked across the street from her residence in the two weeks leading up to the attack. She usually noticed it there starting at 4:00 AM. An older-model green Ford appeared in that spot a few times as well.

Early or Mid-March 1978
Three suspicious men were seen running down the street right by the victims' house. They ran down Meadow Avenue, turned north on Coral Lane, and then the witnesses lost sight of them. As with most sightings, it's unknown if this was related.

March 11th, 1978
An old faded van was seen in the Rivara Road area and also on Meadow Avenue near the victims' house. The van went by houses very slowly and the driver appeared to be studying the neighborhood. The driver was described as a white male, about twenty years old, with blonde, shoulder-length hair.

March 11th, 1978 Evening
A babysitter working on Rivara Road heard a prowler in the backyard. She investigated the sounds, but he was gone.

March 13th, 1978 11:30 PM
A young family saw a suspicious man walking near their house on Meadow Avenue. They described him as a white male, about thirty years old.

March 14th, 1978 Night
In the middle of the night, the victims heard someone kick or slam against the air conditioner in their backyard. They didn't notice any other signs of a prowler.

March 15th, 1978 10:30 PM
The ten-year-old daughter of the woman who had been seeing the faded VW van near her house on Rivara Road saw a figure at her bedroom window. She told her father about it immediately, and he checked the perimeter of the house but didn't find anything out of the ordinary.

March 15th, 1978 Night
The young family on Meadow Avenue that had seen the suspicious man heard noises in their backyard. It sounded like a prowler was moving around. They investigated but didn't find anything.

March 16th, 1978

The male victim noticed that the lock leading from the garage into the kitchen wasn't working properly. Depsite the lock being engaged, the door could be opened by turning the knob to the left.

March 16th, 1978

The phone rang at a neighbor's house, and a twenty-eight-year-old mother of two children answered it. On the other end was a man whispering "I need someone to talk to while I masturbate. Would you be interested?" She wasn't interested, so she hung up.

March 16th, 1978 Night

The daughter of another family that had seen the old, faded VW van heard someone in their backyard. The girl checked into it but didn't see anything out of the ordinary.

March 17th, 1978 9:30 PM

A neighborhood couple living on Meadow Avenue saw a flashlight shining briefly into their backyard. They heard noises out there as well.

March 17th, 1978 10:00 PM

A neighbor on Meadow Avenue heard a big thud at the side of his house. He investigated but didn't find anything wrong.

March 17th, 1978 10:30 PM

A twenty-six-year-old woman living nearby heard a "rattling noise" at the side of her house.

March 17th, 1978 Night

A neighbor living nearby spotted a suspicious man getting out of a green Ford Pinto (probably a 1972 model) parked at the curb of a nearby house. The man went to the trunk, removed a gas can, and then walked down the street with it. None of the neighbors saw him return, and they weren't sure when the car left. The man was described as a white male, late teens, 5'10", 150 lbs, clean-shaven, with blonde collar-length hair. He was wearing a white t-shirt and blue jeans.

March 17th, 1978 11:30 PM
The neighbor who had seen the flashlight in his backyard saw a suspicious man getting out of a small vehicle parked just to the east of their home. The car had a carrier-rack on the back of it. She saw the man remove something from the trunk of his car. He was described as a white male, early twenties, 5'10", 170 lbs. His hair was straight, blonde, and collar-length. He had on a light-colored nylon jacket.

March 18th, 1978 12:15 AM
A twenty-four-year-old woman living nearby awoke to find someone fiddling with her sliding glass window. She woke her husband up, but by the time she roused him, the man was gone.

March 18th, 1978 12:30 AM
A seventeen-year-old girl saw the beam of a flashlight shining into her window. She was the daughter of the family who'd seen a flashlight in their backyard and who had seen the man on the street with the car.

The Attack
The couple went out for the evening and spent time in Old Sacramento, an area of downtown themed to resemble a small town at the turn of the century. They arrived home at 1:00 AM and went to bed soon after.

A bright light shining in their eyes brought them back to consciousness. A masked intruder was standing directly over them, pointing a flashlight straight down into their eyes.

"I won't hurt you, just be quiet. All I want is your money and food so I can live a little longer. I won't hurt you, just be quiet."

A gun was in his right hand, and he waved it around. "This is a .357 Magnum you see and I'll blow your head off. Get on your stomachs."

He walked over to the man, placed the gun against his head, and cocked it. "Turn your head. Put your hands behind your back and cross them." He motioned toward the woman. "You. You, get up and don't look at me. Don't turn around. Tie him up." He threw a brown shoelace at her. "One move, one flinch, and I'll blow your fuckin' head off."

She complied. "Tighter. Tighter," he urged. He held another shoelace in front of her face. "Tie him again. Tighter, and go around again."

When she was finished, he ordered her onto her stomach. "Don't flinch or I'll blow your head off." He pushed the point of the of the gun between her shoulder blades. "Put your hands behind your back and cross them."

He tied her hands tightly, then he pulled the blankets off of both of their legs. "Cross them," he ordered. "One hand under the pillow, one hand under the mattress and you're dead." He tied the man's ankles. "Where's your money?"

"My purse is on the kitchen counter," the woman answered. "My wallet is on the coffee table in the living room," the man added.

"One squeak of the bed and you're dead." He left, and they heard him ransacking the house. Then they heard him tearing a towel into strips. He came back and put the gun to the man's neck.

"It isn't there. Where's you're wallet?"

"Maybe it's in the kitchen," the man replied.

"Oh man," the intruder whispered as he left the room. A moment later, he was back.

"Get up and get away from him," the intruder barked at the woman. "Don't look at me or I'll blow your head off. Walk and be quiet."

He pulled her to her feet and began pushing her out of the bedroom. He forced her down the hall and into the living room.

"On your stomach. Turn your head and don't look at me or I'll kill you. Cross your feet." He tied her ankles loosely. "Pull your head up." He tied a blindfold around her face. "Don't make a sound or I'll kill you."

He left, went into the kitchen, and then went back to the bedroom. He placed a dish and a bowl on the man's back. "If I hear these move, I'm going to kill your girlfriend." He placed the gun to the man's head again and cocked the weapon.

He returned to the living room. The woman was upset and crying.

"Do you like to fuck?" he asked her.

He sat on her back with his full weight and placed his entire genitals into her hands and told her to "make it good." He made her touch him for a few moments, and then he rubbed his lubricated penis up and down her back.

He turned her over and began raping her. As he did, she felt a shoulder holster hit her knee. She was still crying.

"Shut up," he said. "This is how me fuck."

He raped her for a few more moments, then pulled out without climaxing. Throughout the ordeal, the victim felt that he hadn't achieved a full erection at any point. He picked up her foot and began rubbing it all over his genitals.

He then turned her over, slathered suntan lotion between her legs and began sodomizing her. While he did this, he achieved a full erection.

She felt him pull out, and he got up and went to the kitchen. He opened the refrigerator and moved some things around, then he returned and put a plate and a bowl on her back. "One click, one small noise, and he's dead," he told her.

He went out onto the patio. She heard him walking around, and then she heard him begin to cry and sob. He went into the garage and started hyperventilating and breathing loudly. While he was in the garage, she thought she heard someone else walking around on the patio. Then he left.

Immediate Aftermath

March 18th, 1978 Early morning

Anywhere from between a few minutes to about an hour after the assailant possibly left, the neighbors who had seen a flashlight shining in their backyard heard someone running down Meadow Avenue. Shortly after that, they heard a car leaving. They looked out the window but didn't see anything. The car had loud mufflers and was possibly a VW.

The method of entry used by the assailant was an unlocked door leading from the garage to the kitchen.

Two empty beer cans were found in their yard. Thirteen dollars were stolen from the woman's purse, along with her driver's license, $150 in coins that had been kept in two jars, and rings, earrings, and a watch. Also stolen was an old high school photo of the victim. The police discovered that the assailant had also made a knot in a nylon stocking and poked a hole through the crotch, just like at the other Stockton attack.

Suspect Description

The female victim described him as a white male, mid-twenties, 5'10", 160 lbs, with a small, round potbelly. The male victim felt he was maybe 6'1" and slim. His penis was described as small, perhaps three inches long.

He wore a full-faced ski mask, a black cotton button-up shirt, and black leather gloves that had a fur lining. He wore a shoulder holster on the right side of his chest.

The assailant spoke quickly and in a whisper. Both victims thought that he had an accent, perhaps a "refined Mexican accent."

Context and Analysis

The assailant returned to Stockton and committed his final known attack in the area. It's theorized that if he had in fact killed the Maggiores, a trip to Stockton might've sounded like a good idea to him while things settled down up in Sacramento. After this attack he returned to Sacramento one last time for his final attack there (aside from a one-off visit in 1979), and then he began moving around the state.

It did seem that he had his eye on these victims for awhile. Plenty of stalking and odd activity throughout March, which might indicate that the offender was living in the area at this time. It's even possible that he was commuting to Sacramento from Stockton ever since the first Stockton attack (#23). Many of the incidents between the two Stockton assaults seemed to have minimal stalking or some other kind of a different flavor to them, and they seemed a bit more opportunistic and clumsy.

This attack played out like so many of the other attacks on couples, but as usual, there were several differences. Whether these are significant or not is hard to say, but they do add a few brush strokes to the portrait of an emerging killer.

The first difference was that the assailant wasn't standing in the doorway or standing a few feet away (or even at the foot of the bed) when he woke them up. He was standing *right over* them. "All I want is your money and food so I can live a little longer," is an odd statement, somewhat in the same category as some of the dramatic phrases that he'd been known to say previously. He called the man her "boyfriend" instead of her "husband," which was basically accurate (the relationship was more of a common-law husband and wife). Was it the presence of kids in the house, or the lack thereof, that determined whether he said "boyfriend" or "husband"? Or did he really know?

The assailant tied a nylon stocking and poked a hole through the crotch again, just as he had done at the other Stockton attack. Strangely, he didn't do it at any of the other attacks in the entire multi-year case history. Is there some kind of symbolism to this, or was this something deviant that he perhaps did as a child? Like the chewed gum that supposedly was *only* found in Orangevale attacks, this was another oddity that happened only in a certain geographical area that was hit in a non-consecutive order. Out of sixty or so attacks, why would these these anomalies be tied to certain geography? Or was that just coincidence? Is there perhaps some weird overlapping memory/reporting stuff that's going on, and it only happened one time but it appeared twice in the records?

More sobbing by the assailant, and then the hyperventilating that usually seemed to follow it. By now the pattern is emerging—it happened pretty consistently after raping or attempting to rape the victim. As we discussed earlier, in some of the attacks the sobbing seems to serve a purpose. In others, like this one, it seems to serve no purpose at all—which makes these particular instances appear more genuine.

"Shut up. This is how me fuck." That's got to be the *strangest* thing he said in any of the attacks, especially for an assailant who was sometimes described as intelligent-sounding and articulate. Perhaps it was some of his immaturity showing through. We're always on the lookout for instances where the assailant might show a sense of humor or some irony, sarcasm, playfulness, or basically *any* part of his real personality or any kind of peek beneath the mask. This might show a bit of that. Other examples might be the wearing of the stocking cap in Attack #2 and the occasional accosting of motorists (which really shows a mean streak that could've been evident in everyday life—perhaps the offender got pleasure out of just being plain old mean and scary). It's still a strange quote, though. Was he acting like he had developmental problems? Did he say that to anger the victim or get a rise out of her?

There were a few other oddities. Instead of straddling over the victim and kind of hovering like he usually did, he put his full weight on her. He put his entire genitals in her hands instead of just his penis. After raping her, he rubbed her foot all over his genitals. It's odd, almost like fleeting evidence of a foot fetish. If you'll remember, in Attack #16 he placed high-heeled shoes on the victim. If he had a foot fetish we'd probably have seen more of this type of behavior, but you never know. Just another couple of strange things that didn't happen very often.

The two sightings of a strange man with a small vehicle getting something out of the trunk were probably sightings of the same event, or at least the same man. The timing and location make it possible that this was the assailant. We also have more weird, indirect evidence of an accomplice. The three men running down the street could be nothing, but it's still notable. And then we possibly have someone walking around on the patio while the assailant was in the garage? Perhaps he brought a dog with him (there's some evidence that he had a dog with him at one or two scenes in Southern California). Or perhaps it was a trick of the acoustics? Maybe there really *was* someone out there. It's just more things that are hard to rationalize, but also hard to write off.

One final note. The time frame of the phone calls that the victims received in December and January (where the caller would ask by name for a person who didn't live at the residence) coincided with the timing of the phone call that Victim #1 received on January 2nd, 1978. She too got a call from someone asking for someone who didn't live there, too. Later that night she got a call from the East Area Rapist.

Attack #31

Date: April 14th, 1978 9:50 PM to 10:10 PM
Victim: 15-year-old girl
Location: Casilada Way, South Sacramento

Pre-Attack Events

Mid-February 1978
Hang-up phone calls started at the victim's residence. The victim worked as a babysitter for several evenings every month, but the calls only occurred at her home—not anywhere that she babysat.

Late March through Early April 1978
A suspicious vehicle was seen a few times in the area of the attack. It was described as a 1960 Cadillac, black vinyl over blue, ragged top, with no body damage.

April 1st or 2nd, 1978
The victim's house received a phone call. Her sister answered, and a male voice said "I've fucked your sister."

Early April 1978
In the two weeks leading up to the assault, a neighbor who lived near the scene of the attack noticed several times that her side gate had been left open by a prowler.

April 11th, 1978
The woman who lived in the house where the victim would be attacked was watching television with her fourteen-year-old daughter. They heard a sudden noise at the back door, and then the sound of someone on the patio. The women were too scared to investigate the sounds. The husband was away, and the two younger girls that lived at the house were asleep.

April 12th, 1978
The phone rang at the victim's house. The male voice on the other end said "Let me sell you out."

April 13th, 1978 11:00 PM
A neighbor on Rio Lane heard scratching sounds at a side window. The noises stopped when the dog began to bark. Rio Lane was a street located a couple blocks northeast of the attack site, but it ran parallel to Casilada Way and up to the same bike trail.

April 14th, 1978 9:15 PM
The 1960 Cadillac that had been seen in the area was seen again, this time pulling into the driveway of the attack site (and only thirty minutes before the attack would happen, too). When a neighbor drove by, the Cadillac pulled out and left.

April 14th, 1978 9:30 PM
A young housewife living on Casilada Way heard her dog barking in the backyard. Her husband wasn't home, so she didn't investigate.

April 14th, 1978 9:35 PM
A neighbor (near the house where the victim was babysitting) heard his dog barking at something in the backyard.

The Attack

The victim was asked to babysit for the evening. She'd babysat for the family before, so arrangements were made quickly for her to watch the couple's eight-year-old daughter. The child's parents were going out to dinner, and their other children were staying with friends.

The victim arrived around 9:00 PM. She put the girl to bed around 9:30 PM and then went to the living room to watch a movie.

Shortly after the babysitter had left the room, the little girl saw two flashes of light on her bedroom wall. Ten minutes later, she heard two loud noises at the back door, and then a man's voice. It was much higher in pitch than her father's. She hid quietly in her bedroom.

The second loud noise had been the back door crashing open. An intruder had kicked through the dead-bolted door. The babysitter turned to see a masked man with a gun running toward her.

"Don't move or I'll kill you. Don't talk or say anything. Lie on the floor on your stomach and put your hands behind your back."

The girl tried to think of a way to keep her eight-year-old charge safe. "There's a little girl in the other room sleeping and the dog's barking. Can I get him?"

"No." The intruder grabbed her arms, pulled them back, and tied her wrists tightly. "Don't move or I'll stab you with my ice pick."

"What are you doing? What do you want? Are you going to hurt me?"

"I'm not going to hurt you. I'm just going to take food and money and then I'll leave. Just don't talk or move."

With the victim now secured, he began rummaging through the kitchen. After awhile he came back and pulled her up to her feet. He took a blanket from the couch and tied it around her face to blindfold her. He pushed her into another room.

"Lay on your stomach," he said. She did, and then she felt him tying her feet together. The intruder then began rummaging through the rest of the house. He found her purse, and he started going through it. Then he returned.

"Don't move. Be quiet." He pressed his gun against her head and then he rolled her over onto her back. He untied her ankles and unzipped her pants. She cried out for him to stop.

"Be quiet or I'll kill you," he said. He pulled her pants off. "Keep quiet." He lifted her shirt up. "Relax or I'll kill you."

He spread her legs apart. "I've wanted to rape you for a long time." And then he said her name.

As he attempted to enter her, the phone rang. He waited, and they listened to it ring ten times. Unbeknownst to the girl and the rapist, the couple she was babysitting for was on the other end of the phone. After several rings and no answer, the couple tried again. With still no answer, they became concerned and called the girl's parents.

Meanwhile, the assailant had left the room, and moments later, he had returned. He rubbed lotion between her legs, then removed her socks. "Relax, don't scream or yell or I'll kill you." He was about to try again to rape her when the phone rang a third time.

He pulled her to her feet and started pushing her toward the phone. She stumbled because of the blindfold, and as they walked to the phone, he made her hold onto his penis.

"Say hello," he ordered, holding the phone up to her mouth. She mumbled "hello" and then he hung up the phone.

That time, the girl's parents were on the other end of the phone. The strange way in which she'd answered the phone and then the line cutting off immediately made them very concerned. They got into their car and drove over to the residence on Casilada Way as quickly as they could.

After hanging up the phone, the assailant turned her around, repositioned his penis in her hands, and told her to "touch it."

The phone rang again (it was the mother of the child the girl was babysitting for). The assailant ignored it and led the victim outside to the patio, pushed her down, and again tried to rape her.

As he did, there was the sound of a car pulling the driveway. "Who's there?" a man shouted. It was the victim's father. She cried out for him.

He rushed to his daughter's aid. By the time he got to her, the assailant had completely disappeared. The girl had no idea which direction the offender had gone off in because he'd run away silently, and the blindfold had prevented her from seeing him leave.

Immediate Aftermath

<u>April 14th, 1978 10:15 PM</u>
A woman had been fishing with her husband and nephew at the "Minnow Hole," a fishing spot on the Sacramento River. They were done for the day, and the woman was on her way back to the car. She was startled by a man running by her on the levee. "Did you catch any fish?" he asked. "No, I didn't get any," she replied. "Oh, my wife is going to be mad," he said, and he continued running in the direction of the apartments on Riverside Blvd. She described him to police as a white male, mid-twenties, 5'8", medium build, with collar-length brown hair and a mustache. He was wearing a light-colored shirt (possibly a t-shirt). He wasn't dressed for jogging, and he was very out of breath.

The victim was taken to Sacramento Medical Center. Luckily, there had been no penetration and no sperm was found during the rape examination.

Suspect Description
White male, maybe in his twenties or early thirties, not much taller than 5'6". His penis was "not very large" and was not fully erect.

He had on a mask, a blue plaid flannel shirt, a dark blue windbreaker, and gloves.

He wielded an ice pick in his right hand.

His voice was deep and quiet and a bit nervous-sounding. He didn't appear to disguise his voice at all and he didn't talk through clenched teeth.

Context and Analysis

The night before the attack happened, a neighbor heard scratching sounds at a side window that stopped when the family dog began to bark. Incidents like this, and some scratch marks found on windows on Attacks #37 and #38, have led to a theory that the EAR would sometimes scratch on screens to see if residents (or a dog) would respond to the noise. There's not nearly as much evidence that he did this as people seem to believe, but it's a popular theory because it makes sense. There's more evidence that he'd simply just start prying at a residence he wanted to get into and then leave if a dog barked. But this is why police officers often tell people that a family dog can be a good deterrent for burglars and robbers. Obviously it's not foolproof, because the EAR was still able to hit houses that had dogs, but we've detailed many instances throughout the book where dogs were alerted to a prowler's presence when the humans were unaware (Attack #19 in particular comes to mind), so it's still good advice.

This victim was clearly being stalked, at least by phone, and it appears that the area was being stalked by the EAR as well. What's odd is that the house where she babysat had a prowler, and somehow the EAR knew that the girl he was *already* stalking was in that house later on (or else he wouldn't have attacked it)... so how did that happen? It would be easy to write this off as him prowling the area and then attacking opportunistically, but it seems he'd stalked her in advance (by phone, at least). Perhaps it *was* an opportunistic attack, and the phone calls only gain relevance because she *was* eventually attacked. It's worth thinking about the logistics of how he came to attack her at that particular residence that night, and it's worth noting that this is one of the earliest attack times (occurring well before midnight). And for some reason, in Sacramento he'd begun moving away from attacking couples and reverting back to attacks that resembled his first assaults. He forced his way through a door again, just like in Attack #29. And the phone call to the sister was weird... somehow he knew that the victim's sister answered the phone and not some other relative or the victim herself. It's a bit uncanny, really.

The employment of the victim's parents share some common themes with other victims. Her father worked for the State of California Department of Water Resources (interestingly, the other South Sacramento victim had very similar employment—this could definitely be significant!), and her mother taught at Sacramento City College (just like the mother in Attack #29—again, possibility significant). The victim had been to see her doctor at Kaiser a couple weeks before the attack and she'd had dental or orthodontic work done five days before the attack. She often went skiing with the Tioga Ski Club, an organization that picked her up from school (skiing was *also* a tie in Attack #29—the parallels start to add up after awhile). There are plenty of connections here to work with for the motivated sleuth.

The "Minnow Hole" sighting is one of the most interesting sightings in the entire history of the case. "Oh, my wife is going to be mad," he said, a statement that could be taken a few different ways. Was this the East Area Rapist? If so, then yeah, your wife is going to be mad. The exact location of where this sighting occurred has been lost in the mists of time, but the general consensus is that it's about half a mile from the Riverside Blvd on-ramp to Interstate 5, which would mean that the assailant left the attack house and ended up southwest of it near the river, and then he doubled back a bit and traveled along the river going east. His approximate location when he was sighted would've been somewhere to the southeast of the place called "Chicory Bend," possibly near Seamas Avenue. This is only a logical guess of course... the witnesses have passed away and it's impossible to piece it together for sure.

You'll note that we placed this attack on Casilada Way. Apparently even some members of Law Enforcement are confused about where the attack actually occurred (whether the victim lived on Piedmont Drive and was attacked on Casilada Way, or vice-versa). The reason for this is that one of the original reports seems to have gotten it backwards. We were able to confirm through other reports, old records, and phone books that the victim was indeed attacked on Casilada Way, and she lived on Piedmont Drive.

The newspapers at the time mention an April 6th attack in Rancho Cordova, but it was determined that the assailant there was a copycat and that the crime was unrelated.

This was the second attack in the southern part of Sacramento, and this would be the final attack attributable to the East Area Rapist in the Sacramento area for the rest of 1978. After this attack, the assailant would move his rampage to Modesto, Davis, and then to several different towns in and near Contra Costa County. Eventually he moved to Southern California, where the crime spree took a deadly turn.

Could the close call that the assailant had with the victim's father in this attack be part of the reason that he finally left town? And not only did he leave town, but he didn't attack at all for nearly two months. He'd been thwarted and he'd been sighted, and not only that, but good-quality composites of the Maggiore killer were starting to appear in the newspaper. If he had anything to do with that double-homicide, Sacramento was not a good place for him to be. As the next section will show, apparently he began prowling his new territory (Modesto and Davis) right after this failed attack.

Attack #32

Date: June 5th, 1978 3:00 AM to 3:45 AM
Victims: Wife (27 years old) and husband (24 years old).
The couple's young child was asleep in another room.
Location: Fuchsia Lane, Modesto

Pre-Attack Events

April 1978 through Early/Mid-May 1978
During this time period, the couple received a lot of hang-up phone calls. Toward the middle of May, the phone calls became obscene. The final call was received in mid-May, and the caller said "I want to cum on your lap." This was about three weeks before the attack occurred.

The Attack
A tapping sound at the doorway woke the couple up. A masked intruder blinded them with a flashlight.

"Wake up, motherfuckers. Get on your stomachs and put your hands behind your backs. I've got a .357 Magnum and if you flinch, I'll blow your fuckin' brains out."

They complied. He threw a shoelace at the woman and it landed near her face. "Tie him up. Tie him tight."

She obeyed.

"Get on your stomach," he commanded. She did, and then her arms were pulled back behind her and her wrists tied tightly. He pushed her ankles together and tied her feet, then he went and retied the man. He placed the gun against the man's head and cocked it.

"Don't flinch. All I want is money and food to put in my van and then I'll leave." They heard him leave the room, and then they heard him rummaging through the house. He came back.

"One move and there's going to be two dead people."

He walked over to the woman and put a knife to her body. "Get off the bed." He used the knife to cut the shoelace that bound her ankles, then he went around to the husband and placed the gun against his head. "If you make a move, I'm going to blow up your fuckin' kid." He was referring to the couple's young child, who was asleep elsewhere in the house.

He led the woman to another room, then disappeared into the kitchen for a moment. He went back to the husband, placed dishes on his back, and threatened him again. At the end of his threat, he leaned in close and said "I'm going to rape your wife." Then he made his way toward the living room, where the wife was bound.

And... at this point, we don't have any other details on what occurred during the attack, other than some information on Law Enforcement from Sacramento going over what was said and done during the attack and concluding that it was definitely the East Area Rapist. The rapist did stutter at times, and at one point he paced back and forth very intently and it seemed that he was sobbing. The couple mentioned hearing "a hammer" or "a pistol" being cocked and released.

After the sexual assault, the assailant demanded money and stole $1,500.

Immediate Aftermath

June 5th, 1978 3:50 AM
A neighbor living very close by heard a vehicle. It was the loud exhaust of a sports car roaring to life somewhere on Fuchsia Lane. Unfortunately, She was in a part of the house that didn't have a window to the street so she didn't see the car. This was at exactly the time that the assailant left the victims' residence.

After examining the scene, the police determined that the assailant had entered through an unlocked sliding glass door.

Suspect Description

White, mid-twenties, 6', with a medium build. He seemed fit and didn't have fat around his midsection.

He wore a ski mask, and his clothing was dark and appeared to be a one-piece jumpsuit (or something similar). The gloves were made of rough leather or possibly even plastic.

The assailant spoke in a whisper, and he stuttered when he seemed angry. Based on his vocabulary and grammar, the victims felt that his education level was low. The assailant spoke with a Spanish accent, but both victims felt that it was fake. He did not speak through clenched teeth and they felt that he did not go through great effort to disguise the sound of his voice. There were times during the attack when he breathed very heavily and sounded like he was hyperventilating and crying.

The assailant smelled like beer.

Context and Analysis

There isn't as much information available to us on the Modesto and Davis attacks as there is for other jurisdictions, but we've pulled together what we can. Aside from the murder series that occurred in Southern California, this is the string of attacks that interests us the most. Modesto is roughly seventy-five miles south of Sacramento. Davis (the next place he hits, and then he begins alternating between the two) is about fifteen miles west of Sacramento, and they're about ninety miles apart from each other (with the most logical route between the two actually using Sacramento as a hub to change freeways). The most direct route to Modesto is to take State Route 99 down from Sacramento. It's possible to take Interstate 5, but there's a switch over to 99 in Stockton. Stockton is about thirty miles north of Modesto, which makes it a bit clearer how he ended up in Modesto to begin with—he simply kept moving outward. To continue in that direction would take you to Visalia, which is a place that we've talked about as potentially having a connection to the assailant. To keep going past that would take you to Bakersfield, which is a place that he mentioned a couple of times. Past that is the area that the murders began taking place about a year and a half after this attack. Before he would do that though, he'd turn west and attack in Contra Costa County.

But the EAR *didn't* keep going, at least not yet. For some reason he stopped in Modesto, an area which seemed to contain many tactical advantages for a criminal of this type. In roughly a period of one month, he covered an incredible amount of ground and committed five assaults, with a possibly two more that have never been fully brought into the fold. He seemed to flip back and forth between Modesto and Davis, a pattern he was comfortable with on a much smaller scale even in the beginning, when he was going back and forth between Rancho Cordova and Carmichael. The assaults played out like this:

Attack #32: 6/5/78 Modesto
Attack #33: 6/7/78 Davis
Attack #34: 6/23/78 Modesto
Attack #35: 6/24/78 Davis
Attack #36: 7/6/78 Davis

Another possible attack occurred in Modesto on 6/27/78, which would fill in the gap where there "should" be a Modesto attack if the pattern were followed to the letter. We're not clear on the date of the other possibly-related Modesto attack, so until we can confirm it, we're excluding it.

The assailant covered so much ground in this time period, it's quite incredible to think that he was able to stalk, plan, and coordinate all of these attacks. As we look at them closer, we'll try to figure out how he did it, but consider yourself warned—there are more questions than answers.

It seems the hang-up phone calls started right around the time of the last Sacramento attack, possibly even a little bit before that attack even occurred. This gives us a full timeline that has no breaks in it, and he remarkably was able to drop off in Sacramento and pick right up in Modesto.

"Don't flinch" is something he said a couple times in this attack, and that's a fairly new phrase for him. He said it in Attack #10 and in Attack #30, but he wasn't nearly as fond of it in those assaults as he was in this one. Another new thing that he did was that he actually *told* the husband he was going to rape the wife. With new territory came some new courage, apparently.

The assailant smelled like beer, which was a pretty rare description considering the amount of scenes where beer cans were found. He brought his own shoelaces to the attack. Again there was crying and sobbing, and actually this Modesto/Davis series of attacks has a higher percentage of crying and tears than any other series in the East Area Rapist canon. Whatever was making him do this was in full swing during this series. He also stuttered in this attack, something that hadn't happened in awhile, but it's a part of the case that keeps coming back. He didn't disguise his voice very much, and he hadn't worked very hard to disguise it in the previous attack, either.

A few other interesting points to cover: the house was located in the northeastern part of Modesto, and the victims owned and operated their own dry cleaning business.

The assailant stole $1,500, which was a pretty sizable amount in the late 1970s. He was in a new jurisdiction, so it's possible he was moving to the area and needed cash. Or, did he move to Davis instead? Or neither? Had he given up working for a little while and decided to spend all of his time on his attacks? With the schedule he kept over the summer of 1978, it would be hard to imagine anyone holding down a regular job. Was the end of April and May spent gathering all of the intel, and then June and early July spent executing the plans?

A short chart showing the times and days of the week that he hit during this series reveals a few interesting things :

#32 Modesto: 3:00 AM (Sunday Night / Monday Morning)
#33 Davis: 3:55 AM (Tuesday Night / Wednesday Morning)
#34 Modesto: 1:30 AM (Thursday Night / Friday Morning)
#35 Davis: 3:15 AM (Friday Night / Saturday Morning)
Possible Modesto Attack: Tuesday (time unknown)
#36 Davis: 2:50 AM (Wednesday Night / Thursday Morning)

He basically hit on every possible day of the week. Looking at the data like this makes it almost look intentional, as if he were completely obfuscating anything that might be gleaned by trying to analyze his work schedule (or lack thereof). Looking deeper at the times and dates of possible sightings might paint a more accurate or vivid picture, because those are the times where the assailant didn't expect to be seen. Those are also the times, however, that we can't be sure if we're dealing with the actual perpetrator or with just a random, suspicious individual.

Being in a new territory brings a new set of circumstances and new clues to analyze. He'd continue to attack couples for a lot of them, but as we've seen in the 1978 attacks we've explored so far, he was starting to find new types of victims in new types of situations. The next attack, the first EAR assault in Davis, is an example of that. But first we'll take a brief stop in Woodland, California.

Woodland, California

Before we move to Davis, we need to look at a couple things in a town ten miles north of there called Woodland. There were no confirmed East Area Rapist assaults in this town, but there was some activity that might've been related.

March 1978
A suspicious van stopped in front of a young man working in his yard. The driver stepped out of the vehicle and offered to fix a dent in the young man's VW. He declined, so the driver got in his van and left. The vehicle was very distinctive, and was described as a cream-colored van with portholes on the side. The driver was described as a white male, 5'10", slender build, with dark hair (worn combed back), sideburns, and no facial hair. He was wearing a white t-shirt, blue jeans, and cowboy boots. He spoke with an "Okie" accent.

March 1978 through Mid-May 1978
The van was sighted three more times by witnesses living in the same household, with the last sighting occurring in mid-May.

Early June 1978 11:30 PM to 11:45 PM
A woman (living in the same household as the witnesses who had seen the strange van) observed something incredibly suspicious and possibly quite significant. In the middle of the night, she saw a man in front of her house wearing dark clothing and a ski mask. He was simply walking by the house, and after he'd passed her house he

crossed the street and vanished behind a neighbor's residence. The neighbor who lived there was a young woman who lived by herself. Unfortunately, this witness didn't call the police or notify the resident about what she'd seen. Later that night, the commotion of several police cars pulling up to the house across the street woke up the witness. The woman looked out the window and saw that all of the lights were on in the house where she'd seen the prowler, and she saw police going in and out of it.

About an hour after the police left (about 2:00 AM at this point), she heard a vehicle drive up the street and stop. She heard a door slam, and then the sound of the vehicle pulling away. The sequence of noises gave the impression that someone was being picked up. She looked out her window just in time to see an orange-colored van with porthole windows on the side. Flames or some kind of pattern was painted on it. The van was exactly like the one the other witnesses living in the household had described, though the paint was different. She didn't see the driver or any occupants of the vehicle.

She described the masked man as about 5'8" to 5'10" and 150 to 165 lbs. His ski mask was dark with white stripes above the eyes. He seemed to be wearing an all-black jumpsuit. He had on a belt with a large, silver, oval-shaped western-style belt buckle.

Context and Analysis

The activity in this area began during the era of the final Stockton attack and the final Sacramento attack of 1978. There were no EAR attacks for almost six weeks after the assault in mid-April, and since the assailant hit Modesto and Davis so rapid-fire in June, it's likely that he spent most of May doing reconnaissance in new areas. Obviously he chose Modesto and Davis for his next assaults, but it's very possible that he was scouting Woodland as well. Woodland was a little different socioeconomically and architecturally from the other areas he'd hit up to this point in the crimes, so it's possible that he didn't take to the area as well as he did the other two towns and that's why it was spared—except for the one interesting and possible exception detailed above.

We've been unable to find a police case or report that might give us details on what happened across the street from the witness. It would be very interesting to find out if this was an EAR-style assault, wouldn't it? The statute of limitations on whatever happened there has no doubt been up for a very long time, however.

The other sightings in Woodland are interesting, as well. EAR had shown streaks of a Western persona before, based on the belt buckle seen in the first Stockton attack, the occasional Western phrases ("give me a good drop," "gone in the night"), the various holsters and guns, and even the various accents that were reported. It could explain why the suspect was usually described as speaking so slowly and deliberately.

In the Davis assault detailed in the next section, notice that the description of a suspicious man seen in the Davis attack area matches the suspicious man seen in Woodland very closely. Given the geographical and chronological proximity, and the presence of a ski-masked prowler in Woodland, this should be explored further to see what can be developed.

Attack #33

Date: June 7th, 1978 3:55 AM to 4:20 AM
Victims: 21-year-old woman
Location: Wake Forest Drive, Davis

Pre-Attack Events

May 30th, 1978

A janitor at the victim's apartment complex noticed a strange man observing the victim from a distance. The man was positioned on a third-floor balcony, and the victim was in the swimming pool below. After watching her intently for a few minutes, the man left and reappeared down at the pool. The janitor felt sure that he was trying to study the victim without being noticed.

June 5th, 1978

While checking her mailbox in the community area at her apartment complex, the victim seemingly saw the same man that the janitor had seen. When she walked from the mailbox area to her apartment, he seemed to follow her, but he kept quite a distance away and walked in a different direction at one point (while still keeping her within his sight). This man was described as a white male, 6', light-complected, with a mustache and dark hair worn brushed back. He was wearing a white t-shirt and blue jeans. The janitor's description and the victim's description matched exactly.

The Attack

The victim was asleep. She was awakened by a hand clamped over her mouth.

"Cooperate and you won't be hurt. All I want is food and money, or I'll kill you." She felt something sharp dig into her back. "Put your hands behind your back or I'll blow your brains out."

Initially, she thought it was her boyfriend playing a trick on her, especially since they'd just had a discussion about violent crime and how to be prepared for it. She playfully put one of her hands behind her.

The intruder dug deeper into her back with his weapon and violently jerked her other arm back. He tied her quickly with shoelaces. She complained that it was too tight, and suddenly realized that she was not being taught a lesson by a misguided boyfriend. The threat was real.

The assailant trained one of his weapons, a flat-head screwdriver, over her left eye. "All I want is food and money," he snarled.

She began pushing against him and physically resisting. The assailant became angry and pulled her hair so violently that her head lifted off the pillow. "Don't move or you won't see any of your friends ever again," he said.

She started to scream, but the assailant shoved a pair of panties that he had found on the floor into her mouth to gag her.

He pulled the covers off of her legs and pulled her underwear off. She kicked at him as hard as she could and connected solidly.

He became more violent and continued trying to bind her. He was able to tie her feet together and reinforce the ligatures with the belt from her bathrobe and with some towels. Now that his victim secured, he turned his back to her and began to rummage through drawers. While he did, she struggled against her bindings and tried to work the gag out of her mouth. She also took time to study the assailant's appearance. She was just barely able to free her feet when he turned around.

As he approached, she continued to struggle against him. He retaliated violently by jumping on top of her and pummeling her in the face repeatedly. Then he grabbed her by the hair and pulled her head up with his right hand and punched her again with his left. The gag fell out and she started to scream. He punched her with his left hand three more times, then smashed her face back down onto the bed. She still fought, and he fought back, cutting her several times with a nail file. She raised her head and attempted to scream, and as she did, he slammed her so hard that it broke her nose.

"Don't move, don't scream," he panted, out of breath. "Or you won't see any of your friends again. And I mean *any* of your friends."

He began rummaging through her residence. The victim lay still, her face throbbing in pain and the breath knocked out of her. He went to the kitchen, and then he returned to the bedroom. He went over to her and jabbed the nail file into her face near her left eye so hard that it punctured her. She screamed as blood started to flow quickly. He brought the nail file down to her neck.

"I told you to be quiet or I'll kill you!" he growled.

He straddled her and placed his penis in her numb, bound hands. It wasn't erect. "Play with my dick," he said.

She continued to try to resist. He got off of her, and she heard him applying lotion to himself. He climbed on top of her again and attempted to rape her. She squirmed and tried to stop his efforts, but his semi-erect penis was still able to penetrate her.

A moment later, he got up and then left the bedroom. He didn't return.

Immediate Aftermath

The victim was so injured that she had to be taken to the hospital. She was treated for contusions, a broken nose, a black eye, and a concussion.

Suspect Description

White male, 6', 175 lbs. He had light brown hair. He had taken off his gloves and the victim felt his bare thumbs, which were heavily calloused. She described his fingernails as very short. His penis was described as small, and it was never fully erect.

313

His mask was a dark blue or black nylon stocking that went down past his neck. He supplemented it with a knit ski cap. The shirt he wore was a dark blue t-shirt, and he wore it inside-out. She didn't mention any tattoos on his arms. His pants were a thick, light-brown corduroy with a zipper. He wore tennis shoes.

He was armed with a nail file and a flat-head screwdriver.

His voice was a harsh whisper through clenched teeth.

Context and Analysis

Something had brought the East Area Rapist to Davis, a fairly small college town located fifteen miles west of Sacramento along Interstate 80. This attack wasn't a typical EAR assault as far as location went, since he'd never been tied to any activity in Davis before. Between that, the attack happening in an apartment, the victim being a student at UC Davis, and the odd choice of weaponry, the police had a difficult time connecting this to the East Area Rapist at first.

The offender had never been met with much resistance from his victims. A few of them had fought back, but not to this extent. Victim #13 (attacked in 1977) had fought him had been beaten badly. This victim (attacked in 1978) was beaten even *more* severely. Victims in 1979, starting with Robert Offerman and Debra Manning, were apparently *killed* when they retaliated. For those who have difficulty relating to the horror of the rapes, these types of beatings hopefully help bring into focus what a sadistic and horrifying animal this offender truly was.

The Woodland sightings, which precede this attack, are interesting because the descriptions of the suspicious man seen in the apartment complex and at in the Woodland sightings come out to a close match. Added together with the sighting of the runner after Attack #31 (who had a mustache, just like the suspicious man tied to this attack), we may (or may not) have a decent idea of what the assailant looked like at the time.

It's not often that we get a description of the perpetrator's hands, but this observant young woman added the important detail of the callouses on his thumbs. In other attacks his hands were described as quite smooth, which taken together could be an indication of seasonal work or a specific kind of labor that leaves someone with calloused thumbs but doesn't affect the rest of the hand. Perhaps some of those victims mistook very smooth surgical gloves for his bare hands at some of the attacks, so it's hard to draw any definitive conclusions.

The victim was a textiles major and was able to explain that the offender's pants were a thick, light-brown corduroy (but not brushed corduroy), and that they had a zipper (not always common for those types of pants). An investigator on the case noted that these details about the pants were significant, and it appeared that the pants were rare among the general population.

The victim lived alone in her apartment. At the time of the attack, she was getting ready to accept a job in Oakland and she was hunting for a house or apartment in Berkeley.

Attack #34

Date: June 23rd, 1978 1:30 AM to 3:00 AM
Victims: Wife and husband
Location: Grandprix Drive, Modesto

June 22nd, 1978 Evening
A cab driver was parked at the United Airlines terminal in Modesto.
A man approached his cab. The driver didn't see this man get off of a
flight, but a flight had just landed.

The cab driver asked him where he wanted to go, and the man
said "Sylvan and Coffee." The cab driver told him to get in. The man
said that he needed to get his luggage, and then the man entered the
cab. They headed out.

As they were headed northbound on Coffee (and nearing the
Sylvan intersection), the man told the driver to "turn west on Sylvan."
Right after turning, the man said "This is fine, stop here," or "Good
enough." The exact spot where they stopped was the northeastern
corner of Sylvan and Coffee. The man exited the cab, grabbed his
luggage, and walked northbound through a vacant field. This was in
the the direction of the victims' house, which was located roughly
half a mile away. The only other buildings nearby were homes under
construction.

The man was described as a white male, early thirties, 5'9", with a
medium build. His hair was light brown, and he was dressed in dark
clothing. Unfortunately, no composite was made.

The Attack

The husband was the first to wake up. The dog was was barking and growling at something in the doorway.

"Shut the fucking dog up!" a strange voice whispered. A light flashed across the husband's face. He squinted and was able to see a masked man standing in the doorway pointing a gun at him.

"Shut the fucking dog up!" the man repeated. "One flinch and I'll blow your fucking head off."

The wife continued to sleep through the commotion, up until the husband reached over her and dragged the dog over her body. "What's the matter?" the wife asked.

"Shut up," the intruder hissed at her. "Roll over." She was fully awake now. The couple complied.

"Tie his hands behind his back. Don't flinch and don't try anything."

He tossed shoelaces at her. She sat up and began tying her husbands wrists. "Tighter, tighter," the man ordered.

"Lay back on your stomach," he said once she was finished. He went to the closet, pulled out the husband's tennis shoes, and started taking the laces out. He went back to the couple and pulled the covers off of the man's feet and started tying his ankles.

"Lie still or you'll get your fuckin' heads blown off. All I want is food and money for my van. If you try and kick me, I'll blow your fucking brains out. If you're going to make your move you better make it good because I'm going to blow your fucking brains out."

He then went and tied the woman's hands and feet, then he went back to the husband and put the gun to his head. "If you try anything, I'll kill your fuckin' wife and it will be your fault."

The intruder left them and began rummaging through the house. The victims noticed that he had a bag with him, and as he ransacked the house, they heard the bag's zipper opening and closing.

After nearly forty-five minutes, he stormed back into the bedroom.

"Get away from him! You're trying to get him free!" He untied the woman's feet and then pulled her from the bed.

He turned toward the husband. "If you flinch, I'll kill your wife." Then he turned to the wife. "And if you try anything, I'll come back and kill him." He began pushing her from the room and down the hallway.

The husband listened intently, but he couldn't hear what was going on. The intruder suddenly came back, rummaged through the room, and opened drawers. He found the husband's .357 Magnum in the nightstand, threatened him, and then left the room.

A few minutes later, the intruder was back once more, only this time carrying dishes. He started stacking them on the bed and he tied some towel around the husband's face as a blindfold. "I'm putting these dishes on the bed and if I hear them rattle, I'll kill your wife. I'll blow her fuckin' brains out."

Details of the sexual assault are unavailable to me, but I do know that he continued to threaten them, often using a knife that he had taken from their kitchen. At the end of the assault, he stole their wedding rings, along with the .357 Magnum revolver that belonged to the husband.

Immediate Aftermath

The method of entry was apparently an aluminum sliding glass window in the kitchen. The couple was certain they had locked it (along with all of the other doors and windows), but there was no sign of prying or forced entry.

Suspect Description

White male, early twenties, less than 6', slender build. His penis was described as small.

He had on a dark knit ski mask. He was probably wearing a t-shirt, tennis shoes, and he seemed to be carrying a bag that had a zipper.

He had a revolver and a flashlight with him, and he used a knife that he had taken from the victims' kitchen.

He spoke in whispers and had a Spanish accent that the victims felt was probably fake.

Post-Attack Event

<u>July 7th, 1978 5:00 PM</u>
The .357 Magnum stolen in this attack was found in a large cement-lined canal (creatively named "Lateral Number One"). The location where it was found was right behind Palmilla Drive, roughly two miles to the west of the attack. Interestingly, some of the land between the attack house and where the gun was found is still undeveloped to this day.

Context and Analysis
So... is the EAR flying to attacks now? If so, one has to wonder where he's coming from, because if he's coming from Sacramento, it doesn't seem very time-efficient to fly. Nonetheless, we have to follow every lead no matter how odd it may seem. To that end, we've tried to find a flight schedule from the evening of June 22nd, 1978, to see what the arriving flights were, but so far we haven't found anything. There probably wouldn't be any way to get a comprehensive listing anyway, with small private planes being so common.

The timeline between this attack and the next is tight and it can get confusing (especially with there being an airport reference here and also an airport reference in the next one), so here are the timeline details, assuming that the man at the airport is in fact the rapist:

<u>Davis:</u>
June 22nd, 1978 - Suspicious man seen on Shire Lane.

<u>Modesto:</u>
June 22nd, 1978 Evening - Man at airport hails cab, gets dropped off near attack site.

<u>Modesto:</u>
June 23rd, 1978 1:30 AM to 3:00 AM - EAR attacks on Grandprix Drive.

Davis:
June 23rd, 1978 8:30 PM: - Man seen peeping over a fence.

Davis:
June 24th, 1978 3:15 AM to 4:15 AM - EAR attacks on Rivendell Lane. Dog tracks suspect to nearby UC Davis airport.

Some folks theorize that EAR flew into Modesto, committed an attack there, got to Davis somehow during the day, committed his crime there, and then flew out. We don't think this was entirely the case, but no explanation put forth at this point can account for all of the oddities. We'll explore the UC Davis airport situation in the next attack, but for now it's important to look at the timing between these events and ponder the logistics. We do feel that it's likely that the man at the Modesto airport was the fact EAR, given the drop-off point at Sylvan and Coffee and the timing of the attack that night. If it *was* him, we're stumped as to how he got out of the area and made it back to Davis by 8:30 PM that night. It's a tight timeline, given that regardless of what he did, somewhere in there he probably had to find somewhere to sleep. It's possible that he was living in Modesto at the time, or that he had somewhere to stay, and that he'd flown in from somewhere nearby. It's possible that he didn't fly in at all, and it's even possible that the person from the airport wasn't even him. As with everything in this case, just because there are a couple of clues pointing in a certain direction doesn't mean that we can jump to a conclusion, so the situation could actually be quite different from what it seems. We could speculate further, but it would probably just confuse things and lead us too far away from the known facts.

Again he used the word "flinch" during the attack, just like in the first Modesto attack. It's a logical word to use but just unique enough to be noticeable. It serves as an interesting commonality between the two Modesto attacks.

"If you're going to make your move you better make it good because I'm going to blow your fucking brains out" was a rare provocation by the assailant. Usually the victims were told to not even move and put under a blanket of similar threats. This sounded more like a dare than a threat—it's possible that even at this stage, the assailant was partially hoping for a chance to use his gun.

We've mentioned this before, but we don't think too highly of the assailant's burglary skills. His "success" rate is quite good and there's no arguing with the overall effectiveness of his methods, but his actual technical skills are quite brutish and sloppy. However, here we have an attack where the point of entry remains a question mark. The couple was certain that they had locked their doors and windows, but there was no sign of forced entry. Either they were mistaken, or something gave way quite easily. If he had advanced burglary skills that allowed him to slip in and out of homes completely undetected like that, then he would've done it more often. One could argue that maybe he *did* do it more often, and that there are burglaries and recon entries that we're unaware of. Anything is possible, but if he had the skills to enter like a ghost, why did he leave a trail of sloppy entries, broken doors, and cracked windows? It doesn't make sense to do something like that as an intentional misdirection because there's not much to gain from it. Whether the police thought he was a great burglar or not didn't have much effect on what it is he was trying to do.

Something that puzzles us about the entire Modesto/Davis series of attacks is how he found the time to select and properly stalk all of these victims when they were located so far apart. There must be something very important to discover related to this, *or* he simply familiarized himself very well with the areas ahead of time and then on the particular night that he decided to attack he found a suitable victim opportunistically. This particular couple had moved into their house in April, so they'd only been living there for a little over two months. The houses around them were either built very recently or were still under construction.

Both victims worked for the Modesto City Hospital. A strong medical connection, just like so many victims before them.

Attack #35

Date: June 24th, 1978 3:15 AM to 4:15 AM
Victims: Wife (32 years old) and husband. Their ten-year-old
son and two small children were also in the house.
Location: Rivendell Lane, Davis

Pre-Attack Events

June 18th, 1978
A neighbor saw a man between her house and a neighbor's house. She
asked him what he was doing, and he told her that he worked for a
developer and that the developer was interested in "solar homes." She
talked to him for a few minutes and came away with the impression
that he didn't know much about solar power, which made his
presence in the neighborhood quite suspicious.

June 22nd, 1978
On Shire Lane, a street just one hundred feet southeast of where the
attack would take place, a woman saw a strange man in her yard. He
was peering into windows. A composite was made of this man.

June 23rd, 1978 8:30 PM
A neighbor spotted someone looking over her fence the night before
the attack. She didn't get a good look at him, and he melted out of
sight before she could investigate further.

The Attack

The husband and wife were sleeping soundly, but they awoke to the sound of loud, strained breathing and a man whispering orders at them. The light from a flashlight was shining brightly into their eyes.

"Don't you fuckin' move. Don't you fuckin' move. Put your hands behind your backs and don't you fuckin' move or I'll shoot your fuckin' heads off. I have a .357 Magnum and I'll shoot your fuckin' heads off."

The couple was ordered to roll onto their stomachs, and the intruder continued issuing threats at them.

"Don't move or I'll kill every person in the house. I'll kill every fuckin' person. I'll shoot you and splatter blood all over the walls. All I want is food and money. Food and money. I got to have money for gas. I got to have food."

He moved a bit closer. "You, tie him up. Tie his hands up."

The woman looked at the intruder and started to ask him what she was supposed to use to tie him with, when the light focused on the husband's back. Two shoelaces were rolled into an oval shape and laid out on top of him.

She started to tie her husband.

"Run it between his hands," the intruder ordered. She was afraid and couldn't keep her hands steady. The intruder started to become angry. "Between his hands!" he repeated.

She was eventually successful. The assailant tied her wrists tightly.

He then began rummaging through the closet, looking for shoes and pulling laces out of them. He went back to the man and retied his wrists. He then tied the woman's ankles, somewhat loosely compared to how he had tied the husband's hands.

He pressed the gun against the woman's back. "Don't you say one fuckin' word or I'll kill everybody in the house."

He hit the man's foot with the barrel of the gun. "You. Where's the money?"

"In my pants," the man answered.

He hit the woman's foot with the gun. "Where's your purse?"

"It's in the kitchen. There's forty-five dollars in it."

"Shut up," he barked. They heard him leave the room.

A short time later, they heard a sound that terrified them—their ten-year-old son's voice coming from the hallway. The boy had gotten up to go to the bathroom, and he'd encountered the intruder along the way. The EAR pushed him into the bathroom and ordered him not to move or make any noise. The attacker went to the kitchen, retrieved a cup and saucer, and placed the cup over the doorknob on the outside of the bathroom door.

He stormed back into the bedroom a few moments later and pointed something sharp into the woman's back. "That kid better stay in that bathroom or I'm going to push this ice pick into your back. He'd better stay in the bathroom. I'll kill every person in this house. I'll shoot all your fuckin' heads off. All I want is food and money." Then he stormed out.

When he returned, they heard towels being torn into strips. Moments later, he blindfolded them.

"Move over," he said, tapping the woman's foot with the gun. "On the floor."

She rolled off the bed quickly and anto the floor. The intruder lifted her to her feet. The shoelaces from her ankles were loosened and she was led out of the room.

He took her down the hall and into the living room, then carefully lowered her face-down to the floor.

Moments later, she heard lotion being pumped from a bottle, and then after a minute or two he straddled her and placed his penis into her hands.

"All I want is to feel good. You'd better make it feel good." While he moved his penis back and forth in her hands, he uncharacteristically rubbed her back with soft motions.

After a few moments of this, he rolled her over and forced her to orally copulate him.

"You'd better not bite me or this knife will go six inches into your back," he told her. Then he uncharacteristically brushed her hair out of her face.

He savagely raped her. He fondled her breasts, gently at first but then very hard. During the rape, he called her by her nickname. That name wasn't spoken while the assailant was there, nor was it written down anywhere in the house, which made the use of it quite terrifying.

After raping her, he told her that he needed money. Then she heard him take several steps back and begin sobbing and crying.

He left the house shortly thereafter.

Immediate Aftermath
The assailant had entered through an unlocked door or window. Shoe prints were found around the victims' house and in neighboring yards. The assailant had used their bottle of Vaseline Intensive Care lotion, and he had taken over a dozen rolls of pennies from the home.

A bloodhound was used to track the offender, and the dog followed a trail for about two miles heading south. The trail ended near the private airport at UC Davis.

Suspect Description
White male, 5'10", with a thin to medium build. He had big thighs, a hairy butt, and his breath was very "sour." His penis was not fully erect. It was long and thin. The victim was sure that it was circumcised.

He wore a ski mask and dark clothing.

He had a .357 Magnum revolver and an ice pick. He may have had a long-bladed knife, according to the newspapers.

He spoke in an angry whisper through clenched teeth. He breathed heavily and seemed to "pant" a lot.

Post-Attack Event

June 24th, 1978 Morning
A few hours after the attack, the woman who had talked to the strange man about "solar homes" found a jacket on her walkway. It hadn't been there the day before. It was navy blue, made of a heavy suede material, and fit just at the waist like a bomber jacket. The

collar and cuffs were knit and had two gold-colored stripes. It was "Golden Bear Sportswear" brand, model 300 or 303. The jacket hadn't been produced in a very large quantity, but despite the small number of sales, the investigators were unable to match it to a customer fitting the EAR's description.

Context and Analysis

The assailant wasn't often very original with his threats (usually repeating the same ones over and over again), and in this attack he was *very* repetitious.

The attack occurred in a two-story home, and in a house with a floor plan unlike anything he'd attacked before. This was an anomaly. The neighborhood was somewhat dense though. It was wooded, and it had a lot of walking trails, which *were* features that seemed to draw him into certain areas.

The assailant had a .357 Magnum, which was the same kind of gun stolen in Attack #34. It's unknown if it he used the weapon that he'd stolen in that attack or if was a different one. If it was the same one, he went back to the general attack area in Modesto and disposed of it sometime before the evening of July 7th, 1978. Most likely, though, he'd ditched that gun on the night of that attack, and looking at where he dropped it would probably tell us a little about his escape path from that particular scene.

The solar power man was pretty suspicious, but it might have just been a solar power man who was really bad at his job. Davis was a pioneering community when it came to solar power, and the technology was not a commodity back then. Several houses on the victims' street were outfitted with solar panels in the years following the attack.

The assailant was not as violent with the female victim as he usually was in a few segments of the attack, though that in no way diminishes the trauma of the event. It's just something that needs to be noted for comparison's sake. He cried and sobbed again in this attack.

In a puzzling turn of events, the assailant called the female victim by her nickname. Since it wasn't spoken while he was there or written down in the house, it opens up all kinds of possibilities. This, and the jacket, are the standout pieces of evidence from this event. The nickname is one of the pieces of evidence used to show that the EAR most likely *did* spend time stalking victims in these locations before attacking them (at least in some cases), which makes the busy timeline of his attacks during this phase even tighter.

Speaking of the jacket, there's a little bit more information available about that. It was manufactured in San Francisco, and investigators were able to determine that it had been made about five years before the attack. Not very many were made, because that particular color/style combination didn't sell well and it was discontinued fairly soon after being produced. Jackets similar in style to it continue to be made by that manufacturer even to this day, but at the time, only a few stores stocked it. At least one of them was in Sacramento (a store called Bluebeards), and the others were either in the city of San Francisco or a short ways away in Berkeley (where a Bluebeards store also operated). None of the stores were able to assist investigators or provide sales records. One of the latter two stores carried S&M merchandise in their store windows and generally catered to homosexuals. Bluebeards ended up closing in 1992.

The dogs tracked the suspect to the UC Davis private airfield. It's tempting to make more of this than maybe we should, given the possible airline connection in the previous attack. On the surface, it seems he could've flown into Modesto, somehow got to Davis, and then flown back to wherever he came from. Maybe he did. But after unpacking the different accounts of where the bloodhound trail ended up in this attack, I'm inclined to think that he drove to this one. By all accounts, the trail ended far away from any action related to the airplanes—not at all in a place conducive to getting on a flight If he'd made his way anywhere near a hangar, building, or runway, the dogs would've picked up the scent. Instead, they ended at an out-of-the-way place where most likely a car had been parked. Of course, we can't always take everything at face value. Perhaps he was a master of misdirection. Several attacks in the rape series *and* the murder series occur near airfields. Which again, might mean nothing. With so many attacks, there are groups of incidents that occur near almost everything.

Attack #36

Date: July 6th, 1978 2:50 AM to 4:00 AM
Victim: 33-year-old woman. Her two sons, ages 5 and 7,
slept through the attack.
Location: Amador Avenue, Davis

Pre-Attack Events

July 3rd, 1978 Night
A neighbor noticed a suspicious male on a bicycle appearing throughout the neighborhood, particularly on Amador Avenue. Amador Avenue was very close to the house from Attack #35, situated geographically just on the other side of Arlington Blvd (but not connected to it).

July 4th, 1978 Evening
As evening was setting, the same neighbor noticed a strange man walking east on Buckleberry Road toward Arlington Blvd and toward the section where it connected with Rivendell Lane. The man looked very suspicious and appeared to be wearing some sort of disguise. He was about thirty years old, had a beard that looked fake, walked with a cane, and wore a piece of engraved metal usually common in Western-wear. The police were called, but by the time they reached the area, the man was gone. This sighting was about half a mile to the west of the victim in this attack, and just over a hundred feet from Attack #35.

The Attack

The victim had been on a date, and she returned home at about 1:00 AM. She went to bed. Later that night, a flashlight shining in her eyes woke her up.

"Don't move or I'll blow your fuckin' head off. I'm going to blow your fuckin' head off. Do you see this gun?"

She didn't reply, but she was wide awake due to the drastic nature of the threats.

"I'll blow your fuckin' head off," he repeated, and then he threatened to "kill her kids" if she didn't cooperate. He told her to roll over onto her stomach. She rolled over, and he pulled her hands behind her back and tied them tightly. Then he crossed her ankles and tied those as well.

He threatened to kill her two sons. "All I want is food and money for my van," he told her, adding that he wanted "money for gasoline." He told her again that he'd "blow her fuckin' head off" if she made a noise.

He ransacked part of the house, stopping in occasionally to threaten her with a knife. As the attack wore on, he blindfolded her, lubricated himself, and masturbated. He asked her what she thought he was doing while he did this. He straddled her and put his penis into her hands, then ordered her to masturbate him. He continued threatening her, and he stuttered occasionally when he did so.

Then he raped her. As he assaulted her, he kept repositioning his weight. The victim felt that he was having trouble maintaining an erection and reaching a climax, and he seemed frustrated. He grabbed her breast briefly. His frustration seemed to grow, and he pulled out and put his head down on the pillow next to her. He began crying.

"I hate you. I hate you. I hate you Bonnie," he sobbed.

He got up, rummaged through the house again, and left.

Immediate Aftermath

The victim was taken to Davis Community for the rape examination.

A side gate at a residence on Westerness Road was found to be open, indicating that the EAR had come from that direction. Entry had been made by breaking a small hole in the glass lock of a kitchen window, probably with a screwdriver. The plants that had been inside the house on the windowsill were found lined up neatly against the outside of the house, and the window screen was found behind some bushes near the fence. A herringbone tennis shoe print was found in the mud just outside the kitchen window, and a muddy herringbone footprint was found on the kitchen counter next to the sink.

Inside the residence, it was noted that some of the rooms in the house had been extensively ransacked, and some had been left untouched. There were shoelaces, some torn towels, and an open bottle of Keri Lotion inside. Police also found a large kitchen knife on the dresser in the master bedroom.

Twenty-seven dollars in cash and some postage stamps were stolen.

Suspect Description
The assailant's penis was three to four inches long and close to the diameter of a half dollar. It was never fully erect. The victim was sure that he was circumcised.

He had a ski mask, a gun, and a flashlight. He smelled like cigarette smoke.

Post-Attack Event

July 14th, 1978
A man was house-sitting for the victim while she was out of town. He was cleaning out her refrigerator and made a surprising discovery related to the attack—a knife hidden inside of a Velveeta Cheese box.

Context and Analysis
This assault is *very* near Attack #35. If you take a bird's eye view of this area, it's audacious that he came back to this tiny pocket to attack again. Something initially drew the EAR here to the neighborhood, and for some reason he stayed for awhile. If it was a particular victim

that drew him there, it must not have been the one from Attack #35 because it appeared that he hung around even after he'd attacked that victim. There were strange prowlers on Shire Lane, Amador, Buckleberry, etc. He seemed to be prowling the area, not a particular victim. The signs of him zeroing in on one household and stalking it excessively (like he did in the Sacramento attacks) didn't seem to be present here. Or perhaps the assailant had simply gotten better at it and operated in a subtler fashion.

Much has been made about the assailant saying "I hate you, Bonnie." He'd cried for "mommy" before, which sounds like "Bonnie," but the victim really thought he was saying "Bonnie." The idea has been explored as possibly the name of a relative, a wife, a teacher's wife, a sister, and various other possible relationships. So far, nothing has come of it. If there's a "Bonnie" out there who recognizes any of the behaviors in this book, Law Enforcement would love to talk to you.

The assailant stuttered while threatening her, something that he'd done before. Hiding a knife inside of a Velveeta Cheese box, though… that was new. Things had been squirreled away under couches and in a few other places and things had been moved around in the fridge before, but it's possible that the intent of this action was a little different. This was something that was done, in our opinion, to instill fear at a later date. The victim would go to get cheese and be terrified to find a weapon. Luckily, someone else found it and she didn't have to go through that.

The victim was a student at Sacramento State College. She was estranged from her husband, who was a doctor, and they'd been separated for a long time. This attack had an open green space near it, and like Rivendell Lane, it had a main street nearby. The street connected easily with Interstate 80.

After such a frenzy of attacks in Modesto and Davis, the communities braced themselves for more assaults. Particularly Davis. Meetings and open forums were held to discuss the situation. The police chief remarked that he hadn't seen such involvement from the community since the Vietnam War.

Thankfully for Modesto and Davis, the East Area Rapist went on a three month hiatus from attacking after this assault. When he reappeared, Modesto and Davis were in his rearview mirror.

He'd picked up his tour of terror nearly seventy miles to the south—in Contra Costa County.

Attack #37

Date: October 7th, 1978 2:30 AM to 4:40 AM
Victim: Wife (26 years old) and husband (29 years old). Their
infant was in the house as well.
Location: Belann Court, Concord

Pre-Attack Events

September through Early October 1978
All throughout this time period, streets like Minert Road, Oak Grove
Road, Belann Court, and even streets as far away as Hollis Court
experienced open side gates, dogs barking in the middle of the night,
prowlers, and a lot of obscene phone calls.

September 1978
The doorbell rang at the victims' house, and standing at the front
door was a man and a woman claiming to be from the Mormon
Church. The couple seemed suspicious and didn't fit the mold of the
typical Mormon missionaries that had been in the area before.

September 23rd or so, 1978 11:30 PM
A neighborhood couple heard strange noises outside. They went out
to investigate, and in the process, startled two men at the side of their
house. The two men ran to an older-model blue or black Ford
Falcon, got in, and drove away. The car had a loud exhaust. The
couple checked the perimeter of their residence and discovered that
the screens on their windows had been cut near the window locks.

September 27th or so, 1978

There was a predator in the nearby Ygnacio Valley Park. A teenage girl who lived very close to the victims' house was at the water fountain when a man came up behind her, grabbed her, pinned her arms to her side, and started pulling on her. Luckily, joggers came by and the man ran off. Later on, she spotted the same man driving a 1966 Chevrolet pickup with white and gray faded paint and a chain necklace hanging in the rearview mirror. He was a white male, clean-shaven, with a muscular build and a very deep voice. Sometime earlier in the month, that man had actually raped a local girl. The victim he had raped decided not to report her attack to the police, but she shared it with some of her friends.

September 30th, 1978

In the early morning hours, while it was still dark outside, a neighbor caught a glimpse of someone running through a neighbor's yard. The subject hid behind a large planter for a period of time. He was described as having brown corduroy pants and tennis shoes, and the witness had actually assumed it was the paperboy at the time of the sighting.

Late September and Early October 1978

A teenager saw a faded green Chevrolet Fleetside model truck parked on Minert Road near the victims' house. The vehicle was spotted several times, always parked at the same location. The truck couldn't be traced to anyone on the street.

October 1st, 1978 Afternoon

A neighbor spotted a man sitting in a tree and noticed that he was surveilling her yard. The tree was located behind her house, near the parking lot of the Most Precious Blood Church. She could see that he was a white male but couldn't make out any other details.

October 2nd, 1978 Evening

A neighbor on Minert Road (a street that intersects with Belann Court) was leaving to go to the store when she noticed a car parked across the street from her house. The driver was slouched in his seat and he appeared to be studying houses. His look and demeanor scared her.

October 2nd and October 3rd, 1978

A twenty-nine-year-old woman who lived on Hollis Court (over half a mile away from the victims' house) heard a prowler in her yard for two nights in a row. There were noises in the backyard, scratching noises at her screen door, and noises at her windows. Her side gate was left open. Police investigated and found that the screen from one of her windows had been removed, and the screen had been cut near the lock of a sliding glass door

October 4th, 1978 12:00 AM

Neighbors living very close to the victim heard a prowler enter their house in the middle of the night. The husband sprang to action before the prowler could reach the bedroom and chased him away. The wife, from her vantage point upstairs, saw two men running through their yard. They jumped over the fence and ran into the parking lot of the Most Precious Blood Church. Both men were described as white and in their twenties. One of them was about 6' and was dressed in a white t-shirt and blue jeans.

October 4th, 1978, 1:30 AM

A seventeen-year-old girl living on Minert Road with her father spotted a prowler in the backyard. She woke her father, and as she did, both of them heard footsteps on strips of aluminum that were kept in the backyard. They looked out the window, but the prowler was gone. Moments later, the noises were heard again. The father grabbed his shotgun, went back to the window, and that time he was able to spot the prowler. He opened the window and pointed the gun at him.

"What the fuck are you doing out there?"

"I'm looking for a friend," the man replied.

"Get out of my yard or I'll blow your fuckin' head off."

The man ran from the yard toward the front of the house. The father gave chase, running to the front door and into the front yard. By that time, the prowler had completely vanished. No footsteps were heard, nor was a vehicle heard or seen. The side gate had been left open.

The prowler was described as a white or possibly hispanic male, 5'9, 175 lbs, wearing a light beard and a Hawaiian-style shirt. Aside from the light beard, several parts of the description of this man matched the rapist/kidnapper spotted in Ygnacio Valley Park.

October 6th, 1978 Night

The woman living on Hollis Court again heard a prowler in her yard and noises at her doors and windows. The sounds occurred just a couple of hours before the victims were attacked. When investigators examined the perimeter of her house, they noticed that tiny scratch marks had been made in the corners of her screens, just like ones that would be found at the victims' house. The scratch marks were not pry marks—they were visible, intentional, deliberate markings made for some unknown purpose.

The Attack

The victims returned home around 11:30 PM. As they did, they noticed a strange vehicle, possibly a Volkswagen, parked on Minert Road near their house.

The wife put their baby to bed, and the husband noticed that one of the doors inside the house, which was always left open, had been closed. He checked all of the locks in the house and discovered that a deadbolt was mysteriously unlocked. He locked it and went to bed.

A couple hours later, he felt someone steadily tapping his foot. He opened his eyes and spotted a masked man near the foot of the bed. The intruder was shining a flashlight at them with his left hand and pointing a revolver at them with his right.

"I just want food and money, that's all. I'll kill you if you don't do as I say. Get on your stomachs." He moved closer to the husband and pressed the gun against his head. "Put your hands behind your back."

He threw shoelaces at the wife. "Tie his hands." She began tying her husband's wrists.

"Tighter. That's not tight enough. Tighter."

Once she had finished tying her husband's hands, the intruder ordered her onto her stomach, and then he went and retied the husband's hands. Then he tied the wife's, and he also tied her ankles. Her ankles were tied loosely.

"If you look at me I'll have to kill you." He searched the room for a moment, grabbed the husband's shoes, removed laces from them, and returned to their side.

"Keep lying face down. If you look at me, I'll kill you. I'll blow your fucking head off." He tied the husband's ankles tightly, then began rummaging through their drawers.

"Where's your wallet?"

The husband told him that it was on the bathroom counter.

"Where's your purse?"

The woman told him that it was in the kitchen.

He disappeared and then came back. "Is that all the money you have?"

They told him that it was.

He began rummaging and ransacking through the rest of the house. He returned to the bedroom and placed dishes on both of their backs. "If I hear these, I'll blow your fucking heads off." He began ransacking the house again.

When he returned to the bedroom, he went to the woman's side, untied her ankles, and took the dishes off of her back.

"Stand up. Don't look at me or I'll cut your fuckin' head off." He pulled her up to her feet, held a knife to her throat, and began pushing her toward the living room.

"If you don't do everything I tell you, I'll kill you and everyone in the house. Lie down."

He turned on the television and muted it, then put a blanket over the screen. She heard him walk off toward the bedroom.

"If these dishes fall, I'll kill everyone in the house." He placed even more dishes on the man's back. "My main man wants gold and silver."

He was now back in the living room. "If you don't give me a good fuck, I'll kill everyone. I'll cut off your baby's ear and bring it to you." Her nightgown was cut off and removed piece by piece.

He was behind her now, and she heard him lubricating himself with lotion and masturbating.

He called her by name, and then said "I've been seeing you for a long time." Then he raped her, but didn't climax while doing so. He also forced her to orally copulate him, and he climaxed into her mouth.

After the sexual assault, he walked away from her and huddled into the corner of the living room. The victim heard him crying. A few moments later, he got up and began ransacking the house again. He went back and forth from the house to the garage a few times, and then he went into the backyard.

A few minutes passed, and the victim realized that he had left.

Immediate Aftermath

Entry had been made by prying the screen off of the living room window, breaking a small hole in the glass, then reaching in and unlocking it. He'd attempted to enter the side door to the garage by chipping away at the deadbolt, but was unable to open it due to a wooden beam that the victims had been using to secure the door.

Investigators at the scene noticed distinctive scratch marks on the corner of the window screens. They were very visible, and they were not pry marks. These types of scratches were found at another house, the one mentioned earlier on Hollis Court over half a mile away. Scratches of this type only appeared at residences related to this attack and the next one.

Thousands of dollars in appliances, fine china, salt and pepper shakers, forks, knives, electronics, and jewelry were stolen.

A bloodhound was brought in, and the dog tracked the EAR's trail to Minert Road.

The husband underwent hypnosis to try to remember additional details from the attack. Under hypnosis, he mentioned catching a close glimpse of the assailant's gun, and it indeed had several bullets in the chamber. He was also able to recall details of the vehicle he had seen in the vicinity of his house as he was driving home. He described a box-shaped van, light in color (maybe white, teal, or aqua-green). It had a rear chrome bumper, no windows on the sides, and two windows on the back. A suspicious man was near the vehicle. He was white with dark hair, and he wore a white t-shirt and light blue pants.

Suspect Description

The assailant was wearing a ski mask, corduroy pants, and gloves. Under hypnosis, the victim recalled that the gloves were made of a brushed suede.

He had a flashlight and a revolver. The husband, under hypnosis, recalled seeing four bullets in the gun's cylinder.

Under hypnosis, the husband described the attacker's voice in detail. The assailant's sentences were short and stilted. His voice was a whisper through clenched teeth. He breathed loudly and quickly, and at times it sounded like he was hyperventilating.

The assailant had a distinctive smell, "like cinnamon."

Post-Attack Event

October 7th or 8th, 1978

A neighbor nearby found a small security officer's badge in his yard. It was in the shape of a seven-point star, and it had the seal of the State of California and said "Special Officer." It didn't belong to anyone in the area, and it had possibly been dropped by the assailant.

Context and Analysis

There were no attacks for three months after Attack #36 in Davis. What was going on during that time? Was the assailant stalking new areas, like the towns in Contra Costa County? Or did he have some kind of employment that took him offshore, out of the area, or kept him otherwise occupied during this time? All we know is that, possibly as early as September, the assailant had turned up in new territory.

Why Concord? What drew the assailant there? It's impossible to know for sure, but viewing Sacramento as a "home base" of sorts, it's a logical place for him to land. The assailant had already taken Interstate 5 out of town and ended up in Stockton, the first big stop along the way. Continuing on I-5 and jumping over to 99, or just taking 99 out of Sacramento, the first big stop along the way is Modesto, another place he'd hit. Taking Interstate 80 out of Sacramento, the first big town is Davis, yet another place he'd hit. Continuing on Interstate 80, which swings into Interstate 680, he arrived in what was apparently very fertile hunting grounds—the Contra Costa County area. The first geographical stop on this highway? Concord, California.

Now as you take I-80 out of town, in order to get to Concord you do pass through Solano county and the towns of Vacaville and Fairfield. These were places with a population numbers fairly comparable to some of the other places he'd hit (Vacaville's population in 1978 was close to 40,000, and Fairfield's was 50,000), but it doesn't appear EAR stopped in these areas, at least not to attack. Maybe he scoped them out and didn't like them, which was why there's no sign of him during most of July and August.

While looking at the Concord assaults and the other assaults that occurred in Contra Costa County, we tried to determine if it was likely that the offender maintained a residence in Sacramento and commuted to these attacks, or if he actually took up residence in the area he was offending in. It's only about seventy miles between Concord and Sacramento, a distance that's doable and a bit easier in many ways than the distance between Sacramento and Modesto. But the fact that he seemingly bypassed Fairfield and Vacaville (places which weren't *exactly* like he'd been hitting but which *did* offer viable targets), plus the sheer amount of attacks and stalking incidents that happened in the Contra Costa County area, it leans us toward the opinion that the offender actually relocated to this area. Some rough

GIS profiling we did with a research partner put his residence most likely in the Walnut Creek area, but there are hardly enough solid data points to make any actionable conclusions.

Another reason that makes us think that he'd relocated to the area is the variety of items that he stole from these victims. He stole fine china, utensils, and appliances, not to mention some other big ticket items like jewelry and camera equipment. For an offender who usually liked to take cash and odd keepsakes, this time it seemed more like he was shopping to fill his coffers. Either he had a new residence to furnish, or he lived through stealing and hadn't been active for awhile.

Rather than simple hang-up phone calls, many of the calls in this area were of the obscene variety. Several of them related to attacks leading up to this one had been obscene, and they had been getting more vocal and nastier. Now it almost seemed like the norm, at least during this part of the series.

Many of the pre-attack events here seem very EAR-esque, but instead of *one* prowler, some of them have *two* individuals involved. New town, new partner? Two men were never seen at an actual EAR attack, but here we have two attempted robberies, both with two suspects. These events happened close by, and only a short time before the EAR attack. At the one that happened in late September, a blue or black Falcon was sighted. There was a Falcon possibly associated with Attack #26 (a sighting that happened about eleven months before this one). The second event produced a sighting of two men running away after breaking into the house, and they disappeared into a parking lot that'd had some suspicious activity already. One of the men had on a white t-shirt and blue jeans, an outfit which had been associated with suspicious men sighted around EAR attacks a few times already (most notably Attack #30, Attack #33, and possibly Attack #29). The logistics of there being a lookout or accomplice in these attacks is an interesting idea, and it's not one that changes the investigation *too* much unless you start getting into the what-ifs regarding DNA and the difficulties of ruling out one or the other because of an alibi or even a prison term. There's not enough evidence to begin entertaining these theories too heavily but it's hard to dismiss them entirely. And seeing as how the EAR *did* steal quite a bit more than usual at this attack, it's possible that he truly *was* getting his "main man" some extra "gold and silver."

As the husband took a sweep through the house before bed, a door in the house was closed that shouldn't have been, and a deadbolt was unlocked. The EAR had been in his house. This is a good example of the EAR breaking in and preparing the scene, something the assailant might've done often, but we don't usually have concrete proof of it.

Let's go back to "my main man wants gold and silver." That's something that someone who watches a little too much television might say. But again, quite a bit was stolen. Much of what the assailant said is often suspected of being intentional misdirection. He may have been lying about several things, but with most criminals, their actions almost always betray them. We like to look at what the assailant *did* rather than what he *said*. This time, his actions and his words seemed to match up. The stolen goods may not have been for his "main man," but the EAR stole so much during his crime spree that it's difficult to believe that he didn't fence *some* of it. Maybe some of it was deconstructed or melted down, or perhaps he really did keep all of the things that he stole as mementos. He may have discarded almost all of it and used the thefts as a ruse. If he fenced any of it, the clock has just about run out on finding a fence that would remember such a transaction. Serial rapists and other such criminals have been caught before because of their association with a fence, so despite the age of the lead, it's still one that can't be completely forgotten about.

"I'll cut off your baby's ear and bring it to you." That was one of his favorite threats toward the end of the Sacramento attacks, and apparently he brought the phrase to Concord to help us tie him back to Sac. He cut off the victim's nightgown piece by piece, which was reminiscent of a few other past attacks as well.

The assailant cried at the scene, making it the third attack in a row that he'd done this. Forgive us if we don't feel sorry for him.

In a possible (but fairly unlikely) example of mimicry, the

neighbor that pointed his shotgun at the suspicious man in his yard told the intruder that he'd "blow his fuckin' head off." Then, at the attack, the EAR threatened the couple with the exact phrase "blow your fuckin' head off." We're not reading too much into this though, because he'd used the same phrase in Attack #34 and Attack #36, and before that it was "blow your brains out" in Attack #32 and Attack #33. It's interesting how the phraseology would stay the same for some consecutive attacks, then change a little bit and remain the same again for a little while.

When attacking couples, the EAR was consistently armed with a gun. Since he had never used it during an attack, there was always the question about whether the gun was actually loaded or not. Of course in the victims' situation, the smartest thing to do would be to assume that it *was* loaded, but thanks to the post-attack hypnosis session on the husband, the question was finally answered. Yes, the EAR's gun was *loaded*. His killing spree could've started at any moment.

The distinctive scratches found in the corner of the window screens are understandably a source of much confusion. The assailant had pried at *many* screens over the years, so why are these scratches in particular such a big deal? They were distinctive, almost like a signature or a taunt, and they only appeared at the attacks/prowlings in Concord. These scratches were not pry marks. The screens were loose-fitting and did not need to be pried in that way, and the marks were made on the aluminum screen itself, not the frame. They were small, visible, deliberate, distinctive scratches made for some purpose known only to the assailant. All of the scratches appeared near the bottom left corner of the screen. They appeared on the houses associated with this attack and on the two houses associated with the next one. What interests us the most is that, again, these scratches only seemed to appear in the two Concord attacks, making this activity unique to that town. Perhaps it was a tool being used by the assailant to mark target houses in an unfamiliar area. It was not being used by the assailant to mark entry points, because the scratches appeared on every screen around the house and not just one particular window.

The security badge that was found in a neighbor's yard could be a great lead. The assailant had not attacked in three months, and he had never attacked that far away from Sacramento before, and he'd never attacked in Contra Costa County before. It's possible that this badge could be a clue to employment, a disguise, or something significant. It's also possible that it could be unrelated to the EAR, or that it could be an intentional misdirection by the assailant. It was found in the yard near a house on Belann Court. It didn't belong to any of the neighbors. There was surface-wear all over it, indicating that it had been used and/or carried around for quite some time. The badge was a model "B-617" with an air-dried enamel surface. It was manufactured by up to twelve different companies, one of the most prominent ones being the Hookfast Company in Rhode Island. The manufacturer told police that the badge could have been purchased directly from their company or from any of the thousands of salesmen that stocked it. It had the state seal of California in the middle, and the words "Special Officer" around the edge. Several security companies from San Francisco to Concord and surrounding areas were asked about the badge, but none of them required their employees to wear that particular model.

And as we wrap up with this attack, for those of you keeping track of the statistically high amount of medical connections, you'll be interested to know that the male victim in this attack was a pharmacist at Mount Diablo Medical Center.

Attack #38

Date: October 13th, 1978 4:30 AM to 5:30 AM
Victim: 29-year-old woman and her 30-year-old boyfriend.
Her young daughter was also in the house.
Location: Ryan Road, Concord

Some of the geography in this area can be difficult to keep straight, so before reading please note that there is a "Ryan Court" and a "Ryan Road" involved in this attack. The victims lived on "Ryan Road."

Pre-Attack Events

Late September through Mid-October 1978
In addition to the prowlers and open side gates described below, there were several obscene phone calls in the area.

Early October 1978
For two nights in a row, different neighbors on Ryan Road heard strange noises in their backyards.

October 12th, 1978 10:00 PM
Neighbors on Lyon Circle, a street running between Minert Road and Ryan Road, found that their fence boards had been broken by a prowler. Neighbors nearby had heard commotion and prowling.

October 12th, 1978 11:00 PM
Other neighbors on Lyon Circle heard a prowler and discovered that their side gate had been broken.

October 12th, 1978
The neighbors on Ryan Road who'd heard noises in their backyards earlier in the month also heard noises on the night of the attack. A side gate was left open by a prowler. After the attack occurred, police investigated and discovered that someone had been trying to break into one of the houses. A window screen was removed, another one had been pried, and yet another one had been cut near the lock. There were footprints in the yard.

October 13th, 1978 7:00 AM
A woman living on Ryan Court was leaving for work when she discovered that a bicycle was missing from her backyard. Additionally, her side gate had been left open.

The Attack
The couple went to bed around 11:00 PM. They slept with the windows open in the bedroom and the living room, as they often did.

They woke up several hours later to the sound of their bedroom door being opened violently. The beam of a flashlight was trained on them.

"Don't move or I'll blow your heads off."

The woman screamed.

"If you scream again, I'll kill you. I don't want to hurt you. I just want food and money for my girlfriend and me. Roll over and put your face in the pillow. Put your hands behind your back."

He threw shoelaces at the woman. "You, tie his hands. Tie them real tight or I'll kill you."

When she was finished, he ordered her to lie down on her stomach, and then he bound her wrists tightly and her ankles loosely. He retied her boyfriend.

"If either of you move I'll blow your fuckin' heads off." He held the

347

gun against the boyfriend's head.

The woman's young daughter had been woken up by the commotion, and she went into her mom's room to investigate. When she saw what was happening, she started to scream.

"Tell her to shut up or I'll kill you."

Her mother tried to comfort her, and told her to get on the bed between them. The intruder grabbed the child and ordered her to "get into the bathroom and be quiet." She obeyed, turning the light on as she went in. He grabbed her hand and turned the light back off. Once she was inside the bathroom, he pushed furniture in front of the door so she couldn't escape. Then he began ransacking the bedroom.

He left for a little while, then reappeared at the man's side. He shoved the gun into his head violently. "All we want is food and money and then we'll get the hell out of here." He pulled a blanket over the man's head and then put dishes on his back.

"If you move I'll drive this knife into your back," the intruder said as he began rummaging through the house again. They could hear him slamming drawers loudly.

Several moments passed, and then he was back. He untied the woman's ankles, then forced her out of the bed and began pushing her toward the living room. When they arrived, he ordered her onto the floor and told her to lie on her stomach. He began ransacking the house again, wrestling with what sounded like a plastic garbage bag. He made a few trips back and forth from the attached garage. Then he was suddenly back at her side.

"Do you want to live?"

She answered "yes."

"Then this had better be the best fuck I've ever had or I'm going to kill you." He walked away again, and she heard him in the bathroom. Then he returned and tied a towel around her eyes. He straddled her back.

"Play with it," he hissed, and she felt his wet, flaccid penis in her hands. He began moving back and forth. He rolled her over and reissued his threat, saying "This had better be good or I'm going to kill you all."

He raped her. Then he got up and began going in and out of the garage again with a large plastic bag. "Here, put this in the car," he said to an unknown or imaginary person.

Then he was gone.

Immediate Aftermath

While the attack was happening, a neighbor living a couple houses down heard a "beeping sound" several times during the time-frame of the attack. He felt that it was the type of beep made by a car when the doors get opened while the key is still in the ignition.

Police arrived and examined the scene. The garage light had been turned on by the assailant. Inside the house, they found that the power cable had been removed from the television. Strips of towel were found in the garage and in the bedroom, along with two different types of shoelaces: white ones that the assailant had brought with him and brown ones that he'd removed from a shoe in the house.

Just like the other scene in Concord, this house had distinctive scratch marks on the window screens. They weren't pry marks (or else they would've been on the frame, and also, the screens were easy to remove without prying). The scratch marks appeared in the bottom-left corner of every window screen in the house. They looked exactly like the ones that had been found at two different residences earlier in the month.

Police examined the next-door neighbor's house and found the exact same screen scratches (made the same way and in the same places). One of the screens at this house had been removed and it was leaning against the side of the house. The side gate was open, the garden was trampled, and there were scuff marks on the fence like someone had climbed it.

The California State Highway Patrol put a helicopter in the air to look for the assailant, but the search was unsuccessful.

Suspect Description

The assailant was 5'10". His penis was described as no longer than three inches when fully erect, and the victim felt it was circumcised.

He wore a black ski mask and a plain, long-sleeved shirt (which was tucked in). His pants were black slacks and he wore gray gloves that were made of a thick leather or suede. On his feet were black, round-toed shoes with laces.

His voice was "muffled" and he spoke in a nervous whisper.

Post-Attack Event

October 16th, 1978

The bicycle stolen from the family on Ryan Court was found in some bushes near an apartment complex on Ryan Road, not far from where the victims had been attacked.

Context and Analysis

The assailant hit Concord again, mere days after the first attack and only half a mile to the east of his last hit. That's pretty brazen. And this attack was a little deeper in the neighborhood, possibly making it a little riskier. That might've been why he apparently stole a bicycle from a residence just a few houses away. It's possible that he covered a greater distance to his vehicle or hideout.

The assailant delayed the blindfolding of the female victim for quite awhile in this attack, so she probably got a better look at him than most other victims had in the past. Additionally, the daughter had a brief opportunity to see him with the light on while he was trapping her in the bathroom. She was hypnotized to see if she could remember anything helpful, but unfortunately she didn't get a good look at him.

"All *we* want is food and money and then *we'll* get the hell out of here." "I just want food and money for my *girlfriend and me*." "Here, put this in the car." For some reason he wanted to advertise the fact that he wasn't alone, or at least make them *think* he wasn't alone. He put on such a show of it that the most likely case is that he *was* alone for this attack. When it comes to the comment about putting things in the car, the next-door neighbor heard several beeping sounds happen several minutes apart. It's possible that the EAR's vehicle was on the premises. Which is odd considering that there was a bicycle stolen in relation to this attack. There are a lot of possibilities here, including the idea that maybe the bicycle was stolen to throw police off the potential fact that he'd brought a vehicle. The bicycle was clearly stolen the night of the attack, but how do we explain the beeping of a vehicle?

We get questions from time to time about the size of the strips of towel that the EAR would tear. To answer the question, the strips of towel found at this attack and many others were each about two or three inches wide. Sometimes he'd simply tear a towel in half and use one half as a blindfold and the other as a gag. Other times he'd tear a towel in half and use the pieces to dim lights.

The female victim in this case was an accountant who worked in San Francisco. Her husband was a sheet metal worker. The couple had only been living in their home for two months when the assault took place, which makes a real estate connection more likely in this case than an employment connection, if any connection between the assailant and these victims exists at all.

We discussed the screen scratches in-depth in the last attack. Looking at the four houses that we know of where the scratching occurred, it seems that he was simply marking target houses. This neighborhood was fairly vast, and it seems that this might've been his way of helping himself keep notes in an infamiliar area. But as with anything else, this could be wrong. We've kept all of our theories and our attempts to explain the evidence strictly quarantined into these "Context and Analysis" sections so that you can keep the facts separate from any attempt to explain them. We encourage you to try to make the pieces fit into your *own* theories and frames.

Attack #39

Date: October 28th, 1978 2:30 AM to 4:30 AM
Victim: 23-year-old woman and her husband. Their young
son was also in the house.
Location: Montclaire Place, San Ramon

This attack is connected by DNA.

This attack was the first rape case to be connected through DNA to the Golden State Killer murder series.

The Attack
The female victim awoke to a light shining in her eyes. There was an intruder standing over her with a flashlight in his left hand. It was held up high near his face.

"Don't say anything or I'll kill you. Wake him up. Be quiet or I'll kill you, motherfucker."

Her husband woke up, and the intruder threw shoelaces at her. "Tie his hands." While she prepared to bind her husband's wrists, the intruder leaned over her husband and said "Don't move, motherfucker, or I'll kill you."

She finished tying the knots, and then the intruder ordered her onto her stomach. He tied her up.

"I want your money. All your money. I know you have some. I'll kill you if you don't tell me where it is."

She explained that there was fifty dollars in her purse. "I need more than that," he told her. He left the room for a few moments.

"I also have some silver dollars," she said.

The intruder appeared to get angry. "Where is it? Where is it?" He began rummaging through the house and ransacking drawers. After several minutes of doing that, he came back to the bedroom and told the female victim that he wanted to separate them. He pulled her off of the bed, led her to another part of the house, and forced her to lie down on the floor. He bound her ankles and then began moving through the residence. He went back to the bedroom and placed dishes on the husband's back. The intruder held a gun to the victim's head and told him that if he heard the dishes make a noise that he'd come back and kill him.

The assailant returned to the female victim and turned on the stove light in the kitchen. He paced around the room, telling the her that he'd kill her if she moved.

Then he stood over her. He told her something to the effect of "I've seen you at the lake and you look real good. Every time I see you I get hard."

She asked him which lake, and he responded by saying "Whisper! Whisper, motherfucker."

He tore a towel into strips and blindfolded her with a piece of it. Then he left her side for a moment. The victim pushed her head against the floor to move the blindfold aside a little bit, and when the intruder returned she could see that he didn't have pants on. At one point she even caught a glimpse of him with part of his mask up.

"Suck on it and don't hurt me," he said, kneeling down in front of her. "You hurt me and I'll kill you."

The victim told him that she needed a drink of water before she could do it. He went to the sink, filled up a glass with water, came back, and threw the water in her face.

Then he forced his penis into her mouth. He rocked back and forth for several minutes, then pulled out and ejaculated onto her face. Toward the end of his climax, he forced her mouth open.

He got up and wandered the house for a little while. Again he threatened the husband with a gun and again told him that he'd be killed if he moved.

The assailant returned to the victim and raped her. He didn't climax during this part of the assault.

Afterward, he took interest in a ring that the victim was wearing and called it "unusual." He pulled at it until it came off. A few moments later, he was gone.

Immediate Aftermath

October 28th, 1978 4:45 AM

Behind the victims' house was a large power line corridor with some green space on both sides and a trail at the southern side. The street across the corridor from the victims' house was called Pine Valley Road. To the east of that area was a street called Adams Place. A teenage boy returned home around 4:45 AM and saw a man dressed in dark clothing climb the fence from the backyard of 110 Adams Place and then walk west on Pine Valley Road (in the direction of the victims' house).

October 28th, 1978 5:20 AM

A man dressed in dark clothing was seen on Pine Valley Road. He stopped and hid behind some trees when a car went by and then continued walking.

Entry had been made through an unlocked door by the garage. The assailant had left through the back sliding glass door. There were scrape marks on the fence indicating that he had arrived at the residence from the rear. Footprints were found in the backyard. They were a herringbone pattern, size nine and a half.

An empty carton of Coors beer had been placed on the kitchen counter. The phone cord had been cut.

The victim was taken to John Muir Hospital in Walnut Creek for a rape examination.

Suspect Description

White male with light olive skin, late twenties, 5'10" to 6', 165 lbs with a little bit of flab on his stomach, medium build, with a larger upper body and thinner legs. His legs were very light, thin and not particularly muscular, and they had a moderate amount of dark hair on them.

The mask looked like beige or tan nylon pantyhose. He wore a blue nylon jacket that was missing a button and heavy, loose-fitting tan suede gloves. He wore dark blue cotton ribbed dress socks and royal blue brushed suede tennis shoes with a white stripe over the toe (and as mentioned earlier, size nine and a half).

The victim caught a glimpse of a section of the assailant's face. He appeared to have a small, distinctive nose with a high, arched bridge. His lips appeared to be thin, not full. There was possibly a mole on the left side of his mouth or chin. He had a short neck and possibly a slight double chin. He had close-set eyes.

The assailant talked through clenched teeth. He didn't appear afraid or nervous at all. When he walked, his gait had a scuffle to it. The assailant was never fully erect, even when he climaxed.

White shoelaces were used in this attack.

Context and Analysis

Traveling south on Interstate 680 for a little over fifteen miles takes us to San Ramon, the site this attack. Continuing down I-680, we pass Walnut Creek and Danville, places that the EAR also attacked.

From an evidence standpoint, this is one of the most important incidents because physical evidence containing DNA was preserved long enough to connect it to two other Northern California attacks and several of the Southern California murders. These crimes as a whole are so enigmatic that over the years many folks have come up with theories about there being two rapists, or about some of these attacks being copycats, or some other theory to explain some of the oddities related to the series. There's nothing wrong with exploring theories like that, but rest assured that everything you read about the man in this attack is for *sure* the same man who went on to begin murdering. DNA proves it.

There were two interesting leads regarding vehicles in this attack, but unfortunately neither of them panned out. The first was a cream-colored Toyota Celica that was in the vicinity of the attack site at suspicious moments. This car and driver was later identified and cleared by Law Enforcement. He was merely searching the area for a house to purchase.

The second vehicle was a van, or a large V8 engine, that was heard struggling to start up shortly after the assailant left the victims' house. The motor eventually started up and the vehicle left soon afterward. It was discovered that this noise was made by a neighbor who was leaving for work very early in the morning.

With those two events finally cleared by police, we're all able to focus on the two sightings of the suspicious man moving through the area shortly after the assault occurred. Assuming these sightings were of the EAR, the path that the assailant took out of the neighborhood could hold some clues. It seems he probably hopped the victims' back fence or went through the front and walked east on Springdale Lane and turned right on Broadmoor Drive, then traveled through the yards between Adams Place and/or Ramon Place, then backtracked west on Pine Valley Road. He must've either lived or parked somewhere near this road. Assuming that the timestamp on the second sighting is accurate, it's possible that he hid out for a little while. Police arrived at the scene at 5:00 AM, so he might've had to (or wanted to) den up and observe things. For all we know, he could've routinely hung around and watched the scene unfold, and then got out if he heard or saw that tracking dogs were coming. Either that, or in this case he moved very slowly down Pine Valley Road for some reason. Perhaps he made a quicker escape, and the times are off a bit. Attack #26, where he seemingly reappeared to get a bike out of a trailer, has made us wonder if he prowled or did something else after an attack on occasion. Perhaps he had to wait around for someone to pick him up.

In fact, the last idea is somewhat plausible. The assailant might've actually left the victims' house earlier than he'd planned to. Toward the end of the attack, the female victim told him that they were going to be picked up by a taxi at 5:30 AM. To throw in some wild speculation, maybe there was a getaway driver that hadn't arrived yet, and that's why he hung around in the area a little longer. Strange vehicles were sometimes heard while he was in the house or toward the end of an attack. Even going all the way back to Attack #7 where he said "I need to know what time it is." We've always wondered *why* he said that, because the victim's husband was out of town, so he didn't have to be in a hurry if he didn't want to be. It was probably just an odd way of ending an odd conversation. The facts of this case are so malleable and unique that almost anything is possible.

The victims were in the process of moving out of the house, and the night that they were attacked was actually scheduled to be their last night in that house. Did the assailant know it in advance, and was that why he decided to attack on that particular night? If he wanted to attack those victims, it would've been his last chance to do it in that area.

The husband was positive the assailant hadn't entered the child's bedroom, so as usual, the assailant didn't bother children during the assault.

The husband worked for Marina Heating and Air Conditioning in Hayward, and the wife worked as a travel agent (also in Hayward). There were a few small associations between victims/relatives and travel agencies in this case, but not many.

According to an article published on October 31st, 1978 in the Contra Costa Times, there were a few members of Law Enforcement who thought that this attack might've been a copycat. DNA evidence has obviously closed the book on that line of thinking (or, for folks who are prone to wild theories, it's opened up a whole *new* can of worms).

In early December, the Oakland Tribune published a three-page article interviewing the female victim in this case. This was one of the most extensive articles about the crime series written from a victim's perspective.

This was the only time that the East Area Rapist / Golden State

Killer attacked anyone in San Ramon. There's plenty of prowling activity off and on for almost a year here, and about six weeks after this attack a couple discovered signs that the EAR might've been staging an attack in their house, but there are no other confirmed attacks. He usually hit a town twice or more, so this makes San Ramon unique.

Attack #40

Date: November 4th, 1978 3:45 AM to 4:35 AM
Victim: 34-year-old woman. Her infant son was in the house
as well.
Location: Havenwood Drive, San Jose

The Attack
The victim woke up to find an intruder in her bedroom. He told her
not to "make a sound" or he'd kill her "with a knife." She began
screaming and crying, which made the intruder angry. "Don't you
understand?" he asked her. He told her he was hungry. "All I want is
food and money."

He pressed a knife against her temple and turned her over. Then
he pulled her hands back behind her back and tied them. Then he tied
her ankles. He tore towels into strips and used them to blindfold and
gag her.

He lubricated himself with baby lotion, masturbated, and then
sexually assaulted her.

Suspect Description
The victim felt that the assailant was Asian, but she didn't have any
specific reason for thinking so. She also mentioned that he carried a
knife and had a small penis.

Context and Analysis
The offender had attacked twice in Concord, then moved about
fifteen miles south down I-680 to attack in San Ramon, and now he

moved close to forty miles south of *there* and attacked in San Jose. San Jose was the main city in Santa Clara County, so it was outside of the jurisdictions he had hit in the previous three assaults.

There are very few details available to us (or anyone, really) about this attack. Some of the commentary elsewhere on this case explains that the investigation wasn't handled well, and that this was not initially recognized as an East Area Rapist case. Only after close inspection, and with the commission of another EAR crime in San Jose, did investigators pick up on things like the phrase "All I want is food and money," and some of the other details that seemed to fit.

The residence was a two-story house, located directly off the North Capital exit from I-680. Getting into the area and back out again would have been incredibly easy. For extra cover during an approach or exit, directly behind the residence there was a school.

We're not sure what happened during the attack that made the victim think that the assailant might be Asian. The victim *herself* was Asian, if that has any bearing on it. It's possible that the offender thought that there was a language barrier when he issued his ultimatum and she didn't comply, which was why he asked "Don't you understand?"

The next attack, occurring about a month later, would also take place in San Jose. Thankfully, that one would be investigated more thoroughly and there's a lot more information available.

Attack #41

Date: December 2nd, 1978 2:00 AM to 4:00 AM
Victims: Wife and husband
Location: Kesey Lane, San Jose

The Attack

It was the middle of the night. The female victim woke up when the beam of a flashlight hit her face. She began screaming, which woke up her husband.

"Shut up or I'll kill. Don't look at me."

The husband started to jump out of bed, but as he was freeing his legs from the blankets, the intruder hit his shins with the barrel of a gun.

"Don't move, motherfucker, you try that again, motherfucker, and I'll shoot you. All I want is food and money and I'll leave in my van." He pulled out shoelaces from a pocket or a holster. "Tie his hands. Behind his back. Tight." He threw them at the woman.

"On your stomach, motherfucker." He hit the husband again. The husband turned over and his wife tied his wrists.

"On your stomach," he ordered the woman. He pulled her arms back and tied them tightly, then tied her ankles loosely. He retied the husband's wrists and then tied his ankles.

"Don't move. Shut up and don't move or I'll fuckin' shoot you both."

He began ransacking the house. After several minutes, he returned.

"I only want money and food because I'm hungry." They told him that they had food in the kitchen and money in a closet in the hallway. He left and began rummaging through the hallway closet. It was quiet for a little while, and then he was back. He held torn strips of towel in his hand, and he used them to blindfold and gag them. In an uncharacteristic gesture, he arranged the woman's gag carefully to make sure that she could breathe. Then he untied her ankles and pulled her up from the bed.

"Don't you move, motherfucker," he said as he forced the wife out of the room. He took her to the living room, pushed her to the floor, and ordered her onto her stomach. Then he went to the kitchen, where he opened and closed some drawers and cupboard doors loudly.

He returned to the husband and placed dishes on his back. "If these fall, I'll hear them. I'll kill you if I hear them fall."

The intruder went back to the living room and stood over the victim. "I've been watching you for a long time." And then he called her by name. "I've been wanting to fuck you for a long time." He straddled her and put his penis in her hands. "Play with it," he said. It was lubricated and fully erect.

After a few moments, he stood up. He pulled her up into a sitting position and then hit her hard on the side of the head. Her body slammed to the floor.

"You better not hurt it," he said, pulling her up to a sitting position again. He put a knife against her neck. "You better make it feel nice or I'll cut your throat." He placed his penis on her lips.

About a minute later, he pushed her to the floor. "If you scream, I'll blow your brains out." He put the gun to her head.

The victim was menstruating, but it didn't deter him. He removed the tampon and threw it down next to her. Then he entered her.

He was in for only a few seconds, and then he pulled out. He stood up and went to the kitchen, where he began pacing and crying. "You motherfucker. You motherfucker," he sobbed.

Then there was silence. The victim waited for a few minutes and wondered if the assailant was gone. She sat up.

"Lie still or I'll kill you," he said out of nowhere.

Back in the bedroom, the husband moved a little bit. The dishes crashed down to the floor, and the assailant was back with blinding speed. "Just try that again, motherfucker, and I'll shoot your wife first, then you." He put the gun to the husband's head, then replaced the dishes.

He went back to the female victim and raped her again. As soon as he was done, he went straight to the kitchen and sobbed deeply for several minutes. He said a few things under his breath, but the victim couldn't hear what he was saying. The dishes crashed to the floor in the bedroom again, and once more the assailant ran in and threatened the man. After that, it was fairly quiet, though they thought they heard him crying for a third time.

The assailant began walking through the house once more, only this time he gave the impression that he was retracing his steps to make sure that he hadn't dropped anything. Then, there was silence.

Immediate Aftermath

The method of entry was the sliding glass door to the living room, though he had pried at several other entrances. He'd knocked out some glass from the window to the extra bedroom and reached in and unlocked it, but the window would only open a few inches. There were signs that he'd tried to force his way through the window anyway, but was apparently unsuccessful. He'd also tried chipping away the wood near the lock on the door leading to the garage. He broke the glass near the lock to the sliding glass door near the living room to gain entry.

Shoe prints of a herringbone pattern were found, and the assailant had eaten a box of Nabisco crackers. He'd also stolen seventy dollars, the husband's "gold nugget" wedding ring, a "General Electric digital clock radio," and a six-pack of Coors beer.

Suspect Description

The rapist was probably in his twenties. His penis was described as five to six inches long and circumcised.

He wore a navy blue nylon jacket and gloves.

He disguised his voice, speaking in a loud, harsh whisper through clenched teeth. His voice and actions seemed nervous.

The couple described him as a black male, though they didn't see any of his skin. They felt that his voice "sounded like a black man's, particularly when he cursed." The assailant had good vocabulary and diction and they felt he was probably college-educated.

Context and Analysis

This attack was located about two miles to the northwest of the previous assault in San Jose. It was still close to I-680, and this time a nice park called Cataldi Park, located to the south of the residence, could've provided cover (or a way to stalk the area). We don't know if that park existed in the same form back then, but the area was definitely a green space of some kind.

He was very determined to get into this house... look at all the entrances he pried and picked at. Failing at one window or door never seemed to deter him much, which makes us think that the difficulty of a door or window lock probably wasn't the most important variable he considered when casing a residence, even if it turns out that most of his crimes were indeed crimes of opportunity.

The female victim noted that the assailant, brutal as he was, did have a small amount of consideration when he gagged her. He made sure that the gag wasn't choking or suffocating her. In previous assaults, he typically hadn't cared if he'd partially restricted the airways of victims or not.

The assailant's penis was fully erect when he forced the victim to touch it, which was rare at this stage of the crime spree. This attack was also notable because it was the last one that he cried at. He did it twice, maybe three times at this scene, sobbing "you motherfucker" at one point. Despite seeing this behavior nearly a dozen times, we still don't understand it. Most people are quick to dismiss it, but too many victims felt it was genuine, and the behavior kept coming back over a long period of time (and long after it had served what was possibly the initial purpose, which was probably to make him seem insane or unstable). It doesn't really work as a device to instill terror, so that probably wasn't the rationale behind it. We wouldn't be surprised at all if there was a genuine psychological component to this behavior.

He called the victims by name in this attack. It's thought that he'd usually get their names from their driver's licenses while rummaging, but he could've easily gotten it from their trash, their mail, or perhaps the phone book. Whether it was part of the fantasy, a way to instill terror, or a way to throw off the police though, we don't know.

The wife worked as a registered nurse at the Stanford Hospital, providing us with yet another attack connected to the medical field. The husband and wife were both Asian, like the other victim in San Jose.

The victims in this case felt that the assailant was possibly African-American, based on the sound of his voice and the words that he used. Since the victim in the other San Jose attack thought he was Asian, it's possible that he was experimenting with voices, or trying to make his voice sound like different ethnicities in these attacks. This was the furthest away from Sacramento that the offender had ever ventured, and because of the difficulty in conecting the San Jose crimes and because of the different descriptions of his possible ethnicity, we have to wonder if it was intentional on his part. In previous attacks, there had been several victims who felt that he was faking an accent or that he genuinely had an accent, so the idea isn't too far-fetched. Additionally, in the Witthuhn murder, there's possible evidence that he called her house and disguised his voice to sound like an older African-American male's voice.

Attack #42

Date: December 9th, 1978 2:00 AM to 4:00 AM
Victim: 32-year-old woman
Location: Liberta Court, Danville

This attack is connected by DNA.

This is the second attack with DNA evidence that connected the East Area Rapist crime series to the Golden State Killer crime series.

Pre-Attack Events

December 8th, 1978 11:30 PM
Someone at a neighbor's house spotted a dark-colored van parked in the victim's driveway. The victim was told about it later, and she explained to police that she didn't know anyone with a van matching that description.

December 9th, 1978 2:30 AM
The woman who lived directly behind the victim was awakened by her two-year-old daughter, who was frightened and hysteric. It took the mother an hour to get her to calm down. The child had never acted like that before. The police later investigated the house and couldn't find any sign that EAR had been in her yard, though they noted that the mother fit the profile of an EAR victim and the timing overlapped with the attack.

The Attack

The victim woke up with a start and realized that someone was straddling her and pushing on her face. She felt a knife at her throat.

"Don't scream. Don't make any noise. I won't hurt you. All I want is money and food for my van. Put your hands behind your back. If you make a sound, I'll kill you." He pulled her wrists behind her and tied them tightly, then tied her ankles loosely.

"Where's the money? Where's the money?"

He began rummaging through the bedroom. She heard him click a flashlight on and off. After awhile, he turned on a lamp to see better. A few minutes later, she was blindfolded.

"I'm not going to hurt you. I just need food and money for my van." She told him that there was money in her purse, which she had left in the kitchen.

He roamed through the residence, but unlike other attacks, he didn't ransack it or tear it apart. He closed the drapes on all of the windows in the house.

Then he was back at her side. She heard a noise, and realized that he was masturbating. He untied her ankles and then undressed her.

"Do you you like to fuck?" he asked, adding her name to the end of the question. She told him "no."

"Do you like to raise dicks?" Again, she told him "no."

"Then why do you raise mine every time I see you?"

He pulled her shirt up and raped her.

When he was finished, he left the room. After a lengthy period of time went by, he returned and raped her again.

Immediate Aftermath

The victim was taken to John Muir Hospital.

The phone cord in the bedroom had been cut, and two strips of orange towel (tied together) were found on the edge of the bed. For the most part, the house hadn't been ransacked. Entry had been made by prying open the patio door near the kitchen.

The assailant had unplugged a stereo that the victim had left on before she went to sleep, and he'd turned off the heater. He'd left the lamp by her bedside on. Some promising fingerprints were found on the lamp, but these were later determined to belong to someone else.

The victim's driver's license, a ring, two pendants, and an antique stickpin were stolen from the house. The assailant had taken another ring, but it was found near the stereo that had been unplugged.

A bloodhound was called in. The dog picked up the scent immediately, touring the living room, going down the hallway to the master bedroom, looking at drawers and the closet, then going to the sliding glass door and out into the backyard. The dog followed the trail to the corner of the yard and came to a stop at the fence. The handler put the animal over the fence, and the dog followed the railroad tracks behind the victim's house going south, stopping and sniffing several backyards along the way (indicating that the assailant had been in those backyards). The dog stopped at a curb on Hansen Lane, a street which has changed names to Rhett Place and has been rerouted a bit. In all, the dog traveled close to half a mile.

A second bloodhound was brought in, and the dog followed the same trail, although he went a little bit further because the wind had moved some of the scent. A third bloodhound was brought in, and the animal went even further.

A startling discovery was made at the end of the scent trail. There were three pages torn from a spiral notebook. One of them was a hand-drawn map of a neighborhood, with some illegible words scrawled on the back (one of the words appears to read "punishment"). Another page was a handwritten essay about the author hating his/her sixth-grade teacher, and the third was a handwritten essay about General Custer.

Suspect Description

The assailant was between 5'9" and 5'11", 150 to 160 lbs, with brown hair and hairy legs. She saw him without gloves on, and his hands looked calloused.

He wore a ski mask that covered his face from the top of his head all the way down to his collar, and he wore a blue nylon windbreaker. She felt that his shoes had soft soles because she couldn't hear any noise when he was walking around the house.

He had a flashlight and a dull butter knife.

The assailant's voice was a controlled, angry-sounding whisper. He was articulate and seemed educated.

White shoelaces were found at the scene.

Post-Attack Event

January 15th, 1979

The phone rang at the victim's house. The man on the other end spoke in a harsh whisper.

Caller: "Do you want to fuck?"

The vicitm hung up the phone quickly. She called the police and identified the voice as that of her attacker.

Context and Analysis

By the time forensic DNA technology became mainstream, most of the physical evidence from the case had been discarded. Only the murder cases and three of the rapes had DNA evidence left to test. All of the samples were tested and compared over a period of years, and they all matched. The attacks connected by DNA include two attacks from 1978, one attack from 1979, and every suspected murder case that had a DNA sample from the killer. Since this attack is connected by DNA, we know for absolute certain that the man you just read about was the same one who attacked Victim #39, the victims in Attack #46, and that he was the same man who killed the Smiths, the Harringtons, Manuela Witthuhn, Greg Sanchez, Cheri Domingo, and Janelle Cruz. We'll get to all of those cases very soon.

The van sighted in the victim's driveway a couple hours before the attack is notbale, because something similar happened in Attack #31 (a 1960 Cadillac that had been seen in the area) and occasionally in other attacks as well (but not in such an obvious way).

He called the victim by her name, a trick he'd been pulling since pretty much the beginning of the crime spree. The victim was sure that she'd never met him before, and she assumed that he'd gotten her name from her driver's license. She didn't get a good look at the assailant, but she did get to see him from the back because he didn't blindfold her right away. He rummaged a little bit, but the house wasn't ransacked extensively at all. Most areas of the house looked as if they hadn't been touched.

The lamp yielded some fingerprints, and it was thought that the assailant had touched it with his bare hands. It took a a couple tenacious investigators a few decades to eliminate those prints, and it's such an interesting saga that it could fill an entire chapter by itself. After several nail-biting eliminations, the prints were finally matched to someone in the witness protection program who had since passed away. The suspect had a long criminal record, including burglaries, so he looked promising. This person *had* been in the victim's house as a guest, but supposedly not while the lamp was there, so investigators jumped through a mountain of paperwork, flew across the country, exhumed the body, did a DNA comparison, used a special technique to make sure that the fingerprints were correct, and then waited for a few weeks while testing was done. The fingerprints matched. The DNA didn't. All of the mysteries about fingerprints in this attack had finally been resolved and unfortunately, the suspect was not the East Area Rapist.

The papers that were found by the tracking dogs are still, to this day, an unresolved lead. There's a hand-drawn map with some illegible words on the back, an essay about General Custer, and a short journal entry piece called "Mad is the Word" where the writer complains about a sixth grade teacher. The map and the "Mad is the Word" essay were found folded up together, and the "General Custer" essay was folded on top of them. They'd been torn out of a spiral notebook. While it doesn't appear that this evidence was given much consideration at the time, in recent years it's become one of the most interesting and talked-about pieces of evidence in the entire case. We're currently pinging different organizations in search of photographs of the other writings (such as the writing on the wall at the gas station in Attack #22, or the scrawling in the restroom near Attack #27) to determine if there's a handwriting match between any of the papers and writings. It can't be proven without a doubt that these papers were created by the assailant (they could've been planted intentionally to throw off the investigation, or perhaps their presence was a coincidence) so any link between them and other EAR evidence would help. We've included the text of the essays in a section after this chapter.

Another hotly-debated issue stems from this attack as well related to the tracking dogs. The reaction of the dogs at this scene was more enthusiastic than the handlers were used to, particularly in the bathroom, which has led to countless theories about whether the assailant had some kind of drug dependency or some kind of disease. We had an in-depth conversation with a SAR handler where we presented him with information about the sixteen attacks where dogs were used to track the offender (along with information on which dogs were used multiple times, what all of their reactions were, and whatever details we could come up with). His opinion was that the dogs probably became more excited in the bathroom because of a concentration of scent in there, meaning that the assailant had spent more time in there or even that he ejaculated or went to the bathroom in there. We're not aware of him having ejaculated in the bathroom, but he certainly could've spent a lot of time in there or he could've done something else to leave a higher concentration of scent. The sum total of the data doesn't indicate without a doubt that that the assailant had a disease or drug issue that would aggravate sensitive dogs. The over-enthusiastic reaction doesn't occur at every scene or with every dog. However, the dog at Attack #21 also reacted in a way that its handler thought was enthusiastic, and in Attack #45 one of the dogs did also (it doesn't seem that the other two dogs used in that attack did, though). One of the dogs used in this attack was used in Walnut Creek as well, and the dog actually remembered the scent between Attacks #45 and #47 (a period of a few weeks elapsed between them). Regardless of their reactions or what the reactions might've meant, we've seen SAR dogs in action, and these dogs do love their jobs. We don't know how you'd tell an overly-enthusiastic reaction from a normal one. To us, it looks like they always track with gusto!

A note on the general area of where the scent ended: it was called Hansen Lane, but that street no longer exists. It's now called Rhett Place, and it's located off of Orange Blossom Way. The geography of a few streets in that area has changed since the attack took place.

As mentioned, one of the rings taken from the victim was found to still be in the residence. It had been moved or dropped by the attacker. It's unknown, of course, whether this was done by mistake or whether it was left on purpose.

The police tried something interesting with this attack. A day or two after it had happened, they brought together this victim and Victim #39 and let the women discuss their personal lives in-depth, hoping to find commonalities between them. There didn't seem to be anything that could have been zeroed in on by the assailant in his stalking or attacking. This was an important meeting though because both of these attacks would eventually be connected by DNA.

This victim had been divorced for three years, and had only lived in Danville for two years. She'd previously lived in Chicago. She'd been living alone for about a month, and the house she was living in had been for sale for two months—an obvious real estate connection, though it's unknown whether the assailant was using any real estate angles in his victim selection process or not. There are hints in other attacks that the offender might've posed as a prospective buyer to get the layout of a residence and even to unlock a door or window in advance. There's no indication of that happening in this particular attack and no rock-solid proof that it happened in any of the others, though.

The "Homework" Papers

The following are transcriptions of the two essays that were found near Attack #42. Misspellings were left intact. In some areas the words aren't completely legible, so rather than guess, we simply made note of those passages.

"Mad is the Word"
Mad is the word, the word that reminds me of 6th grade. I hated that year

[several lines left blank]

I wish I had know what was going to be going on during my 6th grade year, the last and worst year of elementary school.

Mad is the word that [illegible] in my head about [the word "it" crossed out] my [illegible] year as a 6th grader. My madness was one that was [illegible] by disapointments that hurt me very much. Dissapointments from my teacher, such as feild trips that were planed, then canceled.

My 6th grade teacher gave me a lot of dissapointments [the word "and" crossed out] which made me very mad and made me built a state of hated in my heart, no one ever let me down that hard before and I never hated anyone as much as I did him. Disappointment` wasn't the only reason that made me mad in my 6th grade class, another was getting in trouble at school especially talking that's what really bugged me was writing sentences, those awful sentence that my teacher made me write, hours and *hours I'd sit and write 50 - 100 - 150 sentence day and night I write those dreadful [short illegible word crossed out] paragraphs which embarrased me and more important it made me ashamed of myself which in turn; deep down in side made me realize that writing sentence wasn't fair it wasn't fair to make me suffer like that, it just wasn't fair to make me sit and wright until my bones ached, until my hand felt every horrid pain it ever had and as I wrote, I got mader and mader until I cried,*

I cried because I was ashamed
I cried because I was [illegible]
I cried because I was mad, and
I cried for myself, kid who kept me having to write those [illegible] sentences. My angryness from sixth grade will [illegible] my memory for life and I will be ashamed for my sixth grade year forever

"General Custer"

Gen George Armstrong Custer. A man well amired, but a man hated very much by many who served him. He became a general at a very young age of 23, [illegible] all took place during the civil war, Custer after the war was dropped to his perminent rank of a captain, as he fought more, he made more enimies, especially fighting against the unions in the south west. IN 1876 the government planned to Round up the SUIX AND Cheynne and put the on reservations. Custer regiment joined the expedition, commanded by general Alfred H. Terry. As Terrys scouts reported in from [illegible] through the Mountain territory, Terry ordered Custer to find [crossed out heavily]. Then as Custer searched for the villages, custer and his men found a vally that ran all[illegible] the little big horn river. Custer, expecting only around 1000, was not expecting around 5000 indians THAT would fight back. It was the [illegible] gathering of [illegible] tribes in [illegible]. This battle would be one of the deadliest and most strangest battles between the Indians and the white man. 225 UNION men, including Custer, died that day by courageous by hostile Indians that would do anything to save there homes and there families

Thunderbird Place Incident

1978 had been an odd year. The offender started it off with a flurry of phone calls to former victims, then regressed from attacking couples to attacking young teens again, then the Maggiore murders happened (which may or may not be related), then he hit atypical areas (Stockton and South Sacramento), and then the bizarre Modesto/Davis summer began. Fall saw him moving into the Contra Costa County area, where Concord was hit twice, San Ramon once, San Jose twice, and then Danville. Knowing the EAR's history, an attack in San Ramon or Danville would surely be right around the corner. We have evidence that it *was*, but that a perceptive and proactive couple saved themselves from it.

December 18th, 1978 6:30 PM
A couple in their thirties, living on Thunderbird Place in San Ramon, had a ritual every afternoon and every night of checking the doors, windows, and even looking under furniture for any subtle signs that the dreaded East Area Rapist had been in their home. The couple's residence backed up to a large green space (the San Ramon Golf Course), and they knew that they were exactly the kind of couple that the EAR had been hitting.

During their afternoon ritual on December 18th, the couple found nylon rope hidden under a couch cushion. They immediately called the police.

The police did a thorough search of their residence and couldn't find any sign of forced entry. Despite the wet, muddy ground around

375

the perimeter of their house, no footprints were found.

In an effort to protect the couple (and in hopes of catching the East Area Rapist in the act), two police officers parked next door and set up a stakeout inside the potential victims' house. Nothing happened that night.

A day or two after the rope had been found, the couple discovered that someone had rifled through one of their drawers, removed an envelope of wedding photos, and dumped them out on top of the other items in the drawer. Again, the police set up shop inside the house. Neighborhood dogs barked for about an hour in the middle of the night, but nothing else occurred. The police staked out the residence one more night, but again, there was no sign of the East Area Rapist.

The wedding photos and the envelope that they had been in were dusted for prints, and over a dozen latent prints were found. None of them were ever tied to any of the other East Area Rapist crime scenes. The rope was analyzed by the crime lab, and even sent out to a specialized facility, but nothing unique or identifying was found.

All of the Law Enforcement documentation that we've seen (even reports generated decades later) seems to regard this as a genuine EAR incident,. The offender *was* known to break in occasionally and remove a screen or leave a deadbolt unlocked for himself, and he occasionally staged crime scenes (especially in the earlier attacks). We don't have direct knowledge of him secreting rope, shoelaces, or twine in a house before an attack, though it's not inconceivable that he might've done that. He'd certainly left some in trees, on bike handlebars, and in other places immediately before an attack. It doesn't sound like the amount of rope that they found would've been enough to bind both of the victims' hands and feet though.

This was the last known possible EAR activity for a few months. Perhaps the fairly obvious stakeout of the San Ramon residence spooked the offender into laying low for awhile, or perhaps something in his personal life kept him away. When he resurfaced, it was for a very strange one-off attack back in Rancho Cordova. After that, he committed a few more rapes, and then he began killing.

Attack #43

Date: March 20th, 1979 5:00 AM to 6:00 AM
Victim: A mother of 12-year-old twins (a boy and a girl), who were also in the house.
Location: Filmore Lane, Rancho Cordova

Pre-Attack Events

March 18th, 1979 6:00 PM
The phone rang at the victim's house, and the son answered it. There was silence on the other end, but he could tell that someone was there.

March 20th, 1979 12:30 AM
The son heard a prowler outside of the house, but he didn't tell his mother or sister.

The Attack
The victim woke up to find an intruder in her room, on top of her and holding her shoulders. She started to scream and the intruder reacted violently, hitting her several times on the left side of her face with some kind of solid, rectangular object that he held in his right hand.

"All I want is your fucking money. I won't hurt you if you shut up."

He ordered her to roll over, and then he tied her hands behind her back. He pulled the blankets over her face and turned on the light.

He began rummaging through her dresser, and she heard him

putting jewelry into a bag. He was breathing in and out heavily while he did this, and he called her "bitch" at the end of a long exhale.

He left the light on in her room and then moved to the kitchen. The victim heard him opening and closing drawers.

He returned to her room and pulled the blankets off of her face, allowing her to see him (though she couldn't make out many of his features due to his mask). He rummaged through the house some more and unplugged a few lamps. He ransacked the house for about forty-five minutes, returning several times to check on her and ask her again about money. He used the word "bitch" and/or "fuck" every time he checked on her.

As the attack wore on, he pulled the blankets all the way off of the victim and pulled at her pajamas. He held onto the elastic waistband of her pajama bottoms and pressed a knife against her back. He told her that it was her "last chance" to tell him where the money was. She begged him not to hurt her and told him that she was telling the truth about not having any money. He stood in silence for several minutes, then let go of her pajama bottoms. They snapped back into place.

"Bitch," he said. He gagged her with a scarf from her dresser drawer, put the blankets back over her head, and then began rummaging through the house again.

An alarm clock went off in the daughter's bedroom. The assailant seemed to take it as his cue to leave. He called her "bitch" one more time and then disappeared.

Immediate Aftermath

Deputies handled the scene, and then later that night EAR investigators interviewed the woman and her children.

There were no signs of forced entry, and the victim was sure that she had locked her windows and doors. He left through the front door, which was open when the victim's children woke up.

She'd been tied up with a nylon cord that the assailant had cut from a tent that was stored in the garage.

Sometime while he was rummaging through the house, or perhaps before he woke her up, he'd closed the door to the daughter's room.

The son's door was already shut.

Three thousand dollars in jewelry was stolen. The assailant did not cut the telephone line, he didn't use lotion, and he didn't sexually assault the victim. She didn't hear him go into the refrigerator or hear him eat.

He'd beaten her pretty badly during the initial confrontation. When investigators talked to her, the left side of her face was swollen, bruised, cut, and her eye was partially closed. Her injuries were so painful that she had difficulty speaking.

Suspect Description

The assailant was 6' and about 180 lbs. He did not appear to be fat.

His mask was made out of nylon, perhaps a stretched-out nylon stocking, and it hung loosely from his face. His gloves were tight-fitting, dark, soft, and made out of leather.

He spoke through clenched teeth, and tried to make his voice sound deeper and "huskier" than it probably was. The victim felt that he spoke slowly and deliberately and thought about every word before he said it. She felt that he was doing it to repress a stutter.

Context and Analysis

Another few months had gone by without an attack, and once again he stole thousands of dollars worth of items upon his return. Clear patterns emerge when you walk through the attacks like we've been doing. It's very likely that he fenced this jewelry, and a few thousand dollars went a long way back in the 1970s. But did he fence it in Sacramento or did he fence it somewhere in Contra Costa County or Santa Clara County? Did he live by stealing?

This is such an odd attack in so many ways, and if you've read this far we don't need to point most of them out to you. He hadn't attacked in three solid months, and when he reappeared he was back in Rancho Cordova? And then in the next attack he goes all the way down to Fremont, and then back to Danville and nearby Walnut Creek. If this attack was truly the East Area Rapist and soon-to-be Golden State Killer, and investigators think it was, then that's exactly what he did. Very odd.

This attack makes you wonder if he still lived somewhere in the Sacramento area during *all* of the attacks, from Stockton to Modesto, Davis, Concord, San Jose, and beyond. It's feasible, though it's probably not the most likely scenario. Perhaps he had some reason to be in Rancho Cordova again and just really "needed" to attack that night. Maybe he'd gone back there to work for awhile or visit family or go to school (this attack could've theoretically occurred on a spring break from classes). Or maybe not, and he needed the money. The fact that this attack came after a long absence opens up even more possibilities. When we're sorting through possible suspects ourselves, every once in awhile we'll see something that makes this particular pattern fit, like one suspect who graduated in 1976 and then started college near San Francisco (relatively close to the Fremont, Walnut Creek, and Danville attacks) in January of 1979 (after taking a couple years off of school), and seeing that the spring break of his college aligned with this attack. There are so many different scenarios that can work, but only one of them is the correct one. Hopefully this book is organizing the information in the most logical and useful way possible so that somehow, some of these things can start to fit together for someone.

The area where this attack happened was very atypical, even though it was back in Rancho Cordova where he'd attacked so many times before. The victim lived in a duplex, and everything around it was a duplex as well. The yards were small and very close together, and the fences were quite low (just a little higher than the average adult's waist). The victim was gagged with a scarf and not a towel. She was bound with nylon cord from the garage. Was it possible that EAR was already experimenting with different types of bindings, rather than relying on shoelaces? In Walnut Creek he would use a different type of binding, and when he moved down south to commit murders he'd definitely begin using different types of ligatures. This was perhaps an effort to keep the police ignorant of the fact that he was in town again, or perhaps he knew that if he were walking around town with shoelaces in Rancho Cordova, it would raise all kinds of questions.

Another note about the location of this attack—it's quite far from the other attacks that took place in Rancho Cordova. The victim's residence was located on the far northeast side of the area. The nearest previous attack site was a good three miles away. It's worth analyzing what this could mean, because this part of Rancho Cordova was a huge part of town that he had avoided— except for this attack. To make matters more interesting, the events with the suspicious man that frequented the 7-Eleven in late 1977 (and reportedly evaded the police stakeout) happened just a bit to the northeast of this area. It's an area worth looking at for suspects if it's truly thought that the EAR never offended directly near his own residence... except for maybe this one and only time?

The woman wasn't sexually assaulted, and she felt that it was because of a large scar on her back. When he stood over her with her pajama bottoms pulled down, she felt that he was staring at it and was bothered by it.

Due to the odd geography, the fact that he didn't seem to care if she saw him, and a few other things, we wouldn't be surprised if we someday find out that this was a copycat attack. That doesn't minimizes the trauma or the pain that was inflicted on this victim in any way, of course. In fact, having yet one more person willing to commit a crime of this nature in the area is even more tragic than just having the same offender be responsible. Unfortunately, the East Area Rapist wasn't the only monster haunting the night.

While the differences are easy to spot, there were similarities to the other EAR crimes too, or else we wouldn't be discussing this assault. He spoke through clenched teeth. He called her "bitch." The victim felt that he behaved on a script and he seemed very sure of what he was doing. She felt that he was trying to repress a stutter.

So with this, nearly three years after he'd begun (perhaps three and a half if the October 1975 attack is tied to him), the East Area Rapist seemingly left Sacramento for good. He would go back down Interstate 680 for a few more attacks, and then resurface in Southern California in a far more deadly incarnation.

Attack #44

Date: April 4th, 1979 12:20 AM
Victims: 27-year-old woman and her boyfriend
Location: Honda Way, Fremont

Pre-Attack Break-In
The neighbors living next door to the victims heard what sounded like the victims' gate being pushed open. It made a loud sound, because there was a pile of bricks against it (which must've taken considerable effort to move). The neighbors clicked on a flashlight and looked around outside, but they didn't see anything. A few minutes later, they heard glass cracking and breaking. Again they looked outside, but they didn't see anything. They didn't call the police. The victims were out for the evening while this occurred.

The Attack
The victims left the house at 6:45 PM to go out to dinner in San Jose, and they returned home at 9:00 PM. When they went inside the house, they noticed that the door to the spare bedroom was closed (they usually left it open), but they didn't think anything about it. They went to bed, had intercourse, and went to sleep.

They woke up to the beam of a flashlight. There was a masked man in their bedroom pointing a gun at them.

"Motherfucker, you're dead. Put your face down or I'll blow your fuckin' head off."

He tossed shoelaces onto the man's back and told the woman "Tie him up. Don't look at me." As she tied the man's hands behind his back, the intruder kept urging her "tighter, tighter." Then he ordered her to lie down. He tied her hands tightly, her ankles loosely, and tied the man's ankles tightly. Then he tied the man's wrists with two more shoelaces, both of them much more tightly than the woman had tied him. "Don't you move or I'll blow your fuckin' head off," he barked as he wove the laces around the man's wrists. "I'll cut your fuckin' head off."

He told them that he was hungry and "just needed something to eat." He left the bedroom but didn't go far—they heard him down the hall tearing towels into strips.

He wandered the house for a minute, then came back into the bedroom and told them once more that he was "hungry" and just needed "something to eat." Then he began wandering the house again.

He returned to the bedroom, told them that he needed money, and asked the female victim where her purse was. She told him that it was in the car, which was in the garage. He promptly left their side and went to the garage.

When he came back, he told them that he wanted them to "get away from each other" and he ordered the woman onto the floor. He stood next to her, and she could tell that he either wearing shorts or had no pants on at all. He told her that he needed to separate them, and he pulled her up off of the floor.

She was led to the living room, put onto the floor, positioned face-down on her stomach, covered with a blanket, and then blindfolded with strips of towel. The intruder then went to the kitchen and grabbed an armful of dishes.

He reappeared in the master bedroom. "Don't move or I'll blow your fuckin' head off," he told the man again. He started stacking a pile of glasses, jars, bottles, and whatever else he could find on the man's back. He gagged him with towel, reinforced the ankle bindings with a severed television cord, tied another shoelace around his wrists, tied some neckties and pantyhose around his wrists and ankles, and then slowly ran a knife down the man's back. "I just need food for my van," the assailant told him. He put several blankets over the man's head and then left the room, closing the bedroom door behind him.

He returned to the woman's side. He whispered something, and she couldn't make it out. She told him that she didn't understand, and he got angry and said "Whisper, motherfucker." He repeated himself, and she still couldn't hear him. He leaned down over her face and whispered "If you do what I want, I'll take the food and money and leave without hurting anybody."

He turned on a television and muted the sound, then took the blanket off of her back and straddled the her without putting down his full weight. He placed his lubricated penis into her hands. Then he stood up, took a step toward her face, took a step back, straddled her, and placed his semi-erect penis into her hands again.

He untied her ankles and flipped her onto her back, then began fondling her breasts. The victim didn't think he had gloves on. He raped her.

She was menstruating, but it didn't seem to deter him. He was inside of her for about a minute. He rolled her onto her side and entered her again. He pulled out. She wasn't sure if he had climaxed or not. He squeezed her left breast very hard, threw the blankets on her again, retied her ankles, and then gagged her with a piece of towel. He used one of her boyfriend's neckties to tie her feet to a bookcase. He turned the television off.

"I'll just get these things together and put them in my van," he said. He wandered the house for a moment, possibly retracing his steps to make sure he hadn't forgotten anything, and then she heard her front door open. He went outside. After a few moments, he came back in and walked around for a bit more. Then it seemed he was gone. Neither she nor her boyfriend heard a car or "van" leave.

Immediate Aftermath

The victim went to the hospital. The local police called for assistance. A few officers from other jurisdictions who were familiar with East Area Rapist crimes arrived to help.

Several doors and windows on the house had been pried. The

assailant had worked on the sliding glass door of the master bedroom the most. He'd gotten past the lock but couldn't get past a deadbolt mounted in the floor. He'd also tried to get through the window to the guest bedroom. He'd pried at it, cracked the glass, but still couldn't get through. The sliding glass door to the family room was what finally gave way. Shoe prints were found all over the perimeter of the house.

The EAR had brought all of the shoelaces with him except one of them, which he had taken from one of the male victim's shoes. He'd stolen stolen sixteen hundred dollars, but strangely there was a lot more cash available that he'd left alone.

Suspect Description
White male, late twenties or early thirties, 5'8" to 6', 165lbs to 180lbs. White legs with brown hair. The female victim thought that he had groped her with his bare hands, and noted that his hands were smooth and not calloused. He hadn't achieved a full erection, and his penis seemed to be only three inches long or so.

He wore a dark ski mask, a dark nylon parka, dark pants, brown checkered socks with stretched elastic, and dirty white tennis shoes or deck shoes.

His voice sounded forced and disguised.

Context and Analysis
Fremont is off of I-680, just like the vast majority of the attacks in this phase. It's situated halfway between San Ramon and San Jose.

One of the things that strikes us with this attack is that the EAR could've been in the house when they got home from San Jose, which is scary to think about. If so, he could've witnessed them having sex, which was something that seemingly became a frequent occurrence once he moved further south and began killing. The fact that this attack shares more in common with the murders than with the rapes is scary enough, and the impeding move to murder is almost foreshadowed in this attack when he wakes the man up and tells them "you're dead."

In this assault and in the previous one, he was described as heavier. Maybe he'd gained weight over the break, or worked out, or maybe he was wearing heavier clothing. One investigator theorized that he wore a bullet-proof vest from time to time. Regardless of any size gains, the male victim in this attack, a large, well-built man, could've *easily* outmuscled him in a fair fight. The assailant tied him multiple times with shoelaces (putting no less than four of them around his wrists), electric cord, neckties, and pantyhose. The offender knew that if the man got free in this one, it would be over.

He pried at this house a *lot*. Just like at the attack in San Jose, and in the first murder scene that's coming up soon in December of this same year, it didn't matter how hard he had to try or how long it took... when he wanted into a particular residence, he kept chipping away at it until something gave. As we noted in another chapter, he seemed to prioritize victim qualifications over ease-of-entry.

He used a lot of glass objects on the man's back, but not dishes per se. He mentioned a van, he fondled her breasts, but he didn't call her a "bitch." He assaulted her while she was on her period. These are all variations from the norm, but they're ones that we've seen before. As usual, he asked where the money was kept, not just so he could steal it, but probably to get a peek at their driver's licenses. Sometimes he'd steal them seemingly for a souvenir, but other times he was just probably just curious about their name or wanted to use this "knowledge" to terrorize them or throw the police off.

He ran the knife down he man's back, and he'd done similar things with the female victims in other attacks. We've assumed before that there was something sexual about the way he'd run his knife over the woman's body, but since he did it to the man in this attack, it's probably more likely that he did it simply to terrorize his victims.

"Whisper, motherfucker," is a direct repeat of a line from Attack #39. Despite some of the minor differences in this attack, exact phraseologies help tie the cases together in unique ways.

The woman worked as a secretary in Burlingame, a town on the other side of the Bay. The boyfriend was a contractor, and they had only planned on living in the house until they could sell it.

Attack #45

Date: June 2nd, 1979 10:30 PM
Victim: 17-year-old girl
Location: El Divisadero Avenue, Walnut Creek

Pre-Attack Events

Early May 1979
The victim and her mother lived on San Carlos Drive, a street that intersected with the house where she would later be attacked. In early May, someone had broken into the home and stolen their address book and a nightgown.

May 1979
All throughout the month, the victim received odd phone calls, some of them at home and some of them at the different places she was babysitting at. Occasionally her mother would receive a call. There were about ten calls total. Several other people connected to the victim received hang-up phone calls and crank phone calls as well.

May 16th, 1979 Evening
In the area between Danville and San Ramon (both towns that EAR had already hit), there continued to be suspicious activity. A thirty-eight-year-old woman was doing laundry in her garage, and as she began walking back into the house, she saw an intruder in her living room. Once the intruder discovered that he'd been spotted, he ran out the patio door, through the open side gate, and began running

west on Joaquin Drive toward Camino Ramon, a street that came right off the highway. This happened about twelve miles south of where this victim would be attacked, but near other confirmed East Area Rapist activities.

Mid-May 1979
Crank phone calls started up at a house near the golf course. Three women lived at this house, and the calls continued from mid-May until the day that the attack happened.

June 1st, 1979
Those same three women had a prowler in their backyard. After the attack happened, one of them noticed that two pictures were missing from the house. One of the photos stolen featured a resident of the house in a bikini.

The Attack
The victim was babysitting for a neighbor. Her charge had gone to bed, and the victim was sitting at the kitchen table doing homework and watching television. Something drew her attention to a nearby hallway. Standing there was a masked man with a large knife and some kind of large, rectangular object in his hand. He ran toward her and pushed her head against the table.

"Don't look at me. Don't make any sounds. Shut up and be quiet. I'll slit your fuckin' throat if you don't do as I say."

He grabbed her arm violently and started forcing her toward the master bedroom. One of his hands pushed her head down as they walked and the other held her arm tightly. He pushed her onto the bed in the master bedroom and said "Shut up. Put your hands behind your back. All I want is money." He bound her hands very tightly with plastic "flex ties."

He started running his knife across her neck and again told her that if she wasn't cooperative, he'd "slit her fuckin' throat." "All I want is money," he said again.

He disappeared for a few moments, and when he returned he was carrying pantyhose and strips of torn towel. He used these instruments to blindfold and gag her, and then he began rummaging through the bedroom. He reinforced some of her bindings with a cloth belt and a knotted shirt. After he finished in the bedroom, he went into the bathroom.

When he returned, he rolled her onto her back and untied the ligatures around her ankles. He undressed her from the waist down, then removed his own pants. She heard a strange sound, and realized that he was masturbating. Then she felt his weight on the bed, and he positioned himself in front of her and ordered her to spread her legs apart.

"Have you ever fucked before?" he asked. He got on her and tried to push his way in, but couldn't. He kept trying to force it in, but it wasn't working. He seemed to get angry and frustrated. A moment went by, and then he rolled her over again. He placed his penis into her bound hands and ordered her to "play it it."

He quickly flipped her over again and and laid on top of her with his full weight. He lifted her sweater up and ripped her bra off, then put his mouth on her left breast. He began biting her nipple. He bit it normally a few times, and then bit it very hard, leaving teeth marks that would last for quite awhile. He raped her.

When he was done, he put her back on her stomach. "Don't move or I'll kill you," he said. He roamed the bedroom for a minute, got dressed, and then put his knife against her.

"I'm going to leave. Don't scream for help or anything or I'll cut your throat." A few moments later, the house fell silent.

Immediate Aftermath

The victim was taken to John Muir for treatment and a rape examination.

Bloodhounds were brought in. The first one found the scent in the master bedroom, went to the bathroom sink, and then went out the sliding glass door in the bedroom. The dog went around the house and through the open side gate, down El Divisadero Avenue (heading south), then turned right near San Carlos Drive heading northwest.

The scent ended on San Jose Court. A second bloodhound became fixed on the scent in the bathroom and followed it down the same path. A third dog followed with the same results. They all ended up at a house on San Jose Court/San Carlos Drive that had a pool under construction and a little curved hideaway for a bike or vehicle.

Suspect Description

White male, 5'6", no body fat.

He had a loose-fitting white mask, a belt with a sheath for his knife, and gloves. He wore a dark windbreaker with writing on the left breast.

He spoke through clenched teeth in a "low, gravelly voice."

Post-Attack Events

June 2nd, 1979 Between 9:30 PM and 11:30 PM

Sometime in the general timeframe of the attack, a bicycle was stolen from Los Banos Court (a street about half a mile to the northwest of this attack). The bicycle was later found damaged in front of a house on El Divisadero Avenue (the street where the attack took place).

June 1979

The suspicious phone calls to the victim's family did not end after the attack occurred. They continued to happen, mostly at the mother's job. She worked for a doctor in Walnut Creek. The phone would ring, she'd pick it up, and there'd be nothing but heavy breathing on the other end.

June 4th or 5th, 1979

The mother spotted a suspicious vehicle near her house. She approached it, but before she could get too close, it drove away. She described the driver as a white male, and the car as a maroon-colored Ford Ranchero or Chevrolet El Camino.

Context and Analysis

Walnut Creek is situated just six or so miles south of Concord, and the offender had been attacking along that stretch of Interstate 680 since October. Living elsewhere, like in Sacramento, while he committed these crimes would be impractical and fairly risky since Law Enforcement would have plenty of time to catch someone on their way back north. If he *was* living elsewhere, then he was at least spending a significant amount of time in these areas from October to December 1978 and from April to early July (and probably through August) 1979. This was perhaps a detail that someone who knew the offender in his regular life might have picked up on, and it's something that might lead to identification even today.

In this particular attack, it's likely that some of the stalking was done at close-range *and* from a bit of a distance, given the fact that the calls seemed to follow the victim around to her different babysitting jobs. While it seems to imply that the offender was in the area consistently at least throughout May 1979, that's not necessarily so. The logistics of him calling her at the different places she was working at leaves a lot of room for questions. The other attack against a babysitter, (Attack #31, the final attack of the Sacramento series except for #43) didn't have those types of calls. How did he know where she'd be, and when she'd be there? Did he observe her house or even follow her? Or did he call different people in the address book, listening for her voice to pick up? Was it some combination of the two? Were the calls really from the offender, or could they be coincidence? There were only a few of them. Would he *have* to do this locally, or could he pull it off from afar? If he was just calling phone numbers from their address book (which may have been designated or marked in a certain way to indicate that certain people were babysitting clients) and doing it in the evening when people would usually have a babysitter, he could've done that from anywhere.

Regardless of how he did what he did (or how often he actually did it), the fact is, he seemingly knew where she'd be the night that she was attacked. The couple that she was babysitting for that night was a regular customer—she'd been babysitting for them every Saturday night for quite awhile, but she hadn't for the month or two leading up to the attack. That makes it very odd that he'd know where she'd be that night, unless he was watching the residence, listening in to phone conversations, knew someone else that she knew, or unless it was a huge coincidence and he was prowling for a random victim that night and spotted her. But this attack doesn't seem random. She was targeted, and it seems he had the place and time figured out.

The phone calls kept coming in even *after* the assault. That was fairly rare. It happened with the first official victim in Rancho Cordova, it happened with the first victim in Stockton (Attack #23), and here it was happening again. It makes me wonder what the true benefit or purpose of the phone calls was. On the surface, they seem to merely be a method of figuring out when people will be in the house. But in some of these later attacks, there also seems to be a psychological purpose to it. Especially the calls that were obscene and the calls that came after attacks. The calls in December 1977 are a whole new level of strange and definitely point to the assailant liking to strike terror, or getting some sort of excitement from contacting victims by phone even after the attack. The calls weren't just a tool to figure out a schedule in these cases—at least not always.

The house where the victim was babysitting was positioned across the street from a school—a common geographical feature in many of the attacks. There was also a vacant house nearby, and it had a real estate sign in the yard that essentially advertised it as such. A walking trail was to the south, and it led all through the area. John Muir Hospital was nearby.

In three of these final attacks (and even the Harrington murder in 1980), there are connections to a grocery chain called the Alpha Beta Market. In this attack, the connection involves a gardner from the Alpha Beta Market who had been to a couple houses in the area, including the victim's house. By itself, this doesn't mean anything, but because of the fact that this attack and the next two attacks have a slight connection to the chain, it's worth noting.

This attack had a couple of differences from the others. The biggest difference was the bindings. They're are a little hard to describe... you might call them plastic wire ties or "plastic cuffs" or something else entirely. Basically, the ligatures were plastic strips that were commonly used to keep bundles of power cords together. Was this something that the assailant had on him for some other purpose, and then he improvised their use? It's more likely that he had them for the specific purpose of using them for the attack, but he had never used a binding like this before and as far as we know, he never would again. Maybe he used them for work, or he found them while prowling.

He bit her nipple, at one point doing it so hard that teeth marks were visible. We don't know if anything strange was noted about his teeth. Aside from the rare occasions where he wore a mask with a hole for the mouth, we don't know much about that part of his face. The only other time we're aware of that his teeth were able to be indirectly examined was in Attack #12, where he had bitten into some cheese.

He also told the victim that he wanted money, but he never seemed to search very hard for it and he never asked her where it was kept. Since this residence didn't have any personal items related to the victim, it's not surprising that his rummaging was kept to a minimum.

When she first saw him, she noticed that he had a rectangular object of some sort in his hand. It was thought to be an Eveready flashlight, but it could've been a small container of some sort or something else entirely.

As was usual with the offender, he didn't disturb the kids in their rooms, and they didn't wake up.

The maroon-colored Ford Ranchero or Chevrolet El Camino spotted after the attack matches the infamous "decal" vehicle seen in Attack #21, only the car from Attack #21 was described as more of a brown than a maroon, and the vehicle spotted at *this* attack may or may not have had a decal on it. The sighting related to Attack #21 was on May 16th, 1977, over two full years before this incident.

The handling of this investigation was done by competent Law Enforcement personnel, *but...* there was a problem. Walnut Creek refused to cooperate with EAR Task Force members. When folks talk about how a lack of communication and a lack of cooperation worked in the offender's favor, this is a perfect example. They did keep good records and they did investigate well, but they did it alone, rather than accept the help of specialists. Part of the assailant's strategy of moving from jurisdiction to jurisdiction was to take advantage of the inherent communication problems that existed among different Law Enforcement agencies. It must've worked, or at least it helped a great deal... otherwise, you wouldn't be reading this.

Attack #46

> Date: June 11th, 1979 4:00 AM to 4:45 AM
> Victims: Wife (35 years old) and husband. Their young child
> was in the house as well.
> Location: Allegheny Drive, Danville

This attack is connected by DNA.

Pre-Attack Events

June 10th, 1979 11:45 PM

A neighbor living on the part of El Capitan Drive next to the highway was startled by the sound of footsteps outside his bedroom window. He looked out and saw a prowler standing just a few feet away. The prowler didn't know that he'd been spotted—his eyes were trained on a neighbor's house. After a few minutes, he jumped the fence. The neighbor got dressed and went outside, where he spotted the suspicious man getting onto a ten-speed bicycle. When the man saw the neighbor, he pedaled away quickly. He traveled east, passing Allegheny Drive and then turning right onto Mustang Drive, headed south. The neighbor described the man as a white male, 6'2", 210 pounds, heavy build, with chin-length dark hair and wearing a dark t-shirt. The police were called out but were unable to locate the man.

June 11th, 1979 12:00 AM

A mother on Delta Drive heard her baby crying in the middle of the night. She got up to attend to her, and didn't notice anything out of the ordinary.

June 11th, 1979 1:30 AM
A woman living on Lehigh Valley Circle heard a noise in her yard. She went to look and spotted a prowler outside her home.

June 11th, 1979 2:30 AM
The couple living next door to the victims heard a noise outside their bedroom window. They looked out but didn't see anything. The next day they discovered that their side gate was open.

The Attack
The wife woke up to a man standing at the foot of the bed with a flashlight and a gun aimed at her. Startled, she nudged her husband awake.

"Neither one of you motherfuckers move or I'll blow your fucking heads off. All I want is money."

He moved to the husband's side, pressed the gun against him, and cocked it. "One move and I'll kill every motherfucker in the house."

The husband started to get up, but the intruder grabbed his legs and forced him back onto the bed. "Don't move again or I'll blow your fuckin' head off. Get on your stomach and put your face in the pillow. Put your hands behind your back."

He threw shoelaces at the woman. "Tie his hands," he said. She complied. "Tighter, tighter," her urged her. When she was done, he ordered her to get on her stomach. He pulled her arms back, tied her wrists tightly with shoelaces, then moved over and retied the husbands hands very, very tightly. He tied the man's ankles the same way, and the woman's ankles loosely.

"Where's the money? As soon as you give us money, I'll go back to the city. Or I can kill every motherfucker here and leave." They noticed that he mixed up singular and plural words in the same sentence ("us" and "I'll").

The wife told him that her purse was nearby, under the bar, and the husband told him that his wallet was in a pocket in his pants.

"Shut up," the intruder said. He rummaged through some pants that were on the floor.

"It's not here. Your wallet's not here. Don't lie to me. Where's your billfold?"

"In my other pants in the den."

"Don't move or I'll kill you." He left the room and returned a few minutes later.

"You moved, didn't you? You tried to untie him, didn't you?" He inspected the man's bindings, and then went over and yanked the woman off the bed. He undid her ankles and then gagged and blindfolded her with pieces of towel. He gagged the husband as well.

He began forcing the woman toward the living room. "Where's your purse? I can't find it. Shut up." Once they reached the living room, he set her on the floor and retied her ankles. Then he went back to the master bedroom to check on the husband. He put a sheet over the man's head and then stacked some perfume bottles on his back. He held the gun against his head and cocked it.

"If I hear the bottles jingle, I'll blow your fuckin' head off. You don't like it do you? There's nothing you can do about it."

He began rummaging through the whole house, opening and closing drawers loudly.

"I'm hungry, I need something to eat," he told the wife as he passed by. She heard him in the kitchen opening one of their beers. A minute or two later, he came back and stood by her.

"I want to fuck you," he told her, and then he called her by name. He straddled her and placed his penis in her hands. "Play with it. Stroke it." She could feel that he wasn't fully erect.

"I want you to suck me," he told her, and then he called her by the wrong name. It was a name similar to hers, but it was off by a letter. He forced his penis into her mouth. His hands were on her skin, and it felt like he wasn't wearing gloves. He palced his hands up and down her body. Then he rolled her onto her back, removed the ligatures from her feet, and raped her.

After a few moments, he got up and began rummaging through the house again.

"I have to take these out to the van," he said when he returned. "Don't move or I'll blow your head off. I'll be back."

A minute or two later, both victims heard a small vehicle, possibly a truck, drive quickly up the street and then screech to a halt in front of their house. The truck idled for close to a minute, then hit the gas again and drove for a very short distance, where it stopped idled for a little over another minute. A car door slammed loudly and then the vehicle sped off.

The male victim assumed that the assailant had been picked up by someone, so he started to work on getting out from under the perfume bottles. Suddenly a voice in the room hissed "Don't move or I'll blow your fuckin' head off." It was the assailant, and he was standing just a few feet away. A few minutes went by. The husband waited and listened, and he didn't hear anything else. Again he started moving. The perfume bottles tumbled off of him.

No response. The assailant was gone.

Immediate Aftermath

June 11th, 1979 5:00 AM

About fifteen minutes after the assailant had left the victims' house, a neighbor leaving for work noticed a suspicious van parked very close to some trees. The van was described as fairly new (no older than five years old, but no newer than three), possibly a Chevrolet, with a double rear door that had small windows and single rectangular tail lights. The van was a dark blue-green color. It was parked near the intersection of El Capitan Drive and Camino Ramon, no more than five hundred feet to the southwest of the attack site and located right at the highway.

When the police arrived, they determined that the point of entry had been an unlocked window in the child's bedroom. Muddy footprints were on the floor in that room. Investigators found strips of yellow towel, white shoelaces, and an empty Olympia beer that he had taken from their refrigerator.

Since the victim felt that he had touched her with his bare hands, a special technique was used to see if any prints could be lifted from her skin. None were found. She was then transported to John Muir Hospital.

A bloodhound was brought to the scene, and the dog followed a trail leading south. It went through almost two dozen yards, going down El Capitan Drive and Delta Way. It didn't lead to where the suspicious van had been parked, but it went near that area. Many shoe prints were found in the yards, and they all matched. Casts were taken to a shoe store and they were identified as having come from the Adidas "Tobacco" model, a casual shoe that had a distinctive woven design on the top. The shoe size was nine and a half.

Suspect Description

The assailant was in his twenties, 5'5" to 5'9", with a stocky or even a "chunky" build. He had soft, light-brown hair and his bare hands were small and felt soft, not calloused.

He was wearing a thick, heavy sweater, and the sweater might've made him look heavier than he really was.

The man spoke in a forced hiss or whisper through clenched teeth. His voice seemed weak, not commanding.

They described his mannerisms as "mocking" and felt that he was trying to act "tough." He smelled like talcum powder, and the scent was described as "feminine."

He tied them with white shoelaces.

Post-Attack Events

June 11th, 1979

On Silver Chief Way, a street very close to where the victims lived, a small car wash ticket was found close to the door of a vacant house. It wasn't there the day before. It was described as being three inches square, and it had "Car Wash 6/9/79" printed on it.

June 16th, 1979

More suspicious shoe prints were found. They had a herringbone pattern and were found on El Capitan Drive and Paraiso Drive (the latter a street located north of the attack and connected to the Iron Horse Regional Trail and to Camino Ramon).

Context and Analysis

This attack is connected by DNA to the other two East Area Rapist crimes that DNA was available for, and to several of the Golden State Killer murder cases. As far as M.O., it's a very important attack because it's *so* similar to so many of the other East Area Rapist attacks on couples that had happened in Sacramento and elsewhere. It leaves very little doubt that the same offender committed all or most of the crimes attributed to him.

Everything seemed very routine to the EAR by now, and it should seem routine to the reader too. There's almost an undercurrent of boredom from the assailant, and also an undercurrent of increasing anger and violence. If we were to tell you that he'd begin murdering couples before the year was over, we doubt you'd be surprised.

There didn't *seem* to be any stalking of this particular family. It seemed that on this night, the EAR was simply out in a semi-familiar area and just wanted to attack, and that he kept looking until he found someone. Many of the Danville incidents seemed to have that same vibe. That's also what he seemed to for most of the murders. It's possible that he was trying to stop stalking or attacking altogether, or that he had grown bored of the stalking part of the attacks, or that he simply didn't have the time to do it anymore due to work, school, or family commitments. Perhaps he wasn't in town long enough, or had gotten so good at it that he was never seen, or something had changed physically and he now stuck out too much in the neighborhoods. Maybe he'd just sit at home until the compulsion became too much. Regardless of what happened, in this attack and in the final two Northern California attacks, it doesn't appear that he had extensively stalked his victims. The victim in the previous attack *had* been extensively stalked though… or at least it seemed that way.

To drive the point home a little bit, notice how he called the victim by the incorrect name the second time. Not only did he probably not know her name before the attack, but after he learned her name it wasn't even important enough to remember properly.

"Where's the money? As soon as you give us money, I'll go back to the city. Or I can kill every motherfucker here and leave." He mixed up singular and plural in the same sentence. The victims remembered him saying "we" a few other times during the attack, and "I" a few other times as well. There was another odd word choice, the word "jingle." "If I hear the bottles jingle, I'll blow your fuckin' head off."

This wouldn't be a proper EAR attack without having an event that defied logic. Toward the end of the attack, when the victims felt that the assailant was leaving, they heard a small vehicle drive quickly up the street and then screech to a stop in front of their house. The vehicle waited for a minute, lurched forward a bit, waited again, a door slammed, and then the vehicle sped off. The husband assumed that the assailant had left but he was there in the room with him still (or he had come *back* into the room). And then the assailant silently left. This wasn't the first time that a strange vehicle had been heard toward the end of an EAR assault. It's definitely the most dramatic and puzzling example, though. Was the assailant being picked up by someone, and went outside to drop some things in their truck (it was thought to be a truck), and then later he left to meet them elsewhere? Was there more than one person involved in some sort of capacity? Or was this a really weird coincidence?

More information was learned about the shoe that made the prints in this attack. As noted earlier, it was an Adidas "Tobacco" model, a casual shoe that had a distinctive woven design on the top. This particular model of shoe had been quite popular, with one and a half million sold in the western side of the country. It had been manufactured since 1971.

The "Car Wash 6/9/79" ticket found a few hours after the attack could mean that he crashing in a vacant house, or at least hanging out in one for awhile. He would do that about six months later during the Offerman/Manning murder, so it's worth considering.

We promised you an Alpha Beta Market connection in this attack and in the next, so here it is: the family did their grocery shopping every two weeks at the one on Diablo Road, which was located fairly near their house. Another similarity with previous victims is that the husband in this attack worked in Hayward (as a division manager for a data/documents company). The victims in Attack #39, another DNA-connected case, both worked in Hayward.

Attack #47

Date: June 25th, 1979 4:15 AM to 4:35 AM
Victim: 13-year-old girl. Her 16-year-old sister and her father were also in the house.
Location: San Pedro Court, Walnut Creek

Pre-Attack Event

June 24th, 1979 Afternoon
The victim and her sister received a hang-up phone call while they were home alone.

The Attack
The young girl awoke to a man straddling her back and putting his hand over her mouth.

"Don't say a word. I'm not going to kill you, all I'm looking for is money. All I want is money." He pressed a knife against her neck and ordered her to put her hands behind her back. He began tying her wrists and ankles and told her that if she didn't stay quiet, he would "stab her." He gagged her with one of her bras and began rummaging through her bedroom.

He stood next to her and again told her "I'm not going to kill you. All I'm looking for is money. All I want is money." Then she heard him pumping lotion.

He straddled her back and put his penis into her hands. "You rub my cock and you better make it good or I'll kill you. I've got my long knife and if I cut you it will be instant death."

403

After a few moments, he got off of her and ordered her to roll onto her back. He blindfolded her, untied her feet, and pulled her clothes off.

"Have you ever been fucked before? I want you to spread your legs far apart. Just do what I want and I won't hurt you. Gimme a good drop or I'll kill you." He raped her.

He climaxed after a few moments and then pulled out. He retied her feet but did it very loosely.

"If I hear one word out of you, I'll kill you while I looky-looky for money, money, *money*," he said. It wasn't a stutter... it was voiced more like a taunt. She heard a few noises, one of which she thought might've been the assailant leaving. She started moving and got her blindfold off, and then was able to get through her bedroom door and into the hall.

"I've been raped!" she cried. She began running down the hall. As she passed the bathroom situated between her room and her sister's, she heard noises coming from inside. She found her father and told him that the assailant might still be in the bathroom, and the father checked it. The bathroom, which opened to the outside, had no one in it and the outside door was closed.

Immediate Aftermath

The bindings used in the attack were a white twine that the assailant had brought with him. Some of the twine that he hadn't used was found on the floor near the victim's bed. More was found outside her bedroom window.

Even though the assailant had claimed he was looking for money, he hadn't gone through her purse. Apparently he had stolen her hairbrush, though. A semen stain on her bedsheets was sent to the crime lab. The sample came back as being from a non-secretor, which was consistent with other EAR crime scenes.

A bloodhound was brought in. The dog remembered the assailant's scent from the other Walnut Creek assault, Attack #45, and got to work immediately. The dog followed a path through the backyard that led around the perimeter of the house, stopping at each window and door, which indicated that the assailant had peeped into every opening of the house. The dog then went through the side gate (which the assailant had left open), and went west and then south on San Pedro Court. The dog turned right onto San Carlos Drive to continue heading west, and then an immediate and short left onto San Jose Court. The trail ended exactly where it had ended on the night of Attack #45, at a house with a pool under construction and a little curved hideaway for a bike or a vehicle.

Suspect Description

White male, late twenties, 6', solidly-build and broad-shouldered.

His mask looked homemade, and the material looked like a doily or a cheesecloth or something similar. It fit very loosely. He wore a light-colored t-shirt and some kind of jogging shorts that looked a lot like swim trunks because of the seams or slits down the sides. The victim was positive that they weren't boxer shorts. She didn't notice any gloves. His hands felt smooth, and if he was wearing gloves they might've been the thin, surgical type.

He spoke in a "scratchy" voice through clenched teeth. He had a slight Spanish accent, but she thought it was fake. His voice sounded angry and nervous. He didn't stutter and he didn't trip over words, but he repeated the "looking for money" phrase at one point and it had an slightly arrogant or mocking tone to it.

Post-Attack Events

Late June 1979

Hang-up phone calls suddenly began in earnest after the attack happened, actually starting a just few hours after the assault had taken place. There were several received at the victim's house, and strangely, the neighbors behind them (a couple in their forties) received several too. The reporting on the calls that the neighbors received is a little unclear, and some of the calls to the neighbor's house might've actually occurred before the attack happened.

Context and Analysis

If you've been finding the attacks up to this point a bit repetitive, then don't worry. As you saw with this attack, things are starting to take some left turns.

This is an odd attack, and not just because the girl is such a young child. It's similar to Attack #3 in many ways, with the assailant entering the younger sister's room while the older sister and a parent slept nearby. It's quite risky with the father and the sister in the house in such close quarters. He didn't bind her feet very well at the end, and he brought his own lotion (the victim recognized the scent as Johnson's Baby Lotion). He was only there for about twenty minutes, but it's possible that he wasn't quite ready to leave yet, and that's why he didn't bind her feet tightly.

The speech pattern was a little different. He didn't curse a lot at her like he did with the adult victims, though we don't know if that had to do with her age or if it's just coincidence. The "looky-looky for money money *money*" was definitely different.

One of the most-analyzed phrases from the entire canon of attacks is the "Gimme a good drop" or "Let it drop easy" phrase uttered to this victim. Clearly we know what he's referring to, but the question is, why refer to it this way? Where did that phrase come from? Where would one hear a phrase like that and make it part of their vocabulary? Folks have noted that it seemed to turn up in Western and Cowboy movies quite a bit. Given a few other pieces of evidence (the possible belt buckle from Stockton and the "Okie" man near Davis, the reference to Jesse James in the poem, other dramatic phrases used by the assailant), that phrase might be a facet of the "character" he was playing or the "headspace" he was in when committing these attacks. Some have noted that the phrase might've appeared in porn movies at the time, which would've also been a very likely place for the offender to hear it.

The bindings in this attack were white twine, and the assailant had brought the twine with him. White twine would be used in the Goleta attacks later in the year. The way that it was scattered about in this attack seems very reminiscent of the way it was scattered in the

Offerman/Manning murder.

The victim lived with her father and her sister, and her mother lived in Concord in an apartment. There's a slight possibility that the perpetrator could've learned of her from Concord, if that's where he resided. A more interesting but only slightly more likely connection is the Alpha Beta Market angle (this was the third victim in a row who had shopped there or been in contact with an employee from there before their attack). The victim had been at the Alpha Beta Market near her house late in the evening before she was attacked. Nothing suspicious happened while she was there, and the trip there occurred *after* her hang-up phone call, if that was related.

It's always interesting when phone calls begin happening in earnest *after* the attack, like they did way back with Victim #1 and later on with a few others. Law Enforcement set up phone traps for many of the victims, but unfortunately they were never able to come up with anything usable.

We mentioned this a little bit in the summary for Attack #45, but there's a little bit more to mention. Within the span of a few weeks, the EAR attacked in Walnut Creek twice, and in case you didn't notice, he *parked in the same spot* both times! If the offender's history tells us anything, it tells us that he liked to offend twice or sometimes more in an area... probably so that his good prowling and "intel" didn't go to waste. It happened in Orangevale, Concord, San Jose, Stockton, Modesto, Davis, and so on (Davis and Concord in particular showed that he liked tiny pockets and could potentially be caught on a return trip). And while he attacked at all hours of the night, he had been gravitating toward the later morning hours for awhile by the time this attack happened. This attack seems more preventable than some of the others, because there's a missed opportunity to nab him at his parking spot. By 1979, after three years of Northern California dealing with this assailant, the EAR Task Force could've advised Walnut Creek on bracing for another attack, especially in areas that he'd already traveled. There's no way of knowing if it could've actually prevented anything or resulted in his capture, but again, this was a missed opportunity. Easy to say with hindsight, and we're not singling this area out for any particular reason other than the fact that the clear anecdotes of their stonewalling makes this an easy example.

That's our soapbox moment. Please understand that we hold Law Enforcement in very high regard and recognize that a lot of superb work was done on this case in most of the jurisdictions, but when you spend enough time with this case, the what-ifs can drive you crazy.

Attack #48

Date: July 5th, 1979 3:57 AM
Victims: Wife and husband
Location: Sycamore Hill Court, Danville

Pre-Attack Events

Early July 1979
In the days leading up to the attack, several neighbors received hang-up phone calls. One of them even saw a prowler at her bathroom window.

July 5th, 1979 2:00 AM
The neighbor next door heard a prowler on her porch. When questioned a few days after the attack, painters working on her house remembered seeing footprints on her porch the day after the attack, but they had cleaned them up and painted over them.

July 5th, 1979 3:50 AM
The next-door neighbor on the other side of the victims heard her sliding glass door open. When she checked it later, it was unlocked.

The Attack
The husband was awakened by a rustling sound on the other end of his bedroom. He opened his eyes, and in the reflection of a mirror he saw a figure in the room slipping a dark mask over his head. Something dangled from the man's gloved hand.

The husband sat up with a start. He and the figure turned toward each other. The husband shot out of bed and began screaming at the top of his lungs.

"Who the fuck do you think you are?" the husband yelled at the intruder. "What the fuck are you doing here?"

The masked man took two steps back and then simply stood there blinking while the husband approached him continued to yell. Due to the commotion, his wife woke up. While her husband blocked the intruder into a corner, the wife ran past them, down the stairs, and out the door. Once outside, she began screaming for help.

The husband weighed his options and decided that he didn't want to risk getting killed by this intruder. He told him "If you leave now, you can leave." The husband then turned and ran as fast as he could down the hall, down the stairs, and outside to join his wife.

Immediate Aftermath

The police searched the immediate area, but they couldn't find the intruder. Neither the victims nor a nearby neighbor who had come out to investigate the commotion saw any sign of him leaving.

About an hour later, a bloodhound was brought in. The dog seemed to pick up a trace of him in the living room, and then picked up a stronger trail in the backyard. Once the dog made it to the gate, she had definitely zeroed in on it. She took the trail south to Morninghome Road, then up to where it became Park Hill Road, and then to the area where it intersected with Old Orchard Drive. There was a heavy patch of ivy there and the ground was muddy, but the dog was a true professional and dove in head-first. Because of the way the dog reacted in the ivy area, the handler felt that the target had been there pretty recently. Hoping that the offender was still in the area, they took the dog back to the starting point and tried again (this was done to give the scent more time to spread out and settle, which helps the dog track it). On this second try, the dog stopped only stopped briefly at the ivy and then continued on to a large greenbelt area behind the condos where the victims lived. She went all the way through the greenbelt area to Sycamore Valley Road, where she lost the scent.

The scene was processed thoroughly. It became apparent that the intruder had rummaged through some of the dresser drawers before being interrupted. He'd also taken some of the man's shoes from the closet. White shoelaces were found on the ground where the confrontation had occurred.

Suspect Description
The husband was able to give a very detailed description of the man he saw. Some of these details came out of an in-depth hypnosis session:

The intruder was a white male, mid-twenties, 5'10" to 6', 160 lbs, and had a thin build with square, athletic shoulders. The man's face appeared to be youthful and lean but not bony or gaunt.

His eyes were round, deep-set, and light-colored—probably hazel. The separation between them was somewhere between medium and wide. They were sleepy-looking with heavy eyelids, despite being held wide open. His pupils seemed big or dilated, and his eyelashes were "full but not feminine."

The mask appeared to be homemade, made out of wool, or something like it. It came down only to the jawline, leaving a tiny bit of his chin and neck exposed. The intruder didn't appear to have a beard.

The jacket was a nylon or vinyl windbreaker. The collar was a "regular design with peaked and pointed folds outside and down." The jacket lining was either fleece or flannel. There was gold (but possibly white) lettering on the left breast. The first letter was "C" and it was about a quarter-inch high. There were at least three other letters after the "C." The victim felt that it said "Corn".

It was unknown if the assailant had a weapon or a flashlight.

Context and Analysis

Finally, right? It was about time the offender invaded the lair of a light sleeper. The male victim in this case, who had military training and physically outmatched the offender by a large margin, later regretted not subduing him. While it's natural to play "what if," this man absolutely made the right call based on what was known to him at the time of their confrontation. The EAR was almost always armed with a gun when he attacked couples, and he likely would've acted desperately to survive and get away.

It's difficult to say how the assailant selected this particular group of condominiums, especially since their layout was so different from his usual hunting grounds. Was there something about these particular victims that drew him there, or was he just prowling the complex and spotted them?

One of the differences between this residence and previous ones included the fact that the master bedroom was not on the main floor. Additionally, the residence was very exposed (in the sense that there were a lot of windows and a lot of glass facing the greenbelt-side of the house). Perhaps the multiple windows could've resulted in the assailant spotting them and deciding to make them a target. It'd happened before, and in the portion of the crime spree immediately following this phase, it appears that voyeurism and the random spotting of vulnerable victims seemed to play a much larger role in his victim selection than in the past. Or perhaps that was always how he'd selected victims, and he'd just stalked them more thoroughly in the earlier attacks after he'd noticed them. If that's correct, and if he wasn't stalking too far in advance anymore, why not? Had he become more confident, or was he simply more impulsive and feeling invulnerable because of his dozens of successful attacks? Had the rush he'd gotten from stalking worn off, and only the thrill of the attack mattered? Looking at the way in which he escalated between June 1979 and December 1979, it seems he wasn't getting the same rush that he used to and that he was needing to up the ante.

There are a couple other interesting things to note about the area. There was a house for sale very close to the victims' residence which had been bustling with prospective buyers. If a real estate connection exists with this case, that's where it might've played out. Another interesting detail was the utility crawlspaces located under the complex. These corridors connected the different condos to each other through openings in the closets. It doesn't appear that the EAR used these though, especially since the door to the victims' crawlspace was blocked with their possessions and unable to be opened.

"Corn" is an odd thing for a jacket to say. "Coach" is bandied about as the most likely word, although every once in awhile we'll come across a "seed corn" jacket that fits the description. Most people lean toward "Coach" even more because of the font style that was used. The style of the letters were the traditional "school block" lettering. In the industry, the style is typically called "Varsity" or "Collegiate," and it resembles the the style of lettering used for verbiage on letterman jackets (on the front, not the script font used on the backs). The color was most likely a "gold" or a mustard-yellow. Industry professionals advised that they letters were probably applied by a silk screening process and not individually applied, meaning that the word, whatever it was, was created as one unit, most likely for mass production.

Every once in awhile the theory of this attack being unrelated to the EAR series is discussed, which is natural, because the offender thankfully didn't get an opportunity to present most of his modus operandi. Also, people are uncomfortable with the notion that the EAR would mask himself so late in the process, and they feel that the layout of the residence was just too atypical for the EAR. Others feel that the intruder's reaction when confronted by the husband was "out of character" for the EAR, or that it didn't quite fit with his past behavior.

No doubt, he's a mean, cold-blooded killer who wouldn't hesitate to destroy anything in his way. But our analysis of this situation is that the EAR was simply taken by surprise during a vulnerable phase of the attack. Victims frequently noted that the offender didn't seem confident until they were bound. When he was out prowling, there appeared to be many times where he was calm and stood his ground and simply stared blankly. Of course, there were other times when he took off running or possibly even shot at a pursuer. It's possible that the type of reaction he would display in a situation probably had a lot to do with what he was planning on doing at the moment he was interrupted or encountered. On the prowling incidents where he felt confident, or he was more familiar with the area, or he hadn't done anything nefarious that he could get in trouble for, those are probably the times we got blank stares or even a "good evening." On nights where he was possibly armed, possibly stalking a victim closely, or even planning to attack, we had a prowler who would run. When pursued, we got one who retaliated with violence if he felt he had no other option. We've touched on this before, but it's an important concept to think about.

We don't know if the intruder in this attack was armed. It does seem that he was completely stunned and utterly bewildered at the turn of events. His victim, all six-feet-two-inches and two-hundred-twenty pounds of him, was up and in his face before he even realized what was happening. The victim described the intruder's reaction as "disbelief." We'd probably agree with that assessment—he'd never been confronted that way before. It's truly hard to tell if there was any kind of fear. Psychopaths are known for not having normal emotions, but we'd think that the basic biological drive for self-preservation most likely exists in spite of almost any psychological condition.

The victim didn't notice a weapon or even a flashlight—only what turned out to be shoelaces. If this was the East Area Rapist, and the majority opinion thinks that it was, who knows what would've happened if he'd had a gun in his hand. The husband likely caught him at the perfect time. Just a few seconds later, and the intruder might've had his mask fully-secured and his gun drawn.

One researcher floated the idea that the couple could've made up this incident, but the bloodhound evidence definitely indicated that *someone* was in their room that night. The surrounding geography of the area (the greenbelt portion in particular), the minor prowling incidents, and Danville being a place the EAR had hit multiple times all seem to support the idea of that man being the East Area Rapist.

One quick note about the mask not being secured until just moments before waking up his victims. You'll notice that in the next EAR incident (his failed attack in Goleta), the victims felt that the intruder wasn't even *wearing* a mask when he woke them up. He most likely entered that house in Goleta with the intention to kill. There's a very slight chance that he had planned to do the same thing in this attack, or was "looking for an excuse" to do it, and thus had become quite lackadaisical with his mask.

This failure likely didn't sit right with the offender, and it certainly seemed to influence his behavior going forward. The next person who got out of bed to confront him, Robert Offerman, was shot to death. That confrontation happened roughly five months after this one.

The failure in this attack (and most likely the possibility that he might've been seen) was probably a main reason for the next East Area Rapist attack happening a full three hundred and twenty-five miles away and why, when the offender resurfaced, he was more dangerous than ever.

August 1979 Sightings

Much is made about the supposed quiet period between the attacks in Northern California and Southern California, but as this chapter and the next will show, strange events and EAR-style prowling incidents were still commonplace in Contra Costa County for about six weeks after the failed attack in Danville. Similar events started up in Southern California shortly after these events stopped.

<u>August 8th, 1979 9:40 PM</u>
A fifteen-year-old girl living with her family on Pine Valley Road in San Ramon noticed her dog barking at the home's rear sliding glass door. She turned on the porch light and was startled by the sight of a man with a large knife standing just a few feet away from the door. After being spotted, he ran to the fence, climbed over it quickly, and disappeared.

She called the police, and their response was immediate. While officers and bloodhounds searched for the subject on the ground, the California Highway Patrol put a helicopter in the air and they searched for him from the sky. They focused their efforts on the golf course and the Christmas Tree farm that bordered the house. Despite the blazingly-fast response by Law Enforcement, the subject was never found. Even though the suspect wasn't located, such an impressive show of force by the police department probably helped chase him out of that immediate area for good.

What makes this incident interesting is the fact that it happened less than a couple thousand feet from both Attack #39 *and* the

Thunderbird Place incident where rope was found under the couch cushion. Prowling activity had occurred in the area earlier in the year as well.

The man was described as a white male, mid thirties, 5'9", with a slender build (and "heavy" legs). He was light-complected and clean-shaven, and had very straight, light-brown, collar-length hair. The subject was wearing a dark nylon jacket with a zipper, faded jeans, and he carried a long-bladed knife. A composite was made of this prowler.

Tennis shoe prints were found near the fence. They were a size nine or ten.

August 12th, 1979 4:20 AM

A man in his sixties living on Plaza Circle in Danville spotted a prowler in his backyard. The subject seemed to be "passing through" and left through the open side gate. The same prowler was spotted later, running near a fence. He was described as a white male, mid-thirties, 160 lbs, wearing a silk stocking over his head, a white t-shirt, and light khaki pants.

Plaza Circle was located at the northwestern portion of the Diablo Country Club Golf Course. Attack #48 occurred about three miles to the southeast, and Attacks #42 and #46 were roughly a mile south of Attack #48.

August 17th, 1979 2:00 AM

A woman living on Plaza Circle spotted a prowler with a flashlight near her yard. He appeared to be sizing up her home. The police were called, but they were unable to locate anyone. Other neighbors were questioned about the incident, and several of them reported hearing strange noises, like someone was prowling around their property.

August 17th, 1979 4:00 AM

A woman living off of Diablo Road (across the golf course from Plaza Circle) heard what sounded like a prowler in the yard. Her sons went outside to investigate, but they didn't notice anything amiss.

Berkeley Road Dog Incident

Goleta, a small town over three hundred miles to the south of Danville, was the next place that EAR would strike. Given the short time span between the events in the previous chapter and the events in this one and the next, it's incredible (or very telling) how quickly the EAR relocated to this new area and was able to learn the intricacies of the roads and creek beds. Either he'd honed his "craft" to the point where he required less time to gain a comfort-level with a new area, or he had some sort of familiarity with this area already.

His next attack would be in Goleta on October 1st, 1979. Before we get to that though, there was this odd incident with a prowler and an injured dog that we need to explore.

<u>September 24th, 1979 Evening</u>
A woman living on Berkeley Road in Goleta (about a mile southwest of where the attack would be, but very, *very* close to where there would later be a Golden State Killer murder) answered a knock at her front door. The man standing there told her that his dog had been injured, and that he'd tried knocking on the house next door but no one was home. He asked her if he could use her phone. She looked at the dog, which was lying on the sidewalk adjacent to her driveway. It appeared to be a large German Shepherd or German Shepherd mix. The man repeated his request to use the woman's telephone so that he could call a friend, and he told the woman that he'd been walking his dog without a leash across the footbridge over the San Jose Creek. The dog had run between the houses, and when he'd reappeared, he'd

collapsed at the man's feet. The woman didn't notice any obvious injury to the dog, and despite a bit of apprehension, she allowed the man to use her telephone. While the man called his friend, the woman looked at the dog a little closer. She noted that the dog did not appear to be badly injured. Sometime later, the man's friend arrived in a flat-bed pickup truck. The man and the dog got in it, and the truck pulled away.

September 24th, 1979 Evening
Later that evening, the woman next door to the one described above returned home to find that someone had turned on the water faucet in her front yard. Her entire yard was flooded. This was the house that the man had said he'd gone to first.

September 25th, 1979 Morning
The woman whose yard had been flooded was leaving her house to go to work. Seemingly out of nowhere, a man and a woman carrying an infant approached her. The man claimed that his dog had been stabbed the previous evening at her home or at the house next to hers. He told her the story that he'd told the other neighbor (that he'd been walking his dog without a leash the night before, and that the dog had gotten away from him and had run between the two houses). There were no fences, and he told her that he'd assumed that the dog had entered one of the backyards. When the dog had returned from between the houses, he'd slumped over at the man's feet, and the man had noticed that the dog was bleeding. He told her that he lived on the west side of San Jose Creek and that he'd walked his dog over the footbridge at Berkeley Road. He also said that he'd taken his dog to the vet for emergency treatment.

The woman next door, the one who had let him use the telephone, came out of the house. She recognized the man from the previous evening. Together they walked to the backyards to look around. There didn't appear to be anything that the dog could have injured itself on, and there was no sign of anything else amiss.

The man told both of them that the veterinarian's opinion was that the dog had been stabbed, and it took seventy stitches to close the wound. The man profusely thanked the woman whose telephone he'd used, and later sent her a single rose as a token of appreciation. The rose was in a decorative vase and was arranged with baby's breath, and the woman felt it had come from a florist.

The man was described as a white male in his late teens or early twenties. The woman with him was described as white, in her mid-twenties, heavyset, with shoulder-length blonde hair. As mentioned earlier, the woman was carrying an infant.

Two and a half years later, the witness who'd let him use the telephone was contacted by police, and she gave a more detailed description of the man. She described him as a white male, early twenties, 5'6" to 5'8", with a very slender build. He had slightly wavy dark brown hair and no facial hair. The witness was shown two composites that were used during the murder investigations in Goleta/Santa Barbara, and the witness said that neither of them matched the man she'd seen.

Context and Analysis

It's unknown for sure if this incident is related or not. The proximity of this both in geography and on the calendar to the upcoming October 1st, 1979 attack, plus the close geographical proximity to the later murder of Cheri Domingo and Greg Sanchez, makes this a very interesting piece of the puzzle. It was thought that perhaps the East Area Rapist had been lurking in one of those backyards and he'd injured the dog when it came along and threatened to harm or expose him. At one point the dog owner *himself* was suspected as possibly being the EAR/GSK. This lead wasn't explored heavily at the time, but years later the man walking the dog was seemingly identified and subsequently cleared by DNA. It's still possible that the East Area Rapist was lurking in one of those backyards that night, and it's even possible that the man with the dog was never correctly identified. It's unknown whether this incident was related at all. Regardless, it's an interesting tale that helps set the stage for some of the strange events that follow it.

The Goleta Attack

Date: October 1st, 1979, 2:00 AM
Victims: Woman and her boyfriend
Location: Queen Ann Lane, Goleta

Pre-Attack Events

September, 1979

It seemed a prowler was afoot in the weeks leading up to the attack. Peepers, open side gates, shoe impressions, and noises in yards were noticed by residents living near the victims. One of the incidents happened on September 5th, reducing the break between prowling incidents in Danville and prowling incidents in Goleta to mere weeks. Most of these incidents, which may or may not be related, are discussed in later chapters.

The "dog incident" on Berkeley Road that we just explored happened about a week before this attack.

The Attack

The couple had gone to bed. They were intimate with each other, and then they went to sleep. A few hours later, the woman awoke to someone at the foot of their bed.

"Wake up! Wake up!" the intruder said as he violently kicked their bed. A flashlight beam darted across the woman's face, then her boyfriend's face, then back to hers. She couldn't see the man very well, but she thought that she saw the outline of his hair. He didn't appear to be wearing a mask.

"Get on your stomachs."

They started to comply.

"Don't move, motherfucker, or I'll kill you. Don't move or turn your head. I gotta have money. Tie his hands." He threw ligatures onto the bed. They were pre-arranged lengths of nylon twine. "Tie it tight or I'll kill you."

She did as she was told, tying her boyfriend's hands and then his feet. The intruder then tied *her* hands, and he retied the bindings on her boyfriend. Both of the victims' hands were tied more tightly and more sadistically than in any of the previous crimes. He tied the woman's ankles loosely.

"I gotta have money. I gotta have money. Don't look at me, motherfucker. I gotta have money." He said that he wouldn't hurt them if they gave him money. She told him that her money was in her purse, located in the kitchen.

He began ransacking the bedroom. After looking around for a bit, he returned to their side and leaned in close. "I'll kill you, motherfuckers." He then left the room. They heard him wandering through the house, rummaging and ransacking as he went. He opened and shut drawers loudly.

Then he was back. "I can't find your purse. One move, motherfucker." He left them again, ransacking the house some more. And then he returned. They could tell that he was wearing a ski mask.

"Where's your purse?" he asked again. "I can't find it." She repeated that it was in the kitchen, on the kitchen sink.

He went to her feet and untied her ankles. "Show me." He grabbed her arm and pulled her off the bed and began dragging her through the house toward the kitchen. When they got to the living room, he pushed her behind the couch and made her lie on the floor. He retied her ankles.

He left for a short time, and then he returned. He had found a pair of tennis shorts, and he placed them over her head as a blindfold. She was ordered to turn over, and she rolled onto her back. Through the shorts, she could see the light of the flashlight beam as he examined her naked body with it. He started masturbating while he did this.

"Now I'm going to kill you," he said. "Cut your throat." And then he walked back into the kitchen.

She heard him rummaging around. "I'll kill 'em. I'll kill 'em. I'll kill 'em. I'll kill 'em. I'll kill 'em." Over and over again he said it. Then she heard him a little bit further away, doing something in the hall.

Afraid for her life, she rolled up onto her feet and, though blindfolded, was able to start hopping in the direction of the front door. She tripped as she got near it and slammed into the wall, then she slid against the wall until she found the doorknob. Luckily, she was able to open it. As she did, the bindings around her ankles came loose. She tore through the door, screaming for help. Unable to see, she ran very hard into the side of the house. She rebounded off of the wall and began stumbling around. A moment later, she felt the assailant's gloved hands on her. He pushed her to the ground, put his thumb in her mouth, and pulled on it.

"I told you to be quiet!" he hissed. He put a knife against her throat, then pulled her to her feet and dragged her back into the house. He pushed her to the floor again and retied her ankles. With his victim secured once more, he went back down the hall to check on the boyfriend. The woman again got to her feet and hopped toward the front door, screaming.

Unknown to everyone in the house, a neighbor had heard the commotion, and he'd already sprung into action. And on the other side of the house, the boyfriend had heard it as well and thought that she was being murdered, so he swung himself off the bed and hopped over to the sliding glass door. He was able to open it and make his way through. He propelled his body into the fence with all of his weight, hoping to knock some boards down and get through it. He was unable to, so he began yelling as loudly as he could. "Help! I'm the neighbor! There's a burglar!" One neighbor, whose lights were on, opened their door, looked outside, and closed it again. Help didn't seem to be on the way, so the victim hopped into the backyard. As quickly as he could, he leapt behind some bushes. From behind those, he was able to roll behind a citrus tree.

The assailant noticed that the boyfriend had disappeared through the open door. He stepped out into the backyard, took a few glances around, and then went back inside without investigating further.

The neighbor who had heard the woman scream and hit the wall was an off-duty FBI agent. He'd been up late reading in front of an open window when the commotion started. He immediately called the emergency number, then the Sheriff's department, and then he grabbed his gun and went to assist.

As he was headed out the door, the woman had just freed her feet again and was able to move her blindfold a bit. She ran into the bedroom to free her boyfriend, but he was gone. She tried to cover herself with a bathrobe and then ran out the front door. The robe fell as she was running. She noticed car headlights and she ran toward them, screaming. They stopped to avoid hitting her.

Immediate Aftermath

Just mere seconds after the woman had run out the door, the FBI agent reached the driveway of the residence. As he did, someone on a bicycle sped past him. The agent only got a fleeting glance at the man: he was not wearing a mask, he had on a dark gray and blue Pendleton plaid shirt, and he wore jeans and tennis shoes.

The agent watched the cyclist turn west on Queen Ann Lane, and then the agent dashed to his car. Unfortunately, the car wouldn't start right away. He tried it a couple more times and luckily, the car roared to life. He quickly made a U-turn and sped after the assailant.

The cyclist had disappeared. His pursuer followed his instincts and turned onto San Patricio. By a stroke of luck, he caught sight of the offender again, still speeding away on his bike. At that point, the bicyclist was only about two hundred yards in front of him. The agent floored it. The bicyclist, knowing that he was going to be caught, jumped the curb and ditched the bike (and the serrated kitchen knife he'd been using the threaten the victims). He took off running. The agent caught a glimpse of the subject jumping a fence into a backyard. The agent followed procedure (and common sense) and didn't pursue the assailant. He got into his car and returned to the scene. The female victim was still in the driveway, nude and screaming. The boyfriend was still hiding in the backyard. Neither of them knew that the FBI agent had chased the assailant away.

The police examined the bicycle. It was a ten-speed, twenty-seven-inch Nishiki bike. It was registered to a Federal Parole Officer who lived on North Patterson, a street just a block or two to the north. It had been stolen from his garage between 7:00 PM and midnight. There was no concrete information about how it was stolen, because the garage was locked down and the door was electronically-operated and could not be opened except without an opener. It was eventually determined that the bicycle must've been stolen before the door was locked down, so it was taken quite early in the evening.

The black-handled serrated steak knife was found where the bike had been left. The fence that the suspect had jumped led to a backyard that was connected to a dry creek bed, which connected to other creeks, which connected to the victims' house. Shoe prints were found in nearby yards, giving clues about the suspect's escape route (he'd basically doubled-back toward a main road). They were determined to be a size eight and a half or a nine Adidas running shoe. Matching shoe prints were found in the victim's backyard and in some neighboring yards as well.

Three dollars had been stolen from the residence. Investigators determined that the intruder had gained entry by prying open the victims' rear sliding glass door with a screwdriver. The issue of entry became a little murky when one witness on the scene recalled with certainty that the victims had left windows open during the night, and that the attacker had gained entry through one of those instead. We weren't able to confirm the statement, so we're simply noting the contradiction.

Suspect Description
White male, 5'10" or 5'11". He might not have been wearing a ski mask when he woke the victims up, and they thought they saw dark hair with curly ends just above the collar. He did wear a ski mask

later in the attack.

He was wearing a Pendleton-type shirt, and had some kind of holster attached to his belt on the right side.

The assailant spoke slowly and seemed to be trying to force his voice into a deeper register.

When the FBI agent saw the suspect, he wasn't wearing a mask. He was wearing a dark gray and blue plaid Pendleton shirt, jeans, and tennis shoes.

Context and Analysis

After spending so many years offending in Northern California, the assailant reappeared in Goleta, a fairly small town located nearly four hundred miles south of Sacramento. What led him to zero in on this fairly small area, with a population of about 15,000 in 1979, is not known for sure. Not only did he zero in on this small town, but he restricted himself to a very tight area of operation *within* this small town. Maybe he had some ties here, but it's just as likely that he was simply driving down US-101 and was scoping out "suitable" coastal towns. One theory is that the expansive Los Padres National Forest, which sprawls out to the north, was an attractive feature of the area. If murder was his intention from the beginning, and if some of the theories about the offender being survivalist who could live in the woods are true, perhaps this would've offered a place to disappear to in a pinch. An odd coincidence emerged when information came to light recently about the the male victim who had foiled the EAR in Attack #48. That man had gone to college at UC Santa Barbara, a school roughly four miles from the streets in Goleta that the EAR/GSK attacked was now attacking. Goleta and Danville were well over three hundred miles away from each other, so that's a pretty odd coincidence.

Regardless of what led him there, with a change in location came a change in methods and perhaps even motive. If the couple was correct and the East Area Rapist was *not* wearing a mask when he woke them up, that speaks pretty clearly about his plans, at least to us. It's very possible that he didn't expect his prey to survive the night. Fortunately, it didn't play out exactly according to plan, so we don't know for sure. This was the most he'd ever talked about killing a couple though, and the next couple he attacks *does* get killed.

This was his second major failure in a row, and some folks point to this fact (and some of his behaviors in this attack) as a possible sign of mental decomposition happening in the offender. That very well may be, but we attribute his loss of control here to the simple notion that he was issuing threats in quite a different way. In previous attacks, he was telling his victims "Give me food or money *or* I'll kill you." "Do this or that *or* I'll kill you." There was some of that here as well, but as this attack wore on, the words "if" and "or" disappeared and he was telling them very definitely that he was going to kill them. The victims no longer had that glimmer of hope that they'd survive if they cooperated. These were the first victims who had been approached in this way—they were the first ones who were absolutely, one-hundred-percent convinced in their hearts that he was going to kill them. Since they were bound, that made "escape" their only option. Also, he didn't mention having a gun and he didn't show it to them, which could've helped make them a little bolder. A gun had been his primary control weapon at the other scenes involving couples.

The portion of the attack that seems a little strange to us is that after the assailant brought the female back into the house, he attempted to run things as he usually did. He even left her alone again. He didn't stack dishes on either of them. Clearly, he wasn't as risk-averse as he'd been in the past, and he seemed a bit distracted. Perhaps the theory about mental decomposition is true, although he still functioned quite highly over the next few years. When he brought her in and resumed the attack, it was close to the part of the attack where he usually *did* place dishes on the man's back. It's impossible to know if this was something that was going to happen in this attack or not, because it fell apart again so quickly.

The "I'll kill 'em" chorus could be taken a few different ways. Was he trying to work up enough nerve to actually kill them? That's the prevailing theory. He also could've been simply enjoying the thought of killing them, and repeating the phrase for his own satisfaction. He might've been saying it simply to strike more terror into his victim, without any intention of killing them at all. If some of the theories are true and the East Area Rapist enjoyed inflicting terror more than he enjoyed raping and thieving, then that could work. After fifty or so attacks, it's logical that he'd need to escalate in *some* way to keep the "buzz" going.

It's likely that he *did* intend to kill these victims, though. There was definitely a sense of escalation. Law Enforcement authorities seem convinced that he was going to kill that night, because every official attack documentation and memo that we've seen from any agency lists this one as "Attempted Homicide."

Two important pieces of physical evidence from this scene matched the next attack, which *was* a murder. The first one was the nylon rope/twine that was used on these victims. These ligatures matched the ones used in the next attack, which seems a little careless and could mean a lot of things. The second piece of matching evidence is the shoe prints. The shoe impressions were determined to be the star-shaped design of the Adidas Runner, which also matched the upcoming double murder in Goleta.

The utilization of a bicycle here is noteworthy. The usage of bikes had been associated with the assailant off and on throughout the series, but not usually as a primary mode of transportation. There's just enough data here to make the logistics involved in getting to and from this attack incredibly interesting. The bicycle was stolen from North Patterson several hours before the attack. How did the assailant get to North Patterson? Did he park nearby? Walk? What did he do after he stole the bike? Did he stash it somewhere while he walked up and down the creek beds looking for suitable victims? Had these victims been stalked in advance, or was he out peeping, looking for couples having sex or looking for women sleeping nude? How well did he know the area, and what does that say about how much time he'd spent there? Did he live in Goleta? When did he spend time prowling and learning the creek beds and side streets? When he escaped, was he returning to a vehicle or was he running back home?

Did he run off toward a comfort zone, or did he go somewhere else to throw off his pursuers? Was he living in Goleta while he committed these crimes? His confirmed attacks in this area include this attack (October 1st, 1979), one in December of 1979, and then another one in July of 1981. Many other incidents and burglaries can be easily tied to him. That's a long span of time to be active off and on in a certain area. Goleta must have been significant in some way, if only for the amount of work put in up front toward learning the creeks and geography.

One of the things that seriously perplexes us is the fact that he took off on his bike through the front area of the house. He didn't know that the FBI agent was there, but still... there was a perfectly good escape route available to him by disappearing into the creek bed on the other side of the residence. Much safer. It's possible that he'd parked his car somewhere and he needed to get to it quickly before the police descended on the area, and he couldn't get there quickly through the creeks. He might've lived nearby and thought that he could bike home before the police arrived.

The story about the FBI pursuing the attacker was one of the most riveting moments in the case. Over the years, armchair analysts have complained about the agent not following the suspect over the fence. Knowing what happened on Ripon Court, it's a good thing that he didn't, though. The agent later explained that he knew that the deputies were on their way, and he knew that the main street, Cathedral Oaks, was only a block away and would almost have to be the street that the criminal took out of town. He'd felt certain that the police were going to catch the attacker in that area. Additionally, chasing a suspect into a blind alley or over a fence is actually against the rules for most Law Enforcement agencies. Many of them have a policy against "solo foot pursuits," and they require officers to stop the chase if they lose sight of the suspect or lose contact with other police officers (unless the suspect poses an immediate threat to others). In this case, the agent would've lost contact with other cops (his radio was in his car), and he'd lost sight of the suspect (the suspect vaulted a fence), and the suspect was on the run, so he didn't pose an immediate threat to others. If the offender was armed, a shootout would've been unavoidable. No matter how you look at it, the agent acted appropriately.

Speaking of the FBI agent, he was hypnotized almost a year later to see if he could remember any more details about the suspect's appearance. Nothing new came from the session.

The victim was a computer programmer, which was not only a fairly new profession at the time, but it was something a little new for the assailant as well. The female victim slept nude, a factor in victim selection that appears to be statistically significant.

The East Area Rapist Task Force up north didn't know about this attack, and since the East Area Rapist had seemingly become quiet or left the area entirely, the once-mighty team was reduced to three members. A few officers familiar with the EAR case did end up hearing about the attack and requested more information, but they were denied access to it for several months, a fact that some retired officers are still understandably upset about.

Night Before the Murders

The night leading up to the first Golden State Killer ("GSK") double-homicide in Goleta was a very active one. A crime wave was systematically making its way through a small area of town, leaving behind a trail of burglaries and destruction that eventually ended tragically in murder.

December 29th, 1979 Between 4:00 PM and 8:00 PM
Sometime between 4:00 PM and 8:00 PM, a prowler attempted to pry open the door to a house on Parejo Drive with a round shank screwdriver. The attempt was unsuccessful. The address was notable because it was so close to Queen Ann Lane, the street where the couple had escaped the killer's grasp a few months before. It was also just a few houses away from the suspicious murder of Eva Davidson Taylor, an event that happened in 1974 and shared several elements in common with other Golden State Killer murders.

December 29th, 1979 Between 5:30 PM and 8:30 PM
Someone broke into a residence on Hannah Drive and burglarized it, forcing open the safe inside the home. Cash and a wedding band were stolen, but some of the expensive jewelry was left behind.

December 29th, 1979 6:10 PM
A girl was babysitting on Queen Ann Lane. She saw a woman at the bottom of her neighbor's driveway and observed her walking to the neighbor's front door. The mysterious woman rang the doorbell with

her right hand. Two or three minutes later, she rang it again. The porch light was on and the neighbor was able to get a good look at the woman. She didn't recognize her.

December 29th, 1979 7:00 PM

Almost an hour later, the babysitter saw a suspicious man approaching the same house. The babysitter was standing on the sidewalk next to the retaining wall and *she* could see the man, but the man could not see *her*. She was roughly thirty yards away from him. She watched as he rang the doorbell with his right hand. The porch light was still on, and she got a decent look at him. He seemed to be looking at the peephole.

December 29th, 1979 7:30 PM

Thirty minutes later, the babysitter observed the man once again. He was in the middle of the driveway of that same house, walking up toward the residence. He walked up the driveway with a fairly strange gait, as if he had a sore left foot. His shoes made a distinctive noise, almost like they had taps on the bottom. He approached the door and rang the doorbell.

These sightings were significant because two hours later, an EAR-style burglary occurred at this house. Below are the detailed descriptions of the suspicious man and woman:

Woman:

The witness' initial description of the woman seen at 6:10 PM was that of a twenty-five-year-old with shoulder-length hair. She was dressed in dark clothing. Later, the witness added that the woman's hair was dark brown, and she was dressed in a t-shirt and jeans.

At an interview two weeks later, the witness added that the woman was about 5'4".

Later, a hypnosis session was done. The description of the woman from that session was as follows: white, late twenties, 5'4", 155-175 lbs, black or brown shoulder-length hair. She wore a light-colored short-sleeved t-shirt, jeans with frayed cuffs, and sandals.

Another description given by the witness added the following details and clarifications: the woman had a large, pointed nose, cotton in her right ear, three earrings in her right ear, a class ring on her right hand, a light-colored watch on her right arm, dark blue jeans, black tennis shoes, and black, wavy hair.

Man:
The witness' initial description was that of a white male, about 5'8", with dark or black hair, round-shouldered, wearing a dark-colored Dacron jacket.

At an interview two weeks later, the witness added that he was probably in his late twenties, 5'6" or 5'8", with neck-length dark hair cut short around the ears, wearing a dark down jacket and jeans.

At a hypnosis session, the following description of the man was put forth: white male, late twenties, 5'8" to 6', dark brown collar-length hair, a mustache, with possibly a growth on his face. He looked like he hadn't shaven for a couple of days, and he had a slight cut on his left hand and a ring on his right hand. He had a watch or a charm bracelet on his right arm. He was wearing a dark blue down jacket that went down to his hips, blue jeans that went past his heel, and possibly a black, knit cap (perhaps a watch cap). He wore light tan boots with a one-inch heel. They seemed to be hard-soled, and made a noise such that the witness thought that he might've have taps on the bottoms of his shoes. He walked like he had a sore left foot.

December 29th, 1979 Between 5:30 PM and 9:30 PM
A burglary occurred at a house on Queen Ann Lane, the house where the two suspicious characters described above had been seen ringing the bell. The man of the house had an affiliation with the UCSB Department of Engineering. A piece of twine, matching the twine

that would be later used in the murders, was found in the backyard.

The inner side door leading from the garage to the residence had been forcefully pried open with a 3/8" rectangular screwdriver. So much force had been used that the door frame was broken, and the metal door jamb was lying three feet from the door inside the garage. There were fresh metal-on-metal scratches.

All of the dresser drawers in the master bedroom had been ransacked. In the closet, a key-lock safe had been pried open and two jewelry boxes had been rummaged through. No prints were found at the scene, and some of the items known to have been handled by the burglar(s) were sent in to be analyzed. No prints were found.

The items that were taken included:

An opal pendant. The opal was a Brazilian green and red, cut to an oval shape with a size estimated at 12 x 16 mm. The mounting of the pendant was a fluted filigreed gold-filled mounting (matching a set of earrings). The particular identifying feature of the pendant was that in addition to its distinctive color and mounting, the stone was backed by fourteen-karat sheet gold (which had been glued to the stone). This was not a standard commercial practice, which made this item somewhat unique.

A dinner ring. The ring was a cluster of pearls mounted in a gold setting. The ring was an unusual design, having been custom made by Pandolfi Jewelers of Santa Barbara. It consisted of between eleven and fifteen pearls, with gold leaves interspersed among the pearls. It was a woman's ring, and an identifying feature was that the ring band had been flattened to properly size the ring.

Another dinner ring. The ring was an emerald-cut Amethyst set in a gold mounting. The stone was quite large, with overall dimensions of approximately 1/2" x 3/4". A flexible ring adjuster was installed in the ring band.

A birthstone ring. The ring was a gold band with a small blue birthstone and two small diamonds mounted into the band.

Plain gold cufflinks.

A small gold tie tack, with a polar bear on the tack.

A coin collection. Three two-dollar bills, three Susan B. Anthony dollars, several Canadian and European bills, three Liberty half dollars (1943, 1944, and 1954), five silver quarters, twelve silver Roosevelt dimes, twelve Buffalo nickels, two hundred pennies, and three Kennedy half dollars (one of them was from 1968).

Flashlight. A silicone-plated flashlight with an attached magnet.

A US Merchant Marine Academy ring. It was a gold class ring with words "United States Merchant Marine Academy-1946" in raised letters around the stone setting. The sides of the ring had a stylized Eagle and Shield on both sides. The ring was approximately eighteen pennyweight and the stone had been replaced with a gold signet inscribed with the initials of the owner. Inscribed inside the ring was the number "44-2714."

A ring. A small, gold man's signet ring with the initials of the owner inscribed on the inside.

December 29th, 1979 6:00 PM to 10:15 PM
A similar burglary happened on Harvard Lane, a street that ran north to south and intersected with Parejo Drive, Hannah Drive, and ended near Berkeley Road and Toltec Drive.

December 29th, 1979 10:20 PM
A couple living on Windsor Court was returning home from the movies, and as they approached the house, they saw someone running out of their living room toward the back of the house. They

entered just in time to hear him jumping over their fence into the yard of the adjacent Mountain View Elementary School. Nothing had been taken from their residence, but their white poodle had been hit on the left side of its face and its eye was injured.

It was determined that the intruder had entered through the sliding door on the southwest side of the house, and he'd pried it open with a screwdriver-type tool. No prints were taken at the residence since nothing had been stolen.

The intruder was described as a white male, in his late teens to early thirties, 5'7", medium build, with a hat on but no hair protruding from the hat. He wore a dark, waist-length jacket that was possibly dark leather, pants that were dark but not as dark as the jacket, and a dark small-brimmed hat (possibly a fisherman's hat). He had been running in a crouched position, and he was not seen carrying anything. As soon as he'd hit the ground on the other side of the fence, the automatic sprinklers came on. Shoe prints were found in the victims' backyard and in the Mountain View Elementary School yard near the fence. The shoe prints matched the shoe prints found at the Offerman/Manning murder scene and at the condo next to it.

The man of the house worked as a teacher at a local high school, and his wife worked as an RN at a hospital. They had a one-year-old son.

December 29th, 1979 Night
A bike was stolen from a house on Avenida Pequena. The theft occurred in the same condominium complex as the murder scene.

December 30th, 1979 1:30 AM
A young woman who lived alone in the same complex as Dr. Offerman was awakened to the sound of someone trying to break in. The prowler left without gaining entry.

<u>December 30th, 1979 Early Morning</u>
The vacant condo next door to Dr. Offerman's condominium was broken into.

In many of the burglaries and prowling incidents described in this section, multiple side gates were found open at the residences and their neighbors. Doors had been pried open at most of the scenes. Due to the matching shoe prints, matching pry marks, and the matching pieces of twine that were found, these burglaries were believed to be the work of the East Area Rapist / Golden State Killer. It appeared that the frenzy of activity was escalating that night, and it would crescendo to a peak in the early morning hours of December 30th, 1979 with his first official double murder.

The Offerman/Manning Murders

Date: December 30th, 1979 3:05 AM
Victims: Robert Offerman (44) and
Debra Alexandria Manning (35)
Location: 767 Avenida Pequena, Goleta

The victims in this case were Dr. Robert Offerman and Dr. Debra Alexandria Manning. They had been seeing each other for only a few weeks at the time of their murders.

Background Information
Dr. Robert Offerman was an orthopedic surgeon, as was Dr. Manning's ex-husband.

Dr. Manning was a clinical psychologist (a neuropsychologist) at a pain clinic. She'd lived in Boston for many years, and had moved to Santa Maria, California in 1976. In Boston, she had worked at the VA, treating patients with brain trauma.

At he time of their deaths, Dr. Offerman was going through a divorce, and Dr. Manning's divorce had just been finalized within days of her murder. Dr. Offerman's divorce was in the "division of property" phase when he was killed.

There was a real estate/property sale on November 30th, 1979, that Dr. Offerman and his soon-to-be ex-wife were both involved in.

Dr. Offerman was partners with a Dr. Mazzetti. They worked out of the Goleta Valley Community Hospital (in what they now call the Goleta office), located at 5333 Hollister Avenue, Goleta.

Dr. Manning and Dr. Offerman had met through a mutual acquaintance. She wasn't living with him, and Dr. Offerman was not dating her exclusively (he was also dating the manager of a travel agency in Goleta).

Timeline

???, 1979
Throughout an unknown period of time, Dr. Manning had received a few hang-up phone calls, and she'd occasionally had the feeling she was being stalked. It's unknown if this was related to her murder.

December 28th, 1979 Evening
Dr. Offerman and Dr. Manning both attended a house party given by acquaintances of theirs. The party was held at a residence on Toltec Place, and the guest list included doctors and lawyers (both of these professions were a common denominator in the murder series). The location was significant, since Toltec Way (a street very close by) would be the site of one of the killer's last known murders (on July 27th, 1981).

December 29th, 1979 Between 4:00 PM and 8:00 PM
A burglary occurred on Parejo Drive (this, and several of the other events listed below, have already been discussed).

December 29th, 1979 Between 5:30 PM and 8:30 PM
A burglary occurred on Hannah Drive.

December 29th, 1979 6:10 PM
A female subject was spotted at a house on Queen Ann that would later be burglarized.

December 29th, 1979 6:45 PM
Offerman and Manning spent the afternoon entertaining another couple in their condo. The couple left around 6:45 PM.

December 29th, 1979 7:00 PM
A male subject was spotted at the same house on Queen Ann.

December 29th, 1979 7:30 PM
The male subject was spotted again.

December 29th, 1979 9:30 PM
The owner of the house on Queen Ann returned to find that the home had been burglarized.

December 29th, 1979 10:15 PM
The owner of a house on Harvard Lane returned to find that the home had been burglarized.

December 29th, 1979 10:20 PM
A Windsor Court couple arrived home to find an intruder in their home. He escaped.

December 29th, 1979 After 10:30 PM
Sometime after 10:30 PM, Dr. Offerman left the condo to go to his ex-wife's house to deliver some ski equipment for his son. It's unknown whether Dr. Manning went with him or not.

December 29th, 1979 Night
A bicycle was stolen from Offerman's neighbor's car port.

December 30th, 1979 12:00 AM
A neighbor heard what she believed to be Dr. Offerman's Porsche pull into the common parking lot. She then heard two men's voices and a woman's voice. She recognized Dr. Offerman's voice but not the other two voices. This neighbor's bedroom window was very

close to Offerman's front door and the witness was very sure that there was another male voice.

December 30th, 1979 1:30 AM

A young woman who lived alone in the same complex as Dr. Offerman was awakened to the sound of someone trying to break in. The prowler left without gaining entry.

December 30th, 1979 3:05 AM

A neighbor heard what he thought was a gunshot, then three more gunshots, then a pause, then a final gunshot. Several other neighbors heard those shots as well. This particular neighbor and his wife went upstairs to get a better view of the area, and they tried to determine where the shots had come from. They looked around and didn't notice anything. The lights were off at Offerman's condo, but they noticed that the sliding door was open. The screen inside was closed.

December 30th, 1979 3:05 AM

After hearing the gunshots, another neighbor went outside to the parking lot, assuming that teenagers were setting off firecrackers near his vehicle. He saw and heard nothing else, and observed no activity near Offerman's condo, although he did notice that Offerman's patio door was open.

December 30th, 1979 3:05 AM

A nearby neighbor heard squealing tires and the sound of a car racing on the northern part of Avenida Pequena.

December 30th, 1979 3:17 AM

The same couple who had gone upstairs to find the source of the gunshots looked out a different window and saw a white, boxy car (similar in size to a Pinto or Honda Civic) without lights on driving slowly out of the common parking lot. Neither they, nor anyone else who had heard the gunshots, called the Sheriff's Department. This couple also had a son, and it was later learned that it was this young man's bicycle that had been stolen during the night for apparent use in this attack.

December 30th, 1979 Between 4:00 AM and 5:00 AM

The paperboy and his mother spotted a vehicle leaving the parking lot of the condo where Offerman and Manning had been shot. They described the car as probably a white Pontiac with a bad paint job. They described the driver as looking like the local LA Times delivery man. Although the car was somewhat similar in description to the other car spotted, there were enough differences in the descriptions to be reasonably sure that the sightings were of two different vehicles.

December 30th, 1979 5:00 AM

Another neighbor heard the sound of squealing tires.

December 30th, 1979 Morning

The couple that had planned on playing tennis with Dr. Offerman and Dr. Manning arrived at the Offerman condo. When they arrived, they noticed that a sliding glass door was open. They went inside and discovered the bodies.

December 30th, 1979

The stolen bicycle was found on Crown Avenue, a street just north of Queen Ann Lane and near North Patterson Avenue (where the bike had been stolen in the October 1st, 1979 Goleta attack).

The Murder Scene

Both victims were found dead. Dr. Manning was nude, lying face-down on the right side of the bed with her hands tied behind her back. There was a bullet wound to the back of her head.

Dr. Offerman was kneeling, with his head on the ground and his backside in the air. Some sheets and a pillow were partially underneath him. He had one bullet wound in his upper chest and three in his back. There was a ligature around his left wrist.

The bindings used on the victims were 1/16" diameter three-stranded strings of white nylon twine. They were in pieces ranging from about nineteen inches to twenty-six inches long. These pieces of twine had been tied together by a series of complicated knots in order to make them long enough to use as a binding. On one particular ligature, three different knots were used. Pieces of twine were found in several areas in and near the victim's residence (eleven pieces in total). The twine matched the bindings used at the October 1st, 1979 attack.

There was no sign of extensive ransacking in the house, though there was some evidence that some of the drawers and closets had been gone through. Dr. Manning's purse had some jewelry, a silver dollar, some credit cards, and some cash inside of it. There was no clear-cut evidence that the purse had been sifted through, though we've heard some folks wonder if the jewelry in the purse was hers or if it had been placed there (like the jewelry being moved around in Attacks #5, #6, #21, etc). All of the lights were off in the residence, and the thermostat was off. There was a plastic bag containing turkey bones and a turkey carcass on the back patio, scraps of turkey near the back door, and a turkey bone inside the residence close to the door.

Stolen from the scene was a large buck knife, a fur coat, the doctor's medical bag, and a Minolta camera.

There were three sliding glass doors in the residence, and all three had pry marks. The one leading into the living room had been pried so hard that the door jamb had come loose from the wall.

Tennis shoe impressions were found, and they were determined to be from an Adidas Runner. They matched the shoe prints found at the October 1st, 1979 attack. The prints were found in the mud in the backyard, and strangely, a dog's paw prints were found along with them. The dog prints appeared to be partial prints. The shoe impressions were also found in a neighbor's yard, but no dog prints were found there. Neither Offerman nor his neighbor owned a dog.

Pieces of white twine were found in the backyard of a neighbor's residence (the one where the bicycle had been stolen). More twine was found in nearby areas as the investigation fanned out.

Physical Evidence
Two rings belonging to Dr. Manning were found stuffed between the mattress and the bed frame. One of them had over a dozen small clear stones around a yellow stone, and the other was gold with one stone. Manning had been wearing one or two necklaces, and they were still around her neck when the coroner arrived. They were removed later.

The killer had used a .38 caliber revolver (probably a Smith and Wesson) loaded with Supervel brand, .38 caliber ammunition with 110 grain jacketed bullets. Ballistics were run, and they didn't match any known case, and they didn't match any of the past or future Golden State Killer cases.

Dr. Manning had not been sexually assaulted, and despite bizarre rumors, neither had Dr. Offerman.

Two blue-green flakes were found on Dr. Manning's big toe, and some loose hairs were found on her back. The media reported "green flakes" sprinkled around her body, and these "green flakes" turned out to be gunpowder residue from the shot that killed her.

Some matches were found at the scene. The matches were similar to ones that would be found at the 1981 Witthuhn murder, another killing that the GSK was responsible for.
An "Apollo Airline" business card was in the master bedroom on the dresser, and while it probably belonged to one of the victims, it was

possible that the killer had brought it with him and had left it intentionally.

The ligatures had dark deposits of some kind on them. Tar from the beach has been suggested as a possibility (a common phenomenon on the beaches near Goleta), and roofing tar has been offered up as a possible explanation as well. If chemical composition analysis was done on it, we don't have the results. One of the pieces of twine found in the condo next to the murder scene was supposedly made of a different material than the others—it appeared to be made of rayon, not nylon. Apparently the rayon was described as being the same kind used for automotive purposes (tires or the cords for drive belts). This was the only rayon found—all of the other pieces of twine found at the murder scene and surrounding areas were three-strand nylon cord.

A Schwinn Varsity Men's ten-speed road bicycle was stolen from a condo in the same complex (the unit to the west of the murder scene). In the yard where the bike had been stolen, two more pieces of twine matching the ligatures from the murder scene were found. The bike was eventually found north of most of the activity that had occurred that night, on a street called Crown Avenue. This location was close to where where the bike had been stolen for the October 1st, 1979 Goleta attack.

More evidence was found two days after the murders, this time on the dirt trails/dry creek beds near the attack location. More pieces of twine, some shoe prints, and the prints of a medium/large dog similar to the dog tracks at the crime scene were found alongside the shoe prints. One piece of twine was found on the east side of the roadway across from 825 North Kellogg. Another piece was found on a segment of the trail that led to a greenbelt area next to 866 North Kellogg. The shoe prints and dog prints passed Norma Lane and then disappeared into the main creek area. Matching twine was also found in the yard of a house on Queen Ann Lane.

The Condo Next Door

In addition to all of the burglaries that the killer had committed earlier in the evening, he had entered the condo next door to the murder scene as well. Several of the drapes were open inside, which allowed anyone to see into the condo and determine that it was vacant. A shoe impression matching the murder scene was found under the bedroom window on the south side of the house, and pry marks were found on every single door and window. The sliding glass door on the north side of the residence had apparently been pried at the most. A window screen from the residence was found on top of eight-foot-tall hedges on the northwest side of the residence. The screen on the back door had been pried at unsuccessfully. The wooden doorframe on the front door had been pried at near the latch and on the striker plate. It had been damaged, and the dead bolt was rendered inoperable. Entry was finally made through the living room window.

The condo was technically still on the market at the time of the murders, and no one was living there full-time. It had been used that night by some young men to play board games. A young man related to the owner was staying there off and on. The condo was in the process of being sold to a young woman who worked as an RN.

Inside the residence, pieces of twine matching the ones found at the murder scene were found scattered about the floor and other places. Some of it was found on the floor in the master bathroom, some of it in a cabinet under the master bathroom sink, some on the floor of the master bathroom, and some of it on the mantle over the fireplace. The twine found on the mantle was slightly different than the others, supposedly being made of rayon instead of nylon (as described earlier).

On the southern edge of this condo's yard was a flowerbed that had been heavily trampled. Shoe impressions matching the murder scene were found there, and matching shoe prints formed a path between the flower bed and the front porch of the vacant condo. Hair or fiber was found on top of the fence in this area. This part of the yard was particularly interesting to detectives, because it appeared that the killer had spent a long time there. It was noted that the killer could have had an unobstructed view of Offerman's master bedroom from that location, and it was theorized that he watched Offerman and Manning have sex. No concrete evidence was found to confirm whether the killer had visited the vacant condo before or after the murders, however.

Official Theory

Investigators theorized that Offerman and Manning were asleep when they were attacked. The speculated that the killer confronted them, and believing that she was about the be robbed, Manning had hidden her rings. They felt that the killer had told Manning to tie Offerman, then tied Manning himself. Offerman possibly then freed himself and confronted the killer, who shot him once. After being shot, there's evidence that Offerman continued to go after the assailant, and so he was shot three more times. Most of the investigators didn't feel that the murder was planned. As mentioned above, some of them felt that the crime was sexually-motivated and that the assailant had possibly peeped in on them having sex.

The official theory detailed above was fleshed out before it was known that this killer was the East Area Rapist, so it's important to note that many of the details they came up with matched the EAR's M.O. very closely before a tie to that offender was even a possibility.

Post-Attack Events

Dr. Manning's ex-husband was on a skiing trip at Lake Tahoe the night she died. He underwent a polygraph examination and no discrepancies were found. He was completely eliminated as a suspect.

On January 4th, 1980, different jewelry and coin shops in Goleta and Santa Barbara were given lists and descriptions of what had been stolen. None of the jewelry taken from the murder scene or any of the burglaries ever surfaced.

Requests by Sacramento police to get information about this homicide and the aborted attack from October 1979 were steadfastly denied until March 1980.

Context and Analysis

As mentioned above, the East Area Rapist was not suspected of this crime, nor was he even on the radar. For some reason, it wasn't tied to the October 1st, 1979 attack right away either, apparently. Those two crimes weren't tied to any of the other rapes or murders for a period of years. It wasn't until 2011 that any physical evidence from any Goleta crimes was officially tied to the EAR/GSK, though at that point investigators had been pretty sure that there was a link for awhile.

For reasons unknown, this attack ended in murder, and from what we can tell, the assailant would never again let a victim survive an attack. This was a game-changer. The offender, who some had thought of only as a "nuisance," had now begun to systematically rob California families of their loved ones.

Before we delve into the attack itself, let's explore some of the common connections, just as we've done with the rape attacks.

There's a real estate connection here, just as there was in so many of the "East Area Rapist" phase of attacks. The vacant condo next door, both being listed for sale and being sold to an RN, almost provides a familiarity to this. The property sale occurring with Offerman and his ex-wife on November 30th, 1979, is another possible connecting point.

The medical connections run rampant here, extending far beyond the fact that the new neighbor was going to be an RN. Both of the victims in this case had made medicine their lives, and they had worked in various parts of the state and country. They spent most of their time in these types of settings, and their social circles were based around doctors and medical professionals. Cottage Hospital, located near the murder scene, has a couple ties to this case as well—the biggest one being that one of the burglary victims that night was employed there. Two of the burglary victims worked in eduction, which is another theme that came up often in the Northern California crimes.

Geographically, Cottage Hospital was about a mile and a half south of the murder scene (you would take North Patterson south to 101 to get there). If you remember, one of the very first Goleta incidents was on North Patterson, and it stands to reason that it would be a street traveled on by the killer on his way into or out of town. Most of the Golden State Killer murders were located near a hospital. It doesn't necessarily mean anything, because most people do live by a hospital of some kind, but the medical angle appears to be statistically significant so it's always worth noting.

Up until this point, the existence of connections to the legal field haven't been discussed, nor have they been prevalent. Starting with the murders though, legal connections abound. Whether that's because most of the victims were more mature in age (and older people have more legal issues), or if there was truly a significant connection there, no one yet knows. In the Offerman/Manning case, the connection was that several lawyers were involved in both of their divorces, and many of their friends were attorneys.

A possible insurance connection deserves to be mentioned as well. Offerman's ex-wife held an insurance policy with a company called Frederic Sauer Insurance Company, a firm that came up again in the Janelle Cruz case. Interestingly enough, the company was based out of Stockton.

Other connections exist, but they're not as solid.

The exact sequence of events in the actual attack are left open to speculation, but using the hundreds of pages before us as a guide, we can make some intelligent guesses as to what possibly occurred. The biggest questions that we have about the sequence of events are whether he ate the turkey before or *after* he killed them, and whether he entered the vacant condo before or *after* the murders. The way he feverishly pried at the vacant condo might tell us something, or it might not. The numerous foot impressions in the flower bed—were those made before the murders occurred? Most of us feel that they probably were, and that he probably watched them have intercourse before he attacked. It's also possible, though, that he fled the murder scene shortly after killing them and hid behind the fence to watch for any sort of police response. The frantic way in which he "had" to get into the condo was rather strange. He could see from the windows that there wasn't anything valuable to steal. Was he trying to get in quickly because he had actually entered the condo *after* the murders, and he wanted somewhere to hide? They were so close together that it probably wouldn't have been a very good hiding spot. It's amazing that he kept trying different doors and windows until one of them gave. Whatever the reason and whenever it happened, the killer felt that he *needed* to enter that empty condo for some reason.

The most likely sequence of events is that he watched them have intercourse, broke into the vacant condo to prepare ligatures, and then went to attack them. If this crime was similar to previous crimes, at least until the shooting, then it's likely that the killer callously ate the turkey after murdering them. It appears, at least to us, that he entered the residence, bound the victims or had them bind each other, did a little bit of ransacking, and then killed Offerman when he broke free and confronted him. We're guessing that Offerman broke free because the killer hadn't had a chance to retie him yet, or the killer's twine ligatures just weren't as good as the shoelaces. We know that the snacking didn't happen right away at least, because the neighbors saw nothing at the sliding glass door after the shots occurred. The dog *might* have been inside the house, since he wasn't seen, or he might've just been out of view, or he might not have even been on the property yet. No dog prints were found inside the house.

And speaking of the dog—the presence of a dog at the scene is strange. A little less so when you consider the Berkeley Road incident, but the relation of that incident to the Golden State Killer attacks is debatable. There was a well-known neighborhood dog, a German Shepherd mix, that frequently wandered around at night (potentially because someone was often letting him out, unbeknownst to the owner), and it's been theorized that perhaps this dog, intrigued by the events of the night, or perhaps because he was familiar with the killer, approached him and was fed. The dog tracks were found with the killer's footprints close to half a mile away as well, so there's something to this angle that we're not understanding.

Look at all of the burglaries he perpetrated before the murder— there's almost no way that he had a dog with him for those. Did he go and retrieve the dog after committing all of the burglaries? Did he go and get the dog specifically for the murder? Was the dog stashed in the vacant condo for any portion of the evening? It would've had to have been after midnight, because that was the approximate time that the owner's son and his friends left the condo. Would the dog be afraid of the gunshots? Does bringing a dog to a murder serve any specific purpose, other than perhaps having a "cover story" if you're caught between houses or doing something that you shouldn't be doing? There was a stolen bike, so how would riding a bike work if you had a dog with you? Wouldn't it be easier to travel with a dog on foot or by car? There are a lot of different possibilities, most of which lead to a lot of convoluted theories and timelines. The most likely scenario is that the dog either happened by, or the killer went and retrieved his own dog (or a dog he was familiar with) in between the burglaries and the murders. The dog prints weren't found in all of the places that the killer went to during the timeline of the murders that night, so it couldn't factor in too heavily.

On the subject of the dog, one of the most talked-about facets of the Goleta scenes is some sketchy information that the prints indicated that the dog had three toes. Everything we've been able to find out about the paw prints, ground conditions, and everything else has led us to conclude that the paw prints were most likely *partial prints*, not the full prints of a dog who mysteriously had a toe missing from multiple paws. That being said, a fairly distinctive German Shepherd from the immediate area was indeed tracked down by Law Enforcement, and the various people associated with it were thoroughly investigated. A small fortune was spent on DNA tests, which conclusively cleared everyone who was known to have any contact with the animal.

One of the biggest questions from that night concerns the second male voice that was heard around midnight speaking with Dr. Offerman. The unknown female voice was most likely Dr. Manning, but even that isn't known for sure. Extensive neighborhood interviews have identified everyone's comings and goings that night, and yet this second male voice remains unidentified, which leads us to believe that it was possibly the killer himself. Perhaps he was prowling and was caught in the act. The witness heard the voices from her bedroom window, which was only a few feet away from where the conversation took place, and she heard it just moments after Dr. Offerman's Porsche pulled up and stopped. It's also possible that it was the voice of one of the young men who had been in the vacant condo that night, and somehow the police just didn't ask the right people the right questions. But if it was the voice of the killer, then that would mean that Offerman had seen his face, and it could be a good enough reason to kill him, from the EAR's point of view.

Was Manning's jewelry hidden under the mattress because she usually kept it there while she slept, or did she hide it there when the killer entered the room and confronted them? If she was initially afraid for her life, we don't see her being too worried about a couple of rings. But if she felt he was simply there to rob her, then quickly hiding the rings might make sense. She didn't bother, or she didn't have time, to remove her necklaces. The killer didn't seem interested in taking them after the murder, perhaps because of blood or some other kind of evidence that might've tied him to the crime if he were caught while escaping. It's probable that the offender started out with his usual "give me food and money" routine. But like the Goleta attack before this one, apparently something was said or something happened to create a sense of great desperation in the victims. Offerman probably did not lightly make the decision to risk his life against an armed intruder. Whether it was threats, demeanor, or something less likely (like Offerman recognizing him), we may never know. Offerman may not have even *known* that the intruder was armed if the EAR/GSK hadn't presented his gun to him yet. He hadn't shown the previous victims his gun, either.

Multiple shots were heard by multiple people in close vicinity, and yet no one reported anything to the police. In their defense, do keep in mind that New Years was close, and at least one witness was convinced that the sounds were fireworks of some kind. Another witness said in her statement that when she didn't hear footsteps running away or any kind of vehicle after the shots were fired, she too assumed they were fireworks. A lucky break for the killer, unfortunately. He'd attacked near the 4th of July before as well, so maybe that was part of a clever strategy.

It's interesting that he attacked a small complex of condos. It's risky, because in general the neighbors *do* live fairly close to each other, and they easily recognize cars and folks that don't belong to the complex. Also, it's far easier to hear gunshots when neighbors are in close proximity like that, which makes firing so many shots a dumb move on the killer's part. It could support the argument that he didn't actually intend to kill his victims that night. Why start your killing spree in such a densely-populated residence with such a noisy weapon?

But honestly, who knows how much planning even went into this. It seems rather spontaneous. Dr. Offerman and Dr. Manning had only been dating for a few weeks, and Manning didn't live with Offerman—she was simply visiting for the weekend. It's still possible that she was targeted and stalked, and there's some evidence that she *was*, but there's no way of knowing if it was the Golden State Killer stalking her or not or if the events were just coincidence (and the fact that she wasn't raped could mean that he had no fantasy-based attachment to her). It's possible that the killer had been around to observe Offerman's bedroom before, if he frequently stalked around at night in Goleta. The condo next door was usually vacant, and if he prowled frequently he could've picked up on that. But given the frantic string of events all around the area that night, it's hard to believe that Offerman and Manning were targeted specifically for any particular reason other than the fact that he was prowling the area feverishly and they fit the bill of what he was looking for. We've mentioned numerous times that voyeurism possibly had a lot to do with the attacks, especially the later ones, and this could easily be an example of that—seeing couples having sex could've been one of the things that flipped his switches. Also, the fact that he tried to break into another condo where a young woman lived *before* he settled on Offerman and Manning is an additional point that leans us toward Dr. Offerman and Dr. Manning simply being in the wrong place at the wrong time.

There were rumors, even among Law Enforcement officials, that Dr. Offerman had been sodomized by the killer, but the rumors are completely false. After Offerman was shot, Offerman continued to go after the killer, which was why he was shot several more times and ended up in that awkward position. In total, he was shot in the neck, twice in the chest, and on his backside. The fatal bullet punctured his lung. Very tragic and terrifying. He was a very brave man for confronting this intruder and doing what he could to save his life and the life of Dr. Manning.

It appears that the killer might've been making attempts to distance himself from being connected to the Northern California attacks. Things such as changing the ligatures, not ransacking extensively, possibly even the idea of killing the witnesses could've been premeditated activities. If murder was truly his intention, then distancing himself from those places up north where he'd left a ton of clues was wise. It's interesting that he didn't care if the Offerman/Manning killings were connected to his previous adventures in Goleta though, which is evidenced by him using the same twine and the same shoes. It could be yet another indication that he hadn't planned on committing homicide that night. We might be giving him too much credit though—perhaps the killer wasn't giving any of these things a second thought and he was simply doing what he wanted to do. Seemingly losing control at three scenes in a row (Danville, Goleta, and now Goleta again) definitely means something though. Either his mind was starting to disintegrate, the victims in Southern California weren't as cooperative as the ones up north, or something else.

Some of the physical evidence at this scene offers tantalizing clues. The dark deposits on the ligatures of unknown origin could offer some insights if more was known about it. Goleta was situated near a beach, and there was a big oil spill about ten years before the crime. Even at the time the murders happened, there was still "beach tar" seeping up through the sand. How the substance, whatever it was, got onto the ligatures is a mystery, whether it was beach tar or not. It's possible that the knife or gloves used to cut or handle the ligatures had the substance on it, and the substance was transferred.

One piece of evidence that *did* have some of its chemical composition determined and made more widely-available was the blue-green paint flakes on Dr. Manning's toe. The paint was determined to be architectural paint, somewhat similar to but not exactly like to the paint evidence found in Sacramento.

Speaking of the paint, there might be a connection with the business card. The Apollo Airline card purportedly left on Dr. Offerman's dresser might be his, or it might've been something deliberately left by the killer as either a message or as something to confuse police. Apollo Airline was a small outfit that operated in Goleta for a few years around the time of the murders. Their logo and lettering was a deep blue—a color almost identical to the paint evidence found in Sacramento. Given the composition of the paint in Sacramento though, it's difficult to imagine any use that Apollo Airline would've had for it.

Some of the literature related to this case states that one of the knots used in this attack was the same knot that was used in the next murder, the Smith case. We don't know this to be true, and if it is, it might be a little misleading. The Smith case is famous for a particular ornate knot that may or may have been a "diamond knot." Some of the literature takes a leap and claims that a diamond knot was used in this case as well, but it's somewhat iffy at this point whether it was even used in the Smith case, much less this one. Other knots were used at both scenes, and it's more likely that one of *those* matched, not the diamond knot, given what we've been able to look at. There were several different kinds of knots used at both scenes.

One more point about the ligatures. Clearly, this perpetrator had shown signs over the years that he was often a meticulous planner in some ways, and he rarely dropped things or made mistakes. The items that he *did* drop might even be construed as intentional or specific messages aimed at victims or police. Why then, did he "drop" so much of this twine everywhere? Never before had he been so careless about leaving behind evidence. A few shoelaces and towel strips were frequently left at the rape scenes, but nothing of this magnitude. Was he trying to distance himself from those crimes, or was he trying to create a false scent trail or false foot trail? Did he simply not care, or was he upping the ante when it came to the potential danger of his attacks? Was he sending a message of some kind? And did he drop those pieces of twine found on the trail and found in the yards before or after the murders? Was he coming or going? Just another mystery, and it's something out of character because he usually covered his tracks really well.

There were a couple sightings of cars in relation to this murder. The more intriguing one was that mysterious car pulling out of the common parking lot within twelve minutes of the gunshots and then driving off slowly without lights on. That car has never been identified or accounted for, which certainly makes it suspicious. The other white car appearing later is fairly suspicious as well. But how does this fit in with the stolen bike, the burglaries, the dog, and the footprints on the trail? And would the killer really park in the parking lot? In the rape series, the EAR seemed to park or position his transportation further away. Maybe the killer didn't know the area as well, or he hadn't planned on making so much noise and needing to leave like that. A car would be easier to transport a dog in, if indeed the dog came and went with him. Depending on where he lived and where he came from, a car would not necessarily be needed. All of the burglary sites were within easy walking distance of each other, and it would be quite possible to use the creek beds to traverse the areas. If he did indeed have a car, that points to someone who isn't quite local to the exact area that he's hitting. The stolen bike might've been there for a quick getaway, or it might've even been stolen and dropped as a red herring of sorts, trying to make the police think that a local person who traveled by bike was committing the crimes (when really someone traveling in a car was). Why the bike, and potentially a car, anyway? The creek beds, which he'd never shied away from using in previous locations, would've been sufficient to do everything that he did that night. He could've parked far offsite. And maybe he did... none of those vehicles have been definitively tied to him.

So many theories and avenues of investigation centered around him being a local, at least for a time, but it's impossible to know if that's true or not. If he was a local, why seemingly spend one night, and one night only, out there prowling, burglarizing, thieving, and killing? Why did it all happen at once? Was his family busy that Saturday night, and it was his only time to escape? Was he trying to quit, but lost control for that one night? We actually think that the limited geographic area he kept himself to in Goleta might imply that he was from out of town and had limited familiarity with the area. And speaking of family, was that strange woman sighted at the burglary actually *with* him? If you recall Attack #24, a female voice was possibly heard during the attack.

A word should be said about the layout of the condo itself. It was more like a group of duplexes than a traditional condominium complex. It was surrounded by green space, and it connected to Cathedral Oaks Road (a main street that provided quick access to North Patterson Avenue, which was the way to get to 101). In addition to the vacant condo next door, there were extensive renovations being done on the *other* side of Offerman's condo. Other than that, for folks looking at the construction angle, it'll be slim-pickings because of a building moratorium that affected much of Goleta at the time. There were a few commercial projects that went on during that time period though, one of which ended up becoming an exciting lead. That project was a shopping center on Calle Real, a nearby street. Investigators looking at the architectural paint lead from the Sacramento crimes discovered that this shopping center was finishing up at the time that the Offerman/Manning murders took place, and that the painting phase would've been undertaken by a commercial sprayer sometime around the time of the

Offerman/Manning murders. Since the paint found in three consecutive EAR attacks was architectural paint from a sprayer (and some architectural paint was found on Dr. Manning's toe), this seemed like an interesting lead for a time. Making it even more interesting was the fact that a Sacramento-based company was the one contracted to do the painting. This lead is still being explored.

Because of all of the incidents surrounding the Goleta area (and because we had addresses for all of them), we enlisted a geographic information systems professional to help us do some work on this attack. We ran different profiling scenarios, some of which included other possibly-related events and some that didn't. Amazingly, many of the passes with this data pointed to a small area near Toltec Way as being an origin point for the offender, which is incredible considering that a year and a half after this murder, another GSK double-homicide would occur right there on Toltec Way! This could mean a great many things, but at the very least, what it means to us is that in 1981, when the Golden State Killer came back to murder, he was familiar with that particular area and he didn't venture into new territory. Whether he was relying on reconnaissance he'd done during the fall of 1979 or if he'd truly never left, we don't know.

Three of the rapes that occurred in Contra Costa County (#39, #42, #46) and the rest of the murders in Southern California are connected by DNA. This particular attack is not. Because of the similarities, and the physical evidence tying it to the other Goleta attack (which was very similar to other EAR attacks), it was considered part of the official canon when the entire series was starting to become a cohesive whole to investigators. In 2011, when the DNA match was made between the 1981 Goleta murders and the rest of the Golden State Killer cases, it proved that he had indeed been to Goleta, and this attack was more or less solidified as an official event.

After trudging through all of this information, at the end of the day, only a couple questions really matter. The first one, of course, is about the identity of the killer. The second one that naturally comes to mind is about motivation. Why and how could someone do this?

And why rape and pillage and plunder in Northern California areas, but murder in Southern California? What exactly happened in SoCal? Did he initiate a change in scenery because he wanted to murder, or did he, in a way, "have" to start murdering because of the change in scenery? Meaning, was he a stranger to Sacramento and the surrounding areas, but possibly a known quantity or a recognizable face in Goleta, Irvine, and elsewhere? Even when he's identified, we still may never know why he did what he did. All we know is that the rapist had officially turned to "killer."

You probably noticed that we dedicated some extra pages to these early Goleta incidents and went a little bit more in-depth. That's because this was a very significant transitionary period, and we believe some very valuable clues exist here. During transitions of this type, it becomes more likely that mistakes were made by the killer.

So many things went wrong in these attacks, and those mistakes could work to our benefit. The sloppiness might imply a level of comfort and complacency, either with this location, or the fact that he'd moved so far away from his previous crimes in Northern California that he felt he was starting over. Interestingly enough though, despite so many things going wrong, he was able to "keep it together" and remain unidentified.

More clues are certainly out there to be found in Goleta, and we'll discuss a few more, and then we'll revisit some of these things again when the killer returns in July 1981 to tragically murder another couple.

Possible Goleta Crimes

We wish there was space in this book to put a high-powered microscope to *all* of the crimes and attacks like we did for Goleta, because there's certainly enough material to fill *several* volumes of this size. But for this book we went with as many relevant details as we could put together and still have a narrative that flowed and made sense. Still, as we mentioned earlier, Goleta is one of the areas that we feel is important to focus on, since this was a very big transitional phase for the killer. It's our one indulgence, and *then* we'll get back to moving the story along.

We want to say up front that purists might want to skip this particular section. None of the following events in this chapter are proven to have anything to do with the Golden State Killer, and indeed, some of them probably do not. The killer was known to be in Goleta for the October 1st attack, the burglaries on December 29th, and the subsequent early-morning murder. He'd return in July 1981 for another double murder. Other than that, we can't officially place him in town, but several of the following events make a good case for him being in town much more frequently. It stands to reason that anything odd during the time period and the location of the attacks has the *potential* to be related. If even *some* of these are able to be connected, it could prove significant—at the very least, it would place the killer in the area for more than just a few nights, and it would show that the same type of prowling activities that occurred in his Northern California crimes also occurred in some of his Southern California crimes.

The following incidents are submitted for your consideration based on close geographical ties, timing, M.O., or because the event was so out of the ordinary for a small, quiet, low-crime town like Goleta.

Special thanks goes to researcher Mark Gardner for many of the key pieces of information for this section.

April 18th, 1974: Eva Davidson Taylor Murder

The Offerman/Manning murders would be the last ones that the killer would exclusively use a gun to kill with, at least that we know of. From that point forward, he bludgeoned his victims to death. In light of this information, a case that happened several years before the Offerman/Manning killings jumps out, especially because it happened in the same small area as the other Golden State Killer crimes in Goleta.

Eva Davidson Taylor, a seventy-three year-old woman, was bludgeoned to death at her Parejo Drive home on April 18th, 1974. The killer used a screwdriver to pry open her sliding glass door, and while inside the house, he killed her. There was no sign of sexual assault, and the killer didn't steal anything of value from the home. There had been reports of prowlers in the neighborhood, and a young man had been seen vaulting her fence at some point before the murder.

Was the killer familiar with Goleta in 1979 because he had been there before in 1974? But if this attack was him, why bludgeon someone to death, and then not do it again for nearly six years? These questions haven't been answered. The manner of death, and the extreme proximity to the other known Goleta crimes, makes this one a tantalizing possibility.

To make it even more intriguing, Taylor's daughter began receiving disturbing phone calls in 1981. Some of them were just crank calls, and some of them were obscene. A few of them were hang-up calls. Even when the daughter moved, the calls followed her. She didn't feel that they were calls from her mother's killer, however—she felt that they were related to her work as a psychiatrist.

Fall 1978: Prowler

A peculiar pair of sightings took place a year before the Offerman/Manning murders. A couple living on Vineyard Road (a street just above North Patterson Road, where the bicycle was stolen for the October 1st, 1979 attack) spotted a prowler in their neighbor's backyard on two separate occasions. Both of the sightings occurred while their neighbors were on vacation, and both sightings occurred around 2:00 AM. A man was seen jumping their fence both times. They couldn't make out his features, but they described him as an adult male, 6' tall, dressed in dark clothing and a cap.

August 28th, 1979: Attempted Rape

A young woman was sunbathing in a secluded area of the More Mesa beach, roughly two and a half miles south of the Offerman/Manning murder site, when a nude man wearing a stocking over his head grabbed her and forced himself on her. He attempted to rape her but was unable to maintain an erection.

September 5th, 1979: Prowler

A young woman living on Berkeley Road was getting ready for bed when she spotted a man watching her through the window. He ran off when he was spotted. Berkeley Road, remember, was where the interesting dog incident happened. It was right in the middle of Golden State Killer territory in 1979 and 1981.

September 24th, 1979: Dog Incident

This was the date of the dog incident described earlier in the book. It's listed here for context.

October 1st, 1979: EAR/GSK Attack

This was the date of the failed Goleta attack. It's listed here for context.

October 24th, 1979 6:00 PM: Rape

A twelve-year-old girl was riding her bike on the Maria Ygnacio Bike Path when she came across a man. He engaged her in conversation. She told him that she was searching for her sisters, and the man claimed to know where they were. He took her into the creek area, produced a six-inch knife, and raped her on a board in the creek. An elderly man walking his German Shepherd came upon the scene and drove the rapist away.

The attacker wasn't wearing a mask, and the girl got a decent look at him. She described him as white, early twenties, with blonde, shoulder-length hair. He had a handlebar mustache, and he was wearing a black shirt and a dark green jacket with a pattern or "stitched design." He had a ring with a dark red gemstone on the ring finger or middle finger of his right hand.

This event happened about a mile away from the Offerman/Manning murder, and it happened a few weeks after the failed attack on Queen Ann Lane. If this was the assailant, perhaps with a move down south, he was contemplating a change in M.O.? Perhaps two failed attacks in a row led to a change in tactics? If it's related, the event kind of harkened back to some of the earlier rapes where he led his victims outside or down a canal.

November 1st, 1979: Phone Call

A young woman who lived off of Calle Real (a nearby street) received a phone call in the middle of the night. The man on the other end made non-specific threats and then hung up.

November 4th, 1979 2:00 AM: Assault

A woman was walking near Cottage Hospital when a man grabbed her from behind and tried to drag her away. Fortunately, the woman was able to break free.

November 7th, 1979: Phone Call

The same young woman who had received the threatening phone call on November 1st received another crank call in the middle of the night. The man on the other end threatened to kill her. It was the same voice that had called previously.

Those calls are interesting, because phone calls of the hang-up, obscene, and threatening variety had been part of the perpetrator's M.O. for many years, but the practice seemed conspicuously absent in Goleta. Perhaps the EAR *did* make those phone calls, and for some reason he chose not to attack that victim.

November 12th, 1979: Rape

A teenager was walking her bike on a trail near San Pesaro Drive when she was grabbed by a man. He ripped off her clothes and raped her near the bike path. This occurred near an area between Calle Real (where the suspicious phone calls happened) and Cathedral Oaks, which connects to the Offerman/Manning murder street.

Mid-November, 1979: Break-in

A prowler entered a garage on Dorado Drive two times in the middle of November and rummaged through the owner's items. This street was right in the heart of Golden State Killer activity, connecting to San Patricio Drive, Cathedral Oaks Road, and situated to the immediate southwest of Mountain View Elementary School and Queen Ann Lane. Events similar to this happened several times during the East Area Rapist phase of the killer's crime spree, which makes these seem to be likely connections.

November 20th, 1979 Afternoon: Phone Call

An obscene phone call occurred on Nueces Drive, a street to the northeast of the More Mesa beach area.

November 22nd, 1979 2:15 AM: Rape

A woman in her mid-twenties, living about eight miles to the east of the Offerman/Manning murder site, was raped in her house by a white male in the early morning hours. The man blitz-attacked her a few minutes after her boyfriend left. We don't have any M.O. details that match up to the Golden State Killer, and the geography would be a bit of an outlier, but it's included here because of the timing.

November 22nd, 1979 11:45 AM: Phone Call
Another obscene phone call occurred, this time on a street right off of Calle Real. The house was only a few yards away from the house that received the obscene phone calls on November 1st and 7th.

November 21st through November 24th, 1979
A woman living just south of Berkeley Road received over a dozen hang-up and obscene phone calls every day for four days straight.

November 28th, 1979: Multiple Break-Ins
Two homes on Berkeley Road were broken into and ransacked during the day. Nothing was found to be stolen. Several homes on Hannah Drive, which would be visited by the Golden State Killer on December 29th, were also broken into and ransacked. Homes on Merida Drive, which connected to Parejo Drive and Toltec Drive (very near where Golden State Killer murders would occur in 1981) were broken into and ransacked as well.

Early December, 1979: Attempted Break-In
A house on Chilon Way, a street between Calle Real and and Hollister Avenue, had a prowler that attempted to break in. The resident was inside the house and raised the alarm, which caused the prowler to flee.

December 29th/30th, 1979: EAR/GSK Attack
This was the date of the multiple EAR/GSK burglaries, and the date of the Offerman/Manning murders. It's listed here for context.

Early January, 1980: German Shepherd
A woman living on Berkeley Road noticed that over a long period of time, someone had been scaling her fence, entering her backyard, and "borrowing" her German Shepherd. It's unknown if this activity occurred the night of the Offerman/Manning murder or not, but the

timing is pretty close.

Early January, 1980: Phone calls

On a day in early January, 1980, a resident living nearby received a dozen obscene phone calls in the early morning hours.

The Smith Murders

Date: March 13th, 1980 Night
Victims: Charlene Smith (33), Lyman Smith (43)
Location: 573 High Point Drive, Ventura

At the time of their occurrence, the murders of Charlene and Lyman Smith were perhaps the most high-profile of all the Golden State Killer crimes. The investigation into this double-homicide was long, grueling, and very public, with the police and the media diving very deep into the lives of these victims and everyone associated with them. As a result, much has been written about their complicated personal lives, and we don't intend to retread the same ground—we'll merely give you a snapshot of why this particular homicde case became so complicated and just how arduous its investigation truly was. We'll spend our time, as usual, discussing the timeline and evidence.

Background
Lyman Smith was born on April 7th, 1936, in Pocatello, Idaho. When he was nine years old, he moved with his family to Citrus Heights. He went to San Juan High School and graduated in 1954. Afterward, he ended up going to the University of California at Berkeley to become a lawyer, and he moved to Ventura County in 1961. He worked as a prosecutor.

Charlene Herzenberg was born on April 17th, 1946, in Ventura County. She graduated from Camarillo High School in 1964.

In 1972, Charlene divorced her second husband, and Lyman divorced his first wife. Charlene ended up working for Lyman as a legal secretary, and the two were married in June 1976. They moved to Santa Paula after they were married.

Charlene ended up filing for divorce from Lyman in August of 1978, and the two were separated for a time. She and Lyman eventually reconciled, and they moved to High Point Drive. Lyman's former wife and his three children lived nearby.

Charlene worked as an interior decorator, and she also sold cosmetics and jewelry at the homes of her friends and at an area near the beach. Lyman dabbled in several different businesses, including an air-cargo business called Maverick International (which was headquartered in New York), a real estate venture in Santa Paula, and an avocado ranch.

Lyman's political career had started to take off. At the time of the murders, the couple was waiting to hear back from the governor about a possible appointment to the Ventura County Superior Court. Charlene was in the middle of decorating a condo, and she was planning to spend time with Lyman's two sons on the ski slopes.

Due to the events of March 13th, 1980, it'll never be known whether Lyman was to be appointed judge or not.

Tragically, the same minister who had conducted their marriage ceremony also conducted their funeral service—less than four years after officiating their wedding.

Timeline

There were several prowling incidents reported in the days leading up to the murders. It seemed that someone was trying to enter homes and was only occasionally successful. When he *did* enter a home, he wouldn't take anything. The witnesses and victims of these incidents had almost nothing to report to the police, because there wasn't anything to list as stolen and there was very little, if any, damage to their homes. Not all of these incidents are in the following timeline.

Interestingly, some of these events actually happened *after* the murders. Almost all of the incidents were very close to the Smith's home, and one was notable because it was next to the church that was situated across the street from the murder scene. The neighborhood was laid out in such a way that several houses overlooked other houses in the neighborhood, which theoretically might've made prowling a challenge. The church, which had a lot of construction going on, seemed to offer a fair bit of cover for a prowler.

Early 1980

Before the murders happened, a meter reader (or someone dressed like one) was caught prowling near the Smith's residence and was seen possibly peeping at Charlene on two occasions. It's unknown if these incidents are related to the murders.

Early March 1980

Charlene's former sister-in-law noticed that Charlene seemed on edge. When a friend came to the door at Charlene's house, Charlene seemed nervous and asked her "is there anybody outside?" Charlene ordered the friend to get into the home quickly, then she immediately locked the door. If Charlene had any specific concerns, she never shared them with anyone.

March 8th, 1980

A neighbor on High Point Drive heard someone prowling in her backyard. The prowler tried a few times to open her bathroom window, but he was unable to open it all the way.

March 12th, 1980 8:00 PM

Lyman's business partner visited him. This partner would later be falsely accused of the murders.

March 13th, 1980 Afternoon
Charlene lunched with a friend at the Gin Mill on Victoria Avenue.

March 13th, 1980 3:00 PM to 5:00 PM
Charlene had an important discussion with a man she'd had a longtime affair with. This man was not considered a serious suspect in the murders.

March 13th, 1980 Evening
Charlene talked to her former mother-in-law on the phone.

March 13th, 1980 10:30 PM
A neighbor on El Malabar Drive, just four hundred feet away, saw a white mid-1970s Pontiac sedan parked near the corner of High Point Drive. It had been there for several hours. The vehicle was not known to anyone in the neighborhood, and in the morning, it was gone.

March 13th, 1980 Night
The couple was intimate sometime during the night.

March 13th, 1980 Night
A neighbor heard a shriek coming from the direction of the Smith's house, and then another one, but the second one was muffled. The exact time is unknown.

March 14th, 1980 2:00 AM
The neighbor who had seen the Pontiac was awakened by screams. The screams came from near the Smith residence. He heard nothing else and went back to sleep.

March 14th, 1980 2:00 AM
The neighbors next door to the Smiths had a Great Dane, and the dog woke them up at 2:00 AM. They let him out, and the dog went directly to the gate leading to the Smith's yard and then just stood

there. He made no sound. That was the only time the dog had ever done that.

March 14th, 1980 Morning
A neighbor spotted a milk carton on the Smith's kitchen counter. It was there all day Friday, Saturday, and Sunday. It made her think something was amiss, because it was very unlike Charlene to leave something like that on the counter.

March 16th, 1980 2:00 PM
Lyman's twelve-year-old son, Gary, arrived to cut the grass. He was the unfortunate person that found the bodies. The side door, which was normally kept unlocked for the gardeners, was strangely locked. The front door, which was usually locked, was open. He entered the residence, heard an alarm clock buzzing, made his way to the bedroom, pulled the sheets back, and found his father's dead body. He turned off the alarm and tried to call his mom from the bedroom. He couldn't reach her, so he called 911. "I think my parents are dead. I need the police," he said. They asked him the address, which he didn't know, so he went outside to get it. He rushed back inside, picked up the extension phone in the family room, and gave the address to the dispatcher.

March 16th, 1980 2:17 PM
Ventura Police arrived at the scene.

March 18th, 1980 Between 12:00 AM and 3:00 AM
A prowler visited a house on High Point Drive. The morning after the incident, the resident found that the window screen to his infant son's bedroom had been removed, and a hole had been cut in the glass near the lock.

March 18th, 1980 4:00 AM
A neighbor's dog on High Point Drive barked for almost forty-five minutes, which had never happened before.

The Murder Scene

The couple was found in bed with the blanket pulled over their heads (officers determined that the killer had pulled the covers over their heads *after* he'd killed them). The alarm clock was making noise in the room when the bodies were found, and probably had been doing so for a couple of days.

Lyman was naked and lying face down on the bed. His ankles were crossed and tied with a single length of nylon drapery cord. Fibers of an unknown origin were found on Lyman's ankles. His wrists were crossed over and bound behind his back, palms upward, with the same type of cord.

Charlene was lying face up and was wearing only a t-shirt. Her hands, wrists crossed, were behind her back and tightly bound. Her feet were also bound, tied together with a white nylon drapery cord. Her wrists had been tied more tightly than Lyman's. The ligatures were still intact and tied when the bodies were found. It was determined that the drapery cord had not come from the house, though it theoretically could've come from some supplies that Charlene kept for her business.

The cords used to bind Charlene were slightly different from those used on Lyman—they contained copper threads at the cores. The knots used on her bindings were reportedly more ornate than those on her husband (or perhaps there were just more knots tied on top of each other). She had been struck twice on the left side of her head, and her husband had been bludgeoned as well. Charlene's bludgeoning had been more violent and brutal. She'd been killed by the first hit, but the offender had hit her once more—the second hit being overkill.

The knots on the wrists were ornate, complicated, and described at more than once as "decorative." The knots on the ankles were square knots, a much simpler knot.

472

Blood had been spattered onto the walls and onto a dresser. Analysis of this blood spattering later concluded that Lyman had been killed before Charlene. A blood-soaked log was found between the victims' bodies. It was approximately 21.5" long and had come from a stack of firewood just outside the master bathroom window (or perhaps from the fireplace, which had been stocked with the same wood). Bark from the log was scattered on the carpet, most of it on Charlene's side of the bed. Also on the bed with the couple was a 28" piece of rope.

There was no indication of a struggle by either Lyman or Charlene, aside from them pushing against their bindings.

Charlene's body had small round bruises on the back of her legs (possibly made by the barrel of a gun, or perhaps something else entirely).

Lyman's clothes were found under the bed, as were Charlene's. There were several small, polished stones on the floor, which had come out of nearby drawer.

At first, it was reported that neither of the victims showed significant bruising on the flesh under the ligatures (implying that they had struggled very little against their bonds or that the knots were tied at or shortly after their deaths). Later, it was reported that there was a good deal of bruising, particularly on Charlene's wrists. This meant that the attack had not been brief and that the bindings had been tied very tightly.

There were signs of ransacking in the house. Drawers had been pulled out and dumped onto the floor.

In the living room, officers noted that cushions on the main sofa had been moved and were standing upright against the back of the sofa. A piece of black cloth was found under one of the cushions. It was thought that the killer had searched under the cushions for valuables, but several items of value at this scene were easily-accessible and were not taken. It was proposed that perhaps he had stashed the drapery cord that he'd planned to use for the murder under the cushions at a pre-attack break-in, or that he'd done it to stage a burglary scene. None of these explanations were satisfactory.

There was no evidence of forced entry. There were no pry marks on the doors, no missing screens, no broken windows, and no damaged locks. The front door and the window in the master bedroom were unlocked. Entry was likely gained through an unlocked door or window, though friends felt that the couple was good about locking doors before bed. As discussed earlier, it was reported that a side door would sometimes be left unlocked for the gardeners.

The phone lines weren't cut. There was milk left on the counter, most likely by the killer.

In the spare bedroom, the mattress and box springs were askew, as if "someone had jumped furiously on the bed." Drawers had been opened in this room, but nothing appeared to be missing. It was suggested that the killer was checking under the mattress for valuables or weapons, but after the cases were tied together, it was suggested that he had removed Charlene from the master bedroom and raped her in the other room.

Charlene had indeed been raped. It was determined that she had been assaulted vaginally, with no evidence of oral or anal assault. DNA from the killer was eventually retrieved from semen samples.

The victim's personal jewelry was taken, but the valuable jewelry that she sold as one of her business ventures was in plain view and left behind.

It was assumed that the killer had threatened the couple with a weapon of some kind, because it appeared that he had been able to easily control the victims.

Context and Analysis

While the first murder might have been reactionary, this one appeared to be quite deliberate and intentional.

The investigation into this particular attack was unlike anything the East Area Rapist or Golden State Killer crime spree had ever seen, or would ever see again. More resources were thrown at these murders than anything else in the history of the case. Lyman Smith was up for a judgeship, and due to his standing in the legal profession, there were friends in high places that were cutting red tape for investigators at every turn. Additionally, eight detectives were assigned to the case full-time. The media swarmed all over it.

But despite the attention and resources, the investigation was anything but easy. The complicated business and personal relationships of the victims created an almost infinite number of possibilities and suspects. Despite the fertile suspect pool, lead after lead was thoroughly investigated and detectives came up empty. Law Enforcement couldn't find anyone related to the Smiths who they could make into a viable suspect. Unfortunately, the investigation got *really* sidetracked with one of Lyman's business partners. They'd found a fingerprint of his on a glass at the Smith residence, which was not terribly surprising considering that the man had been at the Smith's home several times (including a day or two before the murder). The business partner's church pastor falsely told the police that the man had confessed the murders to him, and the man ended up spending about a year in jail while a shaky case was built and a preliminary trial was held. At the preliminary trial, it was found that the minister was actually lying about the false confession, and the man was found innocent. He was set free, but his life had been ruined in the process. Many years later, DNA finally cleared him for good of the crimes. Meanwhile, the Smith case had grown cold, and detectives were left without any solid leads to follow.

The Offerman/Manning murder was looked at as a possible connection, but every detective except one felt that there was no relation (mostly due to the choice of murder weapon and the fact that Manning hadn't been raped). As the investigation wore on and the other Golden State Killer murders occurred, a connection between the Smith case and the other murders was still dismissed despite obvious similarities. At that point, the man who had been falsely accused hadn't been proven innocent yet, and the focus was still on building a case against him.

The investigation wasn't as narrowly-focused as it might sound though—at least not at first. A lot of potential suspects were looked at before they settled on the business partner. Lyman's dealings were multi-faceted, and despite being well-liked by most, he certainly had been in positions where he'd made natural enemies. One of the most obvious possibilities was that the killings were some kind of revenge hit somehow related to Lyman's former life as a prosecutor. Even though he hadn't been in that line of work for quite awhile and most of the people he'd put away were on the older side of the age spectrum, it was thought that it could've been someone *related* to one of the people he prosecuted, or someone from the community who didn't like something that he'd done as a prosecutor.

His airline business, which was based at Stewart Airport in the Hudson River Valley (north of Manhattan), had been in dire straits. Despite $17 million in revenue, its expenses overshadowed earnings and it was operating in the red. Poor business practices and trouble in the Middle East (their primary client) forced the business to shut down in early 1979. A few interesting and colorful suspects were developed from this business venture, but none of them panned out.

As the years wore on, it was eventually determined that the killing was more or less random. The DNA match with the other Golden State Killer cases later confirmed it. Looking back, there was the typical EAR-style prowling in the neighborhood, but there were no phone calls that we know of. A white car was seen, which might've been the same the car from the Offerman/Manning murder.

One of the common themes in this crime and the last one is that there was construction going on near the house. The church across the street from the Smiths was renovating and adding on to their school at the time, and it was quite a project. It's possible that a connection can be made between this project, the construction that went on at the condo next to Offerman's, and perhaps the Calle Real construction in Goleta. No connection has been made yet, but one might possibly exist.

The real estate angle here is promising, as well. Any number of the realtors, painters, construction workers, or associated personnel could've encountered Charlene at her interior decorating jobs and then found out information about her or even followed her home. Lyman had many real estate dealings, and he or Charlene could've piqued someone's interest that way as well.

The legal connections here are obvious due to his profession and the involvement of divorce lawyers. The legal field turned up in the previous attack, this attack, and it turned up in a slightly different way in the next one as well.

A possible military connection here is that the Smiths lived very close to a naval facility. A more distant connection is that Charlene's first husband was in the Air Force.

Lyman Smith spent several years living in Citrus Heights, which, as you know, was a major hotbed of EAR activity. The EAR attacks occurred nearly twenty years after he left it, which makes a connection unlikely, but it's an interesting coincidence. Most theories about these murders involve Charlene being the main target, but with Lyman's eventful life there's a small chance that he had drawn the killer's attention in some way. The Golden State Killer is thought to be much younger than Lyman at the time of the murders, but Lyman's father did live in the Sacramento area during the East Area Rapist phase of attacks (even though Lyman had been gone for quite awhile), and there's a remote possibility that while operating in Sacramento, the killer came across Lyman's father or a reference to Lyman and/or Charlene somehow, and that's what drew him all the way to Ventura (or put them on a list of potential victims). There's really no way of knowing how or why the killer chose Ventura as his target, or how he arrived at their neighborhood.

In fact, the Smith neighborhood was fairly unique because of the hills and the way that the different houses were situated. Each one was competing for an ocean view on this uneven terrain, and in the process, each one was gaining a view of their neighbors as well. There were fences to provide a little bit of privacy, but the topography would make it difficult for someone to maneuver around undetected. The church area that was roughly across the street, and some of the foliage nearby, did seem to add a little bit of cover for the killer if he indeed used it. Perhaps he spent time hiding there, watching the residence, as he did in Sacramento at times. Despite the small alcove of cover, it seemed that there were far safer neighborhood options for the killer, so the motivation to attack in this particular area must've been somewhat strong or there must've been some kind of draw or connection. Perhaps the killer enjoyed the challenge, or was looking to separate himself from his previous M.O. (hence the bludgeoning), because the next neighborhood he chose to kill in for the Harrington murders was quite different from anything else he'd chosen before as well.

The murder scene itself yielded several clues, but it also raised a lot of questions. One of the biggest questions was about where the drapery cord came from. Police felt that it hadn't come from the house, but given Charlene's profession, it's possible that the killer came across some while he was searching drawers.

Some folks have wondered if there was some kind symbolism being displayed by the killer by using drapery cord, and by tying such ornate knots on their wrists, or by using cord with a copper core on Charlene's wrists and regular cord on all of the other bindings. Of course anything is possible, but we think it's quite likely that the killer simply made sure that he reinforced their bindings as well as he could, because apparently Robert Offerman had gotten free in the previous attack. As for the cord on Charlene's wrists being different, it's very likely that either her wrists or her ankles were the last things tied (or retied, rather) by the killer as he completed his attack, and it's possible that he was out of whatever he'd been using and he simply moved on to the next type of ligature that was available to him or that he'd brought with him.

And speaking of knots, the time has come to talk about the infamous "diamond knot." The main ornate knot on Charlene's wrist was examined by a cold case team in the late 1990s and early 2000s, and after consulting a knot expert, their conclusion was that the knot was a "diamond knot," also known as a "Chinese decorator's knot" or a "lanyard knot." If their conclusions are correct and that was the knot used, it's a knot that has interior decorating applications and sailing/nautical applications. This is part of the reason that the "symbolism" theory has taken off. It's been suggested that perhaps those knots already existed on the drapery cord, and that the killer simply utilized cord that had already been tied by Charlene, but we've seen a picture of the ligatures, and it seems very unlikely that this was the case. Some of the current investigators aren't as sold on it being a "diamond knot," which left us in muddy waters while we were trying to make sense of this piece of evidence. To seek clarification, we took a photo of the tied ligatures to a knot expert of our own, who concluded that it *wasn't* a "diamond knot." Regardless of what it is or what we call it, the killer did something fairly complicated with the ligatures. A lot of folks cite the usage of this knot as possible proof that the killer had a connection to the military or the sea, and whether it was exactly a "diamond knot" or not, there's potential evidence for those types of connections regardless of knot identification.

The disarray of the couch cushions has been a source of speculation, particularly among those who think that the EAR could've broken into the house and secreted bindings or even waited for the victims to come home. While the EAR did apparently hide bindings under a couch cushion in the Thunderbird Place incident, it didn't appear to be a common thing for him to do. And plus, why would he need to take *all* of the cushions off, even if that *were* the case? There are other possible reasons as to why the couch cushions could have been removed, and one of the theories is that he could've been looking for valuables. Again, that's kind of an odd theory. Most peoples' cushions have a couple pennies and crumbs. The bed in the extra bedroom was also in disarray. Perhaps he was making sure that he hadn't left anything on a previous break-in. A theory that we touched on earlier that might explain the oddities in either the living room or on that bed is the fact that the EAR often separated the female from the male during the attacks where he raped the female, and that separation may have occurred here. Or perhaps he was trying to stage the scene in some way, or was doing a couple things at the scene that he didn't ordinarily do in order to separate himself from other crimes. There's not enough documentation to know if dishes might've been used on Lyman or Charlene. The kitchen was a mess when the house was finally released to the families, but that appeared to be from the ID technicians on the scene and not from the killer.

The sequence of events, and what might or might not have occurred, is open to speculation. Both victims must've been alive for at least a little while after being bound because of the bruising. It's unknown if Lyman was killed before the sexual assault took place, but because the killer likely got blood spatter on him after bludgeoning the victims and blood trails smears weren't found all over the house, he probably raped Charlene first and killed them roughly at the same time. It's not known for sure which room the rape actually ocurred in. Based on the data from fifty other attacks, we can form an educated guess, but it's possible that M.O. shifts were happening. There didn't appear to be a struggle, so it was assumed that the killer at least had a gun or some method of making sure they were compliant, and it's likely that they weren't in immediate fear of their lives or perhaps there would've been efforts to escape, like in the two Goleta attacks.

There's a misconception that the killer stole suits from Lyman's closet. It's unknown whether this happened or not, and the idea came from Lyman's brother, who thought that it was odd that Lyman only had four suits in his closet. If they were of a certain quality or bespoke, it would make sense that he'd only have a few that he'd rotate. The brother had never been to the house and didn't know the details of Lyman's wardrobe, so it was only an interesting observation made by him, not anything definitive. If indeed suits or clothing of any kind was stolen, the reason might simply have been that the killer got blood on him when he'd killed the couple. The murder weapon was covered in blood, there was blood on the wall and the dresser, and it's likely that there was blood on the murderer. He seemed to learn from this "mistake," and while he continued to murder victims by bludgeoning, from this point forward he would cover them up with sheets before he did it. To many, this indicates that he probably got blood on him during this crime and he learned how to prevent that from happening.

The act of bludgeoning his victims to death is an interesting choice that deserves a lot of analysis. Was it done for "practical" purposes, or was this method of killing actuallly the offender's "preferred" method that matched his fantasies? It's thought by profilers that the killer spent a lot of time thinking about his crimes and planning them. It might have been the case that the gun was too loud, and a knife might've been too difficult, slow, or might have left the killer vulnerable. Bludgeoning might've been preferred as quick and quiet, and wouldn't have required the killer to bring a weapon with him to the scene. If that was indeed his thought process, think about warped that is—sitting around and trying to think of the most "efficient" way to kill someone. The act of bludgeoning reminds us of some of the clubs that the East Area Rapist had used very early in the crime spree. It makes us wonder if hitting, clubbing, and the thought of bludgeoning was part of the equation from the beginning. If that poor animal that was killed in 1974 near Dawes and Dolecetto in Rancho Cordova was him (or the Taylor murder in Goleta in 1974), then that certainly fills in the picture for us.

Many of the attacks involved couples who had been intimate with each other before being attacked. This was definitely a recurring theme in the Southern California attacks on couples. There was plenty of evidence at the Offerman/Manning scene and at a future scene (Domingo/Sanchez) that the killer had held back and watched the couple have sex before attacking. One of the profiles generated of the killer felt that witnessing these events made the woman a "whore" in the killer's mind, which amplified anger that he already felt toward women (and that by raping them he confirmed this "whore" status). In studying this case, we've come to the conclusion that peeping and voyeurism could've been a big part of the EAR/GSK's victim selection process throughout, and that he'd look for things that either excited him or angered him, which would sometimes lead to an attack. In the early days he seemed to plan his attacks, but in these killings, they seem to be quite a bit more spontaneous. The hang-up phone calls and the sightings of prowlers is quite minimal compared to the attacks in the 1970s, though investigators didn't really know to ask about such things.

DNA technology would've made the investigation into this double-murder so much easier if it had existed at the time. But Ventura County got there as quickly as they could—they were actually a pioneer in the use of forensic DNA. A murder took place there in 1988, and for one of the first times in history, DNA was actually used as evidence.

Speaking of Ventura County history, Ventura County was a relatively peaceful and quiet place—not prone to events like this at all. There had been very few homicides. Despite the serenity of the area, sadly, this wasn't the first time that tragedy had struck Charlene's family. Her former brother-in-law, James Doyle, had worked as a police officer and was killed in 1975 at an incident on a college campus.

In previous attacks, we've spent time looking at the chronological spacing between them, and at times we've tried to find anything that appeared significant on the calendar. The timing of this crime in relation to the previous ones deserves to be looked at, because when it comes down to it, geography and timing provide some of the best ironclad evidence in the case.

This murder occurred a little over three months after the previous one. That's longer than the EAR usually took between attacks back when he wasn't killing, but it's still within a fairly normal range for him. In general, his attacks had been becoming fewer and further between. Let's examine the timing (listing appears on the next page):

July 5th, 1979: Danville
October 1st, 1979: Goleta
December 30th, 1979: Goleta
March 13th, 1980: Ventura

When it's presented like that, a regular pattern leaps out. We're looking at fairly regular intervals of roughly three months. What's the significance there? The EAR took three month breaks between attacks several other times in his career, most often when changing jurisdictions. Is there a significance to the "three month" span that occurs over and over? Does it speak to the killer being out of the area for work during regular blocks of time? Is this the general amount of time it took the killer to get "familiar" with another area? Could the three months between Goleta attacks be explained by the killer going to another jurisdiction, things not working out, and him coming back to attack in an area that he'd already familiarized himself with? There are almost endless possibilities, but at the root of them is the simple fact that there appears to be a semi-regular pattern up until this point. We couldn't help but notice that three out of the four attacks listed there occurred during times when school was usually out on break. The actual burglaries before and after the Smith murders spanned roughly a seven-day period that coincided with many spring breaks from local schools and universities.

There was no second attack in Ventura County. Goleta received three, the Irvine area received three (two in Irvine and one in Dana Point), but this one was a one-off. Perhaps the media frenzy inadvertently saved another couple from a horrific fate. As explained earlier, the kind of media attention that these murders received was unlike anything the Golden State Killer had ever experienced. Usually his attacks were met with an article or two in the local papers and then the attention died off. For this case to get such a huge amount of media attention, and then the killer to keep on offending in other jurisdictions, says a lot about his psyche, even if the attention *did* chase him out of Ventura County. We firmly believe that if the

GSK *had* planned on killing again in Ventura, the constant barrage of articles and investigations certainly went a long way in changing his mind. The post-attack burglary proves that he was still active, and perhaps stalking a second victim. But if he was staying or living in Ventura, he probably got out of town rather quickly.

The next time the GSK resurfaced, it was in the Irvine area, and he made that place his final known hunting grounds.

The Harrington Murders

Date: August 19th, 1980 Night
Victims: Keith Harrington (24) and Patrice Harrington (27)
Location: 33381 Cockleshell Drive, Dana Point

This double-murder was one of the strangest chapters in Golden State Killer history. It had been five months since the previous killing, which was a solid length of time for this criminal. Given the media attention on the Smiths, the higher stakes, and the change in scenery, it's easy to understand why he was quiet for a few extra months. For these murders, the killer had moved his activities over 125 miles down the Pacific Coast Highway to an area near Irvine called Dana Point. On the night of August 19th, 1980, he invaded a small gated community and killed yet another innocent couple—Keith and Patrice Harrington.

Background
Keith Eli Harrington was born on October 10th, 1955, in Santa Monica. He attended Pacific Palisades High School, where he was an all-conference shortstop on the baseball team. He graduated in 1973 and went to the University of California at Irvine, where he received his Bachelor of Science degree. In 1977, Keith entered medical school, and at the time of his murder, he was only one semester away from finishing. Keith had three brothers, two of them attorneys and one of them with a Ph.D. working in the field of psychology. This brother worked with patients who had brain injuries (the exact same line of work that Dr. Manning had been involved in). Keith's father

had made a lot of money in 1968 when he'd created and marketed a high-tech security camera to banks across the country.

Patrice Ann Harrington, who was three years older than Keith, had worked for a few years as a pediatrics nurse at UC Irvine Medical Center. She left there in July 1979 to work as a nurse for a well-known couple near her home. After several months of doing that, she began working in Santa Ana at Mercy General Hospital. Patrice's father had spent many years as an officer in the Air Force.

The couple had met at the UC Irvine Medical Center a little over a year before the murders. At the time, "Patti" was still a pediatrics nurse there and Keith was in his third year of medical school (studying emergency medicine). A romance blossomed, and they were married in Laguna Beach on May 17th, 1980. They spent their honeymoon in Hawaii, and then lived in San Francisco briefly while Keith completed some college courses. Keith's father offered them the use of his beach house near Dana Point while Keith finished his final year, and the couple accepted his generous offer. It was a temporary place to live, so even though Keith's father didn't live at the house and the master bedroom was unused, they slept in the guest bedroom.

Timeline

1970-1980

Over the years, there had been several unsolved bicycle thefts in the area. Most of them occurred from 1972 to 1974, but they continued on as the years went by.

Early 1980

While taking the garbage out one night, Patrice was surprised by a stranger. She also had a strange run-in with a suspicious jogger around this time period.

August 13th, 1980
This was the last night that Keith's father spoke with the couple.

Mid-August 1980
A few days before the murder occurred, a security guard for the gated community where the Harringtons lived was fired because he had gotten into a fist-fight with one of the residents. This lead was investigated in relation to the murders, but it didn't appear to be related.

Mid-August 1980
It was reported by neighbors that Patrice had been working out in the yard. Since the killer's victim selection method is still unknown, this might be relevant.

August 19th, 1980 11:00 PM
Patrice talked with her sister on the phone. It was the last time that any friends or family heard from the couple.

August 19th, 1980 Night
The couple was intimate with each other sometime before the murder.

August 19th, 1980
The neighbor living directly behind the couple heard a noise in the bushes near the Harrington's house.

August 19th, 1980
Sometime during the night, a neighbor heard loud screaming.

August 19th, 1980 Night or August 20th, Early Morning
Sometime during the night, the couple was attacked and bludgeoned to death.

August 20th, 1980 Evening

A few days before their murders, the Harringtons had made plans to serve dinner to some friends of theirs on the night of the 20th. The friends arrived on the appointed day (which happened to be the day after they were killed), but no one answered the door. They left a note in the Harrington's mailbox expressing concern.

August 21st, 1980 6:30 PM

Keith's father arrived at the couple's house for a dinner date that they had set. The front door was locked, which was quite odd because no one in the Harrington family locked their front door. There was a spare key located on top of the door frame, which Keith's father used to enter the residence. The house was quiet, and no one seemed to be home. There were two bags of non-perishable groceries from the Alpha Beta Market on the counter. The father searched the house, but he didn't notice anything out of the ordinary, even upon entering the guest bedroom. On a second sweep through the house, he thought he saw something in the bed, so he cautiously pulled back the covers. He tragically found his son, lying on his stomach, with his head turned to the left. His face was purple. Keith's father hurriedly checked the other side of the bed, where he found Patti in the exact same position. Unlike Keith, her head was unrecognizable and there was blood all over her. He ran to another room and called his eldest son for help, then dialed the emergency number.

August 22nd, 1980

A bloodstained left motocross glove was found near the intersection of Taxco Drive and Desoto Way. This intersection was about a mile (if traveling on foot) to the northeast of the scene. Using the roads, it would take two or three miles to arrive at the intersection. Because of the summer heat and the length of time that the glove had been exposed to the elements, the blood on the glove was too degraded for any specialized tests. A basic test confirmed that the blood was human.

September 1980
The Harrington family offered a $25,000 reward for information leading to the killer's apprehension.

October 1996
DNA testing done by the Orange County Sheriff's Forensic Science Division determined that some of the semen samples from the crime scene came from the killer. This DNA sample was eventually matched to the other Golden State Killer murders in Irvine and Ventura County (and in 2011, one of the murders in Goleta).

October 2000
The DNA connection was fleshed out and confirmed by investigators, and the information regarding the connection of the multiple crimes was given to the Harrington family.

The Murder Scene
As mentioned above, the victims were found in bed with the blanket pulled over their heads. They were lying face down with their heads turned to the left. Keith's father, who found them, felt that they were still wearing their pajamas. They had both been killed by blunt force trauma to the back of their heads. Unlike the Smith murders, the killer had pulled the covers over their heads before hitting them, which minimized blood spatter significantly. The sheets and comforter around them were saturated with blood, particularly on Patrice's side of the bed, and there was a large pool of blood on the carpet next to her on the floor under her body.

A small fragment of brass was found in Patrice's skull, most likely from the murder weapon. There was no murder weapon found on the property anywhere, so the police decided that the killer must've taken it with him.

There were clear ligature marks on both of their wrists and on Patrice's ankle, along with plenty of bruises. There was a nondescript mark on Keith's ankle. The medical examiner confirmed that they'd been bound very tightly by ligatures of some kind. The killer had taken the bindings off of them and had removed them from the scene, but at least one length of a brown macramé-type cord was found. Police at the time mentioned an "intricate knot pattern" in relation to this case, so it's possible that one or more of the cords that had been left still had a knot tied in it. There was a notation from a former EAR/GSK investigator stating that one of the ligatures was found on the floor under the bed.

There was no sign of forced entry—the killer had apparently entered through an unlocked door. The shutters were drawn in the room where the victims were found.

Nothing in the house was stolen, there didn't appear to be any rummaging or eating by the killer, no weapons were found on the scene, and there wasn't any sign of a struggle. Fingerprints *were* found at the scene, and no match has ever been made. There was reportedly some hair found near the front door that was taken into evidence.

Semen was found in three places: on vaginal swabs from a rape kit, on the back of Patrice's upper right leg, and on the comforter. The lab learned early on that some of the semen samples from the vaginal swabs belonged to someone other than Keith, because tests falsely indicated that the source of the sample had undergone a vasectomy. Further testing years later revealed that the source hadn't undergone a vasectomy—he was simply a non-secretor. As you'll remember from the discussions about the East Area Rapist attacks, the offender was a "non-secretor," which meant that his blood type couldn't be determined by certain tests because the normal antibodies that indicated his blood type were absent.

The house was sealed off by police for a full week while the scene was processed. The integrity of the police lines around the house were called into question by neighbors, who noted that several unauthorized officers came to take a look at the scene out of curiosity.

Detectives assigned to the case worked very hard, conducting more than two hundred interviews and chasing anything that even tenuously looked like a lead. Nothing could be found to bring resolution to the murders.

Proposition 69

It's very rare that something good comes out of a series of crimes like this, but if there's a silver lining to the legacy of any of it, it's Proposition 69.

As a direct result of the murder of his brother and the frustrating years that followed, Bruce Harrington, Keith's oldest brother, spent $2 million of his own money to help drive home legislation that made it mandatory for a prisoner of the California judicial system (related to sex offenses, murder, and voluntary manslaughter) to submit their DNA to a statewide database. It was through examination of those felons, Bruce felt, that the perpetrator would eventually be found.

Before Proposition 69, violent offenders were technically required to submit their DNA to a database, but many of them refused because the penalty was only a misdemeanor with a $500 fine (which wasn't too scary of a consequence to someone facing a long sentence or life in prison and who probably had tons of legal debt already).

It took over two years to get it signed into law, but with the help of 400,000 signatures and the support of Governor Schwarzenegger, Proposition 69 was placed before voters and approved in 2004.

This law went into full effect in 2009. Unfortunately, the Golden State Killer had apparently not been arrested for a felony and put in prison during the appropriate time frame, because no match was made. But since then, California has created the 3rd largest state DNA database of felons in the country, and many, many cases have been solved. The DNA of the Golden State Killer has been compared against this database on a regular basis for many years. Nationally, the EAR/GSK DNA is also regularly run through CODIS (a national DNA database for offenders) on a regular basis. A DNA match through any of these databases would mean that the case is finally solved.

Context and Analysis

If you thought the double homicide in Ventura County was a head-scratcher, you probably weren't ready for this one. There's very little about this crime that makes sense in light of everything we know about the offender, and that was possibly the point. Who would've looked for him 125 miles down the road? And at a house that was not only insulated by the security (or the false sense of security) that a gated community provided, but it wasn't even on the direct edge of the community? There was *some* prowling activity in this area, but not as much as usual. None of his trademark creek beds or other geographical crutches were present. There was a golf course nearby, but it didn't seem to factor into the attack (if we assume that the glove was his) because it was located in the opposite direction.

As strikingly different as it might appear on the surface, there were some glaring similarities to other attacks. The binding, the bludgeoning, the seemingly random nature of it all. The victims themselves. Criminal profilers believe that the killer was looking for couples having sex, and that box is checked here as well. Entry would've been easy if the Harringtons were truly as cavalier about locking their doors and windows as their friends and family said they were. The house was a corner lot, which was a frequent target of the offender. The bindings were different (they were not shoelaces like the Northern California scenes, and they were not twine like in the Goleta scenes), but different ligatures had been used in the Smith murders as well.

One of the biggest similarities was house itself. The residence was almost a carbon copy of the Smith house, from the floor plan to the view of the ocean. In fact, the Smith case, this one, and the two Irvine murders (Witthuhn and Cruz) all shared similarities when it came to floor plans and architects. The chances of this happening aren't as slim as they sound though, given the California housing situation at the time, but it's an interesting observation nonetheless.

Having the same floor plan might've been what emboldened the killer. Obviously *something* did, because this was a risky house to assault. Not only was the neighborhood somewhat dense in places, but were there guards that occasionally made rounds in the community, and the house itself was a bad target for someone who wanted to prowl around it or sit and observe its occupants for any length of time. There was nothing in the way of fences, there was only one portion of the house that had enough shrubbery to conceal a person, and there were no attached creeks, green spaces, or any other place to hide. Everything around it was either pavement (with other houses in direct view) or a neighbor's backyard with very little to offer in the way of concealment.

It's possible that the risk factor associated with this location, plus the challenge of infiltrating a gated community in general (if he indeed had to infiltrate it and didn't have some legitimate way of getting inside or staying there/hiding), added to the excitement and danger. He had raised the stakes in the ultimate way by moving to murder, and perhaps he wanted something tactically difficult to go along with it.

Or perhaps it was simply a bold move to obfuscate his M.O. and not have the crime attached to him. Given the huge amount of media attention that the Smith crime received, it's easy to imagine him being a little shell-shocked. Obviously though, it wasn't enough to scare him away from committing these types of crimes, which as we've noted says a *lot* about the offender. The profilers and many of the Law Enforcement officials felt that an offender like the GSK was essentially *unable* to stop committing these types of crimes. The compulsion was so strong that they kept doing it until they got caught or died. We'll discuss a five year lull in attacks later on, and expand on some of these ideas once we get to the Cruz murder.

There's yet another possibility as to how he ended up in the neighborhood: he intentionally selected and targeted these particular victims and followed them there with complete ignorance to the neighborhood or geography that he'd end up in. How and where he might've encountered them is anyone's guess. Some of the usual possible connections are present.

The first is the Alpha Beta Market, a chain that's come up a few times before. The particular store that Patrice visited was on Crown Valley Parkway, a decent distance from the couple's home. While it's possible that she could've been targeted there, it seems unlikely to us. The assailant would've had a very difficult job following her home because of the security guard that was posted at the vehicle gate of the community. Anyone not belonging to the neighborhood was stopped and had to explain themselves. Also, since she had just gone to the market before she was killed, it left very little time for planning such a complicated crime.

There are a lot of medical connections in this case, too many to even list. The couple had spent their adult lives working in the medical field, and between the college and the hospitals and the nurse's registry that Patrice had been a part of, the connections were everywhere. Even the inclusion of Keith's brother, who oddly enough was in the same line of work that Dr. Manning had been in while she lived in Boston, added countless medical connections to the case.

Construction turns up in the murder series time and time again, and this case is no exception. Plenty of construction was going on in the area and in the surrounding community. There was also a bit of a real estate angle, with homes for sale in the area (including one inside the community itself).

Legal connections abound in several of the murder cases as well, and in this one it's primarily through Keith's two brothers. It was reported that Patrice's father had become an attorney in Huntington Beach, but we've been unable to confirm that information.

In the Sacramento crimes, it was thought that the assailant would often spot potential victims on the bike trails and on the walking trails near the river. With these first murders happening so close to beach areas, was the killer finding victims at the beach? Some of the same difficulties in tracking the Harringtons to their home exist in this scenario as in others, but with the beach within walking distance it would've been easier to follow them home because the Harringtons probably would've used a pedestrian gate rather than a vehicle gate.

A bit more about the neighborhood: Niguel Shores, the neighborhood that they lived in, was described as a private community of nearly 1,000 homes located just north of the Pacific Coast Highway. The victims' house at the time of the murders was appraised at roughly $280,000 (it recently sold for $1.5 million). There were two main gates that were always manned by security guards, and there were one or more pedestrian gates in the community. Several residents, past and present, have informed us that someone on foot would be able to infiltrate the complex very easily, especially someone like the Golden State Killer who had been scaling fences and wandering through backyards for years. The gates mainly existed to keep cars out and to deter lesser criminals.

It's possible to take the glove location, look at the different low fences and gates in the community, and endlessly speculate about how the killer got from one area to another. Multiple possibilities for traveling by car, bike, or going the entire way on foot exist. Dozens of paths have been proposed for the killer, most of them allowing him to pull this off without being seen. We've come up with several of our own, but we'll spare you the details because there's really no way of knowing. Did he stash a bike right up against one of the stucco walls that surrounded the community and then scale it and go on foot? Did he use a creek bed that existed in the neighborhood where the glove was found to make his way to Niguel Shores? Did he park on a side street there? Why was the glove found so deep inside of that neighborhood, when it would've been safer to park nearer to the exit? Was it dropped there to be deceptive? The best way to approach it is to look at how he operated when he was the East Area Rapist. It seemed he often parked several blocks away, then made his way on foot or perhaps bike. The same was most likely done here. Since so much time had passed between the murder and the finding of the bodies, dogs weren't able to help track him, so we'll probably never know.

One interesting tidbit from the investigation is that the

mysterious and unknown nature of the murders scared the people that Patrice had been working for so much that they moved out of the continental United States.

Throughout the crime spree, the EAR/GSK often struck a new area twice. Ventura County didn't get a second set of murders, most likely because of all of the media coverage and because the investigation team was barking up the wrong tree and the killer was probably more than happy to let them do that. The Dana Point area didn't get a second set of murders either, possibly because he was a lot more evidence conscious (he removed the murder weapon and most of the ligatures in this attack, which was different from the Smith murder), or perhaps because the area was so small. He did move to nearby Irvine, so it could be argued that he didn't exactly leave the area.

One other thing that was mentioned in passing but should be brought back into focus is the fact that the killer covered the victims before bludgeoning them to death. This was apparently to minimize blood spatter, and as mentioned in the previous chapter, it seemed to be a lesson that he learned from the Smith case.

This case wasn't connected to the other murders or the East Area Rapist series at the time. One of the investigators on the Smith case noticed a connection immediately, but it wasn't seriously pursued. There were occasional mentions in the media about it. It should've been looked at a lot more closely than it was, even simply given the statistics of violent crime. In 1980, only about 2.5% of all murders involved more than one victim, and very few of those were bludgeoning deaths. It would only natural to compare them and look for similarities.

The killer apparently had no intention of stopping, and it appeared that he was even learning as he went and taking great care to keep his crimes from being connected. Perhaps he had even settled in the area, or perhaps there was a feeling of invincibility—because his next strike would be only twenty-five miles to the north. Instead of murdering a couple though, this time it would be a lone female in Irvine, California.

The Witthuhn Murder

Date: February 6th, 1981, 2:00 AM
Victim: Manuela Witthuhn (28)
Location: 35 Columbus, Irvine

Half a year later but only a relatively short distance away, the Golden State Killer struck again—this time in Irvine. Like his other murders, his M.O. apparently wasn't distinctive enough to be tied to the nearby Harrington murders, and the crimes weren't solidly connected together until many years later.

Background
Manuela Elenore Witthuhn, a woman of German descent, worked nearby as a loan officer/mortgage broker at the time of her murder. She and her husband David, an assistant parts manager for a Mercedes-Benz shop, had been married for five years.

On the night she was attacked, Manuela was alone in the house. Her husband, David, was in the hospital with a viral infection. Manuela had a general fear of sleeping in the house alone, but despite that, she'd turned down her father's offer to let her borrow his German Shepherd. She slept in a sleeping bag on top of the bed for a feeling of extra comfort and security.

Timeline

Fall 1980
A prowling incident occurred at the Witthuhn household roughly four months before the murder. Distinctive shoe prints were found, and these prints matched the Golden State Killer's shoe impressions found at the house on the night Manuela was killed.

February 3rd or 4th, 1981
David Witthuhn, suffering from a viral infection, was checked into the Santa Ana-Tustin Community Hospital (today, it's called the "Newport Specialty Hospital").

February 4th or 5th, 1981
A mysterious phone call was received at the Witthuhn house. The caller was described as an older-sounding African-American male.

February 5th, 1981
Manuela visited David in the hospital.

February 5th, 1981 11:00 PM
The woman living behind David and Manuela returned home to find that the deadbolt on her door was unlocked. She was sure that she had locked it. She examined the rest of the house and nothing seemed to be amiss, so she ignored the strange occurrence.

February 5th, 1981 Night
Sometime during the night, Manuela was attacked and murdered. The estimated time noted on some reports is February 6th, at 2:00 AM.

February 6th, 1981 Morning
Manuela's employers, thinking it odd that she hadn't shown up for work, contacted her parents. Her husband also became very worried that he couldn't reach her.

February 6th, 1981 11:30 AM
Manuela's parents, who lived nearby, went to the Witthuhns' house to investigate. Her father found her body in the bedroom, bludgeoned to death.

February 6th, 1981
David checked himself out of the hospital AMA ("against medical advice") once he was brought up to speed on the news of Manuela's murder.

The Murder Scene

Manuela was found lying in her sleeping bag on top of the bed. She'd been raped and bludgeoned to death inside of it.

Both of her wrists and her right ankle had bruises and deep ligature marks. The ligatures had been removed from the scene by the killer, along with the murder weapon (which appeared to be either a "cannonball" lamp or a small crystal ball with a wooden stand, both of which were missing from the scene).

A small ball of fibers was found on the victim's lower back. It was theorized that these were from the ligatures that had been used to bind her during the attack.

The killer had possibly made entry by forcing open a sliding door at the rear of the house. Most of the pry marks, curiously, were on the *inside* of the house. There was damage to the frame of the sliding door as well. It was theorized that perhaps the intruder had entered through an unlocked door or window, and then perpetrated some additional (and sloppy) prying to make it look like he had entered through the rear. We've floated the idea that he'd possibly pried at the sliding glass door from the inside merely for practice or for "fun." The sliding glass door was open when the body was discovered.

A flathead screwdriver with a variety of paint smudges on it was found nearby, and it had apparently been brought to the scene by the killer. Analysis revealed that it was a match for the pry marks on the rear sliding door.

A "cannonball" lamp and a crystal ball on a wooden base (measuring about six inches total in height) were missing from the house. The items weighed close to ten pounds each. All of Manuela's personal jewelry was stolen, and curiously, the tape from the answering machine was also missing.

Several distinctive tennis shoe prints were found, closely resembling a type of shoe that would be used for racquetball. These shoe prints were found in the backyard, and they matched the ones found at a prowling incident at the Witthuhn house that had occurred a couple months after the Harrington murders. We've been chasing information for several months now about a lead that seems to tie these particular shoes' origin to Sacramento.

Matches were found at the scene, most of them wooden, but there was a notation about paper matches as well (matches that weren't "strike-anywhere"—ones that clearly came out of a matchbook). Some of them were burnt all the way through, and some seemed as if they'd been lit and snuffed out immediately. Two of the burnt matches were in front of the door leading into the garage, and four of them were found in the flower bed next to the garage. These matches were very similar to the ones found at the Offerman/Manning murder scene.

A television, which had been in the back bedroom, was found on the back patio. The killer had moved it there. One of the initial theories was that the killer had tried to stage the scene as a burglary, but photos of the scene show that most likely, the out-of-practice Golden State Killer had placed it there to boost himsef over the fence.

The rape kit contained semen samples, and DNA from them was later matched with other Golden State Killer cases.

Context and Analysis

There are many, many possible prowling incidents related to this attack that we didn't include because the information so far is kinda sketchy and incomplete. The ones occurring between August 1980 and February 1981 are the most promising of course, but strange burglaries and rapes that occur before or after that time window are worth looking at, too. Specific information on them is hard to come by, even though local Law Enforcement, libraries, history/cultural centers, and other places that we've been in contact with have been very helpful. Digging through the information has been a slow process. *Too* slow. We had hoped to have a few more things to present with this case, but it'll have to wait. There was a promising rape case in Lompoc, a bludgeoning in San Diego, and a lot of interesting details to explore with the prowling near the Witthuhn residence, but we don't have enough confirmed details to present that information in a compelling way, and I don't want to step on any toes regarding something that might be an active lead. It's certainly interesting that we can seemingly place the killer in his victim's backyard a few months before the murder, though. It opens up a world of possibilities as far as his movements and his stalking/prowling activities during the murder series.

A few basic connections worth exploring:

Real estate: Manuela's position at the bank meant that she was in frequent contact with people looking to buy homes, as well as in frequent contact with real estate agents and other people related to the industry. Additionally, there was a home for sale very near the Witthuhn house, and there were some vacant homes in the vicinity (mostly because the surrounding housing developments were relatively new). Real estate connections abound in this case, but leads have been followed without success.

Medical: There was also a good chance that the killer could've encountered Manuela through a medical connection. Her husband was in the hospital at the time, and she'd of course gone to visit him (just a few hours before her murder, actually). Any number of the doctors, nurses, pharmacists, patients, or medical personnel that she or her husband encountered there due to that medical event and/or others could be a viable lead. Indeed, several of the interviews (of which there were over one hundred) that Law Enforcement conducted for this case were of the different medical angles. Nothing has yet to turn up.

Military: The El Toro Marine Base was nearby, keeping this crime in step with most of the other murders (most of them took place near military bases, but there doesn't seem to be big military connection beyond that).

Construction: In discussing the case later on, David Witthuhn had mentioned a contractor that he'd been in brief contact with. David was very adept at home repairs and upgrades himself and rarely used a contractor for anything, so it's unlikely that the contractor did any work at his house. There were several different types of construction crews in the neighborhood off and on for various reasons.

A good case could be made for Manuela's neighbor being a potential target, maybe even the primary target. When the neighbor arrived home and noticed that her deadbolt was unlocked, it was almost certainly because the killer had been in her house. The assailant might've been watching the area from one of the numerous nearby parks (almost all of which offered unobstructed views of the women in the neighborhood through the sparse backyards), waiting to see when she'd be arriving home and if she'd be alone or with another man. He'd probably planned on coming back. By locking the deadbolt, she might've made it too hard for him to get back in, thus unknowingly saving her own life.

After killing three couples in a row and spending so much of his time attacking couples in Sacramento and beyond, it's a little strange that he switched back to a lone female for this murder. It made this crime harder to connect to the others, and maybe that was the intention. It's also possible that he had already stalked this couple, and the virus that landed David Witthuhn in the hospital actually saved his life. The killer certainly could've planned on attacking both of them that night, but simply found Manuela alone and because of some personal reason regarding timing or something else, decided to attack anyway.

It might also be possible that he was finished attacking couples for good. The murder after this one was of a female who didn't expect to have male company that night, and the murder after that (the final one) was of another lone female.

But to confuse you even more, an equally-strong case can be made that he *wanted* to keep attacking couples. Manuela did have a husband that was usually in the house, the next woman did have a male companion, and the final murdered woman had been with a young man that night, but he left shortly before she was attacked (but *after* the killer was apparently on the premesis). It's frustrating that the evidence can take us in either direction. The ambiguities in this case are nothing short of remarkable.

This particular area of Irvine lent itself well to peepers and prowlers. There was plenty of green space, parks bookending many of the streets, backyards that backed up to dark and undeveloped areas, and several cul-de-sacs that backed up to empty lots. The rear of the Witthuhn house was made up almost entirely of glass sliders (the house had three in total). At the time of the murder, the Witthuhn house had a small courtyard or alcove that also had a sliding door. The back fence was a fairly standard height (six feet), but it offered little in the way of privacy due to the sparse landscaping and the green area behind the house (called a "vacant lot" in some documentation) that offered plenty of vantage points for seeing into the house. Several areas near the house had thick trees that offered dense coverage for a man to hide in. A park nearby called Sycamore Park was identified as a probable entry/escape path, although Bubble Gum Park would've offered plenty in the way of cover, as well. In the actual yards themselves, there was very little in the way of bushes or hedges, so the killer would've had to stick to the shadows and away from most of the houses while navigating the streets.

This was the only Golden State Killer case where the husband was away, and thus survived. The aftermath of the murder for David Witthuhn was obviously a time of unimaginable difficulty. Drew Witthuhn, David's brother, was a police officer. One of the most poignant aspects of this attack, for us, involved how a family member with a police background was able to support his devastated brother in unique ways, given his experience and skillset. Once the scene was released and David was given permission to stay in his house again, Drew and another officer spent two nights posted in the house, just in case the killer returned. In addition to using his police training to go over the crime scene many times (looking for additional clues or trace evidence), he was also available to the family as an informed observer of investigative procedure (which surely made things clearer and a little easier for them). When one of us discussed this case with Drew, he had nothing but nice things to say about how thoroughly the officers conducted the investigation and how tenaciously they worked many of the leads which emerged—not to mention the compassion that many of them showed the family even after David Witthuhn's death in 2008.

We've been glossing over an important part of these murder cases up until this point—the aftermath and the difficulties that loved ones had to face, including the actual cleanup of the crime scene after its release. Drew recalls having great difficulty cleaning up the fingerprint dust that had been used all throughout the house. In the Harrington murder, Keith's eldest brother Bruce took charge of cleaning the crime scene, and his most vivid memory was a heartbreaking story about how difficult (on many levels) it was to remove a large blood stain that had been left by Patrice's body. These experiences are just a sampling of the dozens of stories told about the pain and human suffering created by these tragedic attacks and murders.

At the Witthuhn crime scene, by the time it was released back to the family, the mattress and sleeping bag had been removed from the scene. Drawers were open throughout the house, and whether the killer had done it or if Law Enforcement had opened all of them isn't even known. There was possible evidence of forced entry at the scene, which was another way that this murder was unique. This one and the Offerman/Manning case were the only Golden State Killer murders that had any evidence of forced entry. The fact that the pry marks were mostly found on the *inside* of the sliding doors is curious, but just the fact that it's one of the only ones that had *indications* of forced entry could be telling. Was he distancing himself from his own previous M.O., or from the victim? Was there no other way in? It's theorized by many that he actually entered through a bathroom window.

Why did he leave his screwdriver at the scene? Was this intentional or on purpose? Was it his, or had he stolen it? There were smudges of paint on it, the predominant color being brown, but reportedly there were up to four other colors on it. The paint was analyzed and it was determined to have been manufactured by Behr. The paint was basically a commodity, which rendered it impossible to trace to a specific source.

The missing answering machine tape was one of the most interesting pieces of evidence in the murder series, especially given the strange phone call received the day before the murder (which may or may not have been related). Keep in mind that while cassette players were fairly common, answering machines were not widely used until a couple years *after* this murder. They weren't very affordable, and they didn't even reach sales of one million until 1984. David Witthuhn was a "techie" and enjoyed technology, so the Witthuhns were early-adopters.

Why did the killer steal the tape? A popular theory is that he'd left a message on there previously, and he wanted to make sure that there wasn't evidence of it. If not, perhaps it was done to misdirect the police. Maybe he didn't know how they worked, and thought that it might've recorded something that happened at the scene. It's also possible that he *was* the strange caller the day before, and he wasn't sure if those types of machines recorded calls or not. Or perhaps he might've wanted a "souvenir" of his victims' voice. Family doesn't specifically remember, but feels that it was Dave's voice on the "leave a message" portion of the machine. Maybe the killer didn't know that and decided to chance it and hope that Manuela's voice was on it. He did seem to enjoy taking personal items that belonged to his victims (he took photographs sometimes, he took their personal jewelry, he took their driver's licenses sometimes), so maybe this was just a "modern," 1980s way of taking a souvenir. Along that same line of thought, it's worth noting that he also stole all of Manuela's jewelry.

One of the things in this murder that tiptoes toward the "myth" category is Manuela, her parents' dog, and all sorts of convoluted and suspicious reasons for it not being there the night she was killed. The dog (a German Shepherd) was owned by her mom and dad, who lived less than two miles away. David and Manuela would walk it, bring it over to the house for a few hours to play, and feed it at her parents' house occasionally, but it doesn't sound like it was very typical for the dog to stay over. Manuela's father had offered to let her keep it until David returned home, but for whatever innocuous, everyday reason, she declined. The most common explanation given was that she probably didn't want the responsibility of taking care of it by herself for an undetermined amount of time. She *did* mention to a few people that she had a general fear of being home alone, but we have to think that if she had a specific fear or if something unnerving had actually happened, she would've stayed with her parents or at least borrowed the dog. One of the tragic "what-ifs" in this case is the question of what might've happened if she'd accepted. What if the dog had been there that night? Would it have acted as a deterrent?

Irvine police assigned an eight-person task force to this murder, and they turned the Witthuns' life inside-out looking for answers. Hospitals, neighbors, real estate agents, phone records—everything was fair game. People close to the investigation report that nothing terribly helpful was gleaned from any of it. There were enough differences between this murder and the Harrington murders for the police at the time to feel that they most likely weren't connected. The missing answering machine tape, the fact that she was alone, the supposed "staged burglary" (which really wasn't staged—it was the killer doing what he usually did) and various other factors did make it difficult to connect to the other Golden State Killer crimes in an era without forensic DNA capabilities.

In a case like this, it's very common to consider the husband as the number one suspect, even though he had a pretty good alibi. It seems the police did their due-dilligence and investigated David as thoroughly as they could. Angles such as murder-for-hire were even explored and easily dismissed. Despite being fully cleared (and truly, never seriously suspected), the tragic event understandably created a cloud that lasted David's entire lifetime. He stayed in the Irvine house for six more years after the murder before moving away, and just like the sons, daughters, grandchildren, parents, brothers, sisters, friends, and everyone else related to all of these victims, David Witthuhn was deeply affected for the rest of his life. He died in 2008, followed four months later by his mother. As proof that Irvine police never forgot the case, the surviving members of the Witthuhn family received sympathy cards from many members of the Irvine PD.

The Domingo/Sanchez Murders

Date: July 27th, 1981, 3:25 AM
Victims: Cheri Domingo (35) and Greg Sanchez (27)
Location: 449 Toltec Way, Goleta

Background
Cheri Domingo, a thirty-five-year-old mother of two, was living with her daughter on Toltec Way. They were house-sitting for a relative, and the house had been on the market since at least May of that year.

Greg Sanchez, a man Cheri had dated previously, stopped by on the evening of the murder. She and Greg hadn't seen each other in awhile, and they ended up spending the night together. Cheri's fifteen-year-old daughter was staying with a friend in Santa Barbara on the night of the murders—a decision that possibly saved her life.

Timeline

July 26th, 1981
The day before the murders, a real estate agent was showing the victim's house to a prospective buyer. A second, unplanned prospective buyer showed up. While the real estate agent continued to help the first buyer, the second man had unsupervised access to the house, both inside and outside. The only description available of this man mentions a possible scar on his face.

July 26th, 1981 9:45 PM
Two men in the neighborhood spotted a shadowy figure standing behind a large tree located on Merida Drive near the backyard of the Domingo house. They were certain that it was a man, but they couldn't see him well enough to describe him.

July 26th, 1981 Approximately 10:00 PM
Another neighbor living nearby was taking a walk in the neighborhood with his wife when they noticed a man following them, sometimes as close as five to ten feet. He appeared to be young, 5'11", with a slim build and blonde neck-length hair.

July 26th, 1981 10:00 PM
The couple living behind Cheri Domingo heard their doorbell ring. They answered it, but no one was there. A few minutes later they noticed a wad of toilet paper on their front lawn.

July 26th, 1981 11:00 PM
Two women were jogging on Merida Drive (on the part of the street that backed up to Toltec Way). They saw a man with a German Shepherd standing near the driveway of the house directly behind Cheri Domingo's. He was only four feet from the front door. The man and his dog were "frozen" in place, and the older woman felt very strongly that the man "did not belong there." The older woman described him as a white male in his twenties or early thirties, 5'10", 190 to 200 lbs, with a "husky" build and neatly-cut blonde hair. He was wearing white or beige tennis shorts and a light-colored t-shirt. The younger woman described him as a white male in his early or mid-twenties, with brownish hair (maybe with a reddish tint) that was slightly coarse in texture. He appeared to have muscular legs and was wearing white shorts. The younger witness was very social and knew almost everyone in the neighborhood, and she did not recognize the man.

July 27th, 1981 Early Morning
Sometime in the early morning hours, Cheri Domingo and Greg Sanchez were murdered.

July 27th, 1981 2:15 AM
The neighbor living next door to the Domingo residence was awakened by his barking dog. The neighbor got up to investigate, but he couldn't determine what the dog was barking at.

July 27th, 1981 Between 3:20 AM and 3:35 AM
Neighbors living nearby heard a gunshot, and then a woman's scream (which was described as "somewhat long"). No one called the police. The dogs in the immediate area barked for about thirty minutes afterward.

July 27th, 1981 Approximately 4:00 AM
A neighbor woke up with a start, feeling that he'd been awakened by the sound of a gunshot. Then he heard a woman's voice. He described the voice as being fairly normal in tone. "Not panicked." It had an "objective" tone.

July 27th, 1981 12:00 PM
The victims were found by a real estate agent who had arrived to show the house to prospective buyers.

Summer 2011
The bedspread from the crime scene was pulled out of storage and examined. A small semen stain was found. DNA was extracted from it, and testing revealed that the DNA matched the other Golden State Killer cases.

The Murder Scene

Gregory Sanchez was found nude and lying face-down on the floor, his body partially inside the bedroom closet and covered with clothes removed from the closet. The bar or rack at the top of the closet had been removed on one side. Sanchez was dead, having been shot in the cheek and then hit in the back of the head with a blunt object reportedly more than twenty times. Evidence determined that Sanchez had been shot while in a kneeling position. The predominant theory at the time was that he had been hit with the blunt object soon after being shot, but then recovered and was attacked again by the killer and knocked into the closet where he was struck several more times until he was dead.

Cheri Domingo was found on the right side of the bed, completely covered by the bedspread. Like Sanchez, had also been bludgeoned to death while nude and lying face-down. She'd been hit at least twice with a tremendous amount of force. The first blow was most likely enough to kill her, and any subsequent ones were overkill. There were miniscule areas of blood spatter on the ceiling, possibly from when the killer swung the weapon back. It was determined that she had been killed by the same weapon that had killed Sanchez. In the three previous murders, the killer had covered the heads of the victims before he hit them, and it's likely that he did the same in this murder as well.

Domingo's hands were crossed behind her back, and there were ligature marks on both wrists and bruises on her ankles. The patterns of the marks and bruises indicated that she may have been "hogtied," or rather, put in a tortuous position where her ankles were pulled back and bound to her wrists. There was no evidence that Sanchez had been bound. A single piece of "shipping twine" was found on the floor to the right of the bed, but the rest was apparently removed by the killer. The murder weapon, determined later to possibly be a yard tool, had also been removed from the scene. There were some unidentified fibers near Cheri's body.

Ballistics were run on the shot that hit Sanchez, and the information was compared to the shots that killed Offerman and Manning. No match. The firearm manufacturer could not be conclusively determined, but was possibly a Charter Arms (either the .38 Undercover Model or the Target Bulldog model).

There was no evidence of forced entry. A rear sliding door, where unmatched fingerprints were found by technicians, was a possible entry point, but the most likely point of entry was the master bathroom. A small window in that bathroom was open when officers arrived, and the window screen was found a few feet away. The window was too small for a man to crawl through, but it was positioned in a location that allowed someone from the outside to reach in and unlock the door that led from the bathroom to the outside.

Deep foot impressions were found on a rug in the master bathroom. Officers at the scene felt certain that the killer had entered the master bathroom and had hidden himself there for quite awhile before confronting the couple, possibly even long enough to witness sexual activity between them. The door leading from the bathroom to the master bedroom made a loud, distinctive scraping sound (the door didn't have enough ground clearance to swing over the height of the carpet), which may have alerted the couple to the killer's presence before the killer was prepared to attack them. It appeared that Sanchez had gotten out of bed to confront the killer before the GSK was able to restrain him. Sanchez had been in the bed on the side of the room closest to the bathroom door, which would've made for close quarters during a confrontation.

There was a large blood stain near the foot of the bed. Near it was a white metal flashlight and a yellow bathrobe. The yellow bathrobe had a bloody shoe print on it. A matching shoe print was found on Greg Sanchez' left arm. Several other prints matching this herringbone, zig-zag style of shoe were found in and around the house.

Luminol (a chemical spray used in crime scenes that reacts with the iron content in blood and makes trace blood evidence glow brightly) was applied at the residence to try to determine the killer's exit path. It worked. A trail led out of the master bedroom, down the hallway, a few steps into the living room, through the kitchen, then toward the front door of the home, which was located next to the garage and which opened to Toltec Way. It's unknown if the killer actually left through that door or if he simply walked through the house and then back to the bedroom again.

More blood was found outside, near the crime scene. There were "bloody tracks" found on the sidewalk at Merida Drive, going across the street to Toltec Drive and continuing toward the murder scene. The tracks were apparently made by a large dog. Swabs were taken of the blood and it was thoroughly tested, but the results were inconclusive. Weathering and the difficulty of obtaining a proper sample (because the blood had soaked into the concrete) made it difficult to conduct any further tests. The species of the animal or dog couldn't be determined because of degradation.

Some of the strangest evidence connected to this scene related to the pieces of toilet paper found near the Domingo residence. There was a piece of toilet paper in the gutter a couple houses down from the murder scene (at the intersection with Toltec Drive). A piece of toilet paper was found in the bushes just off the sidewalk near the gutter, and yet another piece of was found on *top* of the bushes. The rest of the roll of toilet paper was found beside the wooden footbridge at Berkeley Drive. This was still close to the murder scene, and it was the location of the strange dog incidents that occurred in late September 1979.

There's information regarding a stolen handgun at this scene, but we don't have specifics and we can't confirm it.

An astouning amount of legwork was done in this case, with nearly 1,500 interviews being conducted. Unfortunately, nothing was found that could solve it. A tie to the Offerman/Manning murder was suspected early on, but there was no physical proof. Ties to the other Golden State Killer crimes came much, much later. Thirty years after the murders occurred, traces of semen stains were found on the bedspread, indicating that the killer had achieved some kind of sexual release before or after committing the murders. DNA was extracted and tested, and it finally tied this double-homicide to the other killings.

Context and Analysis

There are several important details to examine in this attack, but the most surprising one is that despite a year and a half absence, the killer returned to the same exact area in Goleta. As we've said before, the geography and timing between attacks becomes paramount when trying to lift the mask off of the killer inch by inch, especially since he left very little physical evidence and very few witness descriptions.

Speaking of having very little physical evidence, it took an incredibly diligent cold case team to find the DNA sample on the bedspread. That was a huge find. The Goleta crimes, which contained compelling M.O. ties but lacked that one conclusive link, were finally brought into the fold. Investigators haven't been as lucky with Offerman/Manning, which still doesn't have any sign of DNA, but with footprint and twine matches between that one and the foiled Queen Ann attack (which was more obviously the work of the EAR/GSK) and the DNA link from this one, it enjoys the same status as the others.

The return to Goleta could mean many things. Perhaps the killer had ties to the area, perhaps he was returning to a place he felt comfortable with because he lacked the time and motivation to stalk new territory, or perhaps something in his personal life (work, family, school schedule) brought him back. Maybe something else entirely was going on.

The presence of the dog, along with the bloody dog tracks, leaves us with a lot more questions than answers. It creates strange parallels with the September 1979 Berkeley Road incident where the dog was injured, and it harkens back to the paw prints that were found at the Offerman/Manning scene. Why do dogs only appear in the Goleta murders and none of the other Goleta crimes or none of the other attacks or murders? The logistics of bringing a dog to a double-homicide don't make a whole lot of sense, but given the sighting of the suspicious man with the dog at 11:00 PM behind the Domingo house, the likely purpose becomes obvious. The dog was possibly a prop or a cover. Extensive neighborhood canvassing (over one thousand homes in the vicinity) didn't shed any light on who this man might've been, or why he was standing at such a close, intrusive distance from the home on Merida. Since a man walking a dog at that time of night would've most likely been a local, and he wasn't identified through the massive canvass, it makes it very likely that the dog-walker was the killer and that he was completely unknown to the immediate area.

Let's say that, based on the sighting, the killer started his approach to the Domingo residence in earnest around 11:00 PM. That would leave him a few hours to deposit the dog somewhere else before he made his approach. If he *did* drop the dog off somewhere, is it proof that the killer was staying somewhere nearby? It's possible, but honestly, he could've commuted from anywhere and brought the dog from wherever he lived, especially if he killed it or injured it after its usefulness to him was over with…

The remote possibility also exists that the killer had somehow trained the animal to listen for sirens or for the approach of someone else, and that the animal acted as a canine "lookout" for him while he committed his crimes.

But like we said above, we feel that the dog was probably there for the express purpose of providing a plausible cover for him while he stalked his next victim and surveyed the area before the attack. A man standing alone on a street in the middle of the night is terrifying, but a man walking his dog in the middle of the night is a common, almost reassuring sight. We feel that the EAR's penchant for smoking while he stalked might've also been part of a cover at times. A man standing under a tree doing nothing is creepy, but a man standing under a tree smoking for a bit doesn't raise alarm bells in the same way. Does the presence of the bloody paw print mean that the dog was "eliminated" that night, and that it's sole purpose in life was to provide cover for a killer? Maybe so. A man who could take the lives of human beings without a care in the world could also do it to animals.

The dog might not have been the only cover story that the Golden State Killer used that weekend. Some investigators are confident that the second prospective buyer that showed up to the open house the day before the murders was actually the killer himself, and that he could've unlocked doors or removed window screens in advance of his attack that night.

Let's explore the idea that he was perhaps the "prospective buyer." In the previous murder, Manuela was alone, but David was "supposed" to be there that night. In this murder, Cheri was with Greg, but Greg *wasn't* "supposed" to be there that night. As near as family and witnesses could determine, Greg hadn't been by to see Cheri in quite some time. If the killer picked his victims solely by prowling, and he knew several days in advance which person or couple he wanted to attack, then it would be reasonable to assume that the killer thought that David would be with Manuela, and that Cheri would be alone. If the killer only knew a day or two in advance who he wanted to attack, then it would be reasonable to assume that he thought both Manuela and Cheri would be alone. If the killer had targeted them *that night*, then he knew that Manuela was alone, and depending on when Greg showed up, he might've known or not known that Greg was in the house. Regardless of the scenario and the killer's preference for a couple or a lone woman, there's almost no way that the killer could've anticipated Greg Sanchez being in the house if the killer was indeed the "prospective buyer" from the open house the day before. If he were the "prospective buyer," that would mean that the Golden State Killer had planned on killing a lone female that night, and it would also mean that the presence of Sanchez didn't deter him from his plans, so the "fantasy" component of attacking a lone female wasn't of paramount importance. It's possible that the killer was already in the house or in the bathroom when Sanchez arrived, as well, and that rather than going out the bathroom door, he went ahead with the attack anyway. The attack didn't go the way he wanted it to, obviously, so Greg's presence might've been a factor that he was unprepared for (and it possibly ended up thwarting him).

All of that was written to simply say that it's impossible to know if he had planned to target a lone female, or if this were a spontaneous attack. Perhaps witnessing intercourse between Cheri and Greg was what flipped his switch.

There's *possible* evidence that Cheri was targeted in advance, however. Apparently people who knew Cheri claimed that she'd felt like she was being watched, and there had been an odd incident with a man outside looking into her window. A singles' ad that she'd placed and a dating service she'd used were explored as possible leads.

One thing to keep in mind is that Cheri had only been living on that street since May, so she couldn't have been targeted *too* far in advance. She couldn't have been spotted in 1979 at least, the last time that the GSK was active in the area. He didn't make a special trip back to the area specifically to attack *her*, so he must've come back to the area to look for new victims, likely without any particular victims in mind. The house she was staying in was located right in the heart of his previous activity in the area, so it's far, far more likely that geography was prioritized over the characteristics of the victim. If the killer had stalked her before she lived in that area, that's one heck of a coincidence that she ended up right in the middle of the small cluster of houses that he'd attacked before.

Cheri's situation would've certainly been attractive to the killer, probably making her one of the more viable candidates in the area. The house she was staying at was very close to green space and creek areas that were certainly familiar to the killer, at least back in 1979.

The house had a high fence and a very dark yard that had thick dichondra ground cover. Murder weapons were easily accessible outside the probable point of entry. These sorts of things, of course, described many of the houses in the area. The house was for sale, which meant that there was a lock box on the front door, but the lock box had a number combination lock and not a key lock, which meant that not just anyone could enter the home. Even so, houses for sale factor into several of the crimes in this series throughout the years, so the combination of the real estate angle, plus the fact that an attractive woman like Cheri was living at the house (along with her attractive teenage daughter, who had been living there but had been away for a couple weeks at the time of the murders but could've been a target herself), might have caused the killer to take notice.

One interesting piece of lore related to the "Creek Bed Killer," as the murderer was known before his Goleta crimes were tied to Golden State Killer series, was the rumor that the killer was only targeting couples who were "living in sin." The failed attack on Queen Ann, the Offerman/Manning case, and then the Domingo/Sanchez case seemed to present a pattern that gave some married couples in Goleta a false sense of security. Now that so many more crimes have been tied together, we can dismiss this aspect of the murders. It's interesting though that the victims in Goleta were unmarried, and his other victims (aside from Cruz) *were*. If anything, that piece of trivia might speak to the killer's transient appearance in the town and his lack of stalking particular victims long-term in that area, rather than any kind of moral objection that the killer might've had. It would've been very difficult for him to know in advance that Manning would be spending the night at Offerman's, or that Sanchez would spend the night at Domingo's. It sheds some light on his stalking methods in Goleta. They weren't long-term couples, so he wouldn't have had opportunities to see them together in advance.

The murder weapon couldn't be determined by the investigators on the scene, but one of their first suspects, Cheri's ex-husband, was able to possibly shed some light on the mystery. Investigators brought him to the actual scene of the crime, making him one of the only civilians to actually enter a room where a GSK homicide had taken place before it had been cleaned up. Based on a dust outline on a tool shelf found outside the door to the master bathroom, he explained to them that he felt the murder weapon was a yard tool used for taming the dichondras that were growing in the backyard. The tool, somewhat similar to a "sod plugger" (about three feet long, with a square base and a curved handle), had been on the shelf at one point but was missing from the residence. The tool may or may not have been the murder weapon. In his eagerness to help investigators make sense of the scene, the ex-husband probably raised suspicions, but he was quickly and completely cleared of any involvement in the crimes (having been in San Diego at the time of the murders).

Just like the other cases, the murders took an unimaginable toll on the victims' families. In recent years, Cheri's daughter, Debbi Domingo, has channeled some of that and become a strong and compassionate advocate for the families that have been affected by the East Area Rapist / Golden State Killer. She (along with many other victims and survivors of these attacks) has done tremendous work to raise awareness for this case and to help bring it closer to resolution.

The Cruz Murder

Date: May 4th/5th, 1986
Victim: Janelle Cruz (18)
Location: 13 Encina, Irvine

Background

Janelle Lisa Cruz, born on July 11th, 1967, was the last known victim of the Golden State Killer. She was only eighteen years old when she was killed, which made her the youngest homicide victim in the case.

At the time of her murder, nearly five years had passed since the Cheri Domingo and Greg Sanchez homicides. Aside from a potential phone call from the killer to a Sacramento victim in 1982, there was no known activity from the offender in the intervening years. Something kept the killer from attacking (at least, in any way that could be connected to him), for quite awhile. Something also drew him back to the Irvine area once more, just two miles away from where he had murdered Manuela Witthuhn in 1981.

Timeline

October 21st, 1982

Victim #24 received a call that she identified as the EAR. The caller said "Hi, it's me again. Remember me? I'm going to come over and fuck you again. You're going to suck my cock again."

The call came a few weeks after an article was printed titled "Where is the East Area Rapist Now?" by John Van Landingham.

Early May 1986
In the days leading up to the murder, Janelle was staying at the house alone. Her sister was at Mammoth Lakes, and her mother and stepfather were vacationing in Mexico.

May 3rd, 1986 Night
Some friends were visiting Janelle at her house, and the scene was described as a small party. Some of them heard a noise outside by the back fence. They went outside to check, but they didn't see anyone or hear anything else.

May 4th, 1986
Janelle spent some time at Laguna Beach. She struck up a conversation with a man (a "bodybuilder type") that she met near the basketball court. Later in the day, she was seen at a Mexican restaurant with an unknown male. We don't have documentation that identifies either of these two men, but it's certainly not out of the ordinary for a young woman to talk to someone at the beach or to go to dinner with a man.

May 4th, 1986 Evening
A male friend of Janelle's visited her in the evening. He had driven his own car to her house, and they had arrived there simultaneously (having left the place where Janelle worked at the same time, driving separately). The visit was not romantic in nature, and there was no sexual activity. While they were in her room talking, they heard noises outside the bedroom window. They looked outside, but weren't able to spot anything out of the ordinary. As the evening progressed, they heard another noise, that time further away. It sounded like a gate closing in the side yard or a door shutting near the garage. The friend felt like Janelle acted nonchalantly about the sounds, but he was unnerved by them.

May 4th, 1986 10:45 PM
Janelle's friend left the house.

May 4th, 1986 11:15 PM
At 11:15 PM, a neighbor heard Janelle's car (a Chevette) pull up to her driveway. She must've left her house sometime after 10:45 PM, and it's not known where she went. The muffler wasn't quite up to par on the vehicle, so the neighbor was sure that it was Janelle because of the distinctive sound that her car made. The neighbor heard one car door slam, then no other noises.

May 4th, 1986 Night
Janelle called her best friend, and she discussed feeling anxious about the noises that she had heard near her house. It's unknown for sure whether this call happened before or after the male friend left. Sadly, the friend that Janelle called that night passed away a few years after Janelle's murder.

May 4th, 1986 Night
Sometime during the night, Janelle Cruz was raped and murdered. While it's possible that the attack occurred before midnight, the official date of Janelle's death is May 5th, 1986.

May 5th, 1986 12:00 AM
One of Janelle's male friends called Janelle's house. There was no answer.

May 5th, 1986 5:00 PM
A real estate agent arrived at the house with a prospective buyer in tow. The agent discovered Janelle's body.

The Murder Scene
Janelle was found in the bedroom, lying diagonally on the bed. She'd been bludgeoned to death. Her shoulders and head were covered with a blanket.

Her bra was pulled down to her waist, and her wrists had small scrapes (though no ligature marks). Blue fibers were found on her body, on the bed, and on the floor. Analysis revealed that the fibers came from fabric that had been ripped apart, most likely a towel or something torn to create soft ligatures (which explained why there were no ligature marks), and possibly a gag. The bindings had been removed from the scene by the killer.

There were traces of blood at the scene, mostly on the wooden shutters and the head of the bed. Blood was also found in the kitchen (on the floor and on the cabinets) and on the floor near the front door of the house. The blood appeared to be transfer from the killer, who had apparently moved through the house and gone to the kitchen and front door after the murder. Blades of grass were found on the bed, particularly near the victim's feet and near her head. There was evidence that Janelle had been raped.

The bludgeoning was quite severe, and it appeared that there may have been a struggle. She had been hit once in the back of the head and more than once in the face. She was beaten so savagely and with such force that she had inhaled her teeth. The most crushing blow was to her forehead. The murder weapon was assumed to be a pipe wrench that was missing from the backyard. The killer had apparently taken it with him when he'd left the scene.

There didn't appear to be any ransacking of the residence. The radio was on in the house, set to a station that Janelle would've set it to.

There was no sign of forced entry. A rear sliding glass door was found unlocked, but every other door and window was shut down tightly. A piece of furniture had been moved to the backyard and placed near the fence, probably to be used as a boost for the aging offender to get over the fence. Vague tennis shoe impressions in the backyard by the fence didn't give investigators much to work with, and neither did the rest of the scene.

Context and Analysis

All of the murders were cold and vicious, and this final attack was certainly no different. What's a bit odd is that the victim in this case wasn't killed "cleanly" like the victims in some of the other cases—he actually *bashed her face in*. Other victims had been bludgeoned in the back of the head. Unless Greg Sanchez had tussled with the killer, this was the only scene where a hand-to-hand struggle was likely, given the injury to the back of her head *and* the blows to her face. This implies two different physical attacks or confrontations.

Up until this point, the offender had disappeared for a few months at a time here and there, and usually after a small break, he reappeared in another jurisdiction. The break between the Domingo/Sanchez murders and this attack lasted nearly *five years*. And, as noted in the intro, when he resurfaced, it was a mere two miles from the Witthuhn murder. It was a similar pattern to the murders in Goleta in 1979 and then 1981, just on a grander scale. More time and a bit more distance. And coincidentally (or perhaps not), both of the Goleta cases were double murders, and both of the Irvine cases were single murders.

A lot could be said about his five year absence, like where he could've been and what he could've been doing. Given the Goleta situation described above (where he killed in Goleta, killed elsewhere, then returned a year and a half later to kill again in Goleta), the fear is that he went to another part of the state or another part of the country and continued killing for a few years. No one knows, of course, *where* he was. Prison records, deployments, school records, and the like have all been looked at thoroughly, and nothing has jumped out yet. Similar cases all over the country have been examined, and a few likely ones have turned up here and there, but nothing is sticking.

It's commonly believed that an offender like this has a *compulsion* to commit these types of crimes, and that he literally can't stop himself unless incarceration, illness, or death prevents him from offending. The beliefs on that are changing, however, as more and more criminals of this type are discovered to have taken extended breaks or to even have "retired" completely. He occasionally displayed restraint and risk-aversion during the main years in which he offended, so it's not unreasonable to think that he could've quit while he was ahead. The October 1982 call implies that he wasn't in prison at that time, at least.

It's possible that something as simple as his failure to control Greg Sanchez and Cheri Domingo could've rattled him enough to make him stop for an extended period of time. Advancing age and an apparent lack of complete control over Janelle Cruz could've convinced him to stop entirely.

Indeed, it appeared that this attack didn't go as smoothly for him as some of the others, given the wounds on both sides of Janelle's head. Perhaps because he was "out of practice," perhaps because he hadn't intended to revert back to killing again that night, or perhaps because he had mentally or physically deteriorated, it wasn't as controlled as a few of his other attacks had been. Maybe he was discovered by the victim before he was "ready" to attack her. Of course, not all of his murders were controlled. In fact, most of his Southern California attempts were somewhat disastrous. The failed attempt on October 1st, 1979, the Offerman/Manning murders, and the Domingo/Sanchez murders all went horribly wrong (from his perspective). But those were all Goleta cases. Something about Goleta never "worked right" for him.

The bludgeoning of this victim's face is extremely significant from a profiling and psychological standpoint. Hitting the front of the face as opposed to the back of the head is said to require more rage and hatred, and it can imply a personal connection of some sort to the victim. Whether any of that is true with this particular killer is hard to say, because he's probably not wired quite like the typical criminal population, but *something* was different here. Either he was too weak to keep her down, or his rage had grown even from what we'd witnessed in the 1970s and early 1980s. Whether it was even intentional or not is a logical question to ask. He could've struck her in the back of the head like the other victims, but the blow was too weak to be fatal and a struggle ensued. Maybe he surprised her somewhere in the house and hit her in the back of the head before even initiating his attack. Regardless of the circumstances or the reasoning, it showed that something about the Cruz attack was different from the others. Any variance in the M.O. of an attacker as regimented as the EAR/GSK deserves to be looked at.

To expand on the point a bit more, it's worth examining the GSK's choice of method when it came to the murders. He didn't choke them or strangle them, and he didn't stab them to death. He didn't use methods that got "up close and personal," and while he did rape them, he didn't physically torture them... at least not as much as he could have. He didn't burn them or do anything of that nature. Even during the rape cases where he would run his knife along their skin, he didn't inflict any kind of serious wound. When he did, it appeared to be accidental. He clearly got off on the psychological torture and the sexual conquest of his victims rather than the physical torment. One could argue that he tied them up sadistically and that's quite true, but it also served a purpose by keeping them from getting away or fighting back. When he killed, he used a gun (not his first choice, clearly) or blundgeoning. While the bludgeoning was brutal, it seems it was chosen more for "efficiency" (or maybe pleasure) rather than torture. There were other ways to kill, some some offenders found those to be more "gratifying." This killer did not. There's something to be learned about him from that.

Before this case was connected to the Golden State Killer series, the investigators had quite a few promising leads. If they'd known what we know now, their work would've been a lot easier. Many members of Janelle's peer group were examined thoroughly, and most of them would've been too young to have committed the other murders in this series (much less the rapes in Sacramento), so a lot of time could've been saved if there had been a way to tie the murders together.

The suspect pool was small, so even after the connection was made, the friend that was with Janelle the night she was killed was eliminated through DNA as a formality (despite his age).

The investigation took many different directions. One young man falsely confessed to the murder, which derailed the investigation quite a bit. He spent several months incarcerated before the facts and evidence led investigators to release him.

Janelle's life was combed over for possible suspects. Her job as a cashier at Bullwinkle's Pizza, her previous job at a deli near the house, and her recent participation with Job Corps in Clearfield, Utah were looked at as places where she might've caught the eye of a killer. A few of those leads are still open, and with the DNA connection to the other Golden State Killer cases, several other possible leads have opened up related to education, the medical field, and the real estate world.

The common EAR/GSK connections are worth examining here. Janelle had enrolled at Orange Coast College with her eye on someday becoming a lawyer. Many of the Northern California victims were students when they were attacked, and Keith Harrington was also a student when he was killed. While the tie to the legal field comes up time and time again in the EAR/GSK case, Janelle's connection to it is fairly tenuous, since she had just started school and hadn't taken any law classes yet. But there had been a few other minor intersections with lawyers and legalities in Janelle's life (particularly the divorce of her parents), so the connection exists. And sometimes we like to look at where some of the common themes intersect. For instance, could the killer have been a law professor or a medical student (thus covering law/medical *and* education)? A salesman for a drug company that moonlighted as a real estate agent, like many people in California did at the time?

Janelle had recently undergone a major dental procedure, and she'd had brief stints in psychiatric care. Both of those offer medical connections. Psychiatry has come up a few times, and a statistically significant number of victims in these cases had direct ties to the medical industry or had recently used medical services. It's possible that doctors, nurses, clerical personnel, or even fellow patients could've zeroed in on her through those channels.

The real estate connection would be the most likely avenue that the killer took to Janelle, assuming that this case wasn't completely random. At the time of the murder, the house Janelle was living in was listed for sale by Century 21. Prospective buyers had visited the residence, perhaps even the killer himself since the case seems to echo Domingo/Sanchez a bit. It's thought that EAR posed as a buyer or took advantage of house listings somehow during his rape series, so this could just be a continuation or evolution of that or even a more brazen approach to it if he was confident that his killings wouldn't be connected. And he probably *was* confident of that. After all, it was 1986, and he'd basically gotten away with his crimes. Adding to this angle is the fact that Janelle's mother dabbled in real estate herself, and the family had lived in various places in Irvine (one of them even *closer* to the Witthuhn house than this one was). And having a real estate agent discover the body in *both* crimes (Domingo/Sanchez and Cruz) is an interesting parallel as well.

One other noteworthy aspect of the real estate angle is the fact that in the MLS listing, there were notes related to the availability of the resdidence which seem to have indicated that the family was out of town. The notation was there to let other agents know that the house was available to be toured. One of the killer's methods was possibly to go out and look at houses that were vacant or available to tour so that he could plan for future attacks. He'd attacked several couples that had just bought a house, and we feel that he could've familiarized himself with the floor plan while it was for sale, then waited to see who moved in, and then attacked them if they met his criteria. This could've been the way that he became aware of 13 Encina (and of Cheri Domingo, for that matter). Finding women staying alone in these houses might've seemed to good to be true. Worthwhile leads in this case include licensed real estate agents in the area (a *very* large number) and any agents/prospective buyers that viewed the house in-person in the weeks before the murder.

It's also worth noting that, as in the Offerman/Manning case, an insurance policy listed with Frederic Sauer Insurance Agency was present in this case. A slim connection, but it turns up in two out of the six murder cases in Southern California.

In later years, Janelle's own sister Michelle was instrumental in tracking down a few persons of interest and helping to facilitate their DNA testing. One of those suspects was a mysterious man that had planned on coming to Janelle's house that night to show her some kittens. When he was finally found, it was determined that he was too young to have committed the other Golden State Killer crimes and he was eliminated.

Indeed, two very big things that have to be kept in mind when looking for leads or connections in this murder: Janelle's age and the location of the murder. The killer, at this point, would *have* to have been roughly ten years older than her or more. If he started the EAR rapes when he was twenty, that would make him thirty in 1986. If he was twenty-five, then he'd be thirty-five. Even a fifteen-year-old offender (extremely unlikely) would be several years older than Janelle at the time of this murder. Not only does that generally exclude him as someone in her peer group, but age makes it unlikely that he spotted Janelle and started an infatuation with her while he was stalking or attacking the Witthuhn residence. Keep in mind, she would've only been thirteen or so at the time. He'd attacked people that young before, but it wasn't his typical victim.

The location of this killing speaks volumes. As mentioned earlier, it was only two miles away from the Witthuhn house. Five years—two miles. It's very similar to how he operated in the EAR days when it came to attacking in one neighborhood, going back to another neighborhood, then returning to the first one. But given the short distance and the very long length of time, there's possibly something significant to uncover, even though he seemed to just be doing what he always did. He wouldn't have had to live in the area to commit these crimes. In fact, having a residence in or having ties to Goleta or Irvine long-term wouldn't have been the wisest move for him to make, seeing as how he'd killed people there and there were extensive homicide investigations going on in very small areas.

An article came out about Janelle's stint in the Job Corps program about six or seven weeks before her murder. While some might feel that she could've been targeted because of this, we're willing to write it off because of the Cruz murder's geographic proximity to

Witthuhn. To us, the Offerman/Manning and Domingo/Sanchez cluster, as well as the Witthuhn and Cruz cluster make it obvious that geography was the biggest influence of who he would target, not whether a victim showed up in the paper or not. It's more likely that he had returned to the area to stalk new prey and had noticed her at the grocery store, park, or some other mundane place in the immediate neighborhood, and then followed her a short distance to her house. If he was picking people from the paper, he would've ended up all over town, not with attacks that were tightly clustered together.

The house at 13 Encina was on a cul-de-sac, like the Domingo house. The expanse of greenery and recreational space behind the home could've offered a dark, secluded area to peep and prepare an attack, and the head of the cul-de-sac had a unique "hedge maze" footpath entrance that would've allowed someone to slip in and out of the street quickly (and make a pursuit by car almost impossible). The entrance led to Culver Drive and the Hicks Canyon Park, which would've offered several places to park and get out of the area quickly. The house itself was the only one-story house on the block, with a small park and tennis court directly behind it.

One of the big puzzles at the crime scene was Janelle's car door. The neighbor had heard it slam, but when the police arrived, the car door was found slightly ajar. The seatbelt was hanging out a bit, and it looked like it had prevented Janelle from closing the door all the way. In the darkness, she might not have noticed. A door can easily still make a loud slamming sound but not close all the way, so it's not *terribly* puzzling, but it's a *little* strange. The killer doing a blitz attack in the driveway, reminiscent of earlier attacks, seems unlikely because of the risk and because a neighbor probably would've heard a scream. Did the killer go through her car after she was killed? If he exited through the front, he may have. There was blood in the kitchen and near the front door. Possible explanations for this could involve a potential struggle between the killer and victim that took them throughout the house, or the killer simply eating in the kitchen and peeking out the front door or leaving through it after the murder.

We've wondered if he even planned on attacking that night at all. He could've regressed to simple intrusions peeping activities due to age or something else, and he could've been engaging in during the "silent" years leading up to the attack. Janelle could've discovered him in her house, and for whatever reason he reverted back. Some of the differences in the crime scene could also be due to the killer's awareness of what he had done in the Witthuhn murder nearby, and him making an effort to give the crime scene some intentional differences so as to not arouse suspicion or allow the crimes to be linked.

It's impossible to know, but one theory that we've held onto for awhile is the theory that the killer saw Janelle and her male friend talking in the bedroom (which would explain the noises they heard around their house), and then he watched them and was hoping to witness them having sex. This seemed to be a common theme in most of the murders, and if he was prowling for excitement that night, he was probably expecting that. Having the "fantasy" ruined could've upset him, or it's possible that when they left the house, he made his way inside thinking that they'd be back and he could lie in wait and watch them from inside (like he probably did with Domingo/Sanchez) and then make his move.

Speculating on any of these points won't do a lot of good because they're fairly trivial. We know that the killer apparently kept quiet for almost five years, committed this final crime, and then aside from some suspicious activity that can't be physically tied to him, seemingly vanished forever. Whether he changed his M.O., got sick or injured, went to prison, got married and had a family, or just got older and realized that he couldn't pull off the crimes anymore, we won't know until he's identified.

By 1986, the crimes of the East Area Rapist were in most people's rearview mirrors. There was an occasional article or musing from someone in the media, and there was occasional chatter that some or all of the murders and rapes were somehow tied together, but for the most part, all was quiet. Perhaps one of those articles scared him into retirement… as careful as he had been, there still had to be a few close calls that we're not even aware of, and there had to be some mistakes that he'd made along the way or at least *wondered* if he'd made along the way. While the compulsion that drives criminals to keep offending must be strong, surely in some of them, the compulsion to stay out of prison or off of death row could be stronger. We're not sure of the reason, but whatever that reason is, it caused him to vanish.

Aside from a couple of phone calls over the years purportedly from the killer, the trail stops here.

Decades have gone by, and Law Enforcement keeps on with the case. The resources of the FBI have recently been added to the hunt, and there's currently so much investigation and activity related to the East Area Rapist / Golden State Killer that it hardly seems like a cold case at all. It's everyone's hope that one of these efforts will finally identify this offender once and for all, and a big part of all of us hopes that he's still alive to face punishment for what he's done.

To that end, Janelle's sister Michelle (or "Shelly") Cruz has courageously joined in alongside other family, survivors, and victims to become an amazing advocate for this case. Surely the killer would've thought twice about his actions if he knew that one of the results of his crimes would be an entire army of selfless people like Michelle stepping up and tirelessly hunting him down at every turn.

Beyond the Murders

October 12th, 1987 10:45 PM

Over a year after the Cruz murder, the town of Oakdale (an area of California about fifteen miles northeast of Modesto) was the scene of a suspicious bludgeoning that probably isn't related, but it often gets included with lists of possible EAR/GSK attacks.

A thirty-one-year-old woman living on Maple Street was asleep in her bed when suddenly she felt herself being pummeled in the head with a blunt object. She began screaming as the intruder hit her again and again. The commotion woke up her ten-year-old daughter. As as the daughter rushed in to see what was happening, the assailant escaped through the back of the house.

The woman lost consciousness for a few moments. The police were dialed at 11:00 PM and despite responding quickly, they were unable to locate the attacker.

The officers surveyed the scene and determined that the point of entry had been the laundry room window. Before entering the residence, the attacker had taken an oak log from a woodpile in the backyard, and this became the weapon used to assault the woman. There was no robbery or sexual component to the attack.

The woman was taken to Memorial Hospital Medical Center in Modesto for treatment. Her skull was fractured in multiple places but fortunately, she survived. She never saw her attacker, and they were unable to determine if the offender was even a man or a woman. Green space and a shallow creek that led to a major road were situated nearby.

This attack, because of the timing, location, and method of assault, does seem quite suspicious on the surface. An investigator for the Golden State Killer series looked at the details of the attack, and determined that it probably wasn't EAR/GSK who had attacked this woman. Detectives in Oakdale eventually determined that it was most likely a crime of passion, and they developed a good suspect. For good measure, that suspect's DNA was compared to the Golden State Killer, and it wasn't a match.

Sometime Between 1990 and 1992
Victim #7 received a phone call, and she recognized the voice on the other end as the voice of the rapist. The caller whispered harshly into the phone, saying "You know who this is" or "Do you know who this is?" The victim was on the line with him for about a minute. There was the sound of children and maybe a woman in the background, which could've potentially come from a television or some other source. There might've been crying in the background. At an interview with police, the victim positively identified the caller as the man who had attacked her in 1976. The family had moved to a few different cities and states over the years, but their phone numbers were usually listed in the places they lived at.

Early 1990s
Burglaries in the style of the East Area Rapist occurred in Irvine. They were never confirmed as being related to the offender, but there were a lot of interesting parallels. As with most things that could be active leads, we're reluctant to print anything else. At least one lead regarding these still looks promising. Incidents occurring in Goleta both before and after the murders have also begun to surface as tantalizing possibilities, so it's very possible that more dots will be connected to the Golden State Killer within the next few years.

October 1996
DNA testing done by the Orange County Sheriff's Forensic Science Division on semen samples from some of the Southern California killings finally determined that the victims in those cases were murdered by the same offender. Evidence from the Smiths, the Harringtons, Manuela Witthuhn, and Janelle Cruz were all matched.

October 2000
The DNA connection was fleshed out and confirmed by investigators, and the information regarding the connection of the multiple crimes was given to the family members of the victims.

March 2001
Paul Holes and the Contra Costa County crime lab had spent a few years searching for any remaining DNA and physical evidence from past East Area Rapist crimes. At the end of the search, the only existing and usable DNA evidence was from three of them: #39 in San Ramon, #42 in Danville, and #46 in Danville. They were tested and compared, and it was determined that not only did all three samples match each other, but they matched the Southern California murders as well. Forensic technology had finally established a linkage between the rape cases and the murder cases. The news was reported on April 4th and April 5th.

April 6th, 2001
Victim #14 received a phone call from a man who whispered "Remember when we played?" She positively identified the man as the voice of the East Area Rapist. This phone call came just two days after the breaking news that the East Area Rapist crimes had been tied by DNA to the murders in Southern California.

This call is believed to be a genuine communication from the EAR/GSK, and it's potential proof that he was still alive in 2001.

<u>Spring 2004</u>

During the first few months of 2004, a massive push to get Proposition 69 wrapped up was being undertaken by Bruce Harrington, the brother of murder victim Keith Harrington. Bruce's primary goal was to use the law of the land to force the California prison system to do a massive DNA sweep to look for his brother's killer. Proposition 69 was successful, but unfortunately, the Golden State Killer was not found.

Michelle Cruz, the sister of murder victim Janelle Cruz, participated in a press conference around this time. Afterward, she received five or six hang-up phone calls a day for a period of two weeks or so. When she answered the phone, the caller wouldn't speak, but the caller wouldn't hang up, either.

<u>May 2011</u>

Trace evidence of a semen stain was found on a bedspread from the Domingo/Sanchez murders. DNA was extracted, tested, and compared with the other Southern California cases. It was a match.

<u>June 2016</u>

After decades of local jurisdictions working the case, the FBI announced their involvement (on the 40th anniversary of the first official EAR crime, no less). Additional resources and new eyes were brought to the case.

The Visalia Ransacker

The following chapter is about persons and events that may or may not be related to the EAR/GSK case.

The town of Visalia is an agricultural community situated off of Route 99 between Fresno and Bakersfield. In the mid-1970s, a portion of it was relentlessly preyed upon by a unique brand of burglar (who later turned vicious killer) known locally as the "Visalia Ransacker."

Starting in May of 1973 and really picking up steam the following year, the "VR" committed a steady stream of odd home intrusions—almost all of them on weekends—where typically only small personal items, coins, jewelry, or redemption stamps were stolen. Several of the burglaries had a sexual undertone.

Toward the end of 1974, the police started special patrols and stakeouts. The results were mixed. The VR remained fairly elusive, despite his penchant for targeting a very small geographical area (a zone more easily measured in blocks than in miles). He was spotted by police and residents several times, and odd behaviors such as "talking to people who weren't there" were consistently observed. The general description of the Ransacker was the same at each sighting: a white male, late twenties or early thirties, average height, stocky or pudgy with a heavier, pronounced lower half (extreme pear shape), short light brown hair (occasionally "oily blonde hair"), light skin that appeared to be completely hairless except for his head, wide limbs and hands, and a very round face that looked somewhat distorted and quite distinctive. When observed or confronted, his behavior was allegedly strange, "bumbling," and very childish.

In the days leading up to the Ransacker's murder of local professor Claude Snelling, he began a string of prowling activities up and down the area of South Whitney. On September 11th, 1975, the Ransacker broke in and attempted to abduct a young woman from her home. Her father, the aforementioned Claude Snelling, came to her aid and was tragically shot to death by the Ransacker. The would-be kidnapper fled the area and escaped.

Amazingly, the ransackings resumed a mere eleven days later. Crank phone calls were added to the VR's repertoire, and his behaviors became a bit more disturbing. Police increased their efforts to catch him. In early December 1975, footprints matching the VR's were found under a young woman's bedroom window—which signaled to officers that there was perhaps going to be another attempted kidnapping. They were ready.

The suspect soon returned to the same street and fell right into the trap. An officer stepped out from the shadows with his weapon drawn and chased after the man they believed to be the Ransacker. The suspect cried out in a high-pitched voice, distracted the officer with one hand, and with the other quickly drew a weapon and fired. The bullet went straight into the officer's flashlight, miraculously wedging itself in and not harming the officer in any serious way. The suspect escaped the police dragnet by doubling back and retreating in the opposite direction of the chase. He added an "attempted homicide" to his rap sheet in the process. The Visalia Ransacker was spotted one month later about two miles to the east, and then he dropped from history.

Or did he? Several researchers and even the occasional investigator have been intrigued by similarities between the modus operandi of the Visalia Ransacker and the East Area Rapist. Despite some important differences in physical characteristics and M.O., the timing between one sexually-motivated burglar stopping and another one starting up a few months later certainly piques interest, even though two hundred miles seperated them. On one hand, several major differences between the two do exist, but on the other hand, some of the overlaps between them create a few tenuous links that are hard to discount entirely when taken as a whole.

Due to a lack of physical evidence (or at least, a lack of *publlic details* regarding physical evidence), it's impossible to know if the two cases are linked together. After spending many, many dizzying hours sorting through source material and everything regarding the behaviors and M.O. of the offenders, it comes down to three simple things for us: the physical description of the assailant, the activities of October 21st, 1975, and the basic fact that EAR committed home-invasion rapes and the VR did not.

The physical descriptions provided by witnesses were very homogenous and they all described a very distinct individual. The East Area Rapist, on the other hand, was physically a chameleon who didn't make much of an impression on anyone and whose features were difficult to capture. It's hard to reconcile the face and body of the VR as described by witnesses with the face and body type attributed to the East Area Rapist. Theories such as the offender losing weight during the Spring of 1976 can make only a tiny dent in it because the physical differences were quite numerous. There's a major gulf to cross with this.

The second issue, and most convincing one for us, hinges on whether or not the October 21st, 1975 attack in Rancho Cordova (described at the beginning of the book) was the East Area Rapist or not. The Visalia Ransacker was *also* active on October 20th and October 21st, 1975... two hundred and fifteen miles to the southeast. Let's step through the timeline of those events, just to be complete:

Visalia | October 20th, 1975 10:00 PM
The Visalia Ransacker ransacked and burglarized a residence on Emerald Street.

Rancho Cordova | October 21st, 1975 4:00 AM to 6:30 AM
An EAR-style home-invasion rape was perpetrated by a suspect that matched the EAR's description.

<u>Visalia | October 21st, 1975 1:30 PM</u>
A prowler was at Royal Oaks Drive at the front door of a residence that was being stalked by the VR.

Technically, there was enough time for him to make the trip between Visalia and Rancho Cordova, but the description of the Rancho Cordova offender does not match the description of the Visalia Ransacker of October 1975 at all. Logic dictates that one of these offenders could be the East Area Rapist, or neither of them could be the East Area Rapist, but they can't both be him. It's far more likely that the October 21st, 1975 attacker was the East Area Rapist due to a nearly exact match in M.O., location, and physical description... which would mean that he couldn't be the VR.

The third issue is that, despite several modus operandi components that the VR shared with the East Area Rapist and various other offenders, the main point to consider is that the East Area Rapist was a home-invasion rapist and the VR was a sexually-motivated burglar and possible kidnapper. Do sexually-motivated burglars become home-invasion rapists? A handful of them do. And a high percentage of home-invasion rapists begin as sexually-motivated burglars. But since we don't have any evidence of the VR committing a home-invasion rape (which is a fairly unique offense), then there's no way of knowing if he ever evolved to that level. Very few home-invasion rapists even exist, and even fewer of them possessed the attack characteristics of the East Area Rapist. Without the VR displaying any of the characteristics that the East Area Rapist did as a home-invasion rapist and home-invasion killer, a convincing argument cannot be made based on a couple dozen small similarities that a significant portion of the criminal population also shares.

But the VR case has been brought forward as a possibly-related case for so long that we understandably get a lot of questions about him. Two of the questions we're asked the most are about the geography of the VR case and the VR's proclivity for stealing grocery-store-issued redemption stamps. Since those questions are asked so frequently, we'll address them here:

Which part of town did the Visalia Ransacker offend in? Was geographic profiling ever done?

The Ransacker generally stuck to the area south of Noble Ave, east of Demaree Street, west of South Court Street, and north of West Whitendale Avenue. This was a relatively small area. Beyond that, geographic profiling shows that the VR's point of origin was likely a small quadrant of town south of West Walnut Avenue, east of South Country Center Drive, North of Whitendale Avenue, and west of Mooney Blvd. A second possible area was south of West Beverly Drive and north of West Tulare Avenue. This was a very, very small area. Despite this narrow field of operation, no one in the area recognized this offender, and extensive canvassing failed to reveal him.

The Visalia Ransacker loved to steal Blue Chip stamps. Did the EAR ever steal stamps like that?

There was no mention of the EAR/GSK ever taking those stamps from any victim that we've come across (same goes for shenanigans with piggy banks—another VR staple). We don't find the stamp issue particularly surprising, though, and we wouldn't hinge too many theories on it. With the EAR, we're talking about the city of Sacramento, not Visalia, and the two cities had different redemption programs. And while in the early 1970s, stamps like Blue Chip and S&H were extremely popular, their popularity waned quite a bit as the decade wore on. 1970 had $126 million in Blue Chip stamp activity, and 1980 had only $19.5 million. In the Northern California areas where EAR attacked, many of the grocery stores leaned toward other types of reward programs. Alpha Beta Markets, which dominated parts of Sacramento, originally used S&H stamps instead of Blue Chip, and then in 1968 they discontinued the use of stamps altogether. Most EAR/GSK victims shopped at grocery stores where stamps weren't in use.

Obviously this point, it's impossible to conclusively link the two criminals together. We'll need quite a bit more evidence before we can tie the VR to the EAR, and it remains an active area of research for some. To help do our part and make a contribution to their endeavors, toward the end of the book there's a list of every known Visalia Ransacker crime. It's technically outside the scope of the book to include this information, but we've become quite invested in the VR case on its own and we're happy to do our part in finding justice for Claude Snelling, the VR's murder victim. Since there's so much overlap in interest between EAR/GSK researchers and VR researchers, we hope that folks will find this extra information useful.

A Final Note

The information contained in this book has been culled and collated from writings and interviews with case detectives (former and present), police reports and documentation, news articles, discussions with victims/survivors, and archived correspondence from various Law Enforcement officials who have worked the case throughout the decades.

Writing a book like this was a team-effort. A special debt of gratitude goes to the community surrounding this case—particularly the dozens of people that we've come to know as friends. These folks spent countless hours helping us poke holes in the evidence until nothing was left but the cold, hard facts. Additionally, many researchers and investigators have been more than generous in sharing information, materials, and experience with us. This book is the sum total of their generosity.

We've done everything in our power to ensure that this information is accurate, but in a forty-year-old case, it wasn't always easy or even possible to find out what's completely accurate and what isn't. In instances where the information was contradictory, we spent as much time as possible on figuring out what actually happened. There will be, of course, numerous situations where someone will be able to point to something in this book and discover that perhaps a victim received *two* hang-up phone calls instead of the *three* that this book says, or that something happened at 3:00 AM instead of 2:00 AM, or something to that effect. Again, we've done our level best to sort through all of it. In a cold case like this, the news articles, the memories of people involved, and the reports are often quite contradictory on small but important details. Thankfully there were several folks who were able to help guide us, and we were able to resolve many of the contradictions. There were several details and events that we simply had to leave out of the book, though, because it was impossible to figure out exactly *what* had happened, where, and when. Sometimes a report said one thing, detectives said another, and correspondence with a victim said yet another. We don't want to risk adding more misinformation to a case that's already rife with it, so again, those things were left out. In instances where a detail was absolutely essential but we weren't able to reconcile the available information, we simply noted the contradiction for the reader.

We also left out a lot of information that hadn't been released for whatever reason and seemed like an active lead. Our goal is to *assist* the investigation, not impede it.

Some people, *most* people perhaps, might have found this book a little dry. We offered very little in the way of grand theories or colorful prose. We didn't attempt to describe what the assailant was thinking or how a victim felt. Most people will be using this book more for reference, not necessarily reading it from cover to cover, so we added information and analysis at the end of every major event to help point out certain things and to help provide context for each event's place in the overall narrative of the case. We threw in a few pointed questions that might be considered theories, but these are only starting points and not cohesive explanations for anything that happened.

No personally identifying information about victims is contained in this book that hasn't already been revealed in other places or hasn't been signed off on by the person involved. Keeping up a privacy standard was a primary goal in compiling this. The victims are, first and foremost, the reason why so many people are working so hard to identify this assailant. Street names, occupations, and sometimes ages are included for the rape victims, but very little more. For the murder victims, we got just a little bit more biographical, but not much.

It pained us, but we had to cut so much interesting material out of this book—mostly because it didn't fit the scope of what we had set out to do. It would be prohibitively expensive for the reader to purchase the type of volume we originally had in mind! If you'd like to keep up with the latest or view more materials related to the case, you can find more at the following venues:

Twitter: https://twitter.com/coldcasewriter
Our Website: https://www.coldcase-earons.com
Discussion: http://earonsgsk.proboards.com/

We hope that you found the information presented here to be useful. The goal was to provide info that can help lead to the identification of the criminal known as the East Area Rapist / Golden State Killer. If for any reason you feel that you have a tip that can help move this case forward, we urge you to use the following information to contact the FBI:

Phone: 1-800-CALL-FBI (1-800-225-5324)
Web: https://tips.fbi.gov/

Mail:
FBI Sacramento Field Office
2001 Freedom Way
Roseville, CA 95678

More Information:
https://www.fbi.gov/wanted/seeking-info/unknown-suspect-21

For questions or comments related to this book, you can reach us at:

E-mail: coldcase.earons@gmail.com

Acknowledgments

This small page near the end of the book doesn't even begin to do justice to the impact and contributions made by so many incredible, selfless, and supportive people. We can't thank you enough for your tireless and unwavering dedication to this case and for your support of our efforts to help bring some clarity and organization to it.

Special thanks goes to Karim Anani, Bill Harticon, Jeff, Mike Morford, Andrew Nelms, Renee, Mason Tierney, and Melissa Trussell. You've all contributed so much, both directly and indirectly, to every word written in this book. The resources we've created together, the discussions we've shared, and the countless hours you've put into it have changed the way that many of us approach a cold case in the twenty-first century. You've truly made a difference.

Thanks also goes to "Archangel76," Tom Box, Jane Carson-Sandler, Larry Crompton, Michelle Cruz, Debra Domingo, Doug French, Mark Gardner, "Guessting," Paul Holes, Erika Hutchcraft, Mike Johns, Ken ("Drifter"), Bryan Mack, Tom Macris, Marjorie, John McGrath, "Neuro," Nick, Anne Penn, Larry Pool, "PortofLeith," Sandia, Jerry Schutte, "Sfbay," Richard Shelby, Sammy T, Captain N. Wade Thomas, Tim, Wesley Vegas, DBW, Margaret Wardlow, Mitchell Wells, and Drew Witthuhn. The contributions you've made (and continue to make), the dedication you show, and in many cases the friendships we've forged have been the foundation of this book and of this case. Thank you for everything.

–Kat Winters and Keith Komos

Supplemental Material

DATES / CITIES / STREETS

Attack	Date	City	Street
1	06/18/76	Rancho Cordova	Paseo Dr
2	07/17/76	Carmichael	Marlborough Wy
3	08/29/76	Rancho Cordova	Malaga Wy
4	09/04/76	Carmichael	Crestview Dr
5	10/05/76	Citrus Heights	Woodpark Wy
6	10/09/76	Rancho Cordova	El Segundo Dr
7	10/18/76	Carmichael	Kipling Dr
8	10/18/76	Rancho Cordova	Los Palos Dr
9	11/10/76	Citrus Heights	Greenleaf Dr
10	12/18/76	Carmichael	Ladera Wy
11	01/18/77	Sacramento	Glenville Cir
12	01/24/77	Citrus Heights	Primrose Dr
13	02/07/77	Carmichael	Heathcliff Dr
NA	02/16/77	Sacramento	Ripon Ct
14	03/08/77	Sacramento	Thornwood Dr
15	03/18/77	Rancho Cordova	Benny Wy
16	04/02/77	Orangevale	Richdale Wy
17	04/15/77	Carmichael	Cherrelyn Wy
18	05/03/77	Sacramento	La Riviera Dr
19	05/05/77	Orangevale	Winterbrook Wy
20	05/14/77	Citrus Heights	Merlindale Dr
21	05/17/77	Carmichael	Sandbar Cir
22	05/28/77	South Sacramento	4th Parkway
23	09/06/77	Stockton	North Portage Cir
24	10/01/77	Rancho Cordova	Tuolumne Dr
25	10/21/77	Foothill Farms	Golden Run Ave
26	10/29/77	Sacramento	Woodson Ave
27	11/10/77	Sacramento	La Riviera Dr
28	12/02/77	Foothill Farms	Revelstok Dr
29	01/28/78	Sacramento	College View Wy

NA	02/02/78	Rancho Cordova	La Alegria Dr
30	03/18/78	Stockton	Meadow Ave
31	04/14/78	South Sacramento	Casilada Wy
32	06/05/78	Modesto	Fuschia Ln
33	06/07/78	Davis	Wake Forest Dr
34	06/23/78	Modesto	Grandprix Dr
35	06/24/78	Davis	Rivendell Ln
36	07/06/78	Davis	Amador Ave
37	10/07/78	Concord	Belann Ct
38	10/13/78	Concord	Ryan Rd
39	10/28/78	San Ramon	Montclair Pl
40	11/04/78	San Jose	Havenwood Dr
41	12/02/78	San Jose	Kesey Ln
42	12/09/78	Danville	Liberta Ct
NA	12/18/78	San Ramon	Thunderbird Pl
43	03/20/79	Rancho Cordova	Filmore Ln
44	04/05/79	Fremont	Honda Wy
45	06/02/79	Walnut Creek	El Divisadero Ave
46	06/11/79	Danville	Allegheny Dr
47	06/25/79	Walnut Creek	San Pedro Ct
48	07/05/79	Danville	Sycamore Hill Ct
GSK1	10/01/79	Goleta	Queen Ann Ln
GSK2	12/30/79	Goleta	Avenida Pequena
GSK3	03/13/80	Ventura	Highpoint Dr
GSK4	08/18/80	Dana Point	Cockleshell Dr
GSK5	02/05/81	Irvine	Columbus
GSK6	07/27/81	Goleta	Toltec Wy
GSK7	05/04/86	Irvine	Encina

EAR/GSK COMMUNICATIONS

March 18th, 1977, 4:15 PM
A call came in to the Sheriff's office.

"I'm the East Side Rapist," the male voice said, and then he laughed and hung up.

March 18th, 1977, 4:30 PM
Another call came in to the Sheriff's office.

"I'm the East Side Rapist," the same male voice said. Again, he laughed and hung up.

March 18th, 1977, 5:00 PM
Once more, the phone rang at the Sacramento County Sheriff's office.

"I'm the East Side Rapist and I have my next victim already stalked and you guys can't catch me." He laughed and hung up. Attack #15 happened just a few hours later.

May 28th, 1977 1:50 PM
Some odd writing was noticed on the stall in one of the restrooms at a gas station on the corner of Florin Rd and Riverside Blvd, located about six and a half miles west of the site of Attack #22. It was found several hours after the attack.

This is a fucked part of town
Next month I start this area
EAR

November 7th, 1977

A message was found scrawled on a wall at California State University. The message was scrawled in the men's restroom on the main floor of the library, in the middle stall on the right-hand side. It said:

The East Side Rapist was here
Will rape my first black girl tonight
Dumb cops will never find me.

Attack #27 happened a few days later, less than two miles away.

Late 1977

The Sacramento Sheriff's Department received a strange phone call, purportedly from the offender himself.

Caller: "You're never gonna catch me, you dumb fuckers. [unintelligible] East Area Rapist. I'm gonna fuck again tonight. Be careful.

December 2nd, 1977, 8:00 PM

A call was received at the police station. The voice on the other end said something to the effect of "I shall commit another rape" or "I'll commit another rape tonight." The voice sounded like a man in his twenties and it was very clear, with no accent and no background noise on the call. The words sounded like they were being read or recited. Attack #28 occurred a few hours later.

December 9th, 1977 5:40 PM

The female victim from Attack #21 received a phone call that she felt was from her attacker.

Caller: "Merry Christmas. It's me again."

December 10th, 1977 9:50 PM

The Sheriff's Department received a phone call.

"I am going to hit tonight. Watt Avenue."

<u>December 10th, 1977 9:52 PM</u>
A second call came in.
   "I am going to hit tonight. Watt Avenue."

<u>December 12th, 1977</u>
Envelopes containing a poem called "Excitement's Crave" were received at the offices of the Sacramento mayor, the editor of the Sacramento Bee, and the KVIE Channel 6 PBS television station.

All those mortals surviving birth
Upon facing maturity,
Take inventory of their worth
To prevailing society.

Choosing values becomes a task;
Oneself must seek satisfaction.
The selected route will unmask
Character when plans take action

Accepting some work to perform
At fixed pay, but promise for more,
Is a recognized social norm,
As is decorum, seeking lore.

Achieving while others lifting
Should be cause for deserving fame.
Leisure tempts excitement seeking,
What's right and expected seems tame.

"Jessie James" has been seen by all,
And "Son of Sam" has an author.
Others now feel temptations call.
Sacramento should make an offer.

To make a movie of my life
That will pay for my planned exile.
Just now I'd like to add the wife
Of a Mafia lord to my file.

Your East Area Rapist
And deserving pest
See you in the press or on T.V.

December 1977
Victim #8 received a phone call from someone who whispered threats.

December 1977
Victim #23 also received a phone call from someone whispering threats.

January 2nd, 1978
Victim #1 had been receiving odd phone calls since around Christmas. The police gave her a tape recorder in hopes that she'd be able to catch the elusive caller's voice. On the evening of January 2nd, the phone rang several times. One of them was a wrong number asking "Is Ray there?" Some investigators think that the caller was probably the rapist.

Later on in the evening, the phone rang at Victim #1's house once more. A voice that she recognized as the East Area Rapist was on the other end.

Caller: "Gonna kill you... Gonna killll you... Gonna killlll you Bitch... Bitch... Bitch... Fuckin' whore..."

There was an extended period of deep, harsh breathing before the threats began.

January 6th, 1978 8:30 PM

A volunteer working at the Contact Counseling Service received a strange call from a man. It may or may not be related to the case.

Caller: "Can you help me?"

Volunteer: "What's the problem?"

Caller: "I have a problem. I need help because I don't want to do this anymore."

Volunteer: "Do what?"

Caller: "Well, I guess I can tell you guys. You're not tracing this call are you?" The voice became violent and angry.

Volunteer: "No, we are not tracing any calls."

Caller: "I am the East Side Rapist and I feel the urge coming on to do this again. I don't want to do it, but then I do. Is there anyone there that can help me? I don't want to hurt these women or their husbands anymore." The voice was pleading, but then became violent again. "Are you tracing this call?"

Volunteer: "We are not tracing this call. Do you want a counselor?"

Caller: "No. I have been to counseling all my life. I was in Stockton State Hospital. I shouldn't tell you that. I guess I can trust you guys." Normal voice, then angry again. "Are you tracing this call?"

Volunteer: "No, we are not tracing the call."

Caller: (very angry) "I believe you *are* tracing this call."

The caller hung up. Law Enforcement officers found it difficult to find a viable suspect from Stockton State Hospital records, especially since the caller had given them very little information to work with.

January 20th, 1978 5:20 AM

The mother of Victim #27 was awakened by a phone call. "Hello?" she asked after picking up the phone.

Caller: "I have not struck in awhile. You will be my next victim. I'm going to fuck you in the butt. See you soon."

January 20th, 1978 5:30 AM
The female victim in Attack #18 had just gotten out of bed for work.

    The phone rang. At the other end of the line was a man:

    Caller: "I have not struck in awhile. You will be my next victim. I'm going to fuck you in the butt. See you soon."

December 9th, 1978
The following are transcriptions of the two essays that were found at Attack #42. Misspellings were left intact. In some areas the words aren't completely legible, so rather than guess, we simply indicated those areas.

"Mad is the Word"

Mad is the word, the word that reminds me of 6th grade. I hated that year

[several lines left blank]

I wish I had know what was going to be going on during my 6th grade year, the last and worst year of elementary school.

Mad is the word that [illegible] in my head about [the word "it" crossed out] my [illegible] year as a 6th grader. My madness was one that was [illegible] by disapointments that hurt me very much. Dissapointments from my teacher, such as feild trips that were planed, then canceled.

My 6th grade teacher gave me a lot of dissapointments [the word "and" crossed out] which made me very mad and made me built a state of hated in my heart, no one ever let me down that hard before and I never hated anyone as much as I did him. Disappointment` wasn't the only reason that made me mad in my 6th grade class, another was getting in trouble at school especially talking that's what really bugged me was writing sentences, those awful sentence that my teacher made me write, hours and hours I'd sit and write 50 - 100 - 150 sentence day and night I write those dreadful [short illegible word crossed out] paragraphs which embarrased me and more important it made me ashamed of myself which in turn; deep down in side made me realize that writing sentence wasn't fair it wasn't *fair to make me suffer like that, it just wasn't fair to make me sit and wright until my bones ached, until my hand felt every horrid pain it ever had and as I wrote, I got mader and mader until I cried,*

I cried because I was ashamed
I cried because I was [illegible]
I cried because I was mad, and
I cried for myself, kid who kept me having to write those [illegible] sentences. My angryness from sixth grade will [illegible] my memory for life and I will be ashamed for my sixth grade year forever

"General Custer"
Gen George Armstrong Custer. A man well amired, but a man hated very much by many who served him. He became a general at a very young age of 23, [illegible] all took place during the civil war, Custer after the war was dropped to his perminent rank of a captain, as he fought more, he made more enimies, especially fighting against the unions in the south west. IN 1876 the government planned to Round up the SUIX AND Cheynne and put the on reservations. Custer regiment joined the expedition, commanded by general Alfred H. Terry. As Terrys scouts reported in from [illegible] through the Mountain territory, Terry ordered Custer to find [crossed out heavily]. Then as Custer searched for the villages, custer and his men found a vally that ran all[illegible] the little big horn river. Custer, expecting only around 1000, was not expecting around 5000 indians THAT would fight back. It was the [illegible] gathering of [illegible] tribes in [illegible]. This battle would be one of the deadliest and most strangest battles between the Indians and the white man. 225 UNION men, including Custer, died that day by courageous by hostile Indians that would do anything to save there homes and there families

January 15th, 1979
Victim #42 received a call that she identified as the EAR.
    Caller: "Do you want fuck?"

557

October 21st, 1982

Victim #24 received a call from a voice that she identified as the EAR's.

Caller: "Hi, it's me again. Remember me? I'm going to come over and fuck you again. You're going to suck my cock again."

Sometime between 1990 and 1992

Victim #7 received a phone call, and she recognized the voice on the other end as the voice of the rapist. The caller whispered harshly into the phone, saying "You know who this is" or "Do you know who this is?" The victim was on the line with him for about a minute. There was the sound of children and maybe a woman in the background, which could've potentially come from a television or some other source.

April 6th, 2001

Victim #14 received a phone call from a man who whispered "Remember when we played?" She positively identified the man as the voice of the East Area Rapist. This phone call came just two days after the breaking news that the East Area Rapist crimes had been tied by DNA to the murders in Southern California.

VISALIA RANSACKER INCIDENTS

This is a comprehensive list of incidents related to the Visalia Ransacker, a criminal who may or may not be related to the East Area Rapist. Since this is an active area of research for many, we've done our best to sift through every inch of official reports and documentation available to us to compile this list. While we've become very adept at reconciling differences and issues in the EAR/GSK case, reconciling issues in the VR case documentation was quite a bit trickier, so this wasn't an easy task. When something was unclear or it didn't sit right, we erred on the side of caution and completely left it out. Anecdotes, contradictory information, and second-hand statements were also left out. Some of the prowling incidents couldn't be confirmed as being the Ransacker, so most of the information about them was also left out. The waters are muddy enough without us adding to them. Most of these incidents were probably the work of the same man, but it's possible that some of them might not be.

It's not our intention to dive as deeply into this as we did the EAR/GSK. This section is more of an inventory of incidents to use as a springboard for your own research. Full addresses are not included.

Nearly all of the burglaries were committed while the owners were away or while they were out for the night.

Most of the VR incidents were very similar... almost identical, in fact. He usually left several doors and windows open so that he had multiple escape options if he was interrupted, and he often took women's panties, bras, and nightgowns and put them on the bed, on the floor, wadded them up, folded them up, or even tore them apart. He frequently stole or broke piggy banks and stole Blue Chip stamps where they were available.

VR #1
May 1973 | S Demaree
A prowler was spotted. It was later learned that this prowler matched the general description of the VR.

VR #2

June 1973 | S Demaree

The same house that had been prowled was broken into and extensively ransacked.

VR #3

September 1973 | W Feemster

A prowler was spotted.

VR #4

September 3rd, 1973 | W Kaweah

A prowler matching the VR's description was spotted.

VR #5

September 10th, 1973 | W Kaweah

A prowler was seen near a residence.

VR #6

January 1974 | W Feemster

A prowler was seen on West Feemster.

VR #7

January 1974 | W Feemster

A prowler was seen on the same night, spotted near the other house on West Feemster that had seen him.

VR #8

March 1974 | W Walnut

A house was ransacked. A piggybank was emptied.

VR #9

April 1974 | S Whitney

A house on Whitney was ransacked. Several items were stolen.

VR #10
April 1974 | S Whitney
Another house on Whitney was ransacked on the same night.

VR #11
April 6th, 1974 | Linda Vista
A residence was ransacked and clothing was dumped onto the floor.
Several items were stolen (including cash from a piggybank).

VR #12
April 6th, 1974 | S Whitney
Another residence was ransacked. Several items were stolen.

VR #13
May 4th, 1974 | S Dollner
A house was broken into. Cash was stolen.

VR #14
May 5th, 1974 | W Feemster
A house was broken into. Money and coins from a piggy bank were
stolen. Jewelry was gone through, clothing was dumped from
drawers, and the screen was left on a bed.

VR #15
May 11th, 1974 | S Whitney
A burglary occurred on Whitney. Money was taken. Women's
clothing was scattered about the house and the screen was left near
the bed.

VR #16
May 11th, 1974 | W Tulare
A house on W Tulare was ransacked. The burglar put some dishes on
the doorknob as a sort of alarm system. Money, a piggy bank, and a
pistol were stolen. The screen was left near the bed.

VR #17

May 17th, 1974 | Emerald

A house was broken into. Cash was stolen. Teenage girls lived at the residence, and they were cheerleaders for the local high school. One of their rings was stolen. Women's clothing was scattered throughout the house, and the screen was left on the bed.

VR #18

May 17th, 1974 | Dartmouth

A house was broken into. A piggy bank was rummaged through and money was stolen. Blue Chip stamps were taken.

VR #19

May 18th, 1974 | W Feemster

A house was ransacked. A piggy bank and cologne were messed with, possibly stolen. An item from the kitchen or yard was used as a rudimentary alarm system at the door. One of the teenage residents belonged to the local high school band.

VR #20

May 18th, 1974 | W Feemster

A house was broken into. Cash was stolen.

VR #21

May 18th, 1974 | Cambridge

A house was lightly ransacked, but nothing was stolen.

VR #22

May 18th, 1974 | W Howard

A house was broken into, but nothing was stolen.

VR #23

May 25th, 1974 | W Cambridge

A house was entered. Cash was stolen, and the piggy bank was disturbed.

VR #24
May 25th, 1974 | Sue Lane
Another house was entered and cash was stolen. Women's clothing was removed from drawers and strewn about. A sliding glass door was pried (seemingly from the inside of the residence).

VR #25
May 25th, 1974 | S Redwood
A house was ransacked. Earrings were stolen, along with money and a piggy bank. The screen was left on the bed.

VR #26
May 26th, 1974 | S Sowell
A house was entered, but nothing was stolen.

VR #27
May 26th, 1974 | W Howard
A house was broken into and cash was stolen.

VR #28
May 26th, 1974 | W Cambridge
A house was forcibly entered. The burglar had found a Playboy and had seemingly used lotion to masturbate. He left fingerprints and palm prints. Money was stolen at this attack.

VR #29
June 23rd, 1974 | S Conyer
A house was entered. Nothing was stolen, but women's underwear was removed from drawers and set on the floor.

VR #30
September 14th, 1974 | Princeton
A house was ransacked. One earring out of a pair was stolen, and women's underwear was taken from drawers and set on the ground.

VR #31
October 16th, 1974 | Verde Vista
A prowler was spotted in a carport.

VR #32
October 19th, 1974 | S Grant
A house was burglarized. A revolver and ammo were stolen, along with some cash.

VR #33
October 19th, 1974 | W Cambridge
A house was ransacked. A piggy bank was tampered with, another piggy bank was broken, and the money from inside it was left behind.

VR #34
October 19th, 1974 | W Cambridge
A house was broken into. Nothing was stolen.

VR #35
October 19th, 1974 | S Oak Park
A house was broken into. Cash was stolen. A .38 revolver was left at the scene.

VR #36
October 23rd, 1974 | S Giddings
A house was broken into. Two cameras and a revolver were stolen.

VR #37
October 23rd, 1974 | S Oak Park
A house was broken into. Money was taken.

VR #38
November 1st, 1974 | W Cambridge
A house was ransacked. Cash was stolen and women's underwear was thrown onto the ground.

VR #39

November 1st, 1974 | W Vassar

A house was ransacked. Money was taken from a piggy bank. Women's underwear was thrown onto the ground.

VR #40

November 1st, 1974 | W Paradise

A house was ransacked. Money was taken from a piggy bank, and a single earring from a pair was taken.

VR #41

November 1st, 1974 | S Giddings

A house was ransacked.

VR #42

November 1st, 1974 | W Vassar

A residence was forcibly entered and ransacked.

VR #43

November 2nd, 1974 | S Mountain

A house was ransacked. Cash was taken, along with Blue Chip stamps.

VR #44

November 2nd, 1974 | W Laurel

A house was ransacked. Dishes were left on a doorknob as an alert system, money was taken, and a single earring from a pair was taken. Glue was also stolen and had possibly been handled or used at the scene.

VR #45

November 2nd, 1974 | S Whitney

A house was broken into. A piggy bank was opened and the money inside was taken. Blue Chip stamps were taken, along with a pack of new men's t-shirts.

VR #46
November 2nd, 1974 | Campus
A house was ransacked. Tennis shoe impressions were found in the backyard.

VR #47
November 29th, 1974 | W Princeton
A house was ransacked. A piggy bank was opened and the money inside was taken. .22 caliber ammunition was stolen from the scene.

VR #48
November 29th, 1974 | Walnut
A house was ransacked. Some money was taken.

VR #49
November 29th, 1974 | W Tulare
A house was ransacked. A piggy bank was opened and the money inside was taken. A single earring from a set was stolen. Photos of the children in the house were moved and a bra was handled.

VR #50
November 30th, 1974 | W Meadow Lane
A house was broken into. Cash was taken. Dishes were left on the doorknob as a warning system.

VR #51
November 30th, 1974 | W Meadow Ave
A house was ransacked. Cash was taken, and a photo of a young man was torn.

VR #52
November 30th, 1974 | S Encina
A house was ransacked. Money from a piggy bank was taken. An item was used on a doorknob as an alarm system.

VR #53
November 30th, 1974 | W Paradise
A residence was broken into, but nothing was taken. The kitchen was ransacked.

VR #54
November 30th, 1974 | W Paradise
Cash, a single earring from a set, and some rings were taken from a residence.

VR #55
November 30th, 1974 | W Paradise
A house was broken into. Cash was taken.

VR #56
November 30th, 1974 | W Myrtle
A house was broken into. Cash was taken.

VR #57
November 30th, 1974
A house was broken into. Cash, drugs, and alcohol was taken from the scene. This attack has an address conflict, to the street isn't listed.

VR #58
November 30th, 1974 | W Cambridge
A house was broken into. Cash was taken.

VR #59
November 30th, 1974 | S Oak Park
A house was broken into. A significant amount of money was stolen.

VR #60
November 30th, 1974 | W Kaweah
A residence was ransacked. Ammunition (.22 caliber and 20 gauge shotgun) was taken. Women's underwear was strewn about.

VR #61
November 30th, 1974 | W Kaweah
A residence was ransacked. Cash was stolen.

December 13th through December 15th, 1974
On these dates, the local police organized stakeouts at key locations in the VR's target areas.

VR #62
December 14th, 1974 | W Vassar
A residence was ransacked. Coins from a piggy bank were stolen. The screen was left in the bedroom.

VR #63
December 14th, 1974 | University
A residence was burglarized. Money was stolen and women's clothing was strewn about.

VR #64
December 14th, 1974 | W Cambridge
A house was entered, but nothing was taken. The teenage daughter's clothing was taken out of drawers and thrown around the room.

VR #65
December 14th, 1974 | W Cambridge
A house was entered. Money was taken.

VR #66
December 16th, 1974 | W Seeger
A house was burglarized. This ransacking was odd because the location was atypical. Women's clothing was strewn about.

December 21st through December 23rd, 1974
Special patrols and stakeouts were conducted by the police again in an effort to catch the Ransacker.

VR #67
December 21st, 1974 | W Meadow Ave
A house was broken into and ransacked. Blue Chip stamps, coins from a piggy bank, and earrings were stolen. Women's underwear was taken out of drawers and thrown around the room.

VR #68
December 21st, 1974 | W Iris
A house was broken into. Coins from a piggy bank were taken. A window or door was pried from the inside. Photos were handled.

VR #69
December 21st, 1974 | S Fairway
A house was broken into. Blue Chip stamps were taken, women's underwear was thrown around, and photos of the residents were strewn about the house.

VR #70
December 21st, 1974 | W College
A house was broken into. An item was used on the doorknob to alert the Ransacker to an interruption. Cash was taken from the scene.

December 22nd through December 30th, 1974
Local police conduct more stakeouts and set traps to try to catch the Ransacker.

VR #71
December 22nd, 1974 | Laurel
The Ransacker took money, a pack of new men's t-shirts, a ring, and handled pajamas at the scene.

VR #72
December 22nd, 1974 | Terri Lane
At this burglary, the Ransacker took money from a piggy bank but left other cash at the scene.

VR #73
December 22nd, 1974 | S Divisadero
A house was broken into. Rings, cash, and a single earring were stolen. An item was left on the doorknob as an alarm system. Screens were pushed out from the inside (probably so that the offender would have multiple escape options).

VR #74
December 22nd, 1974 | Fairview
A house was ransacked. Money from a piggy bank was taken.

VR #75
December 22nd, 1974 | S Oak Park
A prowler was spotted.

VR #76
December 22nd, 1974 | Beverly Dr
A prowler was spotted in the area.

VR #77
December 22nd, 1974 | S Oak Park
There was another sighting of a prowler on S Oak Park. The prowlers spotted on the night of December 22nd, 1974 all matched in description and in odd behavior.

VR #78
January 25th, 1975 | S Verde Vista
Money and Blue Chip stamps were stolen at a ransacking.

VR #79
January 25th, 1975 | Pecan
A house was broken into. Money was stolen.

VR #80

February 2nd, 1975 | S Whitney

A house was broken into. A purse was rummaged through and possibly stolen. Blue Chip stamps and ammunition (.22 caliber) were taken. The burglar left hand lotion at the scene and had apparently used it.

VR #81

February 2nd, 1975 | S Whitney

A house was broken into. Nothing was taken.

VR #82

February 2nd, 1975 | Gist

A house was broken into. The VR was interrupted by the owner and chased off.

VR #83

February 5th, 1975 | S Whitney

Claude Snelling spotted a prowler at his residence. Snelling chased him away. Shoe prints matching the VR were found under the daughter's bedroom window. (See VR#108 and VR#120).

VR #84

February 16th, 1975 | Meadow Lane

A house was ransacked. Money was taken, and an item was used as a warning system.

VR #85

February 16th, 1975 | S Sowell

A burglary occurred. Money was taken, along with one earring from a set.

VR #86
February 16th, 1975 | W Kaweah

A house was broken into. Cash was taken. The VR handled a framed wedding photo of the daughter's wedding and broke it. (The daughter attended the nearby College of the Sequoias, the same school that Claude Snelling taught at).

VR #87
March 1st, 1975 | W Howard

A house was ransacked. Cash and rings were taken, along with an H&R revolver that was broken and couldn't fire. Women's clothes were strewn about the house.

VR #88
April 1975 | S Redwood

A prowler was spotted.

VR #89
May 24th, 1975 | S Mountain

A house was broken into. A .38 revolver was stolen.

VR #90
May 24th, 1975 | W Kaweah

A house was broken into. Cash was taken, and an item was placed on a doorknob to alert the VR to anyone entering the house. Women's underwear was strewn about the residence.

VR #91
May 24th, 1975 | S Mountain

A house was ransacked. Cash was taken and women's underwear was strewn about the house.

VR #92
May 24th, 1975 | S Redwood
A house was ransacked. Blue Chip stamps were taken. Women's underwear was taken from drawers and thrown into the floor.

VR #93
May 31st, 1975 | S Sowell
A house was ransacked, especially the kitchen. A piggy bank was broken and the coins inside were taken. Over a dozen rings were stolen. Curiously, the Ransacker lined up some clothes in the kitchen and then poured orange juice on them.

VR #94
June 1st, 1975 | Harvard
A burglary occurred.

VR #95
June, 1975 | Verde Vista
A prowler was spotted.

VR #96
July 24th, 1975 | W Kaweah
A house was ransacked extensively.

VR #97
July 25th, 1975 | Campus
A house was ransacked. Cash, a credit card, and Blue Chip stamps were taken.

VR #98
July 25th, 1975 | Fairview
A house was ransacked. Shotgun ammunition (20 gauge), a ring, cash, and part of a coin collection was stolen.

VR #99

July 25th, 1975 | S Whitney

A house was pried at, but the would-be burglar was unsuccessful.

VR #100

August 1st, 1975 | W Campus

A house was ransacked. Blue Chip stamps and cash were taken. Piggy banks in the house were dumped out. A single earring was taken. The burglar took lingerie out of the drawers and lined several pieces out in the hallway. The pieces seemed to be staged carefully. Women's underwear was removed from drawers and placed in other locations around the house.

VR #101

August 23rd, 1975 | W Howard

A house was ransacked. Lingerie was taken out of drawers and laid out on the kitchen floor. A golden locket with a photo of a grandchild was taken, along with a photo of the couple's daughter. Cash and Blue Chip stamps were taken. A pin from the local church was destroyed and left on the fireplace in the spot where the locket had been taken. A jar of cherries was taken from the refrigerator and left on a neighbor's lawn.

VR #102

August 23rd, 1975 | W Howard

A house was broken into. Coins from a piggy bank were taken and women's underwear was dumped out of drawers.

VR #103

August 23rd, 1975 | W Feemster

A house was ransacked. A ring, Blue Chip stamps, and some cash was taken. Some of the cash was left behind in plain sight. Ammunition (.22 caliber) was handled but left on the bed.

VR #104

August 24th, 1975 | Princeton

A house was broken into. Coins from a piggy bank were taken.

VR #105

August 24th, 1975 | W Cambridge

A house was ransacked. Coins from a piggy bank were taken.

VR #106

August 29th, 1975 | W Dartmouth

A house was ransacked. A single earring from a set was taken and some rings were taken. Some cash was taken as well. Women's underwear was taken from drawers and set on the floor.

VR #107

August 30th, 1975 | Redwood

A house was ransacked. A photo was removed from a frame or an album but it was left behind. A flashlight was stolen.

VR #108

August 31st, 1975 | Royal Oaks

A house was ransacked. A necklace and a silver dollar were taken. Men's clothing was removed from drawers and lined up in the hallway. The revolver that would be used in less than two weeks to kill Claude Snelling was taken from this scene, along with some ammunition (three hundred .38 caliber bullets, twenty-four 12 gauge bullets). (See VR#83 and VR#120).

VR #109

September 1975 | W Myrtle

A prowler was spotted. The prowler was talking to himself and to an imaginary partner.

VR #110

September 6th, 1975 | W Tulare

A girl's Schwinn bicycle (yellow in color) was stolen. (See VR#121).

VR #111

September 6th, 1975 | S Whitney

A prowler was spotted.

VR #112

September 9th, 1975 | S Whitney

A prowler was spotted. He was seen very clearly, and he matched the description of other sightings of the Visalia Ransacker.

VR #113

September 9th, 1975 | S Redwood

A prowler was spotted.

VR #114

September 9th, 1975 | S Whitney

A house was ransacked.

VR #115

September 10th, 1975 | Cornell

A prowler was spotted.

VR #116

September 10th, 1975 | S Whitney

A prowler was spotted in a garage.

VR #117

September 10th, 1975 | S Whitney

A prowler was spotted in another garage.

VR #118

September 11th, 1975 | Campus

A prowler was spotted.

VR #119

September 11th, 1975 | S Locust

A similar prowler was spotted.

VR #120

September 11th, 1975 2:20 AM | S Whitney

Claude Snelling was murdered during the attempted abduction of his daughter. The daughter had gone to bed around 10:30 PM, and sometime during the night the VR removed the screen to her bedroom window, opened a window and a back door, and made his way inside. Despite the young woman's parents and brothers being in the house, he proceeded to grab her from her bedroom and lead her outside. He didn't blindfold or gag her, so when she resisted him, it alerted her father. Claude.

Claude confronted the man, who immediately threw the daughter to the ground and rapidly shot Claude twice. The killer then trained his gun on the daughter, but lowered it and then kicked her several times. He made a quick escape.

The killer had a black ski mask with white stripes and he spoke in a "growl," which seemed disguised. He appeared to have a medium or slightly heavy build.

In the week and a half following the homicide, a flashlight stolen from VR#107 was found nearby, a screwdriver was found wrapped in a clear plastic raincoat, a bottle of liquid (probably alcohol) was found nearby, and the bike stolen from VR#110 was found nearby. (See VR#83 and VR#108 as well).

VR #121

September 11th, 1975 | S Redwood

A prowler was spotted. The yellow Schwinn bike that had been stolen from VR#110 was found on the lawn.

VR #122
September 12th, 1975 | Gist
A prowler was spotted. The prowler damaged property before fleeing the scene.

September 11th, 1975 | S Whitney
The screen from Snelling's window was found on top of a camper trailer.

September 19th, 1975
The revolver stolen from VR#89 was found in a ditch.

September 20th, 1975 | S Redwood
The flashlight taken from VR #107 was found in a yard.

VR #123
September 22nd, 1975 | Verde Vista
A prowler was spotted several times throughout the night.

VR #124
September 22nd, 1975 | Royal Oaks
A house was burglarized. One or both of the daughters who lived at the residence went to the local high school. One of the daughter's earrings was taken from the scene. Some of the daughter's bras were disassembled, and a pair of her bikini panties were manhandled by the prowler, wadded up, and left on the daughter's bed. Two photos of the daughter were taken, and some of her makeup was stolen as well. The daughter was fifteen years old and had won a local beauty contest.

VR #125
October 3rd, 1975 | S Redwood
A prowler was spotted a few times in the area.

VR #126

October 4th, 1975 | Verde Vista

A burglary was attempted. The prowler pried at the window but couldn't get in.

VR #127

October 6th, 1975 | Verde Vista

A prowler was spotted multiple times.

October 16th, 1975 | Royal Oaks

A crank call occurred. The caller said "I know you are alone and I am going to come over and fuck you." The call was made to the victims from VR#124. (See VR#130).

VR #128

October 20th, 1975 | S Whitney

A prowler was spotted.

VR #129

October 20th, 1975 | Emerald

A house was ransacked.

VR #130

October 21st, 1975 | Royal Oaks

A prowler was seen the same house as VR#124. This was the same location that had received the crank phone call from October 16th, 1975.

October 21st, 1975 | Royal Oaks

Phone calls were received at the house from VR#124, VR#130, and the previous crank call. The first phone call on this date was a hang-up call. The second call said "How would you like to get fucked?" and then the caller used one of the resident's names.

VR #131
October 23rd, 1975 | Emerald
A prowler was spotted.

VR #132
October 24th, 1975 | W Campus
A ransacking occurred. A single earring from a pair was taken, a cufflink was taken, and money was taken. The man's underwear and the women's nightgowns were taken out of drawers and manhandled. Additional items were stolen as well.

VR #133
October 24th, 1975 | W Campus
The house next door was ransacked. Money was taken. A flashlight was found. Several drawers in the kitchen were all opened to exactly the same distance. Items were arranged carefully and specifically. Additional items were stolen as well. At either this scene or the previous one, an antique police-issue baton was stolen.

VR #134
October 24th, 1975 | S Redwood
A house was ransacked, and a hammer was taken.

VR #135
October 24th, 1975 | County Center
A house was ransacked. Cash and earrings were taken. Lotion was used and moved.

VR #136
October 24th, 1975 | County Center
A residence was burglarized.

VR #137
October 24th, 1975 | County Center
A residence was burglarized.

VR #138
October 29th, 1975 | W Kaweah
A house was ransacked. Some food and money was taken.

VR #139
November 2nd, 1975 | Evergreen
A prowler was spotted in a garage. He was seen very clearly, and he matched previous descriptions of the Visalia Ransacker.

VR #140
November 2nd, 1975 | Country Lane
A residence was burglarized. Cash, a ring, and shotgun ammunition was taken. Some underwear was left on a crib.

VR #141
November 2nd, 1975 | Country Lane
A residence was ransacked. Coins from a piggy bank were taken.

VR #142
November 2nd, 1975 | Evergreen
A prowler was spotted in a garage.

VR #143
November 6th, 1975 | W Seeger
A house was ransacked.

VR #144
November 6th, 1975 | W Tulare
A house was ransacked. Antique dishes and canned food were taken. Pictures of a girl and other children were moved. An item was left on the doorknob to act as an alarm mechanism in case the Ransacker was interrupted.

VR #145
November 6th, 1975 | S Oak Park
A house was ransacked.

VR #146
November 9th, 1975 | W College
A prowler was spotted.

VR #147
November 9th, 1975 | W College
A residence was ransacked.

VR #148
November 20th, 1975 | S Wellsley Ct
A prowler was spotted at a house under construction.

VR #149
November 23rd, 1975 | Royal Oaks
A house was ransacked.

VR #150
Between November 30th and December 3rd, 1975 | W College
Sometime while the homeowners were away for an extended period, the Ransacker entered their home.

VR #151
December 1st, 1975 | Beverly
A house was ransacked.

VR #152
December 1st, 1975 | S Central
A house was ransacked.

VR #153
December 1st, 1975 | W Kaweah
A house was ransacked.

VR #154
December 8th, 1975 | Sue Lane
A house was ransacked.

VR #155
December 9th, 1975 | W Kaweah
Footprints matching the Ransacker were found under a teenage girl's window.

VR #156
December 10th, 1975 | W Laurel
A residence was ransacked.

VR #157
December 10th, 1975 | W Kaweah
Officer Bill McGowen was shot at by the Ransacker during a confrontation.

VR #158
January 18th, 1976 | S Burke
A prowler matching the Ransacker's description was spotted.

FREQUENTLY ASKED QUESTIONS

This book was written to address many of the common questions about the case, but we realize that folks are often in need of a quick, succinct answer and that they won't have the time or patience to go sifting through the entire volume looking for that one elusive piece of information. To that end, we've compiled this FAQ section to provide quick responses to common questions about the EAR/GSK.

Which attacks are connected by DNA evidence?

The EAR/GSK crime spree spanned ten years and roughly sixty attacks. When these attacks occurred, forensic DNA was merely a pipe dream, but luckily, evidence containing usable DNA was preserved at several of the later scenes. When the technology became available, Law Enforcement used it to make a solid forensic link between most of the murders and three Northern California EAR rapes.

These are the crimes connected by DNA:

Attack #39 in San Ramon (10/28/78)
Attack #42 in Danville (12/09/78)
Attack #46 in Danville (6/11/79)
Smith murders in Ventura (3/13/80)
Harrington murders in Dana Point (8/19/80)
Witthuhn murder in Irvine (2/5/81)
Domingo/Sanchez murders in Goleta (7/27/81)
Cruz murder in Irvine (5/4/86)

Why can't more attacks be connected to the offender by DNA?

Rape cases can only be prosecuted for a few years, after which they are subject to the statute of limitations. This legal mechanism prevents the cases from being tried after a significant period of time has passed. Whether this is an ideal situation or not is beyond the scope of this book, but it's the situation we're left with. Because most of the East Area Rapist crimes in the 1970s were rape cases and no homicides had yet been tied to the offender (homicides have no statutory limit and the window for prosecution is indefinite), the rape cases fell victim to the statute of limitations. Once the clock was up for the rape attacks, most of the jurisdictions involved in the East Area Rapist case destroyed their physical evidence. This included blood samples, rape kits, shoelaces, and any bedding, towels, or articles of clothing that contained seminal fluid left by the offender.

It could be argued that an exception should've been made in this case due to its historic nature and the epic, sweeping toll of it. It could be argued that there was perhaps ample evidence that the homicides in Southern California or the Maggiore homicides were enough to keep the physical evidence in play, but the link wasn't made and so there wasn't enough there to ensure its safekeeping.

While we don't have the luxury of connecting most of the East Area Rapist crimes to the murders through DNA, there's such a strong modus operandi among most of the attacks that we can operate with relative certainty that they're all committed by the same offender. Not having this concrete physical tie hasn't appeared to have impacted the official investigation. When he's prosecuted, he'll be prosecuted for the murders.

Was any of the offender's blood or semen found and analyzed?
Apparently a little under half of the East Area Rapist crimes had a semen sample from the offender. It appears that not all of these were examined by a lab. The ones that were ended up showing remarkably similar characteristics.

Semen samples revealed that the offender was a "non-secretor" with a PGM 2-1. The "non-secretor" status meant that the offender's blood type could not be determined from a semen sample—the antibodies for his blood were not secreted in most of his bodily fluids. This is a characteristic shared by about 20% of the population.

Because the blood could not be typed from the semen samples, and since forensic DNA was not yet in use, finding physical evidence to tie the crimes together was difficult. Fingerprints didn't help, and while shoe prints provided some consistency, without the blood type it was difficult to eliminate suspects early on.

Luckily, there were blood samples found at Attacks #10, #13, and #14. Additionally, blood was able to be typed from some saliva left on a spoon at Attack #16. Analysis of #10, #13, and #16 revealed that the offender had Type A blood, most likely A+. Results from #14 were lost, and it's unknown what the results were.

Were any fingerprints ever found at the crime scenes?

Yes, prints were found at many of them. Latent prints were systematically lifted and collected at every crime scene, and then those prints were compared against the prints of anyone who had been in the house. One by one, most latent prints were eliminated. At over a dozen East Area Rapist scenes, there were prints remaining that couldn't be accounted for. Most of the murder scenes also had prints that couldn't be eliminated.

As the decades wore on, efforts were made to clear any remaining prints once and for all. Several of the prints and scenes eventually received total clearances thanks to work undertaken by cold case teams. In one case, a print match was made over twenty years later (thanks to advances in computer technology), and a body was actually exhumed to be tested for DNA. No match, unfortunately.

Even now, there's still a handful of unidentified prints, one of them going all the way back to Attack #7. We don't have a clear sense of what is currently done with the others. DNA is a much more robust identification tool and is the preferred way of identifying the assailant, considering that we're not sure any of the prints are actually his. Also, some of the prints may no longer be in a usable format, given that most of what exists from earlier scenes as far as paperwork goes is a copy of a copy.

<u>Which composite sketches of the offender are the most accurate?</u>
The general sense that we get from Law Enforcement is that there's a very low confidence level in the composite sketches as a whole, though that's certainly no fault of the witnesses and forensic artists who went to herculean lengths to create the best possible images. Unfortunately, we're lacking that one reliable sighting of the offender under ideal conditions, and the witnesses who *did* have experiences close to "ideal" reported that the offender had almost nothing in the way of distinctive, identifying features.

What we've ended up with are over forty images generated of suspicious persons who, while there are a few common features among them, simply depict a generic white male. And by all accounts, that's exactly what the offender looked like.

We made the decision to keep the sketches out of the book for a variety of reasons, but the low confidence level in them is the main one. In some ways, we feel that the composite sketches of the offender have the potential to do more harm than good. They're different enough to where even the FBI can't settle on one (the three that they typically use have features that differ wildly), and we know from running our website and fielding literally hundreds of queries and potential tips that there's a general misunderstanding of the composite drawings. The general public gives too much emphasis to finding someone who matches the "look" of one or more of the drawings. Law Enforcement can handle the issue of releasing composite images the way that they see fit—so for now we intend to avoid print publication of them in an effort to reduce confusion on the matter. If you'd like to see them, you can view them on our website at https://www.coldcase-earons.com, where we provide more information and context and can do the subject a bit more justice.

Why won't the FBI use some of the new technology that's available to process the DNA and give us a true sketch of the offender?

There are two main reasons why such endeavors are approached very cautiously. The first is that there's a very, very limited amount of testable DNA left, and anything that would require original material has to be considered carefully. It's a precious resource at this point, and it would be terrible to waste it on technology that's still in its infancy if, five years from now, something much becomes available. Not all of these new technologies require an actual sample, but some of them do.

The second reason is that the same problems inherent in producing/releasing an image of the offender based on a witness description are still more or less inherent in producing and releasing an image based on genetic material. The technology can only produce an approximation, and an "image created by DNA" has the potential of being misunderstood by the public. The person out there who has that one tip that might blow this case wide open might see the image and be discouraged from calling because the person they remember did not "look like" the image.

That being said, there does appear to be movement regarding this. When tests like this are conducted, the image will probably eventually make its way to the public whether Law Enforcement sanctions its release or not. At this point, after forty years of the case being unsolved, the potential benefit may very well outweigh the risk of any negative consequences, so look for it to happen at some point.

Could eyewitnesses spend time looking at yearbook or DMV photos to identify the offender?

Countless hours have already been spent by very patient and cooperative witnesses poring over yearbooks, mug shots, advanced photo systems/repositories, and composite images constructed with Identikits. The results have been mixed, but it's not for lack of trying. One eyewitness viewed one of the most advanced photo systems in the country and selected seven or eight images that looked like a suspect. One victim who saw his face went through yearbooks and found a young man who looked exactly like her attacker. Hundreds of promising leads have been checked out in regard to these efforts and many others. In recent years, DNA tests were even done on leads generated from these activities that had previously been cleared by other means. The killer has not yet been among any of the men identified through these efforts.

With so many years between the original sightings and the present day, making an identification based on a yearbook photo at this point is unlikely. Many investigators do look at a yearbook photo of a person they're interested in toward the end of the process of investigating a "person of interest," just to make sure that there's not something about the subject's appearance that would disqualify them, but photos of that nature are not used as a gold-standard investigative tool at this point—if they're even used at all.

Could you explain the paint evidence?

In 1977, traces of a very specific, uncommon type of paint were found at two or three consecutive EAR attacks in Sacramento. They were described as microscopic chips of blue architectural paint that likely came from someone who had been using a paint sprayer. In the time period of the attacks, paint sprayers were unwieldy (often attached to the beds of trucks) and typically only used by professional painters. This would imply that the offender was possibly engaged in the construction industry, possibly even as a painter.

One of the difficulties with this assumption is that we can't be sure that the EAR was even the one who brought the paint to the scene (it could've been leftover from the vacuum sweeping that was done to collect the samples in the first place, for instance, or a byproduct of local construction). Another difficulty with this assumption is that, while finding matching physical evidence at two different scenes might seem indicative of something, what about the other fifty or more scenes that didn't contain this type of evidence?

Whether this could lead to identification, or whether this was just microscopic transfer from something he'd stepped in, there's no way of knowing. The paint evidence is anything but simple, because other types of paint evidence was found at other scenes, as well. The crime scenes containing paint evidence are detailed below:

Attack #8 in Rancho Cordova (10/18/76)
Yellow paint was found smeared on a towel.

Attack #25 in Foothill Farms (10/21/77)
Traces of blue paint were found on boots in the master bedroom of the residence, on shoelaces, and in vacuum sweepings done by scene technicians. The color was similar to the samples found at the next scene, but to our knowledge, the ones from this scene were never compared (or were, but didn't match). Gray smears of paint were found on a fence and a gate.

Attack #26 in Sacramento (10/29/77)
Traces of blue architectural paint were found at the scene in vacuum sweepings done by scene technicians. Some was also found on shoelaces and on one of the victim's hairs.

Attack #27 in Sacramento (11/10/77)
Traces of blue paint were found in vacuum sweepings of the scene. The small flakes at this scene (measured in microns) matched the paint evidence from the previous scene. Investigators of the era determined that the paint was architectural paint—the kind used on masonry. It had originated from a commercial paint sprayer. Additionally, a very small piece of PVC was found among the trace evidence related to the paint. None of this evidence was ever conclusively tied to the offender.

Offerman/Manning murders in Goleta (12/30/79)
A blue/green dried paint sample was found on Dr. Manning's big toe. This paint didn't match any other samples in color or composition, but it *was* determined at one point to be architectural paint.

Witthuhn murder in Irvine (2/5/81)

A screwdriver left behind by the killer had multiple layers of paint stains on it. The primary one was brown Behr paint.

Again, the existence of the paint evidence led some investigators to entertain the possibility that offender had been traveling around the state to work at construction sites, possibly as a painter. This lead has been explored but so far, nothing has come of it.

A few years ago, it seemed that a small break had been made regarding this. Investigators found that a strip mall section at 5801 Calle Real and a Longs Drug store at 5875 Calle Real in Goleta had used a developer from Sacramento. It was determined that the building was finished in the same time frame as the Offerman/Manning murders and it was assumed that the painting phase was most likely going on at that point. The passage of time and incomplete employment records have made following this lead a bit difficult, and so far nothing has come of it.

Among the paint samples found, the matching blue architectural paint is by far the most interesting. Chemical analysis revealed that the paint was flat, not glossy. It was not of automotive origin, and its composition contained phthalo blue and silicates. The color was a dark blue with a shade of gray.

The important thing to remember about this particular paint is that the applications for it were very limited. Again, it was a heavy-duty architectural paint that likely came from someone who had been using a paint sprayer. The silicates in the paint implied its use as an overcoat, providing any surface that it was applied to with a "lotus effect" (the name of that effect referring to the repellant and self-cleaning properties of lotus flowers and leaves). Certain types of silicates repel the dirt and encourage it to adhere to water, which then rolls the dirt off of the surface. This type of paint was most likely used in construction on building exteriors, probably porous exterior surfaces. Swimming pools and floors were not a typical use for this type of paint. Usage in advertising was probably not likely, unless the branding was done on something architectural.

Automotive use was ruled out (even though this was a common 1971 Ford Fleet color) because usually the colored paint that was used on automobiles dried in what, at a microscopic level, looked like a small mountain range. It's called a capillary texture, and the result is that lots of dirt and grime can wedge itself in. Lots of indoor paints and low-grade commercial paints have this property as well. Overcoats were usually applied to mitigate the amount of dirt that could adhere to the paint.

Also, "silicates" is a broad term and can encompass many minerals and substances. Analysis revealed that we're talking about something more akin to silicate mineral paint. Additional analysis revealed that the paint had mostly likely flaked off of canvas and not a hard tool. It was mentioned by one source that the PVC sample was mostly likely from a machining or drilling chip.

When it comes to composition and formula, remember that we're talking about paint from the 1970s, not any kind of modern-day formulas. Lead paint wasn't even banned until *after* the first few flakes were found, so we're talking about a very different era.

What could the offender's "breaks" tells us about him?

While the EAR/GSK offended on a fairly regular basis for a period of years, there were some noticeable breaks between attack dates that occurred with some consistency and regularity. Here are the four main ones:

(listing begins on the next page)

Attack #21 5/17/77 Sac
Attack #22 5/28/77 Sac
—3 MONTH BREAK—
Attack #23 9/6/77 Stockton

Attack #35 6/24/78 Davis
Attack #36 7/6/78 Davis
—3 MONTH BREAK—
Attack #37 10/7/78 Contra Costa County

Attack #41 12/2/78 Contra Costa County
Attack #42 12/9/78 Contra Costa County
—3 MONTH BREAK—
Attack #43 3/20/79 Rancho Cordova

Attack #47 6/25/79 Contra Costa County
Attack #48 7/5/79 Contra Costa County
—3 MONTH BREAK—
Goleta Attack: 10/1/79 Goleta

As you can see, a geographical shift tended to occur at the end of the break as well.

One theory is that he was out-of-pocket for work or something, maybe even outside of the state, and during that time, rather than keep a house or apartment payment going while he was away, he simply found a new living situation upon his return. On the attack after the first break, he mentioned needing things for his "apartment," and after the next break he actually took a lot of housewares and appliances and other sorts of things that someone would need if they were moving somewhere.

It's also possible that he wasn't gone or busy with anything else, and that it took merely took three months to stalk new areas.

Additionally, attempts have been made to line these up with the schedules of colleges and universities in the area, and some of them match up quite well.

While it's clear that there were certainly regular and seemingly significant breaks between the attack dates, this doesn't mean that there wasn't activity attributable to the offender during the breaks. There was. Sometimes a lot of it, and most of those incidents are detailed in this book. There was rarely a month that went by where he wasn't active *somewhere*. This might punch holes in the theory that he was offshore or out of state, or perhaps some of those events weren't him after all. It does seem that there's something significant to be found regarding these breaks, however.

Are there any other towns that EAR could've hit? Are there any other crimes that could be attributed to him?

Some of the more likely possibilities were presented in this book, but of course, there are many others. There's definitely a strong chance that more crimes were committed by this offender and that they either went unreported or they've never been tied to him. Anything that he might've done out of state would be very difficult to bring into the fold. Any double-murders by bludgeoning across the country deserve to be looked at very closely, because those types of homicides are such a statistical anomaly.

One of our pet projects at the moment is looking for EAR-style attacks that could've occurred from July 1978 to October 1978 in Vacaville and Fairfield. This was a quiet period for the EAR while he widened his geography, and he seemingly breezed past these areas. Even if he didn't attack, we're willing to bet that he at least scoped them out. Finding EAR activity in either of these during the "off" months would go a long way toward clarifying his prowling style, and it might answer some questions about where he was during this "break" period.

Did the offender have a small penis? Could he be identified by his small penis size?

Sadly, this is the #1 most popular question on the site and at the forums. The offender's penis, as described by multiple witnesses, seemed to be on the small side of normal. It wasn't a "micropenis" and it didn't appear to be the result of any kind of illness or disability. In some instances it might've appeared even smaller due to the fact that he didn't always achieve a full erection. There didn't appear to be anything terribly distinctive about it, aside from multiple victims noting that it was circumcised.

He probably can't be identified by penis size. There *were* a few sketchy eliminations made based on penis size long ago, but in an era of DNA, there's no reason anymore to ask a suspect to drop his pants.

Was the offender gay?

Believe it or not, this question is a very popular one as well. There are a few reasons it comes up a lot:

1) Old news articles described the offender as being in a "homosexual panic," a supposed psychological condition that they said made him act out because of fears of his own homosexuality. This was most likely printed simply to taunt the offender, and it was later retracted.

2) There were bizarre rumors that Dr. Robert Offerman was sodomized by the offender because of the way the body was found. The killer did not sodomize Dr. Offerman.

3) The offender's inability to maintain erections at many of the attacks is cited as a reason. This could've occurred for many reasons, with homosexuality being pretty far down on the list.

4) It's sometimes used as a misguided effort to insult the offender. We don't like him any more than you do, but we don't use "gay" as a slur.

595

5) A discarded jacket was found near a scene. The jacket may have been bought at a store which counted homosexuals among its targeted customer base.

The jacket was kind of an odd find, but on its own, it means almost nothing. We've seen the make and model of it and like most jackets, it's just a normal jacket that might be worn by anyone. The offender was probably not gay, and there's not enough evidence about the offender's sexuality to help assist in identification, regardless.

Was the offender affiliated with the military?
It's possible. It was the Vietnam era, the offender began in Rancho Cordova (known for its heavy connections to the military), and there were certain tactics that he used which seemed to have an origin in military or Law Enforcement.

Of course, those things could be adopted and learned by a "military enthusiast" just as well. Speaking from a psychological standpoint, an offender like this would probably have a difficult time in the military. The Air Force connections found in so many of the early attacks can be explained away by simply knowing that the area was rife with those types of connections. For the most part they dissipate once he moves out of the area, which tells us that it probably wasn't through military channels that he was finding his victims—or that at least he didn't rely on those channels full-time.

The offender told victims a few times that he was military, but he wasn't always big on telling the truth.

Unfortunately, given the evidence, there's no way of knowing if he was military or not, just like there's no way of knowing if he was a painter or not despite the occasional presence of paint. Hopefully we'll find out someday soon.

Did the offender have a distinctive smell?

Not consistently. There were a few attacks where he smelled really terrible, but it was fairly rare.

One of the myths in this case appears to be the idea that the EAR/GSK smelled like cinnamon. We're not sure where this comes from, because only one victim in the entire canon of attacks reported that kind of smell. One attack out of so many is an anomaly.

In fact, smells weren't attributed to the offender very often at all, despite his supposed smoking and drinking habit. In each incident, victims were asked about the attacker's smell. Most of them didn't report much of anything. The ones that did are listed here:

Attack #3: smelled like aftershave
Attack #9: had a very bad odor and bad breath
Attack #12: a very bad body odor like he hadn't been bathing
Attack #13: smelled like a sweet aftershave
Attack #23: very bad odor
Attack #24: very bad odor
Attack #35: very bad odor and bad breath
Attack #36: smelled like cigarette smoke
Attack #37: a musty smell, like cinnamon
Attack #46: a feminine smell, like talcum powder

Did the offender have an accomplice?

It's hard to imagine the offender having an accomplice for these crimes. They were so horrific and so focused on a particular brand of neurosis that it's hard to picture another person going along with them. There was usually so little stolen that it wouldn't seem worth it to a fellow criminal, even if they had no scruples about the rapes or murders. What would be in it for them? For the accomplice scenario to work, it would almost have to be someone loyal to the offender or someone controlled by him.

There's very little evidence of an accomplice being involved in any of these crimes. There are, however, a few things that are difficult or almost impossible to ignore. Taken by themselves, most of them don't mean much. But taken together, a few odd patterns emerge.

The following is a list of events that may hint at more people being involved in the crimes in some way—probably a very limited way, if they're involved at all. Whether you think there's something to it or not is up to you. Cases where a car was heard after the assailant left in another direction on foot have been excluded for the most part, and cases where the offender was heard talking to someone who didn't seem to be there were mostly excluded as well.

Attack #13: Two men were seen behaving strangely thirty minutes before the attack.

Ripon Court Shooting: Three men were seen running from the area.

Attack #16: A neighbor saw a small foreign vehicle circling the block several times during the timeframe that the EAR was leaving the victims' house.

Attack #17: A relative of the victim said that she was told that there were actually two rapists, though they were never seen at the same time.

Attack #23: A car squealed its tires in front of the house while the EAR was still inside.

Attack #24: During the assault, the doorbell rang, and the intruder went outside seemingly in response to it. He came back inside and raped the victim for a second time. Then a car horn honked twice, then twice again, and the doorbell rang five times. Someone besides the rapist seemed to knock on the window. Different voices were heard, one possibly a woman's voice.

Attack #30: The victim thought she heard someone else walking around on the patio while the offender was in the garage. There was also an incident with three men running in the area.

Attack #37: There were numerous sightings of prowlers and burglars working in pairs (we encourage you to read the chapter on Attack #37 for detailed information... there's a lot of it).

Attack #46: While the assailant was still in the house, a car screeched to a halt, stayed there for a bit, and then left. The victims thought that he'd been picked up, but the assailant was still in the room.

Offerman/Manning murder: A woman was seen possibly casing the house that the EAR would later break into. A woman was also seen in associated with the Berkeley Road dog incident a few months prior.

Did the bloodhounds react strangely to his scent?

Maybe, maybe not. There were at least two scenes where the handlers noted a stronger reaction than they were used to from the dogs, especially at the scent concentrated in the bathroom. This has led to some theories that the assailant had a drug dependency or a disease, or that something was off with the chemistry of the offender and it bothered the dogs. The theory has even been explored in an official capacity (which doesn't necessarily lend it credibility, because most leads, both inside the box and out, have been officially explored).

We had an in-depth conversation with a SAR handler where we presented him with all of the information we could find about the dogs and their reactions. His opinion based on what was presented to him was that the dogs probably became more excited when they encountered a *concentration* of scent, and that it didn't necessarily have anything to do with the scent itself. Since the same dogs were used at multiple scenes, it's also likely that there was a recognition factor happening at some of the locations. The sum total of the data as we understand it does not conclusively point to the offender having something wrong with him that would aggravate a sensitive dog.

For reference, here's a quick and dirty listing of attacks where a bloodhound was used, with any interesting notes or overtly strange reactions noted:

Attack #5

Attack #7

Attack #12: Same dog that was used in Attack #7

Attack #14: A new, highly-trained bloodhound was used

Attack #15

Attack #16

Attack #18: The Sheriff's Department dog was used

Attack #21: The dog became "excited" by the scent

Attack #22

Attack #26: Multiple dogs used

Attack #35

Attack #37

Attack #42: Two dogs used, then a third brought in later

Attack #45: Three dogs used. One of them became "excited" by the scent

Attack #46

Attack #47: The dog used here clearly remembered the scent from a previous attack it had worked (Attack #45).

Attack #48

Are we looking for a three-toed dog?

Paw prints found at the Offerman/Manning murder in Goleta were described in a news article or two as belonging to a dog with three toes. Everything we've been able to find out about the paw prints, ground conditions, and everything else has led us to conclude that the paw prints were most likely partial prints, *not* the full prints of a dog who had a toe missing. That being said, a fairly distinctive German Shepherd from the immediate area was indeed tracked down by Law Enforcement, and the various people associated with it were thoroughly investigated. A small fortune was spent on DNA tests, which conclusively cleared everyone who was known to have had any contact with the animal.

Despite the apparent debunking of the three-toed dog situation, if someone were to come forward with knowledge of a suspect who owned or borrowed a large three-toed dog, it would be important to still consider this suspect, because there's no way of knowing for sure.

Bloody dog tracks were found at the second Goleta murder (Domingo/Sanchez), but there's nothing noted about those tracks having three toes.

How many times did the offender cry at a crime scene? Was it genuine?

The crying fits were one of the weirdest components of the attacks, and they occurred with some regularity. While some of the initial ones seemed like they were done for the victim's benefit, eventually they started to happen with more spontaneity and in many cases, the EAR went off by himself to do it without putting on too many theatrics. Many victims were positive that these crying jags were genuine.

Starting on the next page, we explore the details from the attacks where the EAR cried, or at least the ones where we're *certain* that he cried. You'll notice that the crying usually happened right after raping his victim. If they were tears of remorse, the feeling didn't last long, because sometimes he'd rape his victim again shortly afterward. It almost appears that the tears were from a frustration at being unable to maintain an erection or achieve a climax, or perhaps from not getting the buzz that he used to get. Even victims as early as the second Orangevale attack noticed that he became very frustrated when he couldn't maintain an erection.

(listing begins on the next page)

Attacks where EAR cried:
Attack #22 5/28/77 South Sacramento
Attack #25 10/21/77 Foothill Farms
Attack #26 10/29/77 Sacramento
Attack #29 1/28/78 Sacramento
Attack #30 3/18/78 Stockton
Attack #32 6/5/78 Modesto
Attack #35 6/24/78 Davis
Attack #36 7/06/78 Davis
Attack #37 10/06/78 Concord
Attack #41 12/02/78 San Jose

Attack #22

The EAR issued a warning, then appeared to break down. "I have something for you to tell the fucking pigs. They got it mixed up last time. I said I would kill two people. I'm not going to kill you. If this is on the TV or in the papers tomorrow, I'll kill two people. Are you l-l-l-l-listening? Do you hear me? I have TVs in my apartment and I'll be watching them. If this is on the news, I'll kill two people." She noticed that he seemed very angry when he used the word "pigs."

Then, to her surprise, he started sobbing a little bit. "It scares my mommy when it's on the news," he cried. He appeared to hold back more sobs, and then repeated it. "It scares my mommy when it's on the news." It sounded to the victim like he cried harder when he said the word "mommy."

Attack #25

He put a knife against the victim's throat, threatened her, and then raped her. He didn't force her to touch his penis with her bound hands. He didn't climax. When he was finished, he immediately went to the kitchen. The victim could hear him crying. While he was in there, he ate some of their food.

The assailant checked on the husband. He put a gun against the man's head and repeated some of his earlier threats. Then he returned to the wife, put a knife to her throat, threatened her, and raped her once more. Again, he didn't force her to masturbate him, and during the rape, he didn't climax. He began crying again immediately after pulling out. He walked away, and she heard him settle elsewhere in the house and sob for awhile.

When he came back, he told her "My buddy is in the car waiting. Tell the p-p-p-p-pigs I'll be back New Year's Eve." And then the house was quiet.

Attack #26

He raped the victim for the second time. Then he sat her up and forced his penis into her mouth. He suddenly withdrew, stood up, and began crying. "I'm sorry. Mom. Mommy. Please help me. I don't want to do this, Mommy." The victim felt the sobbing was genuine. He continued on, sobbing and repeating those phrases, and he began hyperventilating and stumbling around the room a bit. He walked down the hallway, and as he got close to the master bedroom, the husband could hear him say "Oh Mom." Then the assailant began breathing harshly, as if angry. The husband also thought it sounded genuine, like he was sobbing and trying to get control of himself.

Then the EAR made his way back to the living room. Again, he sexually assaulted the woman. And again, he began crying and sobbing afterward. He stood up and stumbled around the room some more. "Mommy, I don't want to do this. Someone please help me."

Attack #29

He raped one of the sisters for less than a minute. He wasn't fully erect and he didn't climax. He climbed off of her and then stood next to the bed. He bound their ankles with shoelaces.

"Don't talk to each other or I'll kill you," he said. Then he left the room.

It was quiet for a moment. The girls listened intently, and they heard whimpering or sobbing. The assailant was in the other room, crying and making high-pitched noises "like a child might make."

Then he came back.

Attack #30
The victim felt him pull out, and he got up and went to the kitchen. He opened the refrigerator and moved some things around, then returned and put a plate and a bowl on her back. "One click, one small noise, and he's dead," he told her.

He went out onto the patio. She heard him walking around, and then she heard him begin to cry and sob. He went into the garage, and he started hyperventilating and breathing loudly. While he was in the garage, she thought she heard someone else walking around on the patio.

Attack #32
The rapist stuttered at times, and at one point he paced back and forth very intently and it seemed that he was sobbing.

Attack #35
After raping the victim, he told her that he needed money. Then she heard him take several steps back and begin sobbing and crying.
He left the house shortly thereafter.

Attack #36
While he raped the victim, he kept repositioning his weight. She felt like he might be having trouble maintaining an erection and reaching a climax, and he seemed frustrated. He grabbed her breast briefly. His frustration seemed to grow, and he pulled out and put his head down on the pillow next to her. He began crying.

"I hate you. I hate you. I hate you Bonnie," he sobbed.

He got up, rummaged through the house again, and left.

Attack #37
After the sexual assault, he walked away from the victim and huddled into a corner of the living room. She heard him crying. Then he got up and began ransacking the house again. He went back and forth from the garage a few times, and then went into the backyard. A few minutes passed, and the victim realized that he had left.

Attack #41

He raped the victim for only a few seconds, and then he pulled out. He stood up and went to the kitchen, where he began pacing and crying. "You motherfucker. You motherfucker," he sobbed.

Then there was silence. The victim waited for a few minutes and wondered if the assailant was gone. She sat up.

"Lie still or I'll kill you," he said out of nowhere.

Back in the bedroom, the husband moved a little bit. The dishes crashed down to the floor, and the assailant was back with blinding speed. "Just try that again, motherfucker, and I'll shoot your wife first, then you." He put the gun to the husband's head, then replaced the dishes.

He went back to the female victim and raped her again. As soon as he was done, he went straight to the kitchen and sobbed deeply for close to five minutes. He said several things under his breath, but the victim couldn't hear what he was saying. The dishes crashed to the floor in the bedroom again, and once more the assailant ran in and threatened the man. After that, it was fairly quiet, though they thought they heard him cry again for a third time. He left a few minutes later.

Was the offender a knot expert?

He certainly liked to tie things and certainly tied many knots during the crime spree, but most of the EAR/GSK knots were very rudimentary. There were three basic knots that he used over and over again. These were the square knot, the "granny" knot (similar to the square knot but not as secure), and the overhand knot. The overhand knot is almost impossible to untie once secured. An incomplete version of the overhand knot, a "half-hitch knot," was used at a few scenes as well.

Very rarely were ornate or complicated knots used. One of the best examples of a complicated knot being used was the Smith murder. The Offerman/Manning murder had a mess of knots that was also described as "ornate," probably due to the nature of the ligatures used.

Usually, multiple types of knots were used at the same crime scene. Our understanding is that the offender most likely did this for added security, possibly thinking that using a couple different knots would be more secure than using the same one multiple times.

What motivated this offender to commit these crimes?

This is the question we all wonder about more than any other. Most of the profiles speculate that a deep hatred for women was at the core of everything that he did. There was clearly something more than a sexual component to these attacks. A compulsion to engage in behavior of this magnitude is not something that's seen very frequently, even in prolific criminals. The amount of risk-aversion and care it must've taken to not get caught goes beyond the attention-span of most offenders. The other behaviors, such as stealing personal and meaningful items (like wedding rings and money clips with the victim's initials on them) surely have a psychological component to them as well.

Even if we had an answer to this question, it's very unlikely that we'd understand it. Questions about motivation and psychological makeup regarding this offender are what draws many to this case. The eventual unmasking may clear it up, and it may not. We all want to know what happened to this man, and what sort of mental processes inside his head allowed for such a horrific chain of events.

Again, it's unlikely that we'll ever understand the answer. All that we're left with is the who, what, where, and when. The "why" will always elude us. This book was created to provide you with the "what," "where," and "when." Hard work will eventually provide the "who." And we'll talk about the "why" for ages.

Until that day comes, join us in praying for justice and in working to peel back the layers of this mystery. For the victims and for everyone who's been hurt by these tragedies, justice can't come soon enough. Forty years is far too long for so many to live without answers.

CPSIA information can be obtained
at www.ICGtesting.com
Printed in the USA
FSHW01n1938260418
47519FS

9 780999 458105